PHILOSOPHICAL ISSUES IN LAW:
Cases and Materials

KENNETH KIPNIS
Lake Forest College

PRENTICE-HALL, INC., *Englewood Cliffs, New Jersey 07632*

Library of Congress Cataloging in Publication Data
Main entry under title:

Philosophical issues in law.

Bibliography: p. 325.
CONTENTS: Strict liability in the criminal law:
United States Supreme Court. United States v. Dotterweich. Hart, H. L. A. Legal responsibility and
excuses. Wasserstrom, R. A. Strict liability in
the criminal law. [etc.]
1. Law—United States—Cases. 2. Law—Philosophy.
KF379.P45   340.1   76-40412
ISBN   0-13-662296-8

Printed in the United States of America

10 9 8 7 6 5 4 3 2

Prentice-Hall International, Inc., *London*
Prentice-Hall of Australia Pty. Limited, *Sydney*
Prentice-Hall of Canada, Ltd., *Toronto*
Prentice-Hall of India Private Limited, *New Delhi*
Prentice-Hall of Japan, Inc., *Tokyo*
Prentice-Hall of Southeast Asia Pte. Ltd., *Singapore*
Whitehall Books Limited, *Wellington, New Zealand*

PHILOSOPHICAL ISSUES IN LAW

For my family

Contents

Preface

From time to time the facts of a particular legal case may raise an issue which forces us to go beyond precedent, beyond statute, and even beyond the task of constitutional interpretation. The facts of such a case may take us to that area where law and philosophy intersect, where we find lawyers thinking like philosophers and philosophers reasoning like lawyers. As we read the cases which raise such issues and as we study articles by philosophers and lawyers which explore them, we can sense that what are being asked are very basic and very important questions about the way our society is to be. Further, we can come to understand that in trying to comprehend and resolve these questions, the profession of law and the discipline of philosophy have much to offer one another.

In editing this anthology, in assembling materials which display and illuminate six such issues, I have tried to convey that, in legal philosophy at least, not all philosophical problems are merely philosophers' problems. Each of the issues arises in the context of legal opinions, and each of the six sections begins with this material. Two of the cases concern substantive criminal law and a third concerns criminal procedure. Another opinion evaluates a zoning ordinance; two others, a law school admissions policy. One of the cases concerns a conscientious violation of the draft law. All of these decisions have affected the quality of our institutions. Following the opinions, each section provides materials which discuss the issue raised by the case. I have selected pieces by jurists, by legal scholars, and by philosophers, pieces that are strongly at odds with one another, that work to dispel the notion that there are merely two sides to every question. The problems here are extremely difficult and more work needs to be done on all of them. It has been my aim throughout to show the importance of that work.

In preparing this book I have tried to keep in mind the reader who does not have a legal background. As much as possible I have avoided legal opinions and articles that are bafflingly technical to the lay reader. The introductions to each section provide a context for the main issue and a general indication of the relationships among the materials. A short glossary has been included to help the reader with difficult and unavoidable legal jargon. An appendix on legal materials will serve to initiate the novice into the mysteries of legal citation and the world of legal literature. Finally, where it seemed helpful, I have included comments on particular items in the selected supplementary readings.

As editor I have favored a no-excerpts policy, endeavoring to let each piece speak for itself. Except for the selections by Patrick Devlin, Joel Feinberg, and Richard Epstein, all of the articles are reprinted in their entirety. Among the cases, only *Dotterweich* and the two *DeFunis* opinions have been substantially shortened. To make the cases somewhat easier to read I have deleted many of the legal citations, marking the locations with a double asterisk (**). Citations for all seven cases are given and, with the help of the "Notes on Legal Materials" at the end of the book, it should not be too difficult to locate the complete opinions in any well-equipped law library.

A word of appreciation is owed to more persons and more institutions than it is possible to list here. But I would be remiss if I did not thank William Leon McBride, Jane Lynch, William McLauchlan, Richard Turkington, Arthur Finck, Maria Loffredo, Terry Pence, Bruce Hirsch, John Bruce Moore, Vivien Clair, and John R. Austin. I have been fortunate to have had the help of a production editor as gifted in his craft as Prentice-Hall's Fred Bernardi. I am indebted to the University of Chicago for generously making available resources without which this book would not have been attempted, let alone completed. Gratitude is especially due Dean Norval Morris of the Law School of the University of Chicago. His encouragement and assistance were invaluable. Finally, it is proper that credit be given to Sara Lyn Smith, whose contributions to the genesis of this work were acts of supererogation.

K.K.

SECTION ONE

Strict Liability
in the Criminal Law

At the very broadest level, the criminal law consists of two parts. One part, the law of criminal procedure, is concerned with the manner in which the various elements of the criminal justice system function in the handling of criminal cases. It is through that system that society imposes its most severe sanctions upon its members. The other part of the criminal law, the substantive criminal law, treats the definition and grading of offenses. The issue raised in this section concerns a small but important part of the substantive criminal law: the "strict liability" offenses. To understand what these offenses are and why they are important, some background is required.

Typically, the prosecutor in a criminal case must be prepared to prove more than the fact that the defendant performed an act prohibited by the substantive criminal law. The general rule in Anglo-American jurisprudence is that the act alone is not criminal unless it be accompanied by some specified mental state. Thus, if Betty shoots and kills Bruce, whether Betty has committed a crime—and, if so, which crime she has committed—will depend upon what she had in mind. It may be that Betty planned the death of Bruce in advance, evaluated the possible and probable consequences of her act, and pulled the trigger intending to kill Bruce. If, in addition to proving that Betty shot and killed Bruce, the prosecutor can prove premeditation, deliberation and intent to kill—common mental elements of first-degree murder—then it may be that a conviction for first-degree murder can be obtained. However, if Betty intended to kill Bruce, but did so with neither premeditation nor deliberation, then a conviction for second-degree murder might be in order. But what if Betty did not intend to kill anyone? Say she was test-firing her gun at the wall, aware that the bullet might penetrate and strike someone on the other side. In such a case, because she was aware that there was an unreasonable and high risk that someone would be killed when she fired her gun, a conviction for manslaughter might be in order. Of course, if Betty, exercising all due care, unintentionally shoots and kills Bruce while trying to save him from being mauled by a mountain lion, it is likely that there is no crime at all. The legal maxim *actus non facit reum, nisi mens sit rea*—the act is not guilty unless the mind be guilty—applies in almost all of the criminal law; virtually every crime includes as one of its elements a *mens rea* (guilty mind) requirement.

There are, however, two important types of exception to this rule. In some jurisdictions Betty would be guilty of manslaughter even if she were *not* aware that there was an unreasonable and high degree of risk that someone would be killed when she fired her gun. Even if she mindlessly discharges the gun without realizing that what she is doing is dangerous, she could be convicted if the reasonable person in the same circumstances would have been aware of the risk. A person can be convicted of such an "objective liability" offense even if there was no subjective awareness that the conduct in question was unreasonable. The prosecutor need only prove that the reasonable person under those circumstances would have known of the risk, and that the defendant engaged in the conduct.

Strict liability offenses represent another exception to the traditional *mens rea* requirement. As with objective liability offenses, strict liability crimes do not contain a *mens rea* element. But it is no defense in a strict liability case—as it would be with objective liability—to show that the defendant was acting as a reasonable person would have acted under the circumstances. Bigamy, for example, has been held to be a strict liability offense in some jurisdictions. Thus, where this is so, if Betty marries Bruce while reasonably believing that Fred, her "former husband," has divorced her, she may still be convicted of bigamy if it happens that her belief is false and her earlier marriage to Fred is legally intact. It would not be a defense to show that the reasonable person would have made the same mistake that she did. Betty may have acted with all the care we expect of people and yet, through strict liability and no fault of her own, she may nonetheless find herself in jail.

There has been a substantial amount of controversy as to whether strict liability offenses are justifiable. The selections of this section are intended as an introduction to this problem. The case with which we begin, *United States* v. *Dotterweich*, illustrates some of the main features of the conflict. Dotterweich is the president of a company which shipped adulterated and misbranded drugs in violation of the Federal Food, Drug, and Cosmetic Act. Though there was neither proof nor even a claim that Dotterweich knew that the drugs were adulterated and misbranded, he has been convicted nonetheless. Justice Frankfurter writes the opinion for the court and stresses the importance and difficulty of designing legislation that would effectively protect "the innocent public who are wholly helpless" from the hazards of "illicit and noxious articles." Referring to "questions of importance in the enforcement of the Federal Food, Drug, and Cosmetic Act" and to the difficulty of subjecting corporations to criminal penalties, the court holds that though "consciousness of wrongdoing be totally wanting" the offense is committed where "the accused shares responsibility in the business process resulting in unlawful distribution."

Frankfurter looks at the conviction of Dotterweich against the background of an insufficient "enterprise liability," that is, the criminal liability of a corporation for the acts of its agents. The four dissenters, however, are troubled by their apprehension of strict liability and "vicarious liability," that is, the criminal liability of an individual for the act of another. They are also troubled by the apparent failure of the Federal act to include language explicitly permitting convictions like that of Dotterweich. On the one hand we have an apparent desire to safeguard the "lives and health of people which, in the circumstances of modern industrialism, are largely beyond self-protection," and on the other, a "tenderness of the law for the rights of individuals."

In "Legal Responsibility and Excuses," H. L. A. Hart discusses how different theories of criminal law have accounted for the presence of *mens rea* elements in criminal offenses. After rejecting both "moral culpability" theories and Benthamite "economy of threats" theories, Hart develops his own "mercantile" theory. This considers the criminal law as a "choosing system" in which individuals are respected as "choosing beings." From the perspective provided by this theory Hart goes on to elucidate the "moral odium of strict liability."

Richard Wasserstrom, in his article "Strict Liability in the Criminal Law," reviews some of the main criticisms of strict liability offenses and finds them wanting. Although he is apparently not convinced that strict liability offenses are desirable, and concedes that some statutes creating them may be undesirable, neither is he convinced that such offenses are the embarrassment which their critics have made them out to be. Notwithstanding the criticisms, Wasserstrom maintains that strict liability may not be inconsistent with the "commonly avowed aims of the criminal law." Moreover, it is not clear that strict liability violates the "accepted standards of criminal culpability." Finally, he warns that some of the arguments used to attack strict liability may do damage to criminal negligence offenses (what we have called objective liability offenses).

UNITED STATES V. DOTTERWEICH

UNITED STATES SUPREME COURT

Mr. Justice Frankfurter delivered the opinion of the Court.

This was a prosecution begun by two informations, consolidated for trial, charging Buffalo Pharmacal Company, Inc., and Dotterweich, its president and general manager, with violations of the Act of Congress of June 25, 1938, c. 675, 52 Stat. 1040, 21 U. S. C. §§ 301–392, known as the Federal Food, Drug, and Cosmetic Act. The Company, a jobber in drugs, purchased them from their manufacturers and shipped them, repacked under its own label, in interstate commerce. (No question is raised in this case regarding the implications that may properly arise when, although the manufacturer gives the jobber a guaranty, the latter through his own label makes representations.) The informations were based on § 301 of that Act (21 U. S. C. § 331), paragraph (a) of which prohibits "The introduction or delivery for introduction into interstate commerce of any . . . drug . . . that is adulterated or misbranded." "Any person" violating this provision is, by paragraph (a) of § 303 (21 U. S. C. § 333), made "guilty of a misdemeanor." Three counts went to the jury—two, for shipping misbranded drugs in interstate commerce, and a third, for so shipping an adulterated drug. The jury disagreed as to the corporation and found Dotterweich guilty on all three counts. We start with the finding of the Circuit Court of Appeals that the evidence was adequate to support the verdict of adulteration and misbranding. . . .

. . . [B]aseless is the claim of Dotterweich that, having failed to find the corporation guilty, the jury could not find him guilty. Whether the jury's verdict was the result of carelessness or compromise or a belief that the responsible individual should suffer the penalty instead of merely increasing, as it were, the cost of running the business of the corporation, is immaterial. Juries may indulge in precisely such motives or vagaries.**

And so we are brought to our real problem. The Circuit Court of Appeals, one judge dissenting, reversed the conviction on the ground that only the corporation was the "person" subject to prosecution unless, perchance, Buffalo Pharmacal was a counterfeit corporation serving as a screen for Dotterweich. On that issue, after rehearing, it remanded the

Locations of deleted citations marked with double asterisk (**). Ed.

cause for a new trial. We then brought the case here, on the Government's petition for certiorari, 318 U. S. 753, because this construction raised questions of importance in the enforcement of the Federal Food, Drug, and Cosmetic Act.

The court below drew its conclusion not from the provisions defining the offenses on which this prosecution was based (§§ 301 (a) and 303 (a)), but from the terms of § 303 (c). That section affords immunity from prosecution if certain conditions are satisfied. The condition relevant to this case is a guaranty from the seller of the innocence of his product. So far as here relevant, the provision for an immunizing guaranty is as follows:

"No person shall be subject to the penalties of subsection (a) of this section . . . (2) for having violated section 301 (a) or (d), if he establishes a guaranty or undertaking signed by, and containing the name and address of, the person residing in the United States from whom he received in good faith the article, to the effect, in case of an alleged violation of section 301 (a), that such article is not adulterated or misbranded, within the meaning of this Act, designating this Act. . . ."

The Circuit Court of Appeals found it "difficult to believe that Congress expected anyone except the principal to get such a guaranty, or to make the guilt of an agent depend upon whether his employer had gotten one." 131 F. 2d 500, 503. And so it cut down the scope of the penalizing provisions of the Act to the restrictive view, as a matter of language and policy, it took of the relieving effect of a guaranty.

The guaranty clause cannot be read in isolation. The Food and Drugs Act of 1906 was an exertion by Congress of its power to keep impure and adulterated food and drugs out of the channels of commerce. By the Act of 1938, Congress extended the range of its control over illicit and noxious articles and stiffened the penalties for disobedience. The purposes of this legislation thus touch phases of the lives and health of people which, in the circumstances of modern industrialism, are largely beyond self-protection. Regard for these purposes should infuse construction of the legislation if it is to be treated as a working instrument of government and not merely as a collection of English words.** The prosecution to which Dotterweich was subjected is based on a now familiar type of legislation whereby penalties serve as effective means of regulation. Such legislation dispenses with the conventional requirement for criminal conduct—awareness of some wrongdoing. In the interest of the larger good it puts the burden of acting at hazard upon a person otherwise innocent but standing in responsible relation to a public danger. *United States* v. *Balint,* 258 U. S. 250. And so it is clear that shipments like those now in issue are "punished by the statute if the article is misbranded [or adulterated], and that the article may be misbranded [or adulterated] without any conscious fraud at all. It was natural enough to throw this risk on shippers with regard to the identity of their wares. . . ." *United States* v. *Johnson,* 221 U. S. 488, 497–98.

The statute makes "any person" who violates § 301 (a) guilty of a "misdemeanor." It specifically defines "person" to include "corporation." § 201 (e). But the only way in which a corporation can act is through the individuals who act on its behalf. *New York Central & H. R. R. Co.* v. *United States,* 212 U. S. 481. And the historic conception of a "misdemeanor" makes all those responsible for it equally guilty, *United States* v. *Mills,* 7 Pet. 138, 141, a doctrine given general application in § 332 of the Penal Code (18 U. S. C. § 550). If, then, Dotterweich is not subject to the Act, it must be solely on the ground that individuals are immune when the "person" who violates § 301 (a) is a corporation, although from the point of view of action the individuals are the corporation. As a matter of legal development, it has taken time to establish criminal liability also for a corporation and not merely for its agents. See *New York Central & H. R. R. Co.* v. *United States, supra.* The history of federal food and drug legislation is a good illustration of the elaborate phrasing that was in earlier days deemed necessary to fasten criminal liability on corporations. Section 12 of the Food and Drugs Act of 1906 provided that, "the act, omission, or failure of any officer, agent, or other person acting for or employed by any corporation, company, society, or association, within the scope of his employment or office, shall in every case be also deemed to be the act, omission, or failure of such corporation, company, society, or association as well as that of the person." By 1938, legal understanding and practice had rendered such statement of the obvious superfluous. Deletion of words—in the interest of brevity and good draftsmanship [1]—superfluous for holding a corporation criminally liable can hardly be found ground for relieving from such liability the individual agents of the corporation. To hold that the Act of 1938 freed all individuals, except when proprietors, from the culpability under which the earlier legislation had placed them is to defeat the very object of the new Act. Nothing is clearer than that the later legislation was designed to enlarge and stiffen the penal net and not to narrow and loosen it. This purpose was unequivocally avowed by the two committees which reported the bills to the Congress. The House Committee reported that the Act "seeks to set up effective provisions against abuses of consumer welfare growing out of inadequacies in the Food and Drugs Act of June 30, 1906." (H. Rep. No. 2139, 75th Cong., 3d Sess., p. 1.) And the Senate Committee explicitly pointed out that the new legislation "must not weaken the existing laws," but on the contrary "it must strengthen and extend that law's protection of the consumer." (S. Rep. No. 152, 75th Cong., 1st Sess., p. 1.) If the 1938 Act were construed as it was below, the penalties of the law could be imposed only in the rare case where the corporation is merely an individual's *alter ego.* Corporations carrying on an illicit trade would be subject only to what the House Committee described as a "license fee for the conduct of an illegit-

---

[1] "The bill has been made shorter and less verbose than previous bills. That has been done without deleting any effective provisions." S. Rep. No. 152, 75th Cong., 1st Sess., p. 2.

imate business." [2] A corporate officer, who even with "intent to defraud or mislead" (§ 303b), introduced adulterated or misbranded drugs into interstate commerce could not be held culpable for conduct which was indubitably outlawed by the 1906 Act.** This argument proves too much. It is not credible that Congress should by implication have exonerated what is probably a preponderant number of persons involved in acts of disobedience—for the number of non-corporate proprietors is relatively small. Congress, of course, could reverse the process and hold only the corporation and allow its agents to escape. In very exceptional circumstances it may have required this result.** But the history of the present Act, its purposes, its terms, and extended practical construction lead away from such a result once "we free our minds from the notion that criminal statutes must be construed by some artificial and conventional rule." **

The Act is concerned not with the proprietory relation to a misbranded or an adulterated drug but with its distribution. In the case of a corporation such distribution must be accomplished, and may be furthered, by persons standing in various relations to the incorporeal proprietor. If a guaranty immunizes shipments of course it immunizes all involved in the shipment. But simply because if there had been a guaranty it would have been received by the proprietor, whether corporate or individual, as a safeguard for the enterprise, the want of a guaranty does not cut down the scope of responsibility of all who are concerned with transactions forbidden by § 301. To be sure, that casts the risk that there is no guaranty upon all who according to settled doctrines of criminal law are responsible for the commission of a misdemeanor. To read the guaranty section, as did the court below, so as to restrict liability for penalties to the only person who normally would receive a guaranty—the proprietor—disregards the admonition that "the meaning of a sentence is to be felt rather than to be proved." ** It also reads an exception to an important provision safeguarding the public welfare with a liberality which more appropriately belongs to enforcement of the central purpose of the Act.

The Circuit Court of Appeals was evidently tempted to make such a devitalizing use of the guaranty provision through fear that an enforcement of § 301 (a) as written might operate too harshly by sweeping within its condemnation any person however remotely entangled in the proscribed shipment. But that is not the way to read legislation. Literalism and evisceration are equally to be avoided. To speak with technical accuracy, under § 301 a corporation may commit an offense and all persons who aid and abet its commission are equally guilty. Whether an accused shares responsibility in the business process resulting in unlawful distri-

---

[2] In describing the penalty provisions of § 303, the House Committee reported that the Bill "increases substantially the criminal penalties . . . which some manufacturers have regarded as substantially a license fee for the conduct of an illegitimate business." H. Rep. No. 2139, 75th Cong., 3d Sess., p. 4.

bution depends on the evidence produced at the trial and its submission —assuming the evidence warrants it—to the jury under appropriate guidance. The offense is committed, unless the enterprise which they are serving enjoys the immunity of a guaranty, by all who do have such a responsible share in the furtherance of the transaction which the statute outlaws, namely, to put into the stream of interstate commerce adulterated or misbranded drugs. Hardship there doubtless may be under a statute which thus penalizes the transaction though consciousness of wrongdoing be totally wanting. Balancing relative hardships, Congress has preferred to place it upon those who have at least the opportunity of informing themselves of the existence of conditions imposed for the protection of consumers before sharing in illicit commerce, rather than to throw the hazard on the innocent public who are wholly helpless.

It would be too treacherous to define or even to indicate by way of illustration the class of employees which stands in such a responsible relation. To attempt a formula embracing the variety of conduct whereby persons may responsibly contribute in furthering a transaction forbidden by an Act of Congress, to wit, to send illicit goods across state lines, would be mischievous futility. In such matters the good sense of prosecutors, the wise guidance of trial judges, and the ultimate judgment of juries must be trusted. Our system of criminal justice necessarily depends on "conscience and circumspection in prosecuting officers," ** even when the consequences are far more drastic than they are under the provision of law before us. See *United States* v. *Balint, supra* (involving a maximum sentence of five years). For present purpose it suffices to say that in what the defense characterized as "a very fair charge" the District Court properly left the question of the responsibility of Dotterweich for the shipment to the jury, and there was sufficient evidence to support its verdict.

Reversed.

Mr. Justice Murphy, dissenting:

Our prime concern in this case is whether the criminal sanctions of the Federal Food, Drug, and Cosmetic Act of 1938 plainly and unmistakably apply to the respondent in his capacity as a corporate officer. He is charged with violating § 301 (a) of the Act, which prohibits the introduction or delivery for introduction into interstate commerce of any adulterated or misbranded drug. There is no evidence in this case of any personal guilt on the part of the respondent. There is no proof or claim that he ever knew of the introduction into commerce of the adulterated drugs in question, much less that he actively participated in their introduction. Guilt is imputed to the respondent solely on the basis of his authority and responsibility as president and general manager of the corporation.

It is a fundamental principle of Anglo-Saxon jurisprudence that guilt is personal and that it ought not lightly to be imputed to a citizen who, like the respondent, has no evil intention or consciousness of wrongdoing. It may be proper to charge him with responsibility to the corporation and the stockholders for negligence and mismanagement. But in the absence of clear statutory authorization it is inconsistent with established canons of criminal law to rest liability on an act in which the accused did not participate and of which he had no personal knowledge. Before we place the stigma of a criminal conviction upon any such citizen the legislative mandate must be clear and unambiguous. Accordingly that which Chief Justice Marshall has called "the tenderness of the law for the rights of individuals" ** entitles each person, regardless of economic or social status, to an unequivocal warning from the legislature as to whether he is within the class of persons subject to vicarious liability. Congress cannot be deemed to have intended to punish anyone who is not "plainly and unmistakably" within the confines of the statute.**

Moreover, the fact that individual liability of corporate officers may be consistent with the policy and purpose of a public health and welfare measure does not authorize this Court to impose such liability where Congress has not clearly intended or actually done so. Congress alone has the power to define a crime and to specify the offenders.** It is not our function to supply any deficiencies in these respects, no matter how grave the consequences. Statutory policy and purpose are not constitutional substitutes for the requirement that the legislature specify with reasonable certainty those individuals it desires to place under the interdict of the Act.** . . .

The dangers inherent in any attempt to create liability without express Congressional intention or authorization are illustrated by this case. Without any legislative guides, we are confronted with the problem of determining precisely which officers, employees and agents of a corporation are to be subject to this Act by our fiat. To erect standards of responsibility is a difficult legislative task and the opinion of this Court admits that it is "too treacherous" and a "mischievous futility" for us to engage in such pursuits. But the only alternative is a blind resort to "the good sense of prosecutors, the wise guidance of trial judges, and the ultimate judgment of juries." Yet that situation is precisely what our constitutional system sought to avoid. Reliance on the legislature to define crimes and criminals distinguishes our form of jurisprudence from certain less desirable ones. The legislative power to restrain the liberty and to imperil the good reputation of citizens must not rest upon the variable attitudes and opinions of those charged with the duties of interpreting and enforcing the mandates of the law. I therefore cannot approve the decision of the Court in this case.

Mr. Justice Roberts, Mr. Justice Reed and Mr. Justice Rutledge join in this dissent.

LEGAL RESPONSIBILITY AND EXCUSES

H. L. A. HART

1

It is characteristic of our own and all advanced legal systems that the individual's liability to punishment, at any rate for serious crimes carrying severe penalties, is made by law to depend, among other things, on certain mental conditions. These conditions can best be expressed in negative form as *excusing* conditions: the individual is not liable to punishment if at the time of his doing what would otherwise be a punishable act he was unconscious, mistaken about the physical consequences of his bodily movements or the nature or qualities of the thing or persons affected by them, or, in some cases, if he was subjected to threats or other gross forms of coercion or was the victim of certain types of mental disease. This is a list, not meant to be complete, giving broad descriptions of the principal excusing conditions; the exact definition of these and their precise character and scope must be sought in the detailed exposition of our criminal law. If an individual breaks the law when none of the excusing conditions are present he is ordinarily said to have acted of "his own free will," "of his own accord," "voluntarily"; or it might be said, "He could have helped doing what he did." If the determinist [1] has anything to say on this subject, it must be because he

Reprinted by permission of the publishers, New York University Press. From DETER-MINISM AND FREEDOM IN THE AGE OF MODERN SCIENCE, edited by Sidney Hook, © 1958 by New York University.

[1] A variety of theories or claims shelter under the label "determinism." For many purposes it is necessary to distinguish among them, especially on the question whether the elements in human conduct that are said to be "determined" are regarded as the product of sufficient conditions, or sets of jointly sufficient conditions, which include the individual's character. I think, however, that the defence I make in this paper of the rationality, morality, and justice of qualifying criminal responsibility by excusing conditions will be compatible with any form of determinism which satisfies the two following sets of requirements.

A. The determinist must not deny (*a*) those *empirical* facts that at present we treat as proper grounds for saying, "He did what he chose," "His choice was effective," "He got what he chose," "That was the result of his choice," etc.; (*b*) the fact that when we get what we chose to have, live our lives as we have chosen, and particularly when we obtain by a choice what we have judged to be the lesser of two evils, this is a source of satisfaction; (*c*) the fact that we are often able to predict successfully and on reasonable evidence that our choice will be effective over certain periods in relation to certain matters.

makes two claims. The first claim is that it may be true—though we cannot yet show and may never be able to show that it is true—that human conduct (including in that expression not only actions involving the movements of the human body but its psychological elements or components such as decisions, choices, experiences of desire, effort, etc.) are subject to certain types of law, where law is to be understood in the sense of a scientific law. The second claim is that, if human conduct so understood is in fact subject to such laws (though at the present time we do not know it to be so), the distinction we draw between one who acts under excusing conditions and one who acts when none are present becomes unimportant, if not absurd. Consequently, to allow punishment to depend on the presence or absence of excusing conditions, or to think it justified when they are absent but not when they are present, is absurd, meaningless, irrational, or unjust, or immoral, or perhaps all of these.

My principal object in this paper is to draw attention to the analogy between conditions that are treated by criminal law as *excusing* conditions and certain similar conditions that are treated in another branch of the law as *invalidating* certain civil transactions such as wills, gifts, contracts, and marriages. If we consider this analogy, I think we can see that there is a rationale for our insistence on the importance of excusing conditions in criminal law that no form of determinism that I, at any rate, can construct could impugn; and this rationale seems to me superior at many points to the two main accounts or explanations which in Anglo-American jurisprudence have been put forward as the basis of the recognition of excusing conditions in criminal responsibility.

In this preliminary section, however, I want to explain why I shall not undertake the analysis or elucidation of the meaning of such expressions as "He did it voluntarily," "He acted of his own free will," "He could have helped doing it," "He could have done otherwise." I do not, of course, think the analysis of these terms unimportant: indeed I think we owe the progress that has been made, at least in determining what "the free will problem" is, to the work of philosophers who have pursued this analysis. Perhaps it may be shown that statements of the form "He did it of his own free will" or "He could have done otherwise," etc., are not logically incompatible with the existence of the type of laws the determinist claims may exist; if they do exist, it may not follow that statements of the kind quoted are always false, for it may be that these

---

B. The determinist does not assert and could not truly assert that we *already know* the laws that he says may exist or (in some versions) *must* exist. Determinists differ on the question whether or not the laws are sufficiently simple (*a*) for human beings to discover, (*b*) for human beings to use for the prediction of their own and others' conduct. But as long as it is not asserted that we know these laws I do not think this difference of opinion important here. Of course if we knew the laws and could use them for the detailed and exact prediction of our own and others' conduct, *deliberation* and *choice* would become pointless, and perhaps in such circumstances there could not (logically) be "deliberation" or "choice."

statements are true given certain conditions, which need not include the nonexistence of any such laws.

Here, however, I shall not attempt to carry further any such inquiries into the meaning of these expressions or to press the view I have urged elsewhere, that the expression "voluntary action" is best understood as excluding the presence of the various excuses. So I will not deal here with a determinist who is so incautious as to say that it may be false that anyone has ever acted "voluntarily," "of his own free will," "could have done otherwise than he did." It will, I think, help to clarify our conception of criminal responsibility if I confront a more cautious sceptic who, without committing himself as to the meaning of those expressions or their logical or linguistic dependence on, or independence of, the negation of those types of law to which the determinist refers, yet criticizes our allocation of responsibility by reference to excusing conditions. This more cautious determinist says that whatever the expressions "voluntary," etc. may mean, unless we have reasonable grounds for thinking there are no such laws, the distinctions drawn by these expressions cannot be regarded as of any importance, and there can be neither reason nor justice in allowing punishment to depend on the presence or absence of excusing conditions.

2

In the criminal law of every modern state responsibility for serious crimes is excluded or "diminished" by some of the conditions we have referred to as "excusing conditions." In Anglo-American criminal law this is the doctrine that a "subjective element," or *mens rea,* is required for criminal responsibility, and it is because of this doctrine that a criminal trial may involve investigations into the sanity of the accused; into what he knew, believed, or foresaw; or into the questions whether or not he was subject to coercion by threats or provoked into passion, or was prevented by disease or transitory loss of consciousness from controlling the movements of his body or muscles. These matters come up under the heads known to lawyers as Mistake, Accident, Provocation, Duress, and Insanity, and are most clearly and dramatically exemplified when the charge is one of murder or manslaughter.

Though this general doctrine underlies the criminal law, no legal system in practice admits without qualification the principle that *all* criminal responsibility is excluded by *any* of the excusing conditions. In Anglo-American law this principle is qualified in two ways. First, our law admits crimes of "strict liability." [2] These are crimes where it is no de-

---

2 For an illuminating discussion of strict liability, see the opinion of Justice Jackson in *Morisette* v. *United States* (1952) 342 U.S. 246; 96 L. ed. 288; 72 S. Ct. 240. Also Sayre, "Public Welfare Offenses," 33 C.L.R. 55; Hall, *Principles of Criminal Law* (Indianapolis: Bobbs-Merrill Co., 1947), Chap. X.

fence to show that the accused, in spite of the exercise of proper care, was ignorant of the facts that made his act illegal. Here he is liable to punishment even though he did not intend to commit an act answering the definition of the crime. These are for the most part petty offences contravening statutes that require the maintenance of standards in the manufacture of goods sold for consumption; e.g. a statute forbidding the sale of adulterated milk. Such offences are usually punishable with a fine and are sometimes said by jurists who object to strict liability not to be criminal in any "real" sense. Secondly, even in regard to crimes where liability is not "strict," so that mistake or accident rendering the accused's action *unintentional* would provide an excuse, many legal systems do not accept some of the other conditions we have listed as excluding liability to punishment. This is so for a variety of reasons.

For one thing, it is clear that not only lawyers but scientists and plain men differ as to the relevance of some excusing conditions, and this lack of agreement is usually expressed as a difference of view regarding what kind of factor limits the human *capacity* to control behaviour. Views so expressed have indeed changed with the advance of knowledge about the human mind. Perhaps most people are now persuaded that it is possible for a man to have volitional control of his muscles and also to know the physical character of his movements and their consequences for himself and others, and yet be *unable* to resist the urge or temptation to perform a certain act; yet many think this incapacity exists only if it is associated with well-marked physiological or neurological symptoms or independently definable psychological disturbances. And perhaps there are still some who hold a modified form of the Platonic doctrine that Virtue is Knowledge and believe that the possession of knowledge [3] (and muscular control) is *per se* a sufficient condition of the capacity to comply with the law.[4]

Another reason limiting the scope of the excusing conditions is difficulty of *proof*. Some of the mental elements involved are much easier to prove than others. It is relatively simple to show that an agent lacked, either generally or on a particular occasion, volitional muscular control; it is somewhat more difficult to show that he did not know certain facts about either present circumstances (e.g. that a gun was loaded) or the future (that a man would step into the line of fire); it is much more difficult to establish whether or not a person was deprived of "self-control" by passion provoked by others, or by partial mental disease. As we con-

---

[3] This view is often defended by the assertion that the mind is an "integrated whole," so that if the capacity for self-control is absent, knowledge must also be absent. See Hall, op. cit., p. 524: "Diseased volition does not exist apart from diseased intelligence"; see also reference to the "integration theory," Chap. XIV.

[4] English judges have taken different sides on the issue whether a man can be said to have "lost control," and killed another while in that condition, if he knew what he was doing and killed his victim intentionally. See *Holmes* v. *D.P.P.* (1946), A.C. at 597 (Lord Simon) and *A.G. for Ceylon* v. *Kumarasinghege* v. *Don John Perera* (1953), A.C. 200 (Lord Goddard).

sider these different cases not only do we reach much vaguer concepts, but we become progressively more dependent on the agent's own statements about himself, buttressed by inferences from "common-sense" generalizations about human nature, such as that men are capable of self-control when confronted with an open till but not when confronted with a wife in adultery. The law is accordingly much more cautious in admitting "defects of the will" than "defect in knowledge" as qualifying or excluding criminal responsibility. Further difficulties of proof may cause a legal system to limit its inquiry into the agent's "subjective condition" by asking what a "reasonable man" would in the circumstances have known or foreseen, or by asking whether "a reasonable man" in the circumstances would have been deprived (say, by provocation) of self-control; and the system may then impute to the agent such knowledge or foresight or control.[5]

For these practical reasons, no simple identification of the necessary mental subjective elements in responsibility with the full list of excusing conditions can be made; and in all systems far greater prominence is given to the more easily provable elements of volitional control of muscular movement and knowledge of circumstances or consequences than to the other more elusive elements.

Hence it is true that legal recognition of the importance of excusing conditions is never unqualified; the law, like every other human institution, has to compromise with other values besides whatever values are incorporated in the recognition of some conditions as excusing. Sometimes, of course, it is not clear, when "strict liability" is imposed, what value (social welfare?) is triumphant, and there has consequently been much criticism of this as an odious and useless departure from proper principles of liability.

Modern systems of law are however also concerned with most of the conditions we have listed as excusing conditions in another way. Besides the criminal law that requires men to do or abstain from certain actions whether they wish to or not, all such systems contain rules of a different type that provide legal facilities whereby individuals can give effect to their wishes by entering into certain transactions that alter their own and/or others' legal position (rights, duties, status, etc.). Examples of these civil transactions (acts in the law, *Rechtsgeschäfte*) are wills, contracts, gifts, marriage. If a legal system did not provide facilities allowing individuals to give legal effect to their choices in such areas of conduct, it would fail to make one of the law's most distinctive and valuable contributions to social life. But here too most of the mental conditions we have mentioned are recognized by the law as important not primarily as *excusing* conditions but as *invalidating* conditions. Thus a will, a gift, a marriage, and (subject to many complex exceptions) a contract may be

---

[5] See for a defence of the "reasonable man" test (in cases of alleged provocation) *Royal Commission on Capital Punishment*, pp. 51–53 (paras. 139–45). This defence is not confined to the difficulties of proof.

invalid if the party concerned was insane, mistaken about the legal character of the transaction or some "essential" term of it, or if he was subject to duress, coercion, or the undue influence of other persons. These are the obvious analogues of mistake, accident, coercion, duress, insanity, which are admitted by criminal law as excusing conditions. Analogously, the recognition of such conditions as invalidating civil transactions is qualified or limited by other principles. Those who enter in good faith into bilateral transactions of the kind mentioned with persons who appear normal (i.e. not subject to any of the relevant invalidating conditions) must be protected, as must third parties who may have purchased interests originating from a transaction that on the face of it seemed normal. Hence a technique has been introduced to safeguard such persons. This includes principles precluding, say, a party who has entered into a transaction by some mistake, from making this the basis of his defence against one who honestly took his words at face value and justifiably relied on them; there are also distinctions between transactions wholly invalidated *ab initio* (void) and those that are valid until denounced (voidable), to protect those who have relied on the transaction's normal form.

3

   The similarity between the law's insistence on certain mental elements for both criminal responsibility and the validity of acts in the law is clear. Why, then, do we value a system of social control that takes mental conditions into account? Let us start with criminal law and its excusing conditions. What is so precious in its attention to these, and what would be lost if it gave this up? What precisely is the ground of our dissatisfaction with "strict liability" in criminal law? To these fundamental questions, there still are, curiously enough, many quite discordant answers, and I propose to consider two of them before suggesting an answer that would stress the analogy with civil transactions.

   The first general answer takes this form. It is said that the importance of excusing conditions in criminal responsibility is derivative, and it derives from the more fundamental requirement that for criminal responsibility there must be "moral culpability," which would not exist where the excusing conditions are present. On this view the maxim *actus non est reus nisi mens sit rea* refers to a morally evil mind. Certainly traces of this view are to be found in scattered observations of English and American judges—in phrases such as "an evil mind with regard to that which he is doing," "a bad mind," or references to acts done not "merely unguardedly or accidentally, without any evil mind." [6]

   Some of these well-known formulations were perhaps careless state-

6 Lord Esher in *Lee* v. *Dangar*, (1892) 2 Q.B. 337.

ments of the quite different principle that *mens rea* is an intention to commit an act that is wrong in the sense of legally forbidden. But the same view has been reasserted in general terms in England by Lord Justice Denning: "In order that an act should be punishable, it must be morally blameworthy. It must be a sin." [7] Most English lawyers would however now agree with Sir James Fitzjames Stephen that the expression *mens rea* is unfortunate, though too firmly established to be expelled, just because it misleadingly suggests that, in general, moral culpability is essential to a crime, and they would assent to the criticism expressed by a later judge that the true translation of *mens rea* is "an intention to do the act which is made penal by statute or by the common law." [8] Yet, in spite of this, the view has been argued by a distinguished American contemporary writer on criminal law, Professor Jerome Hall, in his important and illuminating *Principles of Criminal Law,* that *moral* culpability is the basis of responsibility in crime. Again and again in Chapters V and VI of his book Professor Hall asserts that, though the goodness or badness of the *motive* with which a crime is committed may not be relevant, the general principle of liability, except of course where liability is unfortunately "strict" and so any mental element must be disregarded, is the *"intentional or reckless doing of a morally wrong act."* [9] This is declared to be the essential meaning of *mens rea:* though *mens rea* differs in different crimes there is one "common, essential element, namely, the voluntary doing of a morally wrong act forbidden by penal law." [10] On this view the law inquires into the mind in criminal cases in order to secure that no one shall be punished in the absence of the basic condition of *moral* culpability. For it is just only to "punish those who have intentionally committed moral wrongs, proscribed by law." [11]

Now, if this theory were merely a theory as to what the criminal law of a good society should be, it would not be possible to refute it, for it represents a moral preference: namely that legal punishment should be administered only where a "morally wrong" act has been done—though I think such plausibility as it would have even as an ideal is due to a confusion. But of course Professor Hall's doctrine does not fit any actual system of criminal law because in every such system there are necessarily many actions (quite apart from the cases of "strict liability") that if voluntarily done are criminally punishable, although our moral code may be either silent as to their moral quality, or divided. Very many offences are created by legislation designed to give effect to a particular economic

[7] Denning, *The Changing Law* (London: Stevens, 1953), p. 112.

[8] *Allard* v. *Selfridge,* (1925) 1 K.B. at 137. (Shearman J.) This is quoted by Glanville Williams in *Criminal Law, The General Part* (2nd edn.), p. 31, n. 3, where the author comments that the judge should have added "or recklessness."

[9] Hall, op. cit., p. 149.

[10] Ibid., p. 167.

[11] Ibid., p. 166.

scheme (e.g. a state monopoly of road or rail transport), the utility or moral character of which may be genuinely in dispute. An offender against such legislation can hardly be said to be morally guilty or to have intentionally committed a moral wrong, still less "a sin" proscribed by law; [12] yet if he has broken such laws "voluntarily" (to use Professor Hall's expression), which in practice means that he was not in any of the excusing conditions, the requirements of *justice* are surely satisfied. Doubts about the justice of the punishment would begin only if he were punished even though he was at the time of the action in one of the excusing conditions; for what is essential is that the offender, if he is to be *fairly* punished, must have acted "voluntarily," and not that he must have committed some moral offence. In addition to such requirements of justice in the individual case, there is of course, as we shall see, a different type of requirement as to the *general* character of the laws.

It is important to see what has led Professor Hall and others to the conclusion that the basis of criminal responsibility *must* be moral culpability ("the voluntary doing of a morally wrong act"), for latent in this position, I think, is a false dilemma. The false dilemma is that criminal liability *must* either be "strict"—that is, based on nothing more than the outward conduct of the accused—or *must* be based on moral culpability. On this view there is no third alternative and so there can be no reason for inquiring into the state of mind of the accused—"inner facts," as Professor Hall terms them—except for the purpose of establishing *moral* guilt. To be understood all theories should be examined in the context of argument in which they are advanced, and it is important to notice that Professor Hall's doctrine was developed mainly by way of criticism of the so-called objective theory of liability, which was developed, though not very consistently, by Chief Justice Holmes in his famous essays on common law.[13] Holmes asserted that the law did not consider, and need not consider, in administering punishment what in fact the accused intended but that it imputed to him the intention that an "ordinary man," equipped with ordinary knowledge, would be taken to have had in acting as the accused did. Holmes in advocating this theory of "objective liability" used the phrase "inner facts" and frequently stressed that *mens rea,* in the sense of the actual wickedness of the party, was unnecessary. So he often identified "mental facts" with moral guilt and also identified the notion of an objective standard of liability with the rejection of *moral* culpability as a basis of liability. This terminology was pregnant with confusion. It fatally suggests that there are only two alternatives: to con-

12 "The criminal quality of an act . . . [cannot be] discovered by reference to any standard but one: Is the act prohibited with penal consequences? Morality and criminality are far from co-extensive; nor is the sphere of criminality necessarily part of a more extensive field covered by morality unless the moral code necessarily disapproves all acts prohibited by the State, in which case the argument moves in a circle." Lord Atkin *Proprietory Articles Trade Association* v. *A.G. for Canada* (1931) A.C. 310 at 324.

13 Holmes, *The Common Law,* Lecture II, "The Criminal Law."

sider the mental condition of the accused only to find moral culpability
or not to consider it at all. But we are not impaled on the horns of any
such dilemma: there are independent reasons, apart from the question of
moral guilt, why a legal system should require a voluntary action as a
condition of responsibility. These reasons I shall develop in a moment
and merely summarize here by saying that the principle (1) that it is
unfair and unjust to punish those who have not "voluntarily" broken the
law is a moral principle quite distinct from the assertion (2) that it is
wrong to punish those who have not "voluntarily committed a moral
wrong proscribed by law."

The confusion that suggests the false dilemma—either "objective"
standards of liability or liability based on the "inner fact" of *moral* guilt—
is, I think, this. We would all agree that unless a legal system was as a
whole morally defensible, so that its existence was better than the chaos
of its collapse, and more good than evil was secured by maintaining and
enforcing laws in general, these laws should not be enforced, and no one
should be punished for breaking them. It *seems* therefore to follow, but
does not, that we should not punish anyone unless in breaking the law
he has done something morally wrong; for it looks as if the mere fact
that a law has been voluntarily broken is not enough to justify punishment and the extra element required is "moral culpability," at least in
the sense that he should have done something morally wrong. What we
need to escape confusion here is a distinction between two sets of questions. The first is a general question about the moral value of the laws:
Will enforcing them produce more good than evil? If it does, then it is
morally permissible to enforce them by punishing those who have broken
them, unless in any given case there is some "excuse." The second is a
particular question concerning individual cases: Is it right or just to
punish this particular person? Is he to be excused on account of his mental condition because it would be unjust—in view of his lack of knowledge or control—to punish him? The first, general question with regard
to each law, is a question for the legislature; the second, arising in particular cases, is for the judge. And the question of responsibility arises
only at the judicial stage. One necessary condition of the just application
of a punishment is normally expressed by saying that the agent "could
have helped" doing what he did, and hence the need to inquire into the
"inner facts" is dictated not by the moral principle that only the doing of
an *immoral* act may be legally punished, but by the moral principle that
no one should be punished who could not help doing what he did. This
is a necessary condition (unless strict liability is admitted) for the moral
propriety of legal punishment and no doubt also for moral censure; in
this respect law and morals are similar. But this similarity as to the one
essential condition that there must be a "voluntary" action if legal punishment or moral censure is to be morally permissible does not mean that
legal punishment is morally permissible only where the agent has done
something morally wrong. I think that the use of the word "fault" in
juristic discussion to designate the requirement that liability be excluded

by excusing conditions may have blurred the important distinction between the assertions that (1) it is morally permissible to punish only voluntary actions and (2) it is morally permissible to punish only voluntary
commission of a moral wrong.

4

Let me now turn to a second explanation of the law's concern with
the "inner facts" of mental life as a condition of responsibility. This is
a Benthamite theory that I shall name the "economy of threats" and is the
contention that the required conditions of responsibility—e.g. that the
agent knew what he was doing, was not subject to gross coercion or
duress, was not mad or a small child—are simply the conditions that must
be satisfied if the threat to punish announced by the criminal law is to
have any effect and if the system is to be efficient in securing the maintenance of law at the least cost in pain. This theory is stated most clearly
by Bentham; it is also to be found in Austin and in the report of the
great Criminal Law Commission of 1833 of which he was a member. In
a refined form it is implicit in many contemporary attempted "dissolu-
tions" of the problem of free will. Many accept this view as a common-
sense utilitarian explanation of the importance that we attribute to
excusing conditions. It appeals most to the utilitarian and to the determinist and it is interesting to find that Professor Glanville Williams
in his recent admirable work on the general principles of criminal law,[14]
when he wished to explain the exemption of the insane from legal responsibility compatibly with "determinism," did so by reference to this
theory.

Yet the doctrine is an incoherent one at certain points, I think,
and a departure from, rather than an elucidation of, the moral insistence
that criminal liability should generally be conditional on the absence of
excusing conditions. Bentham's best statement of the theory is in Chapter
XIII of his *Principles of Morals and Legislation:* "Cases in Which Punishment Must be Inefficacious." The cases he lists, besides those where
the law is made *ex post facto* or not adequately promulgated, fall into
two main classes. The first class consists of cases in which the penal threat
of punishment could not prevent a person from performing an action
forbidden by the law *or any action of the same sort;* these are the cases
of infancy and insanity in which the agent, according to Bentham, has
not the "state or disposition of mind on which the prospect of evils so
distant as those which are held forth by the law" has the effect of influencing his conduct. The second class consists of cases in which the law's
threat could not have had any effect on the agent in relation to the
particular act committed because of his lack of knowledge or control.

[14] Williams, op. cit. (1st edn.), pp. 346–7.

What is wrong in punishing a man under both these types of mental conditions is that the punishment is wasteful; suffering is caused to the accused who is punished in circumstances where it could do no good.

In discussing the defence of insanity Professor Glanville Williams applies this theory in a way that brings out its consistency not only with a wholly utilitarian outlook on punishment but with determinism.

> For mankind in the mass it is impossible to tell whom the threat of punishment will restrain and whom it will not. For most [it] will succeed; for some it will fail, and the punishment must then be applied to these criminals in order to maintain the threat for persons generally. Mentally deranged persons, however, can be separated from the mass of mankind by scientific tests. . . . Being a defined class their segregation from punishment does not impair the efficacy of the sanction for people generally.[15]

The point made here is that, if, for example, the mentally deranged (scientifically tested) are exempted, criminals will not be able to exploit this exemption to free themselves from liability, since they cannot bring themselves within its scope and so will not feel free to commit crimes with impunity. This is said in order to justify the exemption of the insane consistently with the tenet of determinism, in spite of the fact that from a determinist viewpoint

> every impulse, if not in fact resisted, was in those circumstances irresistible. A so-called irresistible impulse is simply one in which the desire to perform a particular act is not influenced by other factors (like the threat of punishment). But on this definition every crime is the result of an irresistible impulse.

This theory is designed to fit not merely a utilitarian theory of punishment, but also the view that it is always false, if not senseless, to say that a criminal could have helped doing what he did. So on this theory, when we inquire into the mental state of the accused, we do not do so to answer the question, Could he help it? Nor of course to answer the question, Could the threat of punishment have been effective in his case?—for we know that it was not. The theory presents us with a far simpler conceptual scheme for dealing with the whole matter, since it does not involve the seemingly counter-factual speculation regarding what the accused "could have done." On this theory we inquire into the state of mind of the accused simply to find out whether he belongs to a defined class of persons whose exemption from punishment, if allowed, will not weaken the effect on others of the general threat of punishment made by the law. So there is no question of its being unjust or unfair to punish a particular criminal or to exempt him from punishment.

---

15 Williams, loc. cit. This passage is, however, omitted from the 2nd edition of *Criminal Law, The General Part* (1961).

Once the crime has been committed, the decision to punish or not has nothing to do with any moral claim or right of the criminal to have the features of his case considered, but only with the causal efficacy of his punishment on others. On this view the rationale of excuses is not (to put it shortly) that the accused should, in view of his mental condition, be excused whatever the effect of this on others; it is rather the mere fact that excusing him will not harm society by reducing the efficacy of the law's threats for others. So the criminal's mental condition is relevant simply to the question of the effect on others of his punishment or exemption.

This is certainly paradoxical enough. It seems to destroy the entire notion that in punishing we must be just to the particular criminal in front of us and that the purpose of excusing conditions is to protect him from society's claims. But, apart from paradox, the doctrine that we consider the state of a man's mind only to see if punishment is required in order to maintain the efficacy of threats for others is vitiated by a *non sequitur*. Before a man does a criminal action we may know that he is in such a condition that the threats cannot operate on him, either because of some temporary condition or because of a disease; but it does not follow—because the *threat* of punishment in his case, and in the case of others like him, is useless—that his *punishment* in the sense of the official administration of penalties will also be unnecessary to maintain the efficacy of threats for others at its highest. It may very well be that, if the law contained no explicit exemptions from responsibility on the score of ignorance, accident, mistake, or insanity, many people who now take a chance in the hope that they will bring themselves, if discovered, within these exempting provisions would in fact be deterred. It is indeed a perfectly familiar fact that pleas of loss of consciousness or other abnormal mental states, or of the existence of some other excusing condition, are frequently and sometimes successfully advanced where there is no real basis for them, since the difficulties of disproof are often considerable. The uselessness of a *threat* against a given individual or class does not entail that the *punishment* of that individual or class cannot be required to maintain in the highest degree the efficacy of threats for others. It may in fact be the case that to make liability to punishment dependent on the absence of excusing conditions is the most efficient way of maintaining the laws with the least cost in pain. But it is not *obviously* or *necessarily* the case.

It is clear, I think, that if we were to base our views of criminal responsibility on the doctrine of the economy of threats, we should misrepresent altogether the character of our moral preference for a legal system that requires mental conditions of responsibility over a system of total strict liability, or entirely different methods of social control such as hypnosis, propaganda, or conditioning.

To make this intelligible we must cease to regard the law as merely a causal factor in human behaviour differing from others only in the fact that it produces its effect through the medium of the mind; for it is clear that we look on excusing conditions as something that *protects* the individual against the claims of the rest of society. Recognition of their excusing force may lead to a lower, not a higher, level of efficacy of threats; yet—and this is the point—we would not regard that as sufficient ground for abandoning this protection of the individual; or if we did, it would be with the recognition that we had sacrificed one principle to another; for more is at stake than the single principle of maintaining the laws at their most efficacious level. We must cease, therefore, to regard the law simply as a system of stimuli goading the individual by its threats into conformity. Instead I shall suggest a mercantile analogy. Consider the law not as a system of stimuli but as what might be termed a *choosing* system, in which individuals can find out, in general terms at least, the costs they have to pay if they act in certain ways. This done, let us ask what value this system would have in social life and why we should regret its absence. I do not of course mean to suggest that it is a matter of indifference whether we obey the law or break it and pay the penalty. Punishment *is* different from a mere "tax on a course of conduct." What I do mean is that the conception of the law simply as goading individuals into desired courses of behaviour is inadequate and misleading; what a legal system that makes liability generally depend on excusing conditions does is to guide individuals' choices as to behaviour by presenting them with reasons for exercising choice in the direction of obedience, but leaving them to choose.

It is at this point that I would stress the analogy between the mental conditions that excuse from criminal responsibility and the mental conditions that are regarded as invalidating civil transactions such as wills, gifts, contracts, marriages, and the like. These institutions provide individuals with two inestimable advantages in relation to those areas of conduct they cover. These are (1) the advantage to the individual of determining by his choice what the future shall be and (2) the advantage of being able to predict what the future will be. For these institutions enable the individual (1) to bring into operation the coercive forces of the law so that those legal arrangements he has chosen shall be carried into effect and (2) to plan the rest of his life with certainty or at least the confidence (in a legal system that is working normally) that the arrangements he has made will in fact be carried out. By these devices the individual's choice is brought into the legal system and allowed to determine its future operations in various areas thereby giving him a type of indirect coercive control over, and a power to foresee the development of, official life. This he would not have "naturally"; that is, apart from these legal institutions.

In brief, the function of these institutions of private law is to render effective the individual's preferences in certain areas. It is therefore clear why in this sphere the law treats the mental factors of, say, mistake, ignorance of the nature of the transaction, coercion, undue influence, or insanity as invalidating such civil transactions. For a transaction entered into under such conditions will not represent a real choice: the individual, might have chosen one course of events and by the transaction procured another (cases of mistake, ignorance, etc.), or he might have chosen to enter the transaction without coolly and calmly thinking out what he wanted (undue influence), or he might have been subjected to the threats of another who had imposed *his* choices (coercion).

To see the value of such institutions in rendering effective the individual's considered and informed choices as to what on the whole shall happen, we have but to conduct the experiment of imagining their absence: a system where no mental conditions would be recognized as invalidating such transactions and the consequent loss of control over the future that the individual would suffer. That such institutions *do* render individual choices effective and increase the powers of individuals to predict the course of events is simply a matter of empirical fact, and no form of "determinism," of course, can show this to be false or illusory. If a man makes a will to which the law gives effect after his death, this is not, of course, merely a case of *post hoc:* we have enough empirical evidence to show that this was an instance of a regularity sufficient to have enabled us to predict the outcome with reasonable probability, at least in some cases, and to justify us, therefore, in interpreting this outcome as a consequence of making the will. There is no reason why we should not describe the situation as one where the testator *caused* the outcome of the distribution made. Of course the testator's choice in this example is only one prominent member of a complex set of conditions, of which all the other members were as necessary for the production of the outcome as his choice. Science may indeed show (1) that this set of conditions also includes conditions of which we are at the present moment quite ignorant and (2) that the testator's choice itself was the outcome of some set of jointly sufficient conditions of which we have no present knowledge. Yet neither of these two suppositions, even if they were verified, would make it false to say that the individuals' choice did determine the results, or make illusory the satisfaction got (*a*) from the knowledge that this kind of thing is possible, (*b*) from the exercise of such choice. And if determinism does not entail that satisfactions (*a*) or (*b*) are illusory, I for one do not understand how it could affect the wisdom, justice, rationality, or morality of the system we are considering.

If with this in mind we turn back to criminal law and its excusing conditions, we can regard their function as a mechanism for similarly maximizing within the framework of coercive criminal law the efficacy of the individual's informed and considered choice in determining the future and also his power to predict that future. We must start, of course, with the need for criminal law and its sanctions as at least some check on behaviour that threatens society. This implies a belief that the criminal law's threats actually do diminish the frequency of antisocial behaviour, and no doubt this belief may be said to be based on inadequate evidence. However, we must clearly take it as our starting point: if this belief is wrong, it is so because of lack of empirical evidence and not because it contradicts any form of determinism. Then we can see that by attaching excusing conditions to criminal responsibility, we provide each individual with benefits he would not have if we made the system of criminal law operate on a basis of total "strict liability." First, we maximize the individual's power at any time to predict the likelihood that the sanctions of the criminal law will be applied to him. Secondly, we introduce the individual's choice as one of the operative factors determining whether or not these sanctions shall be applied to him. He can weigh the cost to him of obeying the law—and of sacrificing some satisfaction in order to obey—against obtaining that satisfaction at the cost of paying "the penalty." Thirdly, by adopting this system of attaching excusing conditions we provide that, if the sanctions of the criminal law are applied, the pains of punishment will for each individual represent the price of some satisfaction obtained from breach of law. This, of course, can sound like a very cold, if not immoral attitude toward the criminal law, general obedience to which we regard as an essential part of a decent social order. But this attitude seems repellent only if we assume that all criminal laws are ones whose operation we approve. To be realistic we must also think of bad and repressive criminal laws; in South Africa, Nazi Germany, Soviet Russia, and no doubt elsewhere, we might be thankful to have their badness mitigated by the fact that they fall only on those who have obtained a satisfaction from knowingly doing what they forbid.

Again, the value of these three factors can be realized if we conduct the *Gedankenexperiment* of imagining criminal law operating without excusing conditions. First, our power of predicting what will happen to us will be immeasurably diminished; the likelihood that I shall choose to do the forbidden act (e.g. strike someone) and so incur the sanctions of the criminal law may not be very easy to calculate even under our system: as a basis for this prediction we have indeed only the knowledge of our own character and some estimate of the temptations life is likely to offer us. But if we are also to be liable if we strike someone by accident, by mistake, under coercion, etc., the chances that we shall incur the sanctions are immeasurably increased. From our knowledge of the past career of our body considered as a *thing*, we cannot infer much as to the chances of its being brought into violent contact with another, and under a system that dispensed with the excusing condition of, say, accident (implying lack of intention) a collision alone would land us in jail. Secondly, our choice would condition what befalls us to a lesser extent. Thirdly, we should suffer sanctions without having obtained any satisfaction. Again, no form of determinism that I, at least, can construct can throw any doubt on, or show to be illusory, the real satisfaction that a system of criminal law incorporating excusing conditions provides for individuals in maximizing the effect of their choices within the framework of coercive law. The choices remain choices, the satisfactions remain satisfactions, and the consequences of choices remain the consequences of choices, even if choices are determined and even if other "determinants" besides our choices condition the satisfaction arising from their being rendered effective in this way by the criminal law.

It is now important to contrast this view of excusing conditions with the Benthamite explanation, e.g. discussed in Part 3 of this paper. On that view excusing conditions were treated as conditions under which the laws' threat could operate with maximum efficacy. They were recognized *not* because they ensured justice to individuals considered separately, but because sanctions administered under those conditions were believed more effective and economical of pain in securing the general conformity to law. If these beliefs as to the *efficacy* of excusing conditions could be shown false, then all reasons for recognizing them as conditions of criminal responsibility would disappear. On the present view, which I advocate, excusing conditions are accepted as independent of the efficacy of the system of threats. Instead it is conceded that recognition of these conditions may, and probably does, diminish that efficacy by increasing the number of conditions for criminal liability and hence giving opportunities for pretence on the part of criminals, or mistakes on the part of tribunals.

On this view excusing conditions are accepted as something that may conflict with the social utility of the law's threats; they are regarded as of moral importance because they provide for all individuals alike the satisfactions of a choosing system. Recognition of excusing conditions is therefore seen as a matter of protection of the individual against the claims of society for the highest measure of protection from crime that can be obtained from a system of threats. In this way the criminal law respects the claims of the individual as such, or at least as a *choosing being,* and distributes its coercive sanctions in a way that reflects this respect for the individual. This surely is very central in the notion of justice and is *one,* though no doubt only one, among the many strands of principle that I think lie at the root of the preference for legal institutions conditioning liability by reference to excusing conditions.

I cannot, of course, by unearthing this principle, claim to have solved everyone's perplexities. In particular, I do not know what to say to a critic who urges that I have shown only that the system in which excusing conditions are recognized protects the individual better against the claims of society than one in which no recognition is accorded to these factors. This seems to me to be enough; yet I cannot satisfy the complaint, if he makes it, that I have not shown that we are justified in punishing anyone *ever,* at all, under any conditions. He may say that even the criminal who has committed his crime in the most deliberate and calculating way and has shown himself throughout his life competent in maximizing what he thinks his own interests will be little comforted when he is caught and punished for some major crime. At *that* stage he will get little satisfaction if it is pointed out to him (1) that he has obtained some satisfaction from his crime, (2) that he knew that it was likely he would be punished and that he had decided to pay for his satisfaction by exposing himself to this risk, and (3) that the system under which he is punished is not one of strict liability, is not one under which a man who accidentally did what he did would also have suffered the penalties of the law.

5

I will add four observations *ex abundante cautela.*

(i) The elucidation of the moral importance of the mental element in responsibility, and the moral odium of strict liability, that I have indicated, must not be mistaken for a psychological theory of motivation. It does not answer the question, Why do people obey the law? It does not assert that they obey only because they choose to obey rather than pay the cost. Instead, my theory answers the question, Why *should* we have a law with just these features? Human beings in the main do what the law requires without first choosing between the advantage and the cost of disobeying, and when they obey it is not usually from fear of the sanction. For most the sanction is important not because it inspires them with fear but because it offers a guarantee that the antisocial minority who would not otherwise obey will be coerced into obedience by fear. To obey without this assurance might, as Hobbes saw, be very foolish: it would be to risk going to the wall. However, the fact that only a few people, as things are, consider the question Shall I obey or pay?, does not in the least mean that the standing possibility of asking this question is unimportant: for it secures just those values for the individual that I have mentioned.

(ii) I must, of course, confront the objection which the Marxist might make, that the excusing conditions, or indeed *mutatis mutandis* the invalidating conditions, of civil transactions are of no use to many individuals in society whose economic or social position is such that the difference between a law of strict liability and a law that recognizes excusing conditions is of no importance.

It is quite true that the fact that criminal law recognizes excusing mental conditions may be of no importance to a person whose economic condition is such that he cannot profit from the difference between a law against theft that is strict and one that incorporates excusing conditions. If starvation "forces" him to steal, the values the system respects and incorporates in excusing conditions are nothing to him. This is of course similar to the claim often made that the freedom that a political democracy of the Western type offers to its subjects is merely formal freedom, not real freedom, and leaves one free to starve. I regard this as a confusing way of putting what may be true under certain conditions: namely, that the freedoms the law offers may be *valueless* as playing no part in the happiness of persons who are too poor or weak to take advantage of them. The admission that the excusing condition may be of no value to those who are below a minimum level of economic prosperity may mean, of course, that we should incorporate as a further excusing condition the pressure of gross forms of economic necessity. This point, though possibly valid, does not seem to me to throw doubt on the principle lying behind such excusing conditions as we do recognize at present, nor to destroy their genuine value for those who are above the minimum level of economic prosperity; for the difference between a system of strict liability and our present system plays a part in their happiness.

(iii) The principle by reference to which I have explained the moral importance of excusing conditions may help to clarify an old dispute, apt to spring up between lawyers on the one hand and doctors and scientists on the other, about the moral basis of punishment.

From Plato to the present day there has been a recurrent insistence that if we were rational we would always look on crime as a disease and address ourselves to its cure. We would do this not only where a crime has actually been committed but where we find well-marked evidence that it will be. We would take the individual and treat him as a patient before the deed was done. Plato,[16] it will be remembered, thought it superstitious to look back and go into questions of responsibility or the previous history of a crime except when it might throw light on what was needed to cure the criminal.

Carried to its extreme, this doctrine is the programme of Erewhon, where those with criminal tendencies were sent by doctors for indefinite periods of cure; punishment was displaced by a concept of social hygiene. It is, I think, of some importance to realize why we should object to this point of view; for both those who defend it and those who attack it often assume that the *only* possible consistent alternative to Erewhon is a theory of punishment under which it is justified simply as a return for the moral evil attributable to the accused. Those opposed to the Erewhonian programme are apt to object that it disregards *moral* guilt as a necessary condition of a just punishment and thus leads to a condition in which any person may be sacrificed to the welfare of society. Those who defend an Erewhonian view think that their opponents' objection must entail adherence to the form of retributive punishment that regards punishment simply as a justified return for the moral evil in the criminal's action.

Both sides, I think, make a common mistake: there *is* a reason for making punishment conditional on the commission of crime and respecting excusing conditions, which is quite independent of the form of retributive theory that is often urged as the only alternative to Erewhon. Even if we regard the over-all purpose of punishment as that of protecting society by deterring persons from committing crimes and insist that the penalties we inflict be adapted to this end, we can in perfect consistency and with good reason insist that these punishments be applied only to those who have broken a law and to whom no excusing conditions apply. For this system will provide a measure of protection to individuals

16 Plato, *Protagoras,* 324; *Laws,* 861, 865.

and will maximize their powers of prediction and the efficacy of their choices in the ways that I have mentioned. To see this we have only to ask ourselves what in terms of these values we should lose (however much else we might gain) if social hygiene and a *system of compulsory treatment* for those with detectable criminal tendencies were throughout substituted for our system of punishment modified by excusing conditions. Surely the realization of what would be lost, and not a retributive theory of punishment, is all that is required as a reason for refusing to make the descent into Erewhon.

(iv) Finally, what I have written concerns only *legal* responsibility and the rationale of excuses in a legal system in which there are organized, coercive sanctions. I do not think the same arguments can be used to defend *moral* responsibility from the determinist, if it is in any danger from that source.

STRICT LIABILITY IN THE CRIMINAL LAW

Richard A. Wasserstrom

The proliferation of so-called "strict liability" offenses in the criminal law has occasioned the vociferous, continued, and almost unanimous criticism of analysts and philosophers of the law.[1] The imposition of severe criminal sanctions [2] in the absence of any requisite mental element has been held by many to be incompatible with the basic requirements of our Anglo-American, and, indeed, any civilized jurisprudence.

The Model Penal Code, for example, announces that its provisions for culpability make a "frontal attack" upon the notion of strict, or absolute, liability.[3] Francis B. Sayre, in his classic article on "Public Welfare Offenses," contends that since the real menace to society is the intentional commission of undesirable acts, evil intent must remain an element of the criminal law. "To inflict substantial punishment upon

Stanford Law Review 12 (1960): 731. Copyright 1960 by the Board of Trustees of the Leland Stanford Junior University. Reprinted by permission of the Stanford Law Review, Richard Wasserstrom, and Fred B. Rothman and Company.

[1] The history of those strict liability offenses which are of legislative origin is of quite recent date. One of the first cases in which a statute was interpreted as imposing strict criminal liability was *Regina* v. *Woodrow*, 15 M. & W. 404, 153 Eng. Rep. 907 (1846). For an exhaustive account of the early history of these statutory offenses see Sayre, *Public Welfare Offenses*, 33 Colum. L. Rev. 55, 56–66 (1933).

[2] "Severe criminal sanctions" refer to imprisonment as opposed to the mere imposition of a fine.

[3] Model Penal Code § 2.05, comment (Tent. Draft No. 4, 1955).

one who is morally entirely innocent, who caused injury through reasonable mistake or pure accident, would so outrage the feelings of the community as to nullify its own enforcement." [4] And Jerome Hall, perhaps the most active and insistent critic of such offenses, has consistently denounced the notion of strict liability as anathema to the coherent development of a rational criminal law: "It is impossible to defend strict liability in terms of or by reference to the only criteria that are available to evaluate the influence of legal controls on human behavior. What then remains but the myth that through devious, unknown ways some good results from strict liability in 'penal' law?" [5]

Without attempting to demonstrate that strict liability offenses are inherently or instrumentally desirable, one can question the force of the arguments which have been offered against them. It is not evident, for example, that strict liability statutes cannot have a deterrent effect greater than that of ordinary criminal statutes. Nor, is it clear that all strict liability statutes can most fruitfully be discussed and evaluated as members of a single class of criminality. The notion of "fault" is sufficiently ambiguous, perhaps, so as to obscure the sense or senses in which these statutes do impose liability "without fault." And finally, the similarities between strict liability and criminal negligence are such that it seems difficult to attack the former without at the same time calling the latter into comparable question. Issues of this kind are, then, the explicit subjects for examination here.

THE CONCEPT OF STRICT CRIMINAL LIABILITY

Neither the arguments against the imposition of strict criminal liability nor the justifications for such imposition can be evaluated intelligently until the meaning of the phrase "strict criminal liability" has been clarified. One possible approach—and the one selected here as appropriate for the scope of this analysis—is that of ostensive definition. That is to say, a small, but representative, sample of the kinds of offenses which are usually characterized as strict liability offenses can be described briefly so as to make the common characteristics of this class relatively obvious upon inspection.

At the outset, it is essential that strict liability offenses not be confused with Sayre's "public welfare" offenses, i.e., those which he defines as essentially regulative in function and punishable by fine rather than imprisonment.[6] This inquiry is concerned with those offenses which can-

---

[4] Sayre, *supra* note 1, at 56.

[5] HALL, GENERAL PRINCIPLES OF CRIMINAL LAW 304–5 (1947). See also WILLIAMS, CRIMINAL LAW §§ 70–76 (1953); Hart, *The Aims of Criminal Law*, 23 LAW & CONTEMP. PROB. 401, 422–25 (1958).

[6] Sayre, *supra* note 1, at 83.

not be distinguished from other criminal conduct by virtue of the fact that the punishment involved is consistently less than imprisonment.[7] Thus, the cases here selected as exemplary of strict criminal liability are all cases in which the prescribed sentences are surely not minimal in degree or merely regulative in function.

The landmark case in American jurisprudence is undoubtedly *United States* v. *Balint*.[8] The defendant was indicted under a statute which made it unlawful to sell narcotics without a written order. The defendant claimed that the indictment was insufficient because it failed to allege that he had known that the drugs sold were narcotics. The United States Supreme Court held that his conviction did not deny due process.

Another classic example is *State* v. *Lindberg*.[9] The statute in question provided that "every director and officer of any bank . . . who shall borrow . . . any of its funds in an excessive amount . . . shall . . . be guilty of a felony" [10] The defendant contended that he had borrowed the money in question only after he had been assured by another official of the bank that the money had come from a bank other than his own. But the court held that the reasonableness of the defendant's mistake was not a defense.

The final case, *Regina* v. *Prince*,[11] is famous in both English and American jurisprudence. Prince was indicted under a statute which made it a misdemeanour to "unlawfully take . . . any unmarried Girl, being under the Age of Sixteen Years, out of the Possession and against the Will of her Father or Mother. . . ." [12] One of the defenses which Prince sought to interpose rested upon the reasonableness of his beliefs that the girl in question was over sixteen years old. The majority of the court interpreted the statute to make the reasonableness of a belief as to the girl's age irrelevant, and found Prince guilty.

Assuming these cases to be representative,[13] strict liability offenses might be tentatively described (although not defined) as those in which the sole question put to the jury is whether the jury believes the defendant to have committed the act proscribed by the statute.[14] If it finds that

---

[7] If the offenses were always punishable by something less than imprisonment then it would surely be relevant to ask in what sense they were penal in anything but name. This appears in part to be Hall's criticism of Sayre's article. See HALL, op. cit. *supra* note 5, at 279.

[8] 258 U.S. 250 (1922).

[9] 125 Wash. 51, 215 Pac. 41 (1923).

[10] Wash. Comp. Stat. § 3259 (Remington 1922).

[11] 13 Cox Crim. Cas. 138 (1875).

[12] Offenses Against the Person Act, 1861, 24 & 25 Vict., c. 100, § 55.

[13] Exhaustive enumerations of leading strict liability cases can be found in Sayre, *Public Welfare Offenses*, 33 COLUM. L. REV. 55 (1933).

[14] Jackson, *Absolute Prohibition in Statutory Offences*, 6 CAMB. L.J. 83, 88 (1938).

he did the act, then it is obliged to bring in a verdict of guilty.[15] Whether this characterization of the above three cases is either precise or very helpful is a question which must await further discussion below. For the present, however, it is perhaps sufficient to observe that whatever it is that the concept of *mens rea* is thought to designate, it is this which needs not be shown to be predicable of the defendant.[16]

THE JUSTIFICATION OF STRICT LIABILITY

Before attempting to assess the arguments for and against the notion of strict criminal liability, it should be made clear that the author agrees with most of the critics in not finding many of the usual justifications of strict liability at all persuasive. The fact, for example, that slight penalties are usually imposed, or that *mens rea* would be peculiarly unsusceptible of proof in these cases, does not, either singly or in combination, justify the presence of these offenses in the criminal law. But to reject these and comparable arguments is not necessarily to prove that plausible justifications cannot be located. In fact, it is precisely when the "stronger" arguments of the opponents of strict liability are considered in detail that the case against strict liability is found to be less one-sided than the critics so unanimously suppose.

Critics of strict criminal liability usually argue that the punishment of persons in accordance with the minimum requirements of strict liability (1) is inconsistent with any or all of the commonly avowed aims of the criminal law; and (2) runs counter to the accepted standards of criminal culpability which prevail in the community. They assert that the imposition of criminal sanctions in a case in which—conceivably—the defendant acted both reasonably and with no intention to produce the proscribed events cannot be justified by an appeal to the deterrent, the rehabilitative, or the incarcerative functions of punishment.[17] And,

15 There is, of course, a sense in which the notion of having "committed an act" is far from unambiguous. Depending upon how "act" is defined, it may or may not be true that the sole question is whether the defendant committed the act. The fact that the defendant was sleepwalking or insane at the time might be treated as bearing upon the issue of whether the "act" was committed. There is an obvious sense in which even this determination requires some inquiry into the defendant's state of mind.

16 This would be true whether *mens rea* is interpreted as requiring only that the person "intend" to do the act, or as requiring that the person intend to do something which is morally wrong. The latter interpretation is advanced in Mueller, *On Common Law Mens Rea,* 42 MINN. L. REV. 1043 (1958).

17 One author has suggested that the question of whether a crime has been committed ought to be determined solely by deciding whether the defendant committed the specific act proscribed by the statute. The actor's mental state would be relevant to the separate question of the actor's punishment. Leivitt, *Extent and Function of the Doctrine of Mens Rea,* 17 ILL. L. REV. 578 (1923). This bifurcation is unobjectionable

in fact, they assert the practical effect of strict liability offenses is simply to create that anomalous situation in which persons not morally blamed by the community are nevertheless branded criminal.[18] Although the two lines of criticism are intimately related, for purposes of discussion they will be treated somewhat separately.

The notion that strict liability statutes can be defended as efficacious deterrents has been consistently rejected. It has been proposed, for example, that strict liability offenses cannot be a deterrent simply because they do not proscribe the kind of activity which is obviously incompatible with the moral standards of the community. Thus Gerhard Mueller argues that the substance of common-law *mens rea* is the "awareness of evil, *the sense of doing something which one ought not. . . .*"[19] Since all common-law crimes involved the commission of some act which was known by all the members of the community to be morally wrong, there was, he suggests, no problem in finding the presence of *mens rea* in cases of common-law criminal acts. Such, he insists, is not true of strict liability offenses. They do not punish those activities which a person would know to be wrong independently of the existence of a particular statute. Thus strict liability statutes are to be condemned because they necessarily imply that a person might be punished even though he could not have appealed to that one certain indicia of criminality—the moral laws of the community—to decide whether he was doing something which would violate the law.

If I understand Mr. Mueller's argument correctly, then it clearly proves too much to be of any special significance as a criticism of strict liability offenses. The argument rests upon the obviously sound premise that a person cannot be deterred if he does not know or have reason to believe that his intended action will violate the law. And if this theory about common-law *mens rea* is correct, it only demonstrates that everyone either knew or should have known that certain kinds of activity would be legally punishable. These two points, however, at best imply that ignorance of the law ought—on deterrent grounds—to be always admitted as a complete defense to any criminal prosecution founded upon a statute which does not incorporate an express moral rule or practice

---

insofar as it recognizes that one of the factors to be considered in the sentencing of an individual is his mental state at the time of the crime. The author seems to imply that in the absence of a finding of the requisite mental element it would be proper for the court not to punish the defendant at all. This, too, is perhaps in itself unobjectionable. The question remains then whether it makes any sense to speak of this defendant as having committed a crime.

[18] HALL, GENERAL PRINCIPLES OF CRIMINAL LAW 302–3 (1947); WILLIAMS, CRIMINAL LAW § 76, at 269 (1953); Sayre, *Public Welfare Offenses*, 33 COLUM. L. REV. 55, 56 (1933).

[19] Mueller, op. cit. *supra* note 16, at 1060.

into the criminal law.[20] Concomitantly, if a person knew of the existence
and import of a statute of this kind, it seems wholly irrelevant to distinguish strict liability statutes from those requiring some greater "mental
element." It is just as possible to know that one might be violating a
strict liability statute as it is to know that one might be violating some
other kind of criminal statute. Thus, unless special reasons exist for
believing that strict liability offenses are not effective deterrents, Mr.
Mueller's argument leaves them undifferentiated from many other statutory crimes which do not incorporate the moral law of the community.[21]

Just such special reasons for rejecting the deterrent quality of strict
liability offenses are offered by Jerome Hall, among others. He rejects
the argument that a *strict* liability statute is a more efficacious deterrent
than an ordinary criminal statute for at least two reasons: (*a*) It is not
plausible to suppose that the "strictness" of the liability renders it more
of a deterrent than the liability of ordinary criminal statutes; and (*b*)
persons are not, as a matter of fact, deterred by those penalties usually
imposed for the violation of a strict liability offense.[22]

The first of these objections is, it is submitted, inconclusive. For
there seem to be at least two respects in which strict liability statutes
might have a greater deterrent effect than "usual" criminal statutes. In
the first place, it should be noted that Hall's first proposition is just as
apt to be false as to be true. That is to say, it might be the case that a
person engaged in a certain kind of activity would be more careful precisely because he knew that this kind of activity was governed by a strict
liability statute. It is at least plausible to suppose that the knowledge
that certain criminal sanctions will be imposed if certain consequences
ensue might induce a person to engage in that activity with much greater
caution than would be the case if some lesser standard prevailed.

In the second place (and this calls Hall's second premise into ques-

---

[20] Mueller cites the recent case of *Lambert* v. *California*, 355 U.S. 225 (1957) as
implicitly attacking all strict liability statutes on this ground. Such a reading of the
case seems plainly incorrect. At *most,* the reasoning of the Court can be construed as
suggesting that strict liability statutes of which the defendant neither had nor ought
to have had notice might violate due process. More plausibly, the Court struck down
the conviction in *Lambert* because the statute there reached a very general kind of
activity which the defendant could not reasonably have supposed to be regulated by
statute at all: namely, the mere fact that the defendant came into a city and failed to
register with the sheriff as an ex-convict. Surely, it is reading too much into the opinion
to find a disposition on the part of the Court to group all strict liability statutes in
this class.

[21] It is assumed throughout the remainder of this article that knowledge of the
relevant strict liability statutes is possessed or is readily capable of being possessed by
those subject to the statutes.

[22] "There is, first, the opinion of highly qualified experts that the present rules
are regarded by unscrupulous persons merely 'as a license fee for doing an illegitimate
business.'" HALL, op. cit., *supra* note 18, at 301.

tion as well), it seems reasonable to believe that the presence of strict liability offenses might have the added effect of keeping a relatively large class of persons from engaging in certain kinds of activity.[23] A person who did not regard himself as capable of conducting an enterprise in such a way so as not to produce the deleterious consequences proscribed by the statute might well refuse to engage in that activity at all. Of course, if the penalties for violation of the statute are minimal—if payment of fines is treated merely as a license to continue in operation—then unscrupulous persons will not be deterred by the imposition of this sanction. But this does not imply that unscrupulous persons would be quite so willing to engage in these activities if the penalties for violation were appreciably more severe. In effect, Hall's second argument, if it proves anything, shows only that stronger penalties are needed if strict liability statutes are to be effective.

If the above analysis of the possible deterrent effect of strict liability offenses is plausible, then one of the results of their continued existence and enforcement might very well be that few if any persons would be willing to engage in certain kinds of conduct. The presence of statutes such as that in the *Lindberg* case might have the effect of inducing persons not to engage in banking as an occupation since the risks, one might suppose, are just too great to be compensated by the possible rewards. More plausibly, such a statute might merely have the effect of discouraging bankers from borrowing money—or possibly only from borrowing money from banks. But these effects, too, might conceivably make banking a less attractive occupation, although they would probably not cause the disappearance of banking as an institution in society. However, if we assume the strongest of all results—that a statute of this kind would lead to the disappearance of the institution involved—what conclusions are to be drawn?

The case of socially undesirable activity is easy. If the operation of the felony murder rule has the effect of inducing persons to refuse to commit felonies, there are surely few if any persons who would object to this consequence.[24] Where socially beneficial activities, such as banking and drug distribution [25] are concerned, the case is more troublesome. If

---

[23] Glanville Williams concedes both of these points. WILLIAMS, op. cit. *supra* note 18, § 73, at 258. But he argues in part his kind of deterrent places an "undesirable restraint on proper activities." Ibid. Yet, to a considerable extent, this only succeeds in raising the precise point at issue: namely, whether the restraint which is imposed upon activity is undesirable. The legislature might believe that for certain kinds of activity, at least, the restraint was less undesirable than the production of those consequences proscribed by the statute.

[24] Nor do there appear to be any very serious undesirable societal consequences in discouraging persons from having intercourse with females who may be around the age of sixteen. See *Regina* v. *Prince,* 13 Cox Crim. Cas. 138 (1875).

[25] See the more recent federal case, *United States* v. *Dotterweich,* 320 U.S. 277 (1943), where the defendant, president of a drug company, was indicted and convicted under the Federal Food, Drug, and Cosmetic Act, 52 Stat. 1040 (1938), 21 U.S.C. §§ 301–

it is further assumed that at least some of the strict liability statutes in these areas have been rigidly enforced, it is also to be noted that these institutions have not disappeared from the society. One possible conclusion to be drawn is that these strict liability offenses have been deemed to impose a not unreasonable risk. The fact that banking is still considered an extremely attractive endeavor (despite the possibility of a prison sentence for borrowing money from one's own bank) might be interpreted as evidence that people believe they can be successful bankers without violating this or a comparable strict liability statute. They believe, in other words, that they can operate with sufficient care so as not to violate the statute. Admittedly, the evidence in support of this thesis is not particularly persuasive. Perhaps most people who have gone into banking never even knew of the existence of the statute. Perhaps there is no such statute in most jurisdictions. Perhaps they knew of the statute but believed it would never attach to their conduct. And perhaps they took the statute into account incorrectly and should have been deterred by the statute. In part, the difficulty stems from the fact that there is so little empirical evidence available. It is suggested only that the above interpretation of the extant evidence is just as plausible as are the contrary inferences so often drawn.

The fact that strict liability statutes might cause the disappearance of socially desirable undertakings raises, in a specific context, one important feature of the kind of justification which might be offered for these statutes. If it is conceded that strict liability statutes have an additional deterrent effect, then a fairly plausible utilitarian argument can be made for their perpetuation.

To the extent to which the function of the criminal law is conceived to be that of regulating various kinds of conduct, it becomes relevant to ask whether this particular way of regulating conduct leads to more desirable results than possible alternative procedures. The problem is not peculiar to strict liability statutes but is endemic to the legal system as a whole. Consider, for instance, one such justification of the present jury system. In order to prevent the conviction of persons who did not in fact commit the crimes of which they are accused, it is required that a unanimous jury of twelve persons find, among other things, that they believe the accused did the act in question. Perhaps if the concern were solely with guaranteeing that no innocent man be convicted, a twenty or thirty man jury in which unanimous consent was required for conviction would do a better job. But such is not the sole concern of the criminal law; there is also the need to prevent too many guilty persons from going free. Here, a twelve man jury is doubtless more effective than a thirty man jury. Requiring unanimous vote for acquittal would be a still more

---

92 (1938) for shipping misbranded and adulterated drugs in interstate commerce. There was no showing that Dotterweich personally was either negligently or intentionally engaged in the proscribed conduct. It was sufficient that he was the president of the company.

efficacious means of insuring that every guilty man be convicted. The decision to have a twelve man jury which must be unanimous for conviction can be justified, in other words, as an attempt to devise an adjudicatory procedure (perhaps it is unsuccessful) which will yield a greater quantity of desirable results than would any of the alternatives.

Precisely the same kind of analysis can be made of strict liability offenses. One of the ways to prevent the occurrence of certain kinds of consequences is to enact strict liability offenses, since, *ex hypothesi,* these will be an added deterrent. One of the deleterious consequences of strict liability offenses is the possibility that certain socially desirable institutions will be weakened or will disappear. The problem is twofold: first one must decide whether the additional deterrent effect of the strict liability statutes will markedly reduce the occurrence of those events which the statute seeks quite properly to prevent. And second, one must decide whether this additional reduction in undesirable occurrences is more beneficial to society than the possible deleterious effects upon otherwise desirable activities such as banking or drug distribution. For even if it be conceded that strict liability offenses may have the additionally undesirable effect of holding as criminal some persons who would not on other grounds be so regarded, strict liability could be supported on the theory that the need to prevent certain kinds of occurrences is sufficiently great so as to override the undesirable effct of punishing those who might in some other sense be "innocent."

I do not urge that either or both of these arguments for strict liability offenses are either irrefutable or even particularly convincing. But I do submit that this is a perfectly plausible kind of argument which cannot be met simply by insisting either that strict liability is an inherently unintelligible concept or that the legislative judgment of the desirability of strict criminal liability is necessarily irrational.[26] It is one thing to attack particular legislative evaluations on the grounds that they have misconstrued either the beneficial effects of strict liability or its attendant deleterious consequences, but it is quite another thing to attack the possible rationality of any such comparative determination.[27]

---

[26] In this connection, it has been suggested that there is little evidence that legislatures consciously intend criminal statutes to be strict liability statutes. The most exhaustive examination of this issue is in a recent study conducted by the *Wisconsin Law Review,* 1956 Wis. L. Rev. 625. And while it seems clear that there is little affirmative evidence on this score, what evidence is available seems to indicate that at times the legislature has consciously intended the statute to be a strict criminal liability statute. Cf. id. at 644. Additionally, Glanville Williams argues that Parliament seems to have intended to retain strict liability in the statute interpreted by the court in the *Prince* case. See WILLIAMS, op. cit. *supra* note 18, § 73, at 259–60.

[27] Cf. Note, 74 L.Q. Rev. 321, 343 (1958). "It must always be remembered that the primary purpose of the criminal law is to prevent the commission of certain acts which it regards as being against the public interest and not to punish or to reform a wrongdoer. It may, therefore, be necessary to provide for strict liability when this is the only practical way to guard against the commission of the harmful act."

While I do not feel committed to the view that the primary function of the

As was observed earlier, the second of the two major kinds of criticism directed against strict criminal liability is that punishment of persons in accordance with the minimal requirements of strict liability —the punishment of persons in the absence of *mens rea*—is irreconcilable with those fundamental, long extant standards of criminal culpability which prevail in the community. As usually propounded the thesis is a complex one; it is also considerably more ambiguous than many of its proponents appear to have noted. One possible, although less interesting, implication concerns the notion of criminal culpability. The claim is made that the imposition of strict liability is inconsistent with the concept of criminal culpability—criminal culpability being defined to mean "requiring *mens rea*." But unless the argument is to be vacuous it must be demonstrated that independent reasons exist for selecting just this definition which precludes strict liability offenses from the class of actions to which the criminal sanctions are to attach.[28]

A more troublesome and related question is whether the proposition is presented as a *descriptive* or *prescriptive* assertion. It is not clear whether the imposition of strict liability is thought to be incompatible with the accepted values of society or whether the prevalence of strict liability is inconsistent with what ought to be accepted values.

As an empirical assertion the protest against strict liability on the grounds that it contravenes public sentiment is, again, at best an open hypothesis. Those who seek to substantiate its correctness turn to the fact that minimal penalties are often imposed. They construe this as indicative of the felt revulsion against the concept of strict criminal liability. That judges and juries often refuse to impose those sanctions which would be imposed in the comparable cases involving the presence of *mens rea,* is taken as additional evidence of community antipathy.

The evidence is, however, no less (and probably no more) persuasive on the other side. The fact that most strict liability offenses are creatures of statute has already been alluded to. While few persons would seriously wish to maintain that the legislature is either omniscient or a wholly adequate reflection of general or popular sentiment, the fact that so many legislatures have felt such apparently little compunction over enacting such statutes is surely indicative of the presence of a comparable community conviction. Strict liability offenses, as the critics so persistently note, are not mere sports, mere sporadic legislative oversights or anomalies. They are, again as the critics note, increasing in both number and scope. It may very well be the case that strict liability offenses ought to be condemned by the community; it is much more doubtful that they are presently held in such contumely.

---

criminal law is that of the prevention of certain acts, the writer of the Note seems correct in suggesting that if an essentially utilitarian view of the criminal law is adopted, then the justification of many strict liablity offenses becomes increasingly plausible.

28 Cf. p. 743 *infra.*

"MENTAL" REQUIREMENTS, STRICT LIABILITY
AND NEGLIGENCE

The arguments against strict liability offenses which remain to be examined go to what is conceived to be the very heart of a strict liability offense; namely, the imposition of criminal sanctions in the absence of any *fault* on the part of the actor.

> Since that liability [strict liability] is meaningful only in its complete exclusion of fault, it is patently inconsistent to assert, e.g., that a business man is honest, exercises care and skill; and also, if a misbranded or adulterated package of food somehow, unknown to anyone, is shipped from his establishment, that he should be punished or coercively educated to increase his efficiency.[29]

The actor has, *ex hypothesi*, lacked precisely those mental attributes upon which fault is properly predicated—indeed, proof of his state of mind is irrelevant. Thus, the argument concludes, the vicious character of convictions founded upon strict liability is revealed. Intelligent understanding and evaluation of this objection must await, however, the clarification of several critically ambiguous notions. In particular, the ways in which a strict liability offense may fail to take the defendant's state of mind into account are far from clearly delineated. More seriously, still, there seem to be a variety of alternative meanings of "fault" which should be explored and discriminated.

That certain offers of proof concerning the defendant's state of mind might not be irrelevant even in the case of a putative violation is apparent. Quite apart from the ambiguous meaning of the word "act," [30] there are several other questions about the defendant's mental state which might be permitted in a strict liability prosecution. For example, suppose the defendant in the *Lindberg* case were to offer to prove that he had never intended to become a director or officer of the bank and that he reasonably believed that he was merely becoming an employee. Is it clear that this offer would be rejected as irrelevant? Or, suppose the offer of proof was that the defendant had never intended to borrow any money and reasonably believed that he was receiving a bonus. Would this statement be excluded? Thus, it can be argued that if strict liability statutes are to be characterized as "strict" because of their failure to permit inquiry as to the defendant's state of mind, this description is too broad. More appropriately, each criminal statute must be examined to determine in what respects it is "strict."

[29] HALL, op. cit. *supra* note 18, at 304.
[30] See note 15 *supra*.

The ambiguity in the notion of "fault" can be illustrated by a hypothetical situation. Consider a statute which reads: "If a bank director borrows money in excess of [a certain amount] from the bank of which he is director, then the directors of any other bank shall be punishable by not more than ten years in the state prison." Suppose that there is no connection between the various banks in the jurisdiction, that a director of bank *A* had borrowed money in excess of the statutory amount from his own bank, and that a director of bank *B,* a wholly unrelated bank, was accused and convicted. This, it is submitted, would be a case of "stricter" liability. The example is surely chimerical; the point is not. It serves to illustrate the way in which ordinary strict liability statutes do require "fault."

If the notion of fault requires that there be some sort of causal relationship between the accused and the act in question, it is arguable that the *Lindberg* case takes account of such a relationship. The defendant in the *Lindberg* case by virtue of his position *qua* officer of the bank had considerable control over the affairs of that bank. And he had even greater control over his own borrowing activities. If the element of control is sufficient to permit some kind of a causal inference as to events occurring within that control, then a finding of fault in this sense does not seem arbitrary in the same manner in which a finding of fault in the hypothetical clearly would be.

Admittedly, there is a second, more restricted sense of "fault" which was clearly not present in the *Lindberg* case. This would require that the actor intended to have the particular act—borrowing money *from his own bank*—occur. And yet, there was a conscious intent to engage in just that activity—banking—which the defendant knew or should have known to be subject to criminal sanctions if certain consequences ensued. And there was a still clearer intent to do the more specific act—borrow money—which the defendant knew or should have known to be subject to criminal sanctions under certain specified circumstances. Strict liability offenses can be interpreted as legislative judgments that persons who intentionally engage in certain activities and occupy some peculiar or distinctive position of control are to be held accountable for the occurrence of certain consequences.

It is entirely possible that such a characterization of fault might still be regarded as unsatisfactory.[31] The mere fact that there was control over the general activity may be insufficient to justify a finding of fault in every case in which certain results ensue. The kind of fault which must be present before criminal sanctions ought to be imposed, so the argument might continue, is one which is predicated upon some affirmative state of mind with respect to the particular act or consequence.

There may be good reasons why this more restrictive concept of fault ought to be insisted upon in the criminal law. Indeed, I think

---

[31] HALL, op. cit. *supra* note 18, at 304, clearly regards such a definition as unsatisfactory.

such reasons exist and are persuasive. Furthermore, "deontological" arguments, which rest upon analysis of what ought to be entailed by concepts of justice, criminal guilt and culpability might support the more restrictive definition. Arguments of this nature will not be challenged here, for to a considerable extent this article is written in the hope that others will feel the need to articulate these contentions more precisely. However, there remains one final thesis which must be questioned. That is, that a person who accepts this more restrictive notion of fault can consistently believe that negligent acts ought to be punished by the criminal law. [32]

If the objection to the concept of strict liability is that the defendant's state of mind is irrelevant, then a comparable objection seems to lie against offenses founded upon criminal negligence. For the jury in a criminal negligence prosecution asks only whether the activity of the defendant violated some standard of care which a reasonable member of the community would not have violated.[33] To the extent that strict liability statutes can be interpreted as legislative judgments that conduct which produces or permits certain consequences is unreasonable, strict criminal liability is similar to a jury determination that conduct in a particular case was unreasonable.

There are, of course, important differences between the two kinds of offenses. Precisely because strict liability statutes require an antecedent judgment of *per se* unreasonableness, they necessarily require a more general classification of the kind of activity which is to be regulated. They tend, and perhaps inherently so, to neglect many features which ought to be taken into account before such a judgment is forthcoming. Criminal negligence, on the other hand, demands an essentially *a posteriori* judgment as to the conduct in the particular case. As such, it surely provides more opportunity for the jury to consider just those factors which are most significant in determining whether the standard of care was observed.

In spite of these important distinctions, insofar as strict liability

---

[32] The MODEL PENAL CODE §§ 2.02, 2.05 (Tent. Draft No. 4, 1955) appears to take this approach.

[33] I find highly unpersuasive, attempts to treat negligence as in fact requiring *mens rea*. It has been argued that "in the case of negligence . . . the law operates with an objective standard which, based upon experience, closely approximates that under which the defendant must have operated in fact. In my opinion, therefore, we are here confronted with the use of a schematic and crude way of establishing the *mens rea*, but one which nevertheless evidences the law's concern for the mental attitude of the defendant." Mueller, *supra* note 16, at 1063–64.

If Mueller is suggesting merely that when certain kinds of consequences occur in certain kinds of situations it is reasonable to infer that the defendant in fact had a certain state of mind, then I find nothing objectionable about his claim. But, of course, *mutatis mutandis,* the same can be said for many strict liability offenses. If, on the other hand, he is suggesting that negligence in fact requires the jury to make a determination as to the presence or absence of the defendant's *mens rea,* then I do not understand in what sense this is accurate.

statutes are condemned because they fail to require a mental element, negligence as a category of criminality ought to be likewise criticized. There may be independent reasons for urging the retention or rejection of the category of criminal negligence—just as there may be such reasons for accepting or disallowing strict liability offenses. But the way in which the two kinds of criminal liability are similar must be kept in mind whenever they are evaluated.

CONCLUSION

It is readily conceded that many strict liability statutes do not perform any very meaningful or desirable social function. It is admitted, too, that legislatures may have been both negligent and unwise in their selection of strict criminal liability as the means by which to achieve certain ends. But until the issues raised in the preceding discussion have been considered more carefully and precisely, it will *not* be immediately evident that all strict liability statutes are inherently vicious and irrational legislative or judicial blunders.

SECTION TWO

The Enforcement
of Community Standards

The five selections in this section cluster around an issue which has occasioned a good deal of controversy in recent years. We are concerned here with the general question of whether there are proper limits to the reach of the law. Specifically, we ask whether there are areas of human conduct which are *in principle* properly beyond legal sanction. Is there a point at which it is correct to say that, notwithstanding the morality, the social preferences, the spiritual values and the sensibilities of the public, the suppression of certain actions by the law is not the proper business of government?

The examples that typically come up for discussion when this issue is raised are the well-known "morals offenses": prostitution, homosexuality, fornication, obscenity, and several others. But the issue arises in other, less familiar, contexts as well. For example, the case which begins this section, *Village of Belle Terre* v. *Boraas,* concerns a zoning ordinance which, in effect, prohibits more than two unrelated persons from living together in a single household. The owners of a house in the village of Belle Terre have been served with an "Order to Remedy Violations" as a result of leasing their property to more than two university students, who are thus occupying the house in violation of the ordinance. The case arises when the owners and three of the students challenge the constitutionality of the village ordinance.

In the majority opinion, Justice Douglas endorses a broad interpretation of the public welfare (the purported objective of the ordinance): "The values it represents are spiritual as well as physical, aesthetic as well as monetary." While he suggests that the ordinance may not be perfectly aimed at the objective—"every line drawn by a legislature leaves some out that might well have been included"—Justice Douglas, unlike the dissenting Justice Marshall, finds no reason to require that the ordinance be anything more than "reasonable, not arbitrary."

No suspect classification (such as race) is being employed and no fundamental right is being burdened, according to Douglas. Accordingly, the ordinance is constitutional insofar as it bears a "rational relationship to a permissible state objective."

Because Justice Marshall finds that the ordinance "burdens the students' fundamental rights of association and privacy guaranteed by the First and Fourteenth Amendments," he would apply "strict equal protection scrutiny" to the classification in the ordinance. In his dissent Marshall notes that in order to withstand such scrutiny there must be a "clear showing that the burden is necessary to protect a compelling and substantial governmental interest." It is not enough to show that the ordinance "bears a rational relationship to the accomplishment of legitimate governmental objectives." Marshall finds that in acting "to fence out those individuals whose lifestyle differs from that of its current residents" Belle Terre "has embarked upon its commendable course in a constitutionally faulty vessel."

In American constitutional law the problem of setting limits to the reach of the law has involved, as we have seen, the elaboration of the legal concepts of equal protection, freedom of association, and the right to privacy. Other legal concepts—such as contract, property, freedom of speech, and the free exercise of religion—have also played a role in opinions concerning the limits of law. In modern legal philosophy the discussion is usually considered to begin with the publication, in 1859, of John Stuart Mill's important essay *On Liberty*. Mill's professed object was to assert "one very simple principle":

> the sole end for which mankind are warranted, individually or collectively, in interfering with the liberty of action of any of their number, is self-protection. That the only purpose for which power can be rightfully exercised over any member of a civilized community, against his will, is to prevent harm to others. His own good, either physical or moral, is not a sufficient warrant. He cannot rightfully be compelled to do or forbear because it will be better for him to do so, because it will make him happier, because, in the opinions of others, to do so would be wise, or even right.*

In fact, Mill so qualified his principle and specified so many exceptions to it that commentators are not in agreement about the degree to which Mill can be said to embrace it. Because it is such an important work in this context, both widely read and easily available, the reader is strongly urged to become familiar with *On Liberty*.

In the 1950s the issue emerged in England. A committee had been appointed to examine the laws concerning homosexuality and prostitution and to make recommendations about whether they should be reformed—and, if so, how. The *Report of the Committee on Homosexual*

---

*John Stuart Mill, *On Liberty* (Indianapolis: Bobbs-Merrill Company, Inc., 1956), p. 13.

Offenses and Prostitution ("the Wolfenden Report") appeared in 1957 and took a position which was, in substance, consistent with Mill's principle. It held to the distinction between crime and sin, viewing the criminal law as aimed at the preservation of public order and decency, the protection of the citizen, and the safeguarding of the specially vulnerable. The Report maintained that "there must remain a realm of private morality and immorality which is, in brief and crude terms, not the law's business." Thus, homosexual acts between consenting adults should be taken off the list of criminal offenses, and prostitution should be kept off it.

Patrick Devlin has emerged as the most significant critic of the Mill–Wolfenden Committee position on the criminalization of "private immorality." The view he defends is that "it is not possible to set theoretical limits to the power of the State to legislate against immorality." In the excerpts from "Morals and the Criminal Law" and "Democracy and Morality" which are reprinted here, Devlin argues that since "a recognized morality is as necessary to society as . . . a recognized government, then society may use the law to preserve morality in the same way as it uses it to safeguard anything else that is essential to its existence." Moreover, since in a democratic society the "will of the people must prevail," legislation in matters of morals, especially where it reflects the common sense of right and wrong, is as appropriate as legislation in matters of policy. Though Devlin takes the position that "private behaviour" may be very much "the law's business," he does consider that toleration of individual freedom and respect for privacy should be taken into account when considering the enforcement of morality in particular cases.

Joel Feinberg, in the passages taken from his *Social Philosophy,* discusses some of the main problems that have arisen for those who defend Mill's view that only the prevention of harm to "individual persons" or "institutional practices that are in the public interest" can justify the restriction of liberty. Taking issue with Devlin, Feinberg distinguishes between "legitimate and illegitimate techniques of moral change" and finds the legal enforcement of morality to be "a clear example of illegitimacy." Feinberg is, however, willing to see the law prohibit conduct that is offensive to others where susceptibility to the upsetting effects of such conduct is nearly universal and where these effects cannot be avoided without unreasonable inconvenience. Here it is the offensiveness of the conduct that justifies prohibition, not its immorality. Finally, Feinberg notes that it may not be possible to secure certain "collective goods and indivisible services of an essential kind" unless coercion is used: the "freeloader" might otherwise present an insurmountable problem. Feinberg holds that under such circumstances coercion may be justified by the "harm principle."

The distinction that Feinberg draws between prohibiting conduct because it is immoral ("legal moralism") and prohibiting conduct because it is offensive (the "offense principal") is one that has been deployed against Devlin by H. L. A. Hart in his *Law, Liberty, and Morality.* David A. Conway, in "Law, Liberty and Indecency," which concludes this section, is critical of this distinction. He argues (against Hart) that we do not have good reasons for regulating publicly indecent but not privately immoral actions. He is convinced that a principle which permits prohibition of public actions on the grounds that they are offensive has consequences that are "contrary to liberal intuitions." He maintains that such a principle would not be defended by John Stuart Mill and, indeed, might not be worth a defense. Conway sees only two consistent alternatives: either we side with Devlin or we "set aside our prejudices and admit that nudity, intercourse, etc., even in public, are none of the business of society." Conway opts for the latter, "heroic," alternative, although in a footnote he calls attention to problems that arise for the "extreme libertarian," problems which often involve ordinances very much like the one examined in *Belle Terre.*

VILLAGE OF BELLE TERRE V. BORAAS

United States Supreme Court

Mr. Justice Douglas delivered the opinion of the Court.

Belle Terre is a village on Long Island's north shore of about 220 homes inhabited by 700 people. Its total land area is less than one square mile. It has restricted land use to one-family dwellings excluding lodging houses, boarding houses, fraternity houses, or multiple-dwelling houses. The word "family" as used in the ordinance means, "one or more persons related by blood, adoption, or marriage, living and cooking together as a single housekeeping unit, exclusive of household servants. A number of persons but not exceeding two (2) living and cooking together as a single housekeeping unit though not related by blood, adoption, or marriage shall be deemed to constitute a family."

Appellees the Dickmans are owners of a house in the village and leased it in December 1971 for a term of 18 months to Michael Truman. Later Bruce Boraas became a colessee. Then Anne Parish moved into the house along with three others. These six are students at nearby State University at Stony Brook and none is related to the other by blood, adoption, or marriage. When the village served the Dickmans with an

416 U.S. 1 (1974) Locations of deleted citations marked with double asterisk (**). Ed.

"Order to Remedy Violations" of the ordinance,[1] the owners plus three tenants [2] thereupon brought this action under 42 U.S.C. § 1983 for an injunction declaring the ordinance unconstitutional. The District Court held the ordinance constitutional, 367 F. Supp. 136, and the Court of Appeals reversed, one judge dissenting, 476 F. 2d 806. The case is here by appeal, 28 U.S.C. § 1254 (2); and we noted probable jurisdiction, 414 U.S. 907.

This case brings to this Court a different phase of local zoning regulations than we have previously reviewed. *Euclid* v. *Ambler Reality Co.,* 272 U.S. 365, involved a zoning ordinance classifying land use in a given area into six categories. Appellees' tracts fell under three classifications: U–2, which included two-family dwellings; U–3, which included apartments, hotels, churches, schools, private clubs, hospitals, city hall and the like; and U–6, which included sewage disposal plants, incinerators, scrap storage, cemeteries, oil and gas storage and so on. Heights of buildings were prescribed for each zone; also, the size of land areas required for each kind of use was specified. The land in litigation was vacant and being held for industrial development; and evidence was introduced showing that under the restricted-use ordinance the land would be greatly reduced in value. The claim was that the landowner was being deprived of liberty and property without due process within the meaning of the Fourteenth Amendment.

The Court sustained the zoning ordinance under the police power of the State, saying that the line "which in this field separates the legitimate from the illegitimate assumption of power is not capable of precise delimitation. It varies with circumstances and conditions." Id., at 387. And the Court added: "A nuisance may be merely a right thing in the wrong place,—like a pig in the parlor instead of the barnyard. If the validity of the legislative classification for zoning purposes be fairly debatable, the legislative judgment must be allowed to control." Id., at 388. The Court listed as considerations bearing on the constitutionality of zoning ordinances the danger of fire or collapse of buildings, the evils of overcrowding people, and the possibility that "offensive trades, industries, and structures" might "create nuisance" to residential sections. Ibid. But even those historic police power problems need not loom large or actually be existent in a given case. For the exclusion of "all industrial establishments" does not mean that "only offensive or dangerous industries will be excluded." Ibid. That fact does not invalidate the ordinance; the Court held:

> The inclusion of a reasonable margin to insure effective enforcement, will not put upon a law, otherwise valid, the stamp of invalidity. Such laws

---

[1] *Younger* v. *Harris,* 401 U.S. 37, is not involved here, as on August 2, 1972, when this federal suit was initiated, no state case had been started. The effect of the "Order to Remedy Violations" was to subject the occupants to liability commencing August 3, 1972. During the litigation the lease expired and it was extended. Anne Parish moved out. Thereafter the other five students left and the owners now hold the home out for sale or rent, including to student groups.

[2] Truman, Boraas, and Parish became appellees but not the other three.

may also find their justification in the fact that, in some fields, the bad fades into the good by such insensible degrees that the two are not capable of being readily distinguished and separated in terms of legislation. Id., at 388–389.

The main thrust of the case in the mind of the Court was in the exclusion of industries and apartments and as respects that it commented on the desire to keep residential areas free of "disturbing noises"; "increased traffic"; the hazard of "moving and parked automobiles"; the "depriving children of the privilege of quiet and open spaces for play, enjoyed by those in more favored localities." Id., at 394. The ordinance was sanctioned because the validity of the legislative classification was "fairly debatable" and therefore could not be said to be wholly arbitrary. Id., at 388.

Our decision in *Berman* v. *Parker*, 348 U.S. 26, sustained a land-use project in the District of Columbia against a landowner's claim that the taking violated the Due Process Clause and the Just Compensation Clause of the Fifth Amendment. The essence of the argument against the law was, while taking property for ridding an area of slums was permissible, taking it "merely to develop a better balanced, more attractive community" was not, id., at 31. We refused to limit the concept of public welfare that may be enhanced by zoning regulations.[3] We said:

> Miserable and disreputable housing conditions may do more than spread disease and crime and immorality. They may also suffocate the spirit by reducing the people who live there to the status of cattle. They may indeed make living an almost insufferable burden. They may also be an ugly sore, a blight on the community which robs it of charm, which makes it a place from which men turn. The misery of housing may despoil a community as an open sewer may ruin a river.
>
> We do not sit to determine whether a particular housing project is or is not desirable. The concept of the public welfare is broad and inclusive. . . . The values it represents are spiritual as well as physical, aesthetic as well as monetary. It is within the power of the legislature to determine that the community should be beautiful as well as healthy, spacious as well as clean, well-balanced as well as carefully patrolled. Id., at 32–33.

If the ordinance segregated one area only for one race, it would immediately be suspect under the reasoning of *Buchanan* v. *Warley*,

---

[3] Vermont has enacted comprehensive statewide land-use controls which direct local boards to develop plans ordering the uses of local land, *inter alia*, to "create conditions favorable to transportation, health, safety, civic activities and educational and cultural opportunities, [and] reduce the wastes of financial and human resources which result from either excessive congestion or excessive scattering of population. . . ." Vt. Stat. Ann., Tit. 10, § 6042 (1973). Federal legislation has been proposed designed to assist States and localities in developing such broad objective land-use guidelines. See Senate Committee on Interior and Insular Affairs, Land Use Policy and Planning Assistance Act, S. Rep. No. 93–197 (1973).

245 U.S. 60, where the Court invalidated a city ordinance barring a black from acquiring real property in a white residential area by reason of an 1866 Act of Congress, 14 Stat. 27, now 42 U.S.C. § 1982, and an 1870 Act, § 17, 16 Stat. 144, 42 U.S.C. § 1981, both enforcing the Fourteenth Amendment.**

In *Seattle Trust Co.* v. *Roberge,* 278 U.S. 116, Seattle had a zoning ordinance that permitted a "philanthropic home for children or for old people" in a particular district "when the written consent shall have been obtained of the owners of two-thirds of the property within four hundred (400) feet of the proposed building." Id., at 118. The Court held that provision of the ordinance unconstitutional, saying that the existing owners could "withhold consent for selfish reasons or arbitrarily and may subject the trustee [owner] to their will or caprice." Id., at 122. Unlike the billboard cases (e.g., *Cusack Co.* v. *City of Chicago,* 242 U.S. 526), the Court concluded that the Seattle ordinance was invalid since the proposed home for the aged poor was not shown by its maintenance and construction "to work any injury, inconvenience or annoyance to the community, the district or any person." 278 U.S., at 122.

The present ordinance is challenged on several grounds: that it interferes with a person's right to travel; that it interferes with the right to migrate to and settle within a State; that it bars people who are uncongenial to the present residents; that it expresses the social preferences of the residents for groups that will be congenial to them; that social homogeneity is not a legitimate interest of government; that the restriction of those whom the neighbors do not like trenches on the newcomers' rights of privacy; that it is of no rightful concern to villagers whether the residents are married or unmarried; that the ordinance is antithetical to the Nation's experience, ideology, and self-perception as an open, egalitarian, and integrated society.[4]

We find none of these reasons in the record before us. It is not aimed at transients. Cf. *Shapiro* v. *Thompson,* 394 U.S. 618. It involves no procedural disparity inflicted on some but not on others such as was presented by *Griffin* v. *Illinois,* 351 U.S. 12. It involves no "fundamental" right guaranteed by the Constitution, such as voting, *Harper* v. *Virginia Board,* 383 U.S. 663; the right of association, *NAACP* v. *Alabama,* 357 U.S. 449; the right of access to the courts, *NAACP* v. *Button,* 371 U.S. 415; or any rights of privacy, cf. *Griswold* v. *Connecticut,* 381 U.S. 479; *Eisenstadt* v. *Baird,* 405 U.S. 438, 453–454. We deal with economic and social legislation where legislatures have historically drawn lines which we respect against the charge of violation of the Equal Protection Clause if the law be "reasonable, not arbitrary" (quoting *Royster Guano Co.* v. *Virginia,* 253 U.S. 412, 415) and bears "a rational relationship to a [permissible] state objective." *Reed* v. *Reed,* 404 U.S. 71, 76.

---

4 Many references in the development of this thesis are made to F. Turner, The Frontier in American History (1920), with emphasis on his theory that "democracy [is] born of free land." Id., at 32.

It is said, however, that if two unmarried people can constitute a "family," there is no reason why three or four may not. But every line drawn by a legislature leaves some out that might well have been included.[5] That exercise of discretion, however, is a legislative, not a judicial, function.

It is said that the Belle Terre ordinance reeks with an animosity to unmarried couples who live together.[6] There is no evidence to support it; and the provision of the ordinance bringing within the definition of a "family" two unmarried people belies the charge.

The ordinance places no ban on other forms of association, for a "family" may, so far as the ordinance is concerned, entertain whomever it likes.

The regimes of boarding houses, fraternity houses, and the like present urban problems. More people occupy a given space; more cars rather continuously pass by; more cars are parked; noise travels with crowds.

A quiet place where yards are wide, people few, and motor vehicles restricted are legitimate guidelines in a land-use project addressed to family needs. This goal is a permissible one within *Berman* v. *Parker, supra.* The police power is not confined to elimination of filth, stench, and unhealthy places. It is ample to lay out zones where family values, youth values, and the blessings of quiet seclusion and clean air make the area a sanctuary for people.

The suggestion that the case may be moot need not detain us. A zoning ordinance usually has an impact on the value of the property which it regulates. But in spite of the fact that the precise impact of the ordinance sustained in *Euclid* on a given piece of property was not known, 272 U.S., at 397, the Court, considering the matter a controversy in the realm of city planning, sustained the ordinance. Here we are a step closer to the impact of the ordinance on the value of the lessor's property. He has not only lost six tenants and acquired only two in their place; it is obvious that the scale of rental values rides on what we decide today. When *Berman* reached us it was not certain whether an entire tract would be taken or only the buildings on it and a scenic easement. 348 U.S., at 36. But that did not make the case any the less a controversy in the constitutional sense. When Mr. Justice Holmes said for the Court

[5] Mr. Justice Holmes made the point a half century ago. "When a legal distinction is determined, as no one doubts that it may be, between night and day, childhood and maturity, or any other extremes, a point has to be fixed or a line has to be drawn, or gradually picked out by successive decisions, to mark where the change takes place. Looked at by itself without regard to the necessity behind it the line or point seems arbitrary. It might as well or nearly as well be a little more to one side or the other. But when it is seen that a line or point there must be, and that there is no mathematical or logical way of fixing it precisely, the decision of the legislature must be accepted unless we can say that it is very wide of any reasonable mark." *Louisville Gas Co.* v. *Coleman,* 277 U.S. 32, 41 (dissenting opinion).

[6] *Department of Agriculture* v. *Moreno,* 413 U.S. 528 (1973), is therefore inapt as there a household containing anyone unrelated to the rest was denied food stamps.

in *Block* v. *Hirsh,* 256 U.S. 135, 155, "property rights may be cut down, and to that extent taken, without pay," he stated the issue here. As is true in most zoning cases, the precise impact on value may, at the threshold of litigation over validity, not yet be known.

Reversed. . . .

Mr. Justice Marshall, dissenting.

This case draws into question the constitutionality of a zoning ordinance of the incorporated village of Belle Terre, New York, which prohibits groups of more than two unrelated persons, as distinguished from groups consisting of any number of persons related by blood, adoption or marriage, from occupying a residence within the confines of the township.** Lessor-appellees, the two owners of a Belle Terre residence, and three unrelated student tenants challenged the ordinance on the ground that it establishes a classification between households of related and unrelated individuals, which deprives them of equal protection of the laws. In my view, the disputed classification burdens the students' fundamental rights of association and privacy guaranteed by the First and Fourteenth Amendments. Because the application of strict equal protection scrutiny is therefore required, I am at odds with my Brethren's conclusion that the ordinance may be sustained on a showing that it bears a rational relationship to the accomplishment of legitimate governmental objectives.

I am in full agreement with the majority that zoning is a complex and important function of the State. It may indeed be the most essential function performed by local government, for it is one of the primary means by which we protect that sometimes difficult to define concept of quality of life. I therefore continue to adhere to the principle of *Euclid* v. *Ambler Realty Co.,* 272 U.S. 365 (1926), that deference should be given to governmental judgments concerning proper land-use allocation. That deference is a principle which has served this Court well and which is necessary for the continued development of effective zoning and land-use control mechanisms. Had the owners alone brought this suit alleging that the restrictive ordinance deprived them of their property or was an irrational legislative classification, I would agree that the ordinance would have to be sustained. Our role is not and should not be to sit as a zoning board of appeals.

I would also agree with the majority that local zoning authorities may properly act in furtherance of the objectives asserted to be served by the ordinance at issue here: restricting uncontrolled growth, solving traffic problems, keeping rental costs at a reasonable level, and making the community attractive to families. The police power which provides the justification for zoning is not narrowly confined. See *Berman* v. *Parker,* 348 U.S. 26 (1954). And, it is appropriate that we afford zoning authorities considerable latitude in choosing the means by which to implement such purposes. But deference does not mean abdication.

This Court has an obligation to ensure that zoning ordinances, even when adopted in furtherance of such legitimate aims, do not infringe upon fundamental constitutional rights.

When separate but equal was still accepted constitutional dogma, this Court struck down a racially restrictive zoning ordinance. *Buchanan v. Warley,* 245 U.S. 60 (1917). I am sure the Court would not be hesitant to invalidate that ordinance today. The lower federal courts have considered procedural aspects of zoning,[2] and acted to insure that land-use controls are not used as means of confining minorities and the poor to the ghettos of our central cities.[3] These are limited but necessary intrusions on the discretion of zoning authorities. By the same token, I think it clear that the First Amendment provides some limitation on zoning laws. It is inconceivable to me that we would allow the exercise of the zoning power to burden First Amendment freedoms, as by ordinances that restrict occupancy to individuals adhering to particular religious, political, or scientific beliefs. Zoning officials properly concern themselves with the uses of land—with, for example, the number and kind of dwellings to be constructed in a certain neighborhood or the number of persons who can reside in those dwellings. But zoning authorities cannot validly consider who those persons are, what they believe, or how they choose to live, whether they are Negro or white, Catholic or Jew, Republican or Democrat, married or unmarried.

My disagreement with the Court today is based upon my view that the ordinance in this case unnecessarily burdens appellees' First Amendment freedom of association and their constitutionally guaranteed right to privacy. Our decisions establish that the First and Fourteenth Amendments protect the freedom to choose one's associates. *NAACP* v. *Button,* 371 U.S. 415, 430 (1963). Constitutional protection is extended, not only to modes of association that are political in the usual sense, but also to those that pertain to the social and economic benefit of the members.** The selection of one's living companions involves similar choices as to the emotional, social, or economic benefits to be derived from alternative living arrangements.

The freedom of association is often inextricably entwined with the constitutionally guaranteed right of privacy. The right to "establish a home" is an essential part of the liberty guaranteed by the Fourteenth Amendment.** And the Constitution secures to an individual a freedom "to satisfy his intellectual and emotional needs in the privacy of his own home." *Stanley* v. *Georgia,* 394 U.S. 557, 565 (1969); see *Paris Adult Theatre I* v. *Slaton,* 413 U.S. 49, 66–67 (1973). Constitutionally protected privacy is, in Mr. Justice Brandeis' words, "as against the Government,

---

[2] See *Citizens Assn. of Georgetown* v. *Zoning Comm'n,* 155 U. S. App. D. C. 233, 477 F. 2d 402 (1973).

[3] ** See generally Sager, Tight Little Islands: Exclusionary Zoning, Equal Protection, and the Indigent, 21 Stan. L. Rev. 767 (1969); Note, Exclusionary Zoning and Equal Protection, 84 Harv. L. Rev. 1645 (1971); Note, The Responsibility of Local Zoning Authorities to Nonresident Indigents, 23 Stan. L. Rev. 774 (1971).

the right to be let alone . . . the right most valued by civilized man."
Olmstead v. *United States,* 277 U.S. 438, 478 (1928) (dissenting opinion).
The choice of household companions—of whether a person's "intellectual
and emotional needs" are best met by living with family, friends, professional associates or others—involves deeply personal considerations as
to the kind and quality of intimate relationships within the home. That
decision surely falls within the ambit of the right to privacy protected by
the Constitution. See *Roe* v. *Wade,* 410 U.S. 113, 153 (1973); *Eisenstadt*
v. *Baird,* 405 U.S. 438, 453 (1972); *Stanley* v. *Georgia, supra,* at 564-565;
Griswold v. *Connecticut, supra,* at 483, 486; *Olmstead* v. *United States,
supra,* at 478 (Brandeis, J., dissenting); *Moreno* v. *Department of Agriculture,* 345 F. Supp. 310, 315 (DC 1972), aff'd, 413 U.S. 528 (1973).

The instant ordinance discriminates on the basis of just such a
personal lifestyle choice as to household companions. It permits any
number of persons related by blood or marriage, be it two or twenty, to
live in a single household, but it limits to two the number of unrelated
persons bound by profession, love, friendship, religious or political af-
filiation, or mere economics who can occupy a single home. Belle Terre
imposes upon those who deviate from the community norm in their
choice of living companions significantly greater restrictions than are
applied to residential groups who are related by blood or marriage, and
compose the established order within the community.[4] The town has, in
effect, acted to fence out those individuals whose choice of lifestyle differs
from that of its current residents.[5]

This is not a case where the Court is being asked to nullify a township's sincere efforts to maintain its residential character by preventing
the operation of rooming houses, fraternity houses, or other commercial
or high-density residential uses. Unquestionably, a town is free to restrict
such uses. Moreover, as a general proposition, I see no constitutional
infirmity in a town limiting the density of use in residential areas by
zoning regulations which do not discriminate on the basis of constitutionally suspect criteria.[6] This ordinance, however, limits the density of
occupancy of only those homes occupied by unrelated persons. It thus
reaches beyond control of the use of land or the density of population,
and undertakes to regulate the way people choose to associate with each
other within the privacy of their own homes.

It is no answer to say, as does the majority, that associational interests are not infringed because Belle Terre residents may entertain whom-

---

[4] "Perhaps in an ideal world, planning and zoning would be done on a *regional*
basis, so that a given community would have apartments, while an adjoining community would not. But as long as we allow zoning to be done community by community, it is intolerable to allow one municipality (or many municipalities) to close its
doors at the expense of surrounding communities and the central city." *Appeal of
Girsh,* 437 Pa. 237, 245 n. 4, 263 A. 2d 395, 399 n. 4 (1970).

[5] See generally Note, On Privacy: Constitutional Protection for Personal Liberty,
48 N. Y. U. L. Rev. 670, 740–750 (1973).

[6] See *Palo Alto Tenants' Union* v. *Morgan,* 487 F. 2d 883 (CA9 1973).

ever they choose. Only last Term Mr. Justice Douglas indicated in concurrence that he saw the right of association protected by the First Amendment as involving far more than the right to entertain visitors. He found that right infringed by a restriction on food stamp assistance, penalizing households of "unrelated persons." As Mr. Justice Douglas there said, freedom of association encompasses the "right to invite the stranger into one's home" not only for "entertainment" but to join the household as well.** I am still persuaded that the choice of those who will form one's household implicates constitutionally protected rights.

Because I believe that this zoning ordinance creates a classification which impinges upon fundamental personal rights, it can withstand constitutional scrutiny only upon a clear showing that the burden imposed is necessary to protect a compelling and substantial governmental interest.** And, once it be determined that a burden has been placed upon a constitutional right, the onus of demonstrating that no less intrusive means will adequately protect the compelling state interest and that the challenged statute is sufficiently narrowly drawn, is upon the party seeking to justify the burden.**

A variety of justifications have been proffered in support of the village's ordinance. It is claimed that the ordinance controls population density, prevents noise, traffic and parking problems, and preserves the rent structure of the community and its attractiveness to families. As I noted earlier, these are all legitimate and substantial interests of government. But I think it clear that the means chosen to accomplish these purposes are both overinclusive and underinclusive, and that the asserted goals could be as effectively achieved by means of an ordinance that did not discriminate on the basis of constitutionally protected choices of lifestyle. The ordinance imposes no restriction whatsoever on the number of persons who may live in a house, as long as they are related by marital or sanguinary bonds—presumably no matter how distant their relationship. Nor does the ordinance restrict the number of income earners who may contribute to rent in such a household, or the number of automobiles that may be maintained by its occupants. In that sense the ordinance is underinclusive. On the other hand, the statute restricts the number of unrelated persons who may live in a home to no more than two. It would therefore prevent three unrelated people from occupying a dwelling even if among them they had but one income and no vehicles. While an extended family of a dozen or more might live in a small bungalow, three elderly and retired persons could not occupy the large manor house next door. Thus the statute is also grossly overinclusive to accomplish its intended purposes.

There are some 220 residences in Belle Terre occupied by about 700 persons. The density is therefore just above three per household. The village is justifiably concerned with density of population and the related problems of noise, traffic, and the like. It could deal with those problems by limiting each household to a specified number of adults, two or three perhaps, without limitation on the number of dependent children.[7] The burden of such an ordinance would fall equally upon all segments of the community. It would surely be better tailored to the goals asserted by the township than the ordinance before us today, for it would more realistically restrict population density and growth and their attendant environmental costs. Various other statutory mechanisms also suggest themselves as solutions to Belle Terre's problems—rent control, limits on the number of vehicles per household, and so forth, but, of course, such schemes are matters of legislative judgment and not for this Court. Appellants also refer to the necessity of maintaining the family character of the village. There is not a shred of evidence in the record indicating that if Belle Terre permitted a limited number of unrelated persons to live together, the residential, familial character of the community would be fundamentally affected.

By limiting unrelated households to two persons while placing no limitation on households of related individuals, the village has embarked upon its commendable course in a constitutionally faulty vessel.** I would find the challenged ordinance unconstitutional. But I would not ask the village to abandon its goal of providing quiet streets, little traffic, and a pleasant and reasonably priced environment in which families might raise their children. Rather, I would commend the town to continue to pursue those purposes but by means of more carefully drawn and even-handed legislation.

I respectfully dissent.

MORALS AND THE CRIMINAL LAW

PATRICK DEVLIN

In jurisprudence, as I have said, everything is thrown open to discussion and, in the belief that they cover the whole field, I have framed three interrogatories addressed to myself to answer:

1. Has society the right to pass judgement at all on matters of morals? Ought there, in other words, to be a public morality, or are morals always a matter for private judgement?
2. If society has the right to pass judgement, has it also the right to use the weapon of the law to enforce it?

---

[7] By providing an exception for dependent children, the township would avoid any doubts that might otherwise be posed by the constitutional protection afforded the choice of whether to bear a child.**

From *The Enforcement of Morals* by Patrick Devlin. © Oxford University Press 1965. Reprinted by permission of the publisher.

3. If so, ought it to use that weapon in all cases or only in some; and if only in some, on what principles should it distinguish?

I shall begin with the first interrogatory and consider what is meant by the right of society to pass a moral judgement, that is, a judgement about what is good and what is evil. The fact that a majority of people may disapprove of a practice does not of itself make it a matter for society as a whole. Nine men out of ten may disapprove of what the tenth man is doing and still say that it is not their business. There is a case for a collective judgement (as distinct from a large number of individual opinions which sensible people may even refrain from pronouncing at all if it is upon somebody else's private affairs) only if society is affected. Without a collective judgement there can be no case at all for intervention. Let me take as an illustration the Englishman's attitude to religion as it is now and as it has been in the past. His attitude now is that a man's religion is his private affair; he may think of another man's religion that it is right or wrong, true or untrue, but not that it is good or bad. In earlier times that was not so; a man was denied the right to practise what was thought of as heresy, and heresy was thought of as destructive of society.

The language used in the passages I have quoted from the Wolfenden Report suggests the view that there ought not to be a collective judgement about immorality *per se*. Is this what is meant by "private morality" and "individual freedom of choice and action"? Some people sincerely believe that homosexuality is neither immoral nor unnatural. Is the "freedom of choice and action" that is offered to the individual, freedom to decide for himself what is moral or immoral, society remaining neutral; or is it freedom to be immoral if he wants to be? The language of the Report may be open to question, but the conclusions at which the Committee arrive answer this question unambiguously. If society is not prepared to say that homosexuality is morally wrong, there would be no basis for a law protecting youth from "corruption" or punishing a man for living on the "immoral" earnings of a homosexual prostitute, as the Report recommends.[1] This attitude the Committee make even clearer when they come to deal with prostitution. In truth, the Report takes it for granted that there is in existence a public morality which condemns homosexuality and prostitution. What the Report seems to mean by private morality might perhaps be better described as private behaviour in matters of morals.

This view—that there is such a thing as public morality—can also be justified by *a priori* argument. What makes a society of any sort is community of ideas, not only political ideas but also ideas about the way its members should behave and govern their lives; these latter ideas are its morals. Every society has a moral structure as well as a political one: or rather, since that might suggest two independent systems, I should say

---

[1] Para. 76.

that the structure of every society is made up both of politics and morals. Take, for example, the institution of marriage. Whether a man should be allowed to take more than one wife is something about which every society has to make up its mind one way or the other. In England we believe in the Christian idea of marriage and therefore adopt monogamy as a moral principle. Consequently the Christian institution of marriage has become the basis of family life and so part of the structure of our society. It is there not because it is Christian. It has got there because it is Christian, but it remains there because it is built into the house in which we live and could not be removed without bringing it down. The great majority of those who live in this country accept it because it is the Christian idea of marriage and for them the only true one. But a non-Christian is bound by it, not because it is part of Christianity but because, rightly or wrongly, it has been adopted by the society in which he lives. It would be useless for him to stage a debate designed to prove that polygamy was theologically more correct and socially preferable; if he wants to live in the house, he must accept it as built in the way in which it is.

We see this more clearly if we think of ideas or institutions that are purely political. Society cannot tolerate rebellion; it will not allow argument about the rightness of the cause. Historians a century later may say that the rebels were right and the Government was wrong and a percipient and conscientious subject of the State may think so at the time. But it is not a matter which can be left to individual judgement.

The institution of marriage is a good example for my purpose because it bridges the division, if there is one, between politics and morals. Marriage is part of the structure of our society and it is also the basis of a moral code which condemns fornication and adultery. The institution of marriage would be gravely threatened if individual judgements were permitted about the morality of adultery; on these points there must be a public morality. But public morality is not to be confined to those moral principles which support institutions such as marriage. People do not think of monogamy as something which has to be supported because our society has chosen to organize itself upon it; they think of it as something that is good in itself and offering a good way of life and that it is for that reason that our society has adopted it. I return to the statement that I have already made, that society means a community of ideas; without shared ideas on politics, morals, and ethics no society can exist. Each one of us has ideas about what is good and what is evil; they cannot be kept private from the society in which we live. If men and women try to create a society in which there is no fundamental agreement about good and evil they will fail; if, having based it on common agreement, the agreement goes, the society will disintegrate. For society is not something that is kept together physically; it is held by the invisible bonds of common thought. If the bonds were too far relaxed the members would drift apart. A common morality is part of the bondage. The bondage is part of the price of society; and mankind, which needs society, must pay its price.

Common lawyers used to say that Christianity was part of the law of the land. That was never more than a piece of rhetoric as Lord Sumner said in *Bowman* v. *The Secular Society*.[2] What lay behind it was the notion which I have been seeking to expound, namely that morals—and up till a century or so ago no one thought it worth distinguishing between religion and morals—were necessary to the temporal order. In 1675 Chief Justice Hale said: "To say that religion is a cheat is to dissolve all those obligations whereby civil society is preserved." [3] In 1797 Mr. Justice Ashurst said of blasphemy that it was "not only an offense against God but against all law and government from its tendency to dissolve all the bonds and obligations of civil society." [4] By 1908 Mr. Justice Phillimore was able to say: "A man is free to think, to speak and to teach what he pleases as to religious matters, but not as to morals." [5]

You may think that I have taken far too long in contending that there is such a thing as public morality, a proposition which most people would readily accept, and may have left myself too little time to discuss the next question which to many minds may cause greater difficulty: to what extent should society use the law to enforce its moral judgements? But I believe that the answer to the first question determines the way in which the second should be approached and may indeed very nearly dictate the answer to the second question. If society has no right to make judgements on morals, the law must find some special justification for entering the field of morality: if homosexuality and prostitution are not in themselves wrong, then the onus is very clearly on the lawgiver who wants to frame a law against certain aspects of them to justify the exceptional treatment. But if society has the right to make a judgement and has it on the basis that a recognized morality is as necessary to society as, say, a recognized government, then society may use the law to preserve morality in the same way as it uses it to safeguard anything else that is essential to its existence. If therefore the first proposition is securely established with all its implications, society has a prima facie right to legislate against immorality as such.

The Wolfenden Report, notwithstanding that it seems to admit the right of society to condemn homosexuality and prostitution as immoral, requires special circumstances to be shown to justify the intervention of the law. I think that this is wrong in principle and that any attempt to approach my second interrogatory on these lines is bound to break down. I think that the attempt by the Committee does break down and that this is shown by the fact that it has to define or describe its special circumstances so widely that they can be supported only if it is accepted that the law *is* concerned with immorality as such.

The widest of the special circumstances are described as the provision of "sufficient safeguards against exploitation and corruption of

2 (1917), A.C. 406, at 457.
3 *Taylor's Case,* 1 Vent. 293.
4 *R.* v. *Williams,* 26 St. Tr. 653, at 715.
5 *R.* v. *Boulter,* 72 J.P. 188.

others, particularly those who are specially vulnerable because they are
young, weak in body or mind, inexperienced, or in a state of special
physical, official or economic dependence." 6 The corruption of youth
is a well-recognized ground for intervention by the State and for the
purpose of any legislation the young can easily be defined. But if similar
protection were to be extended to every other citizen, there would be
no limit to the reach of the law. The "corruption and exploitation of
others" is so wide that it could be used to cover any sort of immorality
which involves, as most do, the co-operation of another person. Even if
the phrase is taken as limited to the categories that are particularized
as "specially vulnerable," it is so elastic as to be practically no restriction.
This is not merely a matter of words. For if the words used are stretched
almost beyond breaking-point, they still are not wide enough to cover
the recommendations which the Committee make about prostitution.

Prostitution is not in itself illegal and the Committee do not think
that it ought to be made so.7 If prostitution is private immorality and
not the law's business, what concern has the law with the ponce or the
brothel-keeper or the householder who permits habitual prostitution?
The Report recommends that the laws which make these activities criminal offences should be maintained or strengthened and brings them
(so far as it goes into principle; with regard to brothels it says simply
that the law rightly frowns on them) under the head of exploitation.8
There may be cases of exploitation in this trade, as there are or used to
be in many others, but in general a ponce exploits a prostitute no more
than an impresario exploits an actress. The Report finds that "the great
majority of prostitutes are women whose psychological makeup is such
that they choose this life because they find in it a style of living which
is to them easier, freer and more profitable than would be provided
by any other occupation. . . . In the main the association between
prostitute and ponce is voluntary and operates to mutual advantage." 9
The Committee would agree that this could not be called exploitation in
the ordinary sense. They say: "It is in our view an over-simplification to
think that those who live on the earnings of prostitution are exploiting
the prostitute as such. What they are really exploiting is the whole
complex of the relationship between prostitute and customer; they are,
in effect, exploiting the human weaknesses which cause the customer to
seek the prostitute and the prostitute to meet the demand." 10

All sexual immorality involves the exploitation of human weaknesses. The prostitute exploits the lust of her customers and the customer
the moral weakness of the prostitute. If the exploitation of human
weaknesses is considered to create a special circumstance, there is virtu-

6 Para. 13.
7 Paras. 224, 285, and 318.
8 Paras. 302 and 320.
9 Para. 223.
10 Para. 306.

ally no field of morality which can be defined in such a way as to exclude the law.

I think, therefore, that it is not possible to set theoretical limits to the power of the State to legislate against immorality. It is not possible to settle in advance exceptions to the general rule or to define inflexibly areas of morality into which the law is in no circumstances to be allowed to enter. Society is entitled by means of its laws to protect itself from dangers, whether from within or without. Here again I think that the political parallel is legitimate. The law of treason is directed against aiding the king's enemies and against sedition from within. The justification for this is that established government is necessary for the existence of society and therefore its safety against violent overthrow must be secured. But an established morality is as necessary as good government to the welfare of society. Societies disintegrate from within more frequently than they are broken up by external pressures. There is disintegration when no common morality is observed and history shows that the loosening of moral bonds is often the first stage of disintegration, so that society is justified in taking the same steps to preserve its moral code as it does to preserve its government and other essential institutions.[11] The suppression of vice is as much the law's business as the sup-

[11] It is somewhere about this point in the argument that Professor Hart in *Law, Liberty, and Morality* discerns a proposition which he describes as central to my thought. He states the proposition and his objection to it as follows (p. 51). "He appears to move from the acceptable proposition that *some* shared morality is essential to the existence of any society [this I take to be the proposition on p. 12] to the unacceptable proposition that a society is identical with its morality as that is at any given moment of its history, so that a change in its morality is tantamount to the destruction of a society. The former proposition might be even accepted as a necessary rather than an empirical truth depending on a quite plausible definition of society as a body of men who hold certain moral views in common. But the latter proposition is absurd. Taken strictly, it would prevent us saying that the morality of a given society had changed, and would compel us instead to say that one society had disappeared and another one taken its place. But it is only on this absurd criterion of what it is for the same society to continue to exist that it could be asserted without evidence that any deviation from a society's shared morality threatens its existence." In conclusion (p. 82) Professor Hart condemns the whole thesis in the lecture as based on "a confused definition of what a society is."

I do not assert that *any* deviation from a society's shared morality threatens its existence any more than I assert that *any* subversive activity threatens its existence. I assert that they are both activities which are capable in their nature of threatening the existence of society so that neither can be put beyond the law.

For the rest, the objection appears to me to be all a matter of words. I would venture to assert, for example, that you cannot have a game without rules and that if there were no rules there would be no game. If I am asked whether that means that the game is "identical" with the rules, I would be willing for the question to be answered either way in the belief that the answer would lead to nowhere. If I am asked whether a change in the rules means that one game has disappeared and another has taken its place, I would reply probably not, but that it would depend on the extent of the change.

Likewise I should venture to assert that there cannot be a contract without terms. Does this mean that an "amended" contract is a "new" contract in the eyes of the

pression of subversive activities; it is no more possible to define a sphere of private morality than it is to define one of private subversive activity. It is wrong to talk of private morality or of the law not being concerned with immorality as such or to try to set rigid bounds to the part which the law may play in the suppression of vice. There are no theoretical limits to the power of the State to legislate against treason and sedition, and likewise I think there can be no theoretical limits to legislation against immorality. You may argue that if a man's sins affect only himself it cannot be the concern of society. If he chooses to get drunk every night in the privacy of his own home, is any one except himself the worse for it? But suppose a quarter or a half of the population got drunk every night, what sort of society would it be? You cannot set a theoretical limit to the number of people who can get drunk before society is entitled to legislate against drunkenness. The same may be said of gambling. The Royal Commission on Betting, Lotteries, and Gaming took as their test the character of the citizen as a member of society. They said: "Our concern with the ethical significance of gambling is confined to the effect which it may have on the character of the gambler as a member of society. If we were convinced that whatever the degree of gambling this effect must be harmful we should be inclined to think that it was the duty of the state to restrict gambling to the greatest extent practicable." [12]

In what circumstances the State should exercise its power is the third of the interrogatories I have framed. But before I get to it I must raise a point which might have been brought up in any one of the three. How are the moral judgements of society to be ascertained? By leaving it until now, I can ask it in the more limited form that is now sufficient for my purpose. How is the law-maker to ascertain the moral judgements of society? It is surely not enough that they should be reached by the opinion of the majority; it would be too much to require the individual assent of every citizen. English law has evolved and regularly uses a

---

law? I once listened to an argument by an ingenious counsel that a contract, because of the substitution of one clause for another, had "ceased to have effect" within the meaning of a statutory provision. The judge did not accept the argument; but if most of the fundamental terms had been changed, I daresay he would have done.

The proposition that I make in the text is that if (as I understand Professor Hart to agree, at any rate for the purposes of the argument) you cannot have a society without morality, the law can be used to enforce morality as something that is essential to a society. I cannot see why this proposition (whether it is right or wrong) should mean that morality can never be changed without the destruction of society. If morality is changed, the law can be changed. Professor Hart refers (p. 72) to the proposition as "the use of legal punishment to freeze into immobility the morality dominant at a particular time in a society's existence." One might as well say that the inclusion of a penal section into a statute prohibiting certain acts freezes the whole statute into immobility and prevents the prohibitions from ever being modified.

These points are elaborated in the sixth lecture at pp. 115–16 [Chapter VI of *The Enforcement of Morals*. Ed.].

[12] (1951) Cmd. 8190, para. 159.

standard which does not depend on the counting of heads. It is that of the reasonable man. He is not to be confused with the rational man. He is not expected to reason about anything and his judgement may be largely a matter of feeling. It is the viewpoint of the man in the street—or to use an archaism familiar to all lawyers—the man in the Clapham omnibus. He might also be called the right-minded man. For my purpose I should like to call him the man in the jury box, for the moral judgement of society must be something about which any twelve men or women drawn at random might after discussion be expected to be unanimous. This was the standard the judges applied in the days before Parliament was as active as it is now and when they laid down rules of public policy. They did not think of themselves as making law but simply as stating principles which every right-minded person would accept as valid. It is what Pollock called "practical morality," which is based not on theological or philosophical foundations but "in the mass of continuous experience half-consciously or unconsciously accumulated and embodied in the morality of common sense." He called it also "a certain way of thinking on questions of morality which we expect to find in a reasonable civilized man or a reasonable Englishman, taken at random." [13]

Immorality then, for the purpose of the law, is what every right-minded person is presumed to consider to be immoral. Any immorality is capable of affecting society injuriously and in effect to a greater or lesser extent it usually does; this is what gives the law its *locus standi*. It cannot be shut out. But—and this brings me to the third question—the individual has a *locus standi* too; he cannot be expected to surrender to the judgement of society the whole conduct of his life. It is the old and familiar question of striking a balance between the rights and interests of society and those of the individual. This is something which the law is constantly doing in matters large and small. To take a very down-to-earth example, let me consider the right of the individual whose house adjoins the highway to have access to it; that means in these days the right to have vehicles stationary in the highway, sometimes for a considerable time if there is a lot of loading or unloading. There are many cases in which the courts have had to balance the private right of access against the public right to use the highway without obstruction. It cannot be done by carving up the highway into public and private areas. It is done by recognizing that each have rights over the whole; that if each were to exercise their rights to the full, they would come into conflict; and therefore that the rights of each must be curtailed so as to ensure as far as possible that the essential needs of each are safeguarded.

I do not think that one can talk sensibly of a public and private morality any more than one can of a public or private highway. Morality is a sphere in which there is a public interest and a private interest, often

[13] *Essays in Jurisprudence and Ethics* (1882), Macmillan, pp. 278 and 353.

in conflict, and the problem is to reconcile the two. This does not mean
that it is impossible to put forward any general statements about how
in our society the balance ought to be struck. Such statements cannot
of their nature be rigid or precise; they would not be designed to cir-
cumscribe the operation of the law-making power but to guide those
who have to apply it. While every decision which a court of law makes
when it balances the public against the private interest is an *ad hoc*
decision, the cases contain statements of principle to which the court
should have regard when it reaches its decision. In the same way it is
possible to make general statements of principle which it may be thought
the legislature should bear in mind when it is considering the enactment
of laws enforcing morals.

I believe that most people would agree upon the chief of these
elastic principles. There must be toleration of the maximum individual
freedom that is consistent with the integrity of society. It cannot be said
that this is a principle that runs all through the criminal law. Much of
the criminal law that is regulatory in character—the part of it that deals
with *malum prohibitum* rather than *malum in se*—is based upon the
opposite principle, that is, that the choice of the individual must give
way to the convenience of the many. But in all matters of conscience the
principle I have stated is generally held to prevail. It is not confined to
thought and speech; it extends to action, as is shown by the recognition
of the right to conscientious objection in war-time; this example shows
also that conscience will be respected even in times of national danger.
The principle appears to me to be peculiarly appropriate to all questions
of morals. Nothing should be punished by the law that does not lie
beyond the limits of tolerance. It is not nearly enough to say that a
majority dislike a practice; there must be a real feeling of reprobation.
Those who are dissatisfied with the present law on homosexuality often
say that the opponents of reform are swayed simply by disgust. If that
were so it would be wrong, but I do not think one can ignore disgust if
it is deeply felt and not manufactured. Its presence is a good indication
that the bounds of toleration are being reached. Not everything is to be
tolerated. No society can do without intolerance, indignation, and disgust; [14] they are the forces behind the moral law, and indeed it can be
argued that if they or something like them are not present, the feelings
of society cannot be weighty enough to deprive the individual of freedom
of choice. I suppose that there is hardly anyone nowadays who would
not be disgusted by the thought of deliberate cruelty to animals. No one
proposes to relegate that or any other form of sadism to the realm of
private morality or to allow it to be practised in public or in private. It
would be possible no doubt to point out that until a comparatively short
while ago nobody thought very much of cruelty to animals and also that
pity and kindliness and the unwillingness to inflict pain are virtues

---

[14] These words which have been much criticized, are considered again in the
preface [of *The Enforcement of Morals*, Ed.] at p. viii.

more generally esteemed now than they have ever been in the past. But matters of this sort are not determined by rational argument. Every moral judgement, unless it claims a divine source, is simply a feeling that no right-minded man could behave in any other way without admitting that he was doing wrong. It is the power of a common sense and not the power of reason that is behind the judgements of society. But before a society can put a practice beyond the limits of tolerance there must be a deliberate judgement that the practice is injurious to society. There is, for example, a general abhorrence of homosexuality. We should ask ourselves in the first instance whether, looking at it calmly and dispassionately, we regard it as a vice so abominable that its mere presence is an offence. If that is the genuine feeling of the society in which we live, I do not see how society can be denied the right to eradicate it. Our feeling may not be so intense as that. We may feel about it that, if confined, it is tolerable, but that if it spread it might be gravely injurious; it is in this way that most societies look upon fornication, seeing it as a natural weakness which must be kept within bounds but which cannot be rooted out. It becomes then a question of balance, the danger to society in one scale and the extent of the restriction in the other. On this sort of point the value of an investigation by such a body as the Wolfenden Committee and of its conclusions is manifest.

The limits of tolerance shift. This is supplementary to what I have been saying but of sufficient importance in itself to deserve statement as a separate principle which law-makers have to bear in mind. I suppose that moral standards do not shift; so far as they come from divine revelation they do not, and I am willing to assume that the moral judgements made by a society always remain good for that society. But the extent to which society will tolerate—I mean tolerate, not approve— departures from moral standards varies from generation to generation. It may be that over-all tolerance is always increasing. The pressure of the human mind, always seeking greater freedom of thought, is outwards against the bonds of society forcing their gradual relaxation. It may be that history is a tale of contraction and expansion and that all developed societies are on their way to dissolution. I must not speak of things I do not know; and anyway as a practical matter no society is willing to make provision for its own decay. I return therefore to the simple and observable fact that in matters of morals the limits of tolerance shift. Laws, especially those which are based on morals, are less easily moved. It follows as another good working principle that in any new matter of morals the law should be slow to act. By the next generation the swell of indignation may have abated and the law be left without the strong backing which it needs. But it is then difficult to alter the law without giving the impression that moral judgement is being weakened. This is now one of the factors that is strongly militating against any alteration to the law on homosexuality.

A third elastic principle must be advanced more tentatively. It is that as far as possible privacy should be respected. This is not an idea that has ever been made explicit in the criminal law. Acts or words done or said in public or in private are all brought within its scope without distinction in principle. But there goes with this a strong reluctance on the part of judges and legislators to sanction invasions of privacy in the detection of crime. The police have no more right to trespass than the ordinary citizen has; there is no general right of search; to this extent an Englishman's home is still his castle. The Government is extremely careful in the exercise even of those powers which it claims to be undisputed. Telephone tapping and interference with the mails afford a good illustration of this. A Committee of three Privy Councillors who recently inquired [15] into these activities found that the Home Secretary and his predecessors had already formulated strict rules governing the exercise of these powers and the Committee were able to recommend that they should be continued to be exercised substantially on the same terms. But they reported that the power was "regarded with general disfavour."

This indicates a general sentiment that the right to privacy is something to be put in the balance against the enforcement of the law. Ought the same sort of consideration to play any part in the formation of the law? Clearly only in a very limited number of cases. When the help of the law is invoked by an injured citizen, privacy must be irrelevant; the individual cannot ask that his right to privacy should be measured against injury criminally done to another. But when all who are involved in the deed are consenting parties and the injury is done to morals, the public interest in the moral order can be balanced against the claims of privacy. The restriction on police powers of investigation goes further than the affording of a parallel; it means that the detection of crime committed in private and when there is no complaint is bound to be rather haphazard and this is an additional reason for moderation. These considerations do not justify the exclusion of all private immorality from the scope of the law. I think that, as I have already suggested, the test of "private behaviour" should be substituted for "private morality" and the influence of the factor should be reduced from that of a definite limitation to that of a matter to be taken into account. Since the gravity of the crime is also a proper consideration, a distinction might well be made in the case of homosexuality between the lesser acts of indecency and the full offence, which on the principles of the Wolfenden Report it would be illogical to do.

The last and the biggest thing to be remembered is that the law is concerned with the minimum and not with the maximum; there is much in the Sermon on the Mount that would be out of place in the Ten Commandments. We all recognize the gap between the moral law and the law of the land. No man is worth much who regulates his conduct with the sole object of escaping punishment, and every worthy society sets for its members standards which are above those of the law. We recognize the existence of such higher standards when we use expres-

---

[15] (1957) Cmd. 283.

sions such as "moral obligation" and "morally bound." The distinction was well put in the judgement of African elders in a family dispute: "We have power to make you divide the crops, for this is our law, and we will see this is done. But we have not power to make you behave like an upright man." [16]

DEMOCRACY AND MORALITY

Patrick Devlin

How does the law-maker ascertain the moral principles that are accepted by the society to which he belongs? He is concerned only with the fundament that is surely accepted, for legal sanctions are inappropriate for the enforcement of moral standards that are in dispute. He does not therefore need the assistance of moral philosophers nor does he have to study the arguments upon peripheral questions. He is concerned with what is acceptable to the ordinary man, the man in the jury box, who might also be called the reasonable man or the right-minded man. When I call him the man in the jury box, I do not mean to imply that the ordinary citizen when he enters the jury box is invested with some peculiar quality that enables him to pronounce *ex cathedra* on morals. I still think of him simply as the ordinary reasonable man, but by placing him in the jury box I call attention to three points. First, the verdict of a jury must be unanimous; so a moral principle, if it is to be given the force of law, should be one which twelve men and women drawn at random from the community can be expected not only to approve but to take so seriously that they regard a breach of it as fit for punishment. Second, the man in the jury box does not give a snap judgement but returns his verdict after argument, instruction, and deliberation. Third, the jury box is a place in which the ordinary man's views on morals become directly effective. The law-maker who makes the mistake of thinking that what he has to preserve is not the health of society but a particular regimen, will find that particular laws wither away. An important part of the machinery for hastening obsolescence is the lay element in the administration of English justice, the man in the jury box and the lay magistrate. The magistrates can act by the imposition of nominal penalties; the juryman acts by acquittal. If he gravely dislikes

[16] A case in the Saa-Katengo Kuta at Lialiu, August 1942, quoted in *The Judicial Process among the Barotse of Northern Rhodesia* by Max Gluckman, Manchester University Press, 1955, p. 172.

a law or thinks its application too harsh, he has the power, which from time immemorial he has exercised, to return a verdict of acquittal that is unassailable; and of its unassailability in English law William Penn and Bushell the juror stand as immortal witnesses.[1]

This gives the common man, when sitting in the jury box, a sort of veto upon the enforcement of morals. One of the most interesting features of *Shaw's** case is that (in cases of uncategorized immorality contrary to common law as distinct from offences defined by statute) it confers on the jury a right and duty more potent than an unofficial veto; it makes the jury a constitutional organ for determining what amounts to immorality and when the law should be enforced. I shall return to that later.

What I want to discuss immediately is the reaction that many philosophers and academic lawyers have to the doctrine I have just outlined. They dislike it very much. It reduces morality, they feel, to the level of a question of fact. What Professor H. L. A. Hart calls rationalist morality,[2] which I take to be morality embodied in the rational judgement of men who have studied moral questions and pondered long on what the answers ought to be, will be blown aside by a gust of popular morality compounded of all the irrational prejudices and emotions of the man in the street. Societies in the past have tolerated witch-hunting and burnt heretics: was that done in the name of morality? There are societies today whose moral standards permit them to discriminate against men because of their colour: have we to accept that? Is reason to play no part in the separation of right from wrong?

The most significant thing about questions of this type is that none of the questioners would think them worth asking if the point at issue had nothing in it of the spiritual. It is a commonplace that in our sort of society matters of great moment are settled in accordance with the opinion of the ordinary citizen who acts no more and no less rationally in matters of policy than in matters of morals. Such is the consequence of democracy and universal suffrage. Those who have had the benefit of a higher education and feel themselves better equipped to solve the nation's problems than the average may find it distasteful to submit to herd opinion. History tells them that democracies are far from perfect and have in the past done many foolish and even wicked things. But they do not dispute that in the end the will of the people must prevail nor do they seek to appeal from it to the throne of reason.

But when it comes to a pure point of morals—for example, is homosexuality immoral and sinful?—the first reaction of most of us is different.

1 See *Bushell's* Case (1670), Jones 1, at 13, 84 Eng. Rep. 1123.

* *Shaw* v. *Director of Public Prosecutions.* The case is discussed in *The Enforcement of Morals* at 87–88 and at 97–100. Ed.

2 Hart, "Immorality and Treason," *The Listener*, 1959, vol. 62, pp. 162, 163. Professor Hart's views on this point have been considered by Dean Rostow in "The Enforcement of Morals," *Cambridge Law Journal*, 1960, pp. 174, 184–92. I cannot improve on what the Dean has said; I merely elaborate it in my own words.

That reaction illustrates vividly the vacuum that is created when a society no longer acknowledges a supreme spiritual authority. For most of the history of mankind this sort of question has been settled, for men in society as well as for men as individuals, by priests claiming to speak with the voice of God. Today a man's own conscience is for him the final arbiter: but what for society?

This problem does not arise for one who takes the extreme view that society and the law have no concern at all with morals and that a man may behave as he wishes so long as he respects another's physical person and property. But I believe that there is general agreement that that is not enough and that the law should prevent a man from, for example, corrupting the morals of youth or offending the moral standards of others by a public display of what they regard as vice. The law cannot interfere in these ways except from the basis of a common or public morality. Whatever view one takes of the law's right of intervention—whether it should be no wider than is necessary to protect youth or as wide as may be desirable to conserve the moral health of the whole community—one still has to answer the question: "How are moral standards to be ascertained in the absence of a spiritual authority?"

This question, it seems to me, has received less study than it ought to have. The lawyers have evaded it by means of the assumption, substantially justifiable in fact though not in theory, that Christian morality remains just as valid for the purposes of the law as it was in the days of a universal church. The philosophers seem to have assumed that because a man's conscience could do for him, if he so chose, all that in the age of faith the priest had done, it could likewise do for society all that the priest had done. It cannot, unless some way be found of making up a collective conscience.

It is said or implied that this can be done by accepting the sovereignty of reason which will direct the conscience of every man to the same conclusion. The humbler way of using the power of reason is to hold, as Aquinas did, that through it it is possible to ascertain the law as God ordered it, the natural law, the law as it ought to be; the prouder is to assert that the reason of man unaided can construct the law as it ought to be. If the latter view is right, then one must ask: As men of reason are all men equal? If they are, if every man has equivalent power of reasoning and strength of mind to subdue the baser faculties of feeling and emotion, there can be no objection to morality being a matter for the popular vote. The objection is sustainable only upon the view that the opinion of the trained and educated mind, reached as its owner believes by an unimpassioned rational process, is as a source of morals superior to the opinion of ordinary men.[3]

To the whole of this thesis, however it be put and whether or not

[3] In a letter published in *The Times* (London), 22 March 1961, p. 13, col. 5, a distinguished historian wrote that what clinched the issue in the relationship between morality and the law was "simply that it is impossible to administer justice on a law as to which there is a fundamental disagreement among *educated* opinion." (My italics.)

it is valid for the individual mind that is governed by philosophy or faith, the law-maker in a democratic society must advance insuperable objections, both practical and theoretical. The practical objection is that after centuries of debate, men of undoubted reasoning power and honesty of purpose have shown themselves unable to agree on what the moral law should be, differing sometimes upon the answer to the simplest moral problem. To say this is not to deny the value of discussion among moral philosophers or to overlook the possibility that sometime between now and the end of the world universal agreement may be reached, but it is to say that as a guide to the degree of definition required by the law-maker the method is valueless. Theoretically the method is inadmissible. If what reason has to discover is the law of God, it is inadmissible because it assumes, as of course Aquinas did, belief in God as a law-giver. If it is the law of man and if a common opinion on any point is held by the educated *élite*, what is obtained except to substitute for the voice of God the voice of the Superior Person? A free society is as much offended by the dictates of an intellectual oligarchy as by those of an autocrat.

For myself I have found no satisfactory alternative to the thesis I have proposed. The opposition to it, I cannot help thinking, has not rid itself of the idea, natural to a philosopher, that a man who is seeking a moral law ought also to be in pursuit of absolute truth. If he were, they would think it surprising if he found truth at the bottom of the popular vote. I do not think it as far from this as some learned people suppose and I have known them to search for it in what seem to me to be odder places. But that is a subject outside the scope of this lecture which is not concerned with absolute truth. I have said that a sense of right and wrong is necessary for the life of a community. It is not necessary that their appreciation of right and wrong, tested in the light of one set or another of those abstract propositions about which men forever dispute, should be correct. If it were, only one society at most could survive. What the law-maker has to ascertain is not the true belief but the common belief.

When I talk of the law-maker I mean a man whose business it is to make the law whether it takes the form of a legislative enactment or of a judicial decision, as contrasted with the lawyer whose business is to interpret and apply the law as it is. Of course the two functions often overlap; judges especially are thought of as performing both. No one now is shocked by the idea that the lawyer is concerned simply with the law as it is and not as he thinks it ought to be. No one need be shocked by the idea that the law-maker is concerned with morality as it is. There are, have been, and will be bad laws, bad morals, and bad societies. Probably no law-maker believes that the morality he is enacting is false, but that does not make it true. Unfortunately bad societies can live on bad morals just as well as good societies on good ones.

In a democracy educated men cannot be put into a separate category for the decision of moral questions. But that does not mean that in a free society they cannot enjoy and exploit the advantage of the superior mind. The law-maker's task, even in a democracy, is not the drab one of counting heads or of synthesizing answers to moral questions given in a Gallup poll. In theory a sharp line can be drawn between law and morality as they are—positive law and positive morality—and as they ought to be; but in practice no such line can be drawn, because positive morality, like every other basis for the law, is subject to change, and consequently the law has to be developed. A judge is tethered to the positive law but not shackled to it. So long as he does not break away from the positive law, that is, from the precedents which are set for him or the clear language of the statute which he is applying, he can determine for himself the distance and direction of his advance. Naturally he will move towards the law as he thinks it ought to be. If he has moved in the right direction, along the way his society would wish to go, there will come a time when the tethering-point is uprooted and moved nearer to the position he has taken; if he has moved in the wrong direction, he or his successors will be pulled back.

The legislator as an enforcer of morals has far greater latitude than the modern judge. Legislation of that sort is not usually made an election issue but is left to the initiative of those who are returned to power. In deciding whether or not to take the initiative the relevant question nearly always is not what popular morality is but whether it should be enforced by the criminal law. If there is a reasonable doubt on the first point, that doubt of itself answers the whole question in the negative. The legislator must gauge the intensity with which a popular moral conviction is held, because it is only when the obverse is generally thought to be intolerable that the criminal law can safely and properly be used. But if he decides that point in favour of the proposed legislation, there are many other factors, some of principle and some of expediency, to be weighed, and these give the legislator a wide discretion in determining how far he will go in the direction of the law as he thinks it ought to be. The restraint upon him is that if he moves too far from the common sense of his society, he will forfeit the popular goodwill and risk seeing his work undone by his successor.

This is the method of law-making common to both America and England. The popular vote does not itself enact or veto; rather, the initiative is put into the hands of a very few men. Under this method the law reformer has a double opportunity. He may work upon the popular opinion which is the law-makers' base or he may influence the law-maker directly. At each of these stages the educated man is at an advantage in a democratic society.

Let us consider the first stage. True it is that in the final count the word of the educated man goes for no more than that of any other sort of man. But in the making up of the tally he has or should have the advantage of powers of persuasion above the ordinary. I do not mean by that simply powers of reasoning. If he is to be effective he must be ready to persuade and not just to teach, and he must accept that reason is not the plain man's only guide. "The common morality of a society at any time," says Dean Rostow, "is a blend of custom and conviction, of reason and feeling, of experience and prejudice." [4] If an educated man is armed only with reason, if he is disdainful of custom and ignores strength of feeling, if he thinks of "prejudice" and "intolerance" as words with no connotations that are not disgraceful and is blind to religious conviction, he had better not venture outside his academy, for if he does he will have to deal with forces he cannot understand. Not all learned men are prepared like Bertrand Russell to sit on the pavement outside No. 10 Downing Street. Not all are lucid as well as erudite. Many a man will find satisfaction in teaching others to do what he is not equipped to do himself; but it is naïve for such a man to reproach judges and legislators for making what he deems to be irrational law, as if in a democratic society they were the agents only of reason and the controllers of a nation's thought.

The other advantage which the educated man possesses is that he has easier access to the ear of the law-maker. I do not mean merely by lobbying. When—with such latitude as our democratic and judicial system allows—the law-maker is determining the pace and direction of his advance from the law that is towards the law that ought to be, he does and should inform himself of the views of wise and experienced men and pay extra attention to them.

These are the ways by which well-informed and articulate men can play a part in the shaping of the law quite disproportionate to their numbers. Under a system in which no single question is submitted to the electorate for direct decision, an ardent minority for or against a particular measure may often count for more than an apathetic majority. Recently in England in the reform of the criminal law a minority has had some remarkable successes. In 1948 flogging was abolished as a judicial punishment; [5] it is doubtful whether that would have been the result of a majority vote, and it is still uncertain whether the gain will be held. Some years later much the same body of opinion was very nearly successful in abolishing capital punishment; I do not believe that in the country as a whole there is a majority against capital punishment. In 1959 the common law on obscenity was altered by statute. [6] Notwithstanding that the tendency of a book is to deprave and corrupt, it is a good defence if its publication is in the interests of some "object of general concern," such as literature or art; and the opinion of experts is made admissible on the merits of the work. Under this latter provision in the recent case of *Lady Chatterley's Lover,* [7] thirty-five witnesses distinguished in the fields of literature and morals were permitted to discuss at large the

4 Rostow, op. cit. p. 197.

5 Criminal Justice Act, 1948, 11 & 12 Geo. 6, c. 58, s. 2.

6 Obscene Publications Act, 1959, 7 & 8 Eliz. 2, c. 66, s. 4.

7 The transcript of the trial, somewhat abridged, has been published as *The Trial of Lady Chatterley: Regina* v. *Penguin Books Limited* (Rolph edn. 1961).

merits of the book, and thus a specially qualified body of opinion was brought into direct communication with the jury. On the other hand there has so far been a failure to reform the law against homosexuality. The conclusion of the Wolfenden Committee is an indication—I believe a correct one—that a substantial majority of "educated opinion" is in favour of some modification; but I believe also that the Home Secretary was right in his conclusion that public opinion as a whole was too strongly against the proposed amendments to permit legislation.

FROM SOCIAL PHILOSOPHY

JOEL FEINBERG

LINES OF ATTACK ON MILL

Arguments against Mill's unsupplemented harm principle (his claim that the private and public harm principles state the *only* grounds for justified interference with liberty) have been mainly of two different kinds.[1] Many have argued that the harm principle justifies too much social and political interference in the affairs of individuals. Others allow that the prevention of individual and social harm is always a ground for interference, but insist that it is by no means the only ground.

(i) "No Man Is An Island"

Mill maintained in *On Liberty* that social interference is never justified in those of a man's affairs that concern himself only. But no man's affairs have effects on himself alone. There are a thousand subtle and indirect ways in which every individual act, no matter how private and solitary, affects others. It would therefore seem that society has a right, on Mill's own principles, to interfere in every department of human life. Mill anticipated this objection and took certain steps to disarm it. Let it be allowed that no human conduct is entirely, exclusively, and to the last degree self-regarding. Still, Mill insisted, we can distinguish between actions that are plainly other-regarding and those that are "directly," "chiefly," or "primarily" self-regarding. There will be a

Joel Feinberg, SOCIAL PHILOSOPHY, © 1973, pp. 31–40, 41–45, 52–54. Reprinted by permission of Prentice-Hall, Inc., Englewood Cliffs, New Jersey, and the author.

[1] Cf. H. L. A. Hart, *Law, Liberty, and Morality* (Stanford: Stanford University Press, 1963), p. 5.

twilight area of cases difficult to classify, but that is true of many other workable distinctions, including that between night and day.

It is essential to Mill's theory that we make a distinction between two different kinds of consequences of human actions: the consequences *directly* affecting the interests of others, and those of primarily self-regarding behavior which only *indirectly* or *remotely* affect the interests of others. "No person ought to be punished simply for being drunk," Mill wrote, "but a soldier or policeman should be punished for being drunk on duty." [2] A drunk policeman directly harms the interests of others. His conduct gives opportunities to criminals and thus creates grave risk of harm to other citizens. It brings the police into disrepute, and makes the work of his colleagues more dangerous. Finally, it may lead to loss of the policeman's job, with serious consequences for his wife and children.

Consider, on the other hand, a hard working bachelor who habitually spends his evening hours drinking himself into a stupor, which he then sleeps off, rising fresh in the morning to put in another hard day's work. His drinking does not *directly* affect others in any of the ways of the drunk policeman's conduct. He has no family; he drinks alone and sets no direct example; he is not prevented from discharging any of his public duties; he creates no substantial risk of harm to the interests of other individuals. Although even his private conduct will have some effects on the interests of others, these are precisely the sorts of effects Mill would call "indirect" and "remote." First, in spending his evenings the way he does, our solitary tippler is *not* doing any number of other things that might be of greater utility to others. In not earning and spending more money, he is failing to stimulate the economy (except for the liquor industry) as much as he might. Second, he fails to spend his evening time improving his talents and making himself a better person. Perhaps he has a considerable native talent for painting or poetry, and his wastefulness is depriving the world of some valuable art. Third, he may make those of his colleagues who like him sad on his behalf. Finally, to those who know of his habits he is a "bad example." [3] All of these "indirect harms" together, Mill maintained, do not outweigh the direct and serious harm that would result from social or legal coercion.

Mill's critics have never been entirely satisfied by this. Many have pointed out that Mill is concerned not only with political coercion and legal punishment but also with purely social coercion—moral pressure, social avoidance, ostracism. No responsible critic would wish the state to punish the solitary tippler, but social coercion is another matter. We

---

[2] John Stuart Mill, *On Liberty* (New York: Liberal Arts Press, 1956), pp. 99–100.

[3] Mill has a ready rejoinder to this last point: If the conduct in question is supposed to be greatly harmful to the actor himself, "the example, on the whole must be more salutory" than harmful socially, since it is a warning lesson, rather than an alluring model, to others. See Mill, *On Liberty*, p. 101.

can't prevent people from disapproving of an individual for his self-regarding faults or from expressing that disapproval to others, without undue restriction on *their* freedom. Such expressions, in Mill's view, are inevitably coercive, constituting a "milder form of punishment." Hence "social punishment" of individuals for conduct that directly concerns only themselves—the argument concludes—is both inevitable and, according to Mill's own principles, proper.

Mill anticipated this objection, too, and tried to cope with it by making a distinction between types of social responses. We cannot help but lower in our estimation a person with serious self-regarding faults. We will think ill of him, judge him to be at fault, and make him the inevitable and proper object of our disapproval, distaste, even contempt. We may warn others about him, avoid his company, and withhold gratuitous benefits from him—"not to the oppression of his individuality but in the exercise of ours." [4] Mill concedes that all of these social responses can function as "penalties"—but they are suffered "only in so far as they are the natural and, as it were, the spontaneous consequences of the faults themselves, not because they are purposely inflicted on him for the sake of punishment." [5] Other responses, on the other hand, add something to the "natural penalties"—pointed snubbing, economic reprisals, gossip campaigns, and so on. The added penalties, according to Mill, are precisely the ones that are never justified as responses to merely self-regarding flaws—"if he displeases us, we may express our distaste; and we may stand aloof from a person as well as from a thing that displeases us, but we shall not therefore feel called on to make his life uncomfortable." [6]

(ii) Other Proposed Grounds for Coercion

The distinction between self-regarding and other-regarding behavior, as Mill intended it to be understood, does seem at least roughly serviceable, and unlikely to invite massive social interference in private affairs. I think most critics of Mill would grant that, but reject the harm principle on the opposite ground that it doesn't permit enough interference. These writers would allow at least one, and as many as five or more, additional valid grounds for coercion. Each of these proposed grounds is stated in a principle listed below. One might hold that restriction of one person's liberty can be justified:

1. To prevent harm to others, either
   a. injury to individual persons (*The Private Harm Principle*), or
   b. impairment of institutional practices that are in the public interest (*The Public Harm Principle*);

4 Mill, *On Liberty*, p. 94.
5 Mill, *On Liberty*, p. 95.
6 Mill, *On Liberty*, p. 96.

2. To prevent offense to others (*The Offense Principle*);
3. To prevent harm to self (*Legal Paternalism*);
4. To prevent or punish sin, i.e., to "enforce morality as such" (*Legal Moralism*);
5. To benefit the self (*Extreme Paternalism*);
6. To benefit others (*The Welfare Principle*).

The liberty-limiting principles on this list are best understood as stating neither necessary nor sufficient conditions for justified coercion, but rather specifications of the *kinds* of reasons that are always relevant or acceptable in support of proposed coercion, even though in a given case they may not be conclusive.[7] Each principle states that interference might be permissible *if* (but not *only if*) a certain condition is satisfied. Hence the principles are not mutually exclusive; it is possible to hold two or more of them at once, even all of them together, and it is possible to deny all of them. Moreover, the principles cannot be construed as stating sufficient conditions for legitimate interference with liberty, for even though the principle is satisfied in a given case, the general presumption against coercion might not be outweighed. The harm principle, for example, does not justify state interference to prevent a tiny bit of inconsequential harm. Prevention of minor harm always counts in favor of proposals (as in a legislature) to restrict liberty, but in a given instance it might not count *enough* to outweigh the general presumption against interference, or it might be outweighed by the prospect of practical difficulties in enforcing the law, excessive costs, and forfeitures of privacy. A liberty-limiting principle states considerations that are always good reasons for coercion, though neither exclusively nor, in every case, decisively good reasons.

It will not be possible to examine each principle in detail here, and offer "proofs" and "refutations." The best way to defend one's selection of principles is to show to which positions they commit one on such issues as censorship of literature, "morals offenses," and compulsory social security programs. General principles arise in the course of deliberations over particular problems, especially in the efforts to defend one's judgments by showing that they are consistent with what has gone before. If a principle commits one to an antecedently unacceptable judgment, then one has to modify or supplement the principle in a way that does the least damage to the harmony of one's particular and general opinions taken as a group. On the other hand, when a solid, well-entrenched principle entails a change in a particular judgment, the overriding claims of consistency may require that the judgment be adjusted. This sort of dialectic is similar to the reasonings that are prevalent in law courts. When similar cases are decided in opposite ways, it is incumbent on the court to distinguish them in some respect that will

---

[7] I owe this point to Professor Michael Bayles. See his contribution to *Issues in Law and Morality*, ed. Norman Care and Thomas Trelogan (Cleveland: The Press of Case Western Reserve University, 1973).

reconcile the separate decisions with each other and with the common rule applied to each. Every effort is made to render current decisions consistent with past ones unless the precedents seem so disruptive of the overall internal harmony of the law that they must, reluctantly, be revised or abandoned. In social and political philosophy every person is on his own, and the counterparts to "past decisions" are the most confident judgments one makes in ordinary normative discourse. The philosophical task is to extract from these "given" judgments the principles that render them consistent, adjusting and modifying where necessary in order to convert the whole body of opinions into an intelligible, coherent system. There is no a priori way of refuting another's political opinions, but if our opponents are rational men committed to the ideal of consistency, we can always hope to show them that a given judgment is inconsistent with one of their own acknowledged principles. Then something will have to give.

MORALS OFFENSES AND LEGAL MORALISM

Immoral conduct is no trivial thing, and we should hardly expect societies to tolerate it; yet if men are *forced* to refrain from immorality, their own choices will play very little role in what they do, so that they can hardly develop critical judgment and moral traits of a genuinely praiseworthy kind. Thus legal enforcement of morality seems to pose a dilemma. The problem does not arise if we assume that all immoral conduct is socially harmful, for immoral conduct will then be prohibited by law not just to punish sin or to "force men to be moral," but rather to prevent harm to others. If, however, there are forms of immorality that do not necessarily cause harm, "the problem of the enforcement of morality" becomes especially acute.

The central problem cases are those criminal actions generally called "morals offenses." Offenses against morality and decency have long constituted a category of crimes (as distinct from offenses against the person, offenses against property, and so on). These have included mainly sex offenses, such as adultery, fornication, sodomy, incest, and prostitution, but also a miscellany of nonsexual offenses, including cruelty to animals, desecration of the flag or other venerated symbols, and mistreatment of corpses. In a useful article,[8] Louis B. Schwartz maintains that what sets these crimes off as a class is not their special relation to morality (murder is also an offense against morality, but it is not a "morals offense") but the lack of an essential connection between them and social harm. In particular, their suppression is not required by the public security. Some morals offenses may harm the perpetrators them-

[8] Louis B. Schwartz, "Morals Offenses and the Model Penal Code," *Columbia Law Review*, LXIII (1963), 669 ff.

selves, but the risk of harm of this sort has usually been consented to in advance by the actors. Offense to other parties, when it occurs, is usually a consequence of perpetration of the offenses *in public*, and can be prevented by statutes against "open lewdness," or "solicitation" in public places. That still leaves "morals offenses" committed by consenting adults in private. Should they really be crimes?

In addition to the general presumption against coercion, other arguments against legislation prohibiting private and harmless sexual practices are drawn from the harm principle itself; laws governing private affairs are extremely awkward and expensive to enforce, and have side effects that are invariably harmful. Laws against homosexuality, for example, can only be occasionally and randomly enforced, and this leads to the inequities of selective enforcement and opportunities for blackmail and private vengeance. Moreover, "the pursuit of homosexuals involves policemen in degrading entrapment practices, and diverts attention and effort" [9] from more serious (harmful) crimes of aggression, fraud, and corruption.

These considerations have led some to argue against statutes that prohibit private immorality, but, not surprisingly, it has encouraged others to abandon their exclusive reliance on the harm and/or offense principles, at least in the case of morals offenses. The alternative principle of "legal moralism" has several forms. In its more moderate version it is commonly associated with the views of Patrick Devlin,[10] whose theory, as I understand it, is really an application of the public harm principle. The proper aim of criminal law, he agrees, is the prevention of harm, not merely to individuals, but also (and primarily) to society itself. A shared moral code, Devlin argues, is a necessary condition for the very existence of a community. Shared moral convictions function as "invisible bonds" tying individuals together into an orderly society. Moreover, the fundamental unifying morality (to switch the metaphor) is a kind of "seamless web"; [11] to damage it at one point is to weaken it throughout. Hence, society has as much right to protect its moral code by legal coercion as it does to protect its equally indispensable political institutions. The law cannot tolerate politically revolutionary activity, nor can it accept activity that rips asunder its moral fabric. "The suppression of vice is as much the law's business as the suppression of subversive activities; it is no more possible to define a sphere of private morality than it is to define one of private subversive activity." [12]

9 Schwartz, "Morals Offenses and the Model Penal Code," 671.

10 Patrick Devlin, *The Enforcement of Morals* (London: Oxford University Press, 1965).

11 The phrase is not Devlin's but that of his critic, H. L. A. Hart, in *Law, Liberty, and Morality* (Stanford: Stanford University Press, 1963), p. 51. In his rejoinder to Hart, Devlin writes: "Seamlessness presses the simile rather hard but apart from that, I should say that for most people morality is a web of beliefs rather than a number of unconnected ones." Devlin, *The Enforcement of Morals*, p. 115.

12 Devlin, *The Enforcement of Morals*, pp. 13–14.

H. L. A. Hart finds it plausible that some shared morality is necessary to the existence of a community, but criticizes Devlin's further contention "that a society is identical with its morality as that is at any given moment of its history, so that a change in its morality is tantamount to the destruction of a society." [13] Indeed, a moral critic might admit that we can't exist as a society without some morality, while insisting that we can perfectly well exist without *this* morality (if we put a better one in its place). Devlin seems to reply that the shared morality *can* be changed even though protected by law, and, when it does change, the emergent reformed morality in turn deserves *its* legal protection.[14] The law then functions to make moral reform difficult, but there is no preventing change where reforming zeal is fierce enough. How does one bring about a change in prevailing moral beliefs when they are enshrined in law? Presumably by advocating conduct which is in fact illegal, by putting into public practice what one preaches, and by demonstrating one's sincerity by marching proudly off to jail for one's convictions:

> there is . . . a natural respect for opinions that are sincerely held. When such opinions accumulate enough weight, the law must either yield or it is broken. In a democratic society . . . there will be a strong tendency for it to yield—not to abandon all defenses so as to let in the horde, but to give ground to those who are prepared to fight for something that they prize. To fight may be to suffer. A willingness to suffer is the most convincing proof of sincerity. Without the law there would be no proof. The law is the anvil on which the hammer strikes.[15]

In this remarkable passage, Devlin has discovered another argument for enforcing "morality as such," and incidentally for principled civil disobedience as the main technique for initiating and regulating moral change. A similar argument, deriving from Samuel Johnson and applying mainly to changes in religious doctrine, was well known to Mill. According to this theory, religious innovators deserve to be persecuted, for persecution allows them to prove their mettle and demonstrate their disinterested good faith, while their teachings, insofar as they are true, cannot be hurt, since truth will always triumph in the end. Mill held this method of testing truth, whether in science, religion, or morality, to be both uneconomical and ungenerous.[16] But if self-sacrificing civil disobedience is *not* the most efficient and humane remedy for the moral reformer, what instruments of moral change are available to him? This question is not only difficult to answer in its own right, it is also the rock that sinks Devlin's favorite analogy between "harmless" immorality and political subversion.

[13] Hart, *Law, Liberty, and Morality,* p. 51.
[14] Devlin, *The Enforcement of Morals,* pp. 115 ff.
[15] Devlin, *The Enforcement of Morals,* p. 116.
[16] Mill, *On Liberty,* pp. 33–34.

Consider the nature of subversion. Most modern law-governed countries have a constitution, a set of duly constituted authorities, and a body of statutes created and enforced by these authorities. The ways of changing these things will be well known, orderly, and permitted by the constitution. For example, constitutions are amended, legislators are elected, and new legislation is introduced. On the other hand, it is easy to conceive of various sorts of unpermitted and disorderly change—through assassination and violent revolution, or bribery and subornation, or the use of legitimately won power to extort and intimidate. Only these illegitimate methods of change can be called "subversion." But here the analogy between positive law and positive morality begins to break down. There is no "moral constitution," no well-known and orderly way of introducing moral legislation to duly constituted moral legislators, no clear convention of majority rule. Moral subversion, if there is such a thing, must consist in the employment of disallowed techniques of change instead of the officially permitted "constitutional" ones. It consists not simply of change as such, but of illegitimate change. Insofar as the notion of legitimately induced moral change remains obscure, illegitimate moral change is no better. Still, there is enough content to both notions to preserve some analogy to the political case. A citizen works *legitimately* to change public moral beliefs when he openly and forthrightly expresses his own dissent, when he attempts to argue, persuade, and offer reasons, and when he lives according to his own convictions with persuasive quiet and dignity, neither harming others nor offering counterpersuasive offense to tender sensibilities. A citizen attempts to change mores by *illegitimate* means when he abandons argument and example for force and fraud. If this is the basis of the distinction between legitimate and illegitimate techniques of moral change, then the use of state power to affect moral belief *one way or the other,* when harmfulness is not involved, is a clear example of illegitimacy. Government enforcement of the conventional code is not to be called "moral subversion," of course, because it is used on behalf of the status quo; but whether conservative or innovative, it is equally in defiance of our "moral constitution" (if anything is).

The second version of legal moralism is the pure version, not some other principle in disguise. Enforcement of morality as such and the attendant punishment of sin are not justified as means to some further social aim (such as preservation of social cohesiveness) but are ends in themselves. Perhaps J. F. Stephen was expressing this pure moralism when he wrote that "there are acts of wickedness so gross and outrageous that . . . [protection of others apart], they must be prevented at any cost to the offender and punished if they occur with exemplary severity." [17] From his examples it is clear that Stephen had in mind the very acts that are called "morals offenses" in the law.

It is sometimes said in support of pure legal moralism that the

[17] James Fitzjames Stephen, *Liberty, Equality, Fraternity* (London, 1873), p. 163.

world as a whole would be a better place without morally ugly, even "harmlessly immoral," conduct, and that our actual universe is intrinsically worse for having such conduct in it. The threat of punishment, the argument continues, deters such conduct. Actual instances of punishment not only back up the threat, and thus help keep future moral weeds out of the universe's garden, they also erase past evils from the universe's temporal record by "nullifying" them, or making it as if they never were. Thus punishment, it is said, contributes to the intrinsic value of the universe in two ways: by canceling out past sins and preventing future ones.[18]

There is some plausibility in this view when it is applied to ordinary harmful crimes, especially those involving duplicity or cruelty, which really do seem to "set the universe out of joint." It is natural enough to think of repentance, apology, or forgiveness as "setting things straight," and of punishment as a kind of "payment" or a wiping clean of the moral slate. But in cases where it is natural to resort to such analogies, there is not only a rule infraction, there is also a *victim*—some person or society of persons who have been harmed. Where there is no victim—and especially where there is no profit at the expense of another —"setting things straight" has no clear intuitive content.

Punishment may yet play its role in discouraging harmless private immoralities for the sake of "the universe's moral record." But if fear of punishment is to keep people from illicit intercourse (or from desecrating flags, or mistreating corpses) in the privacy of their own rooms, then morality shall have to be enforced with a fearsome efficiency that shows no respect for individual privacy. If private immoralities are to be deterred by threat of punishment, the detecting authorities must be able to look into the hidden chambers and locked rooms of anyone's private domicile. When we put this massive forfeiture of privacy into the balance along with the usual costs of coercion—loss of spontaneity, stunting of rational powers, anxiety, hypocrisy, and the rest—the price of securing mere outward conformity to the community's moral standards (for that is all that can be achieved by the penal law) is exorbitant. . . .

OBSCENITY AND THE OFFENSE PRINCIPLE

Up to this point we have considered the harm and offense principles together in order to determine whether between them they are sufficient to regulate conventional immoralities, or whether they need help from a further independent principle, legal moralism. Morals offenses were treated as essentially private so that the offense principle

---

[18] Cf. C. D. Broad, "Certain Features in Moore's Ethical Doctrines," in P. A. Schilpp, *The Philosophy of G. E. Moore* (Evanston, Ill.: Northwestern University Press, 1942), pp. 48 ff.

could not be stretched to apply to them. Obscene literature and pornographic displays would appear to be quite different in this respect. Both
are materials deliberately published for the eyes of others, and their
existence can bring partisans of the unsupplemented harm principle
into direct conflict with those who endorse *both* the harm and offense
principles.

In its untechnical, prelegal sense, the word "obscenity" refers to
material dealing with nudity, sex, or excretion in an offensive manner.
Such material becomes obscene in the legal sense when, because of its
offensiveness or for some other reason (this question had best be left
open in the definition), it is or ought to be without legal protection.
The legal definition then incorporates the everyday sense, and essential to
both is the requirement that the material be *offensive*. An item may
offend one person and not another. "Obscenity," if it is to avoid this
subjective relativity, must involve an interpersonal objective sense of
"offensive." Material must be offensive by prevailing community standards that are public and well known, or be such that it is apt to offend
virtually everyone.

Not all material that is generally offensive need also be harmful in
any sense recognized by the harm principle. It is partly an empirical
question whether reading or witnessing obscene material causes social
harm; reliable evidence, even of a statistical kind, of causal connections
between obscenity and antisocial behavior is extremely hard to find.[19]
In the absence of clear and decisive evidence of harmfulness, the American Civil Liberties Union insists that the offensiveness of obscene material cannot be a sufficient ground for its repression:

> . . . the question in a case involving obscenity, just as in every case in-
> volving an attempted restriction upon free speech, is whether the words
> or pictures are used in such circumstances and are of such a nature as to
> create a clear and present danger that they will bring about a substantial
> evil that the state has a right to prevent. . . . We believe that under the
> current state of knowledge, there is grossly insufficient evidence to show
> that obscenity brings about *any* substantive evil.[20]

The A.C.L.U. argument employs *only* the harm principle among liberty-
limiting principles, and treats literature, drama, and painting as forms
of expression subject to the same rules as expressions of opinion. In
respect to both types of expression, "every act of deciding what should
be barred carries with it a danger to the community." [21] The suppression
itself is an evil to the author who is squelched. The power to censor and

19 There have been some studies made, but the results have been inconclusive.
See the *Report of the Federal Commission on Obscenity and Pornography* (New York:
Bantam Books, 1970), pp. 169-308.

20 *Obscenity and Censorship* (Pamphlet published by the American Civil Liberties Union, New York, March, 1963), p. 7.

21 *Obscenity and Censorship*, p. 4.

punish involves risks that socially valuable material will be repressed along with the "filth." The overall effect of suppression, the A.C.L.U. concludes, is almost certainly to discourage nonconformist and eccentric expression generally. In order to override these serious risks, there must be in a given case an even more clear and present danger that the obscene material, if not squelched, will cause even greater harm; such countervailing evidence is never forthcoming. (If such evidence were to accumulate, the A.C.L.U. would be perfectly willing to change its position on obscenity.)

The A.C.L.U. stand on obscenity seems clearly to be the position dictated by the unsupplemented harm principle and its corollary, the clear and present danger test. Is there any reason at this point to introduce the offense principle into the discussion? Unhappily, we may be forced to if we are to do justice to all of our particular intuitions in the most harmonious way. Consider an example suggested by Professor Schwartz. By the provisions of the new Model Penal Code, he writes, "a rich homosexual may not use a billboard on Times Square to promulgate to the general populace the techniques and pleasures of sodomy." [22] If the notion of "harm" is restricted to its narrow sense, that is, contrasted with "offense," it will be hard to reconstruct a rationale for this prohibition based on the harm principle. There is unlikely to be evidence that a lurid and obscene public poster in Times Square would create a clear and present danger of injury to those who fail to avert their eyes in time as they come blinking out of the subway stations. Yet it will be surpassingly difficult for even the most dedicated liberal to advocate freedom of expression in a case of this kind. Hence, if we are to justify coercion in this case, we will likely be driven, however reluctantly, to the offense principle.

There is good reason to be "reluctant" to embrace the offense principle until driven to it by an example like the above. People take perfectly genuine offense at many socially useful or harmless activities, from commercial advertisements to inane chatter. Moreover, widespread irrational prejudices can lead people to be disgusted, shocked, even morally repelled by perfectly innocent activities, and we should be loath to permit their groundless repugnance to override the innocence. The offense principle, therefore, must be formulated very precisely and applied in accordance with carefully formulated standards so as not to open the door to wholesale and intuitively unwarranted repression. At the very least we should require that the prohibited conduct or material be of the sort apt to offend almost everybody, and not just some shifting majority or special interest group.

It is instructive to note that a strictly drawn offense principle would not only justify prohibition of conduct and pictured conduct that is in its inherent character repellent, but also conduct and pictured conduct that is inoffensive in itself but offensive in inappropriate circumstances.

[22] Schwartz, "Morals Offenses and the Model Penal Code," 680.

I have in mind so-called indecencies such as public nudity. One can imagine an advocate of the unsupplemented harm principle arguing against the public nudity prohibition on the grounds that the sight of a naked body does no one any harm, and the state has no right to impose standards of dress or undress on private citizens. How one chooses to dress, after all, is a form of self-expression. If we do not permit the state to bar clashing colors or bizarre hair styles, by what right does it prohibit total undress? Perhaps the sight of naked people could at first lead to riots or other forms of antisocial behavior, but that is precisely the sort of contingency for which we have police. If we don't take away a person's right of free speech for the reason that its exercise may lead others to misbehave, we cannot in consistency deny his right to dress or undress as he chooses for the same reason.

There may be no answering this challenge on its own ground, but the offense principle provides a ready rationale for the nudity prohibition. The sight of nude bodies in public places is for almost everyone acutely *embarrassing*. Part of the explanation no doubt rests on the fact that nudity has an irresistible power to draw the eye and focus the thoughts on matters that are normally repressed. The conflict between these attracting and repressing forces is exciting, upsetting, and anxiety-producing. In some persons it will create at best a kind of painful turmoil, and at worst that experience of exposure to oneself of "peculiarly sensitive, intimate, vulnerable aspects of the self" [23] which is called *shame*. "One's feeling is involuntarily exposed openly in one's face; one is uncovered . . . taken by surprise . . . made a fool of." [24] The result is not mere "offense," but a kind of psychic jolt that in many normal people can be a painful wound. Even those of us who are better able to control our feelings might well resent the *nuisance* of having to do so.

If we are to accept the offense principle as a supplement to the harm principle, we must accept two corollaries which stand in relation to it similarly to the way in which the clear and present danger test stands to the harm principle. The first, the *standard of universality*, has already been touched upon. For the offensiveness (disgust, embarrassment, outraged sensibilities, or shame) to be sufficient to warrant coercion, it should be the reaction that could be expected from almost any person chosen at random from the nation as a whole, regardless of sect, faction, race, age, or sex. The second is the *standard of reasonable avoidability*. No one has a right to protection from the state against offensive experiences if he can effectively avoid those experiences with no unreasonable effort or inconvenience. If a nude person enters a public bus and takes a seat near the front, there may be no effective way for other patrons to avoid intensely shameful embarrassment (or other insupportable feelings) short of leaving the bus, which would be an un-

[23] Helen Merrill Lynd, *On Shame and the Search for Identity* (New York: Science Editions, Inc., 1961), p. 33.

[24] Lynd, *On Shame and the Search for Identity*, p. 32.

reasonable inconvenience. Similarly, obscene remarks over a loudspeaker, homosexual billboards in Times Square, and pornographic handbills thrust into the hands of passing pedestrians all fail to be reasonably avoidable.

On the other hand, the offense principle, properly qualified, can give no warrant to the suppression of *books* on the grounds of obscenity. When printed words hide decorously behind covers of books sitting passively on bookstore shelves, their offensiveness is easily avoided. The contrary view is no doubt encouraged by the common comparison of obscenity with "smut," "filth," or "dirt." This in turn suggests an analogy to nuisance law, which governs cases where certain activities create loud noises or terrible odors offensive to neighbors, and "the courts must weigh the gravity of the nuisance [substitute 'offense'] to the neighbors against the social utility [substitute 'redeeming social value'] of the defendant's conduct." [25] There is, however, one vitiating disanalogy in this comparison. In the case of "dirty books" the offense is easily avoidable. There is nothing like the evil smell of rancid garbage oozing right out through the covers of a book. When an "obscene" book sits on a shelf, who is there to be offended? Those who want to read it for the sake of erotic stimulation presumably will not be offended (or else they wouldn't read it), and those who choose not to read it will have no experience by which to be offended. If its covers are too decorous, some innocents may browse through it by mistake and be offended by what they find, but they need only close the book to escape the offense. Even this offense, minimal as it is, could be completely avoided by prior consultation of trusted book reviewers. I conclude that there are no sufficient grounds derived either from the harm or offense principles for suppressing obscene literature, unless that ground be the protection of children; but I can think of no reason why restrictions on sales to children cannot work as well for printed materials as they do for cigarettes and whiskey. . . .

COLLECTIVE GOODS AND COLLECTIVE ACTION

Despite the presumptive case for liberty, there seem to be numerous examples in which the modern state has no choice but to force (usually by compulsory taxation) both willing and unwilling citizens to support public projects that are clearly in the public interest. In many of these cases those who do not benefit directly from a public service are made to pay as much in its support as those who do, or even more. Thus nondrivers are taxed to support highways and nonparents to support schools. This has the appearance of injustice, and the justification of unhappy necessity. Often the alternative to mandatory taxation—a system of

[25] William L. Prosser, *Handbook of the Law of Torts* (St. Paul: West Publishing Co., 1955), p. 411.

purely voluntary support requiring only users to pay fees—is subject to a fatal defect that forces us to choose between universal compulsory support for the public facility or no facility at all.

Consider, for example, public municipal parks. Suppose the town of Metropolis decides to create a large public park with gardens, woods, trails, and playgrounds. John Doe appreciates living in an attractive community but has no direct personal need for such a park, since he already has a ten acre yard with gardens, picnic tables, tennis courts, and the like. Why, he asks, should he be forced to support something he doesn't need and doesn't want strongly enough to pay for? Suppose, however, that the city charges only those who wish to use the park, and that this group constitutes 90 percent of the population. The richest 10 percent opt out, thus raising the average costs to the remainder. That rise, in turn, forces some of the 90 percent to withdraw, thus raising the cost to the others, forcing still more to drop out, and so on. This process will continue until either a very expensive equilibrium is reached, or, what is more likely, the whole project collapses (as in the case of some voluntary public medical and insurance plans).

It is avoidance of this characteristic escalation effect, rather than paternalism, that provides the rationale for compulsory social security and medicare programs. Here it is important to apply the various principles of liberty distribution not to individual cases, such as the compulsory taxation of John Doe, but to rules and general financing schemes. Compulsory rather than voluntary schemes are justified when the social good in question cannot be secured in any other way. Whether compulsion on this ground accords with the harm principle depends on whether loss of the good would be classified as a social harm or the mere withholding of a benefit (see pp. 29–31 [of *Social Philosophy,* Ed.]). Where the good is security, medical care, or education, there is little doubt that its loss would properly be called a "harm" to those who incur it.

In cases of the sort we have been considering, some people who don't want a given public service are forced to pay for it because there is no other practical way of supporting it, and its loss would be a harm to those who do want it. In a more interesting and troublesome kind of case, *all* of the members of a community or group want some good which is in fact in the interests of each individual equally, and yet it is in no individual's interest to contribute toward the goal unless we are *made* to do so. This paradoxical state of affairs has attracted considerable attention from economists who have noticed its similarity to the condition of a company in an industry that enjoys "perfect competition." So long as the price of a manufactured product on the free market exceeds the marginal cost of production, it will be in the interest of each company to increase its output and thus maximize its profit. But the consequence of increased output will be lower prices, so in the end all companies will be worse off for "maximizing profits" than they might otherwise have been. If any single firm, anticipating this unhappy result, were to restrict its own output unilaterally, it would be in still more trouble, for its restriction of output in a large industry would not prevent the fall of prices, and it would suffer lower sales in addition to lower prices. It is in the interest of each firm that *all the others* restrict output, but, in a purely competitive situation, none of the others dare do that. Where there is no coercion, we have the paradoxical result that it is "rational" for each firm to pursue policies that will destroy its interests in the end. It is more rational still to prefer general coercion.

Problems like that raised by "perfect competition" tend to occur wherever large organizations have come into existence to advance the interests of their members. A great many such organizations, from consumer societies and labor unions to (as many have claimed) the political state itself, exist primarily to advance some common interest in virtue of which the members can be supposed to have banded together in the first place. Now, some of the collective aims to which large organizations are devoted have a very special character. They are directed at goods which, if they are made available to any one member of the group, cannot feasibly be withheld from any other member. Examples of such generalized and indivisible goods are supported prices for companies in the same industry in a not-so-competitive market, the power of collective bargaining for members of a union, and certain goods provided for its citizens by the state, such as police protection, courts of law, armies, navies, and public health agencies. Perhaps it would be technically possible to "sell" these goods only to those willing to pay for them, but it would hardly be "feasible." It is not clear, for example, how an organization, private or public, could eliminate air pollution only for those willing to pay. Nonpayers would breathe the expensively purified air, and there would be no way of preventing this "freeloading" short of banishment or capital punishment. In such cases, it is in each member's interest to let the others pay the bill and then share in consumption of the indivisible benefit; since each member knows that every member knows this as well as he, each has reason to think that he may be taken advantage of if he voluntarily pays his share. Yet if each member, following his own self-interest, refuses to pay, the collective good for which they are united cannot be achieved. Voluntarily submitting to a coercion understood by each to apply to all seems the only way out.

It is in virtue of such considerations that compulsory taxation, at least in support of collective goods and indivisible services of an essential kind, can be justified by the harm principle. That principle would not justify compulsory taxation in support of benefits to private groups, or even of public benefits of the sort whose loss would not constitute a serious harm, but that does not mean that the friends of public libraries, museums, and parks need be driven to embrace the welfare principle (*supra*, p. 33 [p. 74, Ed.]). When persons and groups are deprived of what they *need*, they are harmed; it may not be implausible to insist that the country as a whole, in this and future generations (including people who have no present desire for culture, history, nature, or beauty), *needs* large national parks, wilderness areas, enormous libraries, museums, atomic accelerators for physical research, huge telescopes, and so on. To argue that we need these things is to claim that we cannot in the end get along very well without them. That is the kind of case that must be made if we are to justify compulsion, on liberal principles, to the reluctant taxpayer.

LAW, LIBERTY AND INDECENCY

David A. Conway

I

The distinction between private immorality and public indecency plays a significant and perhaps a crucial role in H. L. A. Hart's argument in *Law, Liberty, and Morality*.[1] This distinction, and the uses to which he puts it, have, however, been largely overshadowed in the "debate" between Professor Hart and Lord Devlin which has centred around such "great" questions as whether a shared morality is necessary for a society. I shall argue that Hart's position, in so far as it is based on that distinction, is quite untenable, and that even if it were to be a possible position, it would none the less be incompatible with the sort of "libertarian" view of society expressed by John Stuart Mill, whose "spirit," at least, Hart believes himself to be defending.

The position that Hart sets out to defend is that society has no right to prohibit any action simply on the ground that it is immoral; the only actions with which society may interfere are those which are likely to cause harm. For instance, no matter how morally abhorrent many, perhaps most, members of society believe homosexual actions to be, homosexuality should not be held subject to regulation by society in the absence of clear and compelling evidence that such actions are harmful.

But there are cases which even the libertarian would intuitively think of as subject to regulation, even though they are not obviously "harmful." In particular, there are the cases which are usually considered

"Law, Liberty and Indecency" by David A. Conway, *Philosophy*, vol. 49, April, 1974, pp. 135–147. © Copyright 1974. Reprinted by permission of the journal, the author, and the Royal Institute of Philosophy.

[1] H. L. A. Hart, *Law, Liberty, and Morality* (New York: Random House, 1966). Hereafter cited as "Hart."

under the heading of "public indecency," such as public nudity, fornication, or sodomy. On the surface, the prohibition of actions of this type would appear to be enforcing the convictions of society that they are morally wrong. Thus, Lord Devlin says: "Why then do we object to the public exhibition of a false morality and call it indecency? If we thought that unrestricted indulgence in the sexual passions was as good a way of life as any other for those who liked it, we should find nothing indecent in the practice of it either in public or in private. It would become no more indecent than kissing in public. Decency as an objective depends on the belief in continence as a virtue which requires sexual activity to be kept within prescribed bounds." [2] Advocates of the libertarian position therefore seem to be faced with a dilemma: either they admit that moral convictions are subject to enforcement in the case of public indecency (and if in this case, why not in others?), or they deny that even such actions as homosexual intercourse in public may be prohibited. The latter appears to be an excessively "heroic" alternative and is not acceptable to Mill, Hart, or many other defenders of "liberty." [3]

Hart does not believe that he is forced to accept either of the unpalatable alternatives. The apparent dilemma arises only if we fail to see that the prohibition of indecency need not involve any moral presuppositions, that judgments concerning what is indecent are logically distinct from judgments concerning what is immoral:

> Sexual intercourse between husband and wife is not immoral, but if it takes place in public it is an affront to public decency. Homosexual intercourse between consenting adults in private is immoral according to conventional morality, but not an affront to public decency, though it would be both if it took place in public. But the fact that the same act, if done in public, could be regarded both as immoral and as an affront to public decency must not blind us to the difference between these two aspects of conduct and to the different principles on which the justification of their punishment must rest.[4]

Mill argued in a similar manner in the single reference to public indecency in *On Liberty*.

> There are many acts which, being directly injurious only to the agents themselves, ought not to be legally interdicted, but which if done publicly, are a violation of good manners and, coming thus within the category of offences against others, may be rightly prohibited. Of this kind are offences against decency; on which it is unnecessary to dwell, the rather as they are

[2] Patrick Devlin, *The Enforcement of Morals* (London: Oxford University Press, 1965), p. 120.

[3] John Wilson is an exception; as I understand him, he does accept the "heroic" alternative. *Logic and Sexual Morality* (Baltimore: Penguin Books, 1965), Ch. 6.

[4] Hart, p. 45.

only connected indirectly with our subject, the objection to publicity being equally strong in the case of many actions not in themselves condemnable, nor supposed to be so.[5]

For both Mill and Hart, then, publicly indecent actions may be condemned because they "cause distress" to others, because they "offend" others, because they are "nuisances." On the other hand, many other actions may be morally condemned, but this sort of condemnation, however justified it may be, can never be sufficient ground for society to prohibit the actions so long as they are practised in private.[6]

A difficulty immediately arises. If in cases of public indecency, the fact that the actions give offence is considered a sufficient reason for regulating them, why should the same not be true of private actions? Hart himself recognizes the possibility of this objection:

> Offence to feelings, it may be said, is given not only when immoral activities or their commercial preliminaries are thrust upon unwilling witnesses, but also when those who strongly condemn certain sexual practices as immoral learn that others indulge in them in private. Because this is so, it is pointless to attend to the distinction between what is done privately and what is done in public; and if we do not attend to it, then the policies of punishing men for mere immorality and punishing them for conduct offensive to the feelings of others, though conceptually distinct, would not differ in practice. All conduct strongly condemned as immoral would then be punishable.[7]

Here we have one version of a traditional objection to Mill's principle, the objection that no significant human actions are "self-regarding." [8]

Little seems to have been accomplished; our original dilemma has reappeared in only slightly altered form. If offence is considered as harm, then immoral private actions will be subject to regulation. If offence is not treated as harm, then there are no grounds for regulating actions considered "publicly indecent."

[5] John Stuart Mill, *On Liberty* (New York: Liberal Arts Press, 1956), p. 119. Hereafter cited as "Mill."

[6] The passage on p. 119 is, however, patently inconsistent with Mill's over-all position in *On Liberty* (see section V of this paper). Also, on pp. 77 and 102 he explicitly contrasts offence with harm in order to deny that offence is sufficient ground for prohibiting an action. Henceforth, I shall not consider the passage on p. 119 as being part of "Mill's position."

[7] Hart, pp. 45-46.

[8] This claim may be made on a number of grounds, not just on the ground that any action may offend others. For a brief survey of some objections to Mill along these lines, see J. C. Rees, "A Re-reading of Mill on Liberty," in Peter Radcliff (ed.), *Limits of Liberty* (Belmont: Wadsworth Publishing Co., 1966), pp. 91–93.

II

As we have seen, Hart is aware of this argument, and he presents it himself; but he thinks there is an answer to it:

> The fundamental objection surely is that a right to be protected from the distress which is inseparable from the bare knowledge that others are acting in ways you think wrong, cannot be acknowledged by anyone who recognizes individual liberty as a value. For the extension of the utilitarian principle that coercion may be used to protect men from harm, so as to include their protection from this form of distress, cannot stop there. If distress incident to the belief that others are doing wrong is harm, so also is the distress incident to the belief that others are doing what you do not want them to do. To punish people for causing this form of distress would be tantamount to punishing them simply because others object to what they do; and the only liberty that could coexist with this extension of the utilitarian principle is liberty to do those things to which no one seriously objects. Such liberty plainly is quite nugatory.[9]

We have, then, three classes of actions which may give offence. We have offence which arises from (*a*) public indecency, (*b*) the bare knowledge that "others are doing wrong," and (*c*) the bare knowledge "that others are doing what you do not want them to do." Now, he says, (*a*) can be regulated, but we must not allow (*b*) to be regulated, for if we do, we must also allow (*c*) to be regulated. Between (*a*) and (*b*) we have a significant difference (public v. private) which enables us to stop the "progression"; between (*b*) and (*c*) we have no such relevant difference.

Anyone of even a slightly liberal persuasion will certainly agree that it is imperative not to regulate private actions simply on the ground that they are disliked. Nonetheless, we must bear in mind that, as Hart himself points out,[10] to question whether society has a right to regulate a certain type of action is to ask a moral question. So, if two classes of actions are to be treated differently in this respect, it must be shown that there is a difference between their regulation which would morally justify the control of one but not the other.

Has Hart given us a moral ground for regulating publicly indecent but not privately immoral actions? It is obvious that, *at least in the absence of further argument,* he has not. The distinguishing mark he has offered is concerned merely with the *locus* of the action, and this is surely irrelevant *in itself* for the question whether the action should be

9 Hart, p. 47.
10 Hart, p. 17.

regulated. (That it is irrelevant is something which I cannot *argue* for, any more than one could argue against a murderer who pleads not guilty on the ground that he shot his victim in the left side of the head rather than the right side. All we can say is, "what difference does that make?") In his understandable eagerness to halt the progression from allowing the regulation of (*a*) to allowing (*c*) to be regulated, he forgets that the progression can only be legitimately halted by a morally relevant difference.

III

It might be objected that my argument is based on a very unsympathetic reading of Hart. Surely, it may be urged, he does not mean that whether an action is performed in one place rather than another is in itself morally relevant. He must mean that there are other features which *accompany* the prohibition of public as against private actions that *are* morally relevant.

First, it may be argued that the crucial difference is in the degree of total offensiveness. While some private actions may be very offensive to those who learn of them, perhaps more offensive than some examples of public indecency, the prohibition against regulating the private actions is justified by the fact that *on the whole* public actions give much more offence than private ones. Such an argument is misconceived, since it assumes that we should follow a rule on all occasions on the ground that the rule leads to the best results on many occasions.

The law must, of course, often "generalize" over cases which are likely to be quite different in their predictable results. Nonetheless, there is no reason for adopting such a "bludgeon approach" in this situation, since it is clearly often possible to distinguish between individual types of actions in regard to their probable offensiveness to others. (E.g., short skirts are permissible, toplessness is not, in most communities.)

Second, Hart seems to endorse the following argument: in not allowing an action to be performed in public, we are not prohibiting that action altogether, since the potential offender is "at liberty to do the same thing in private . . ." [11] Therefore, preventing the action only in public is "utterly different from attempts to enforce sexual morality which may demand the repression of powerful instincts with which personal happiness is intimately connected." [12] This argument, if successful,

---

[11] Hart, p. 48. The omitted words here are "if he can." This appears to indicate that Hart does not attach much importance to the claim that "one is left at liberty to do the same thing in private." Also, on p. 46, he seems to *contrast* this way of making the public–private distinction with his own way of doing so. If, however, he really does not intend to be seriously urging this rationale for the public–private distinction, I fail to see what morally relevant rationale he could possibly have in mind.

[12] Hart, p. 43.

would give a morally relevant rationale for the public–private distinction in terms of the amount of suffering caused by (i) prohibiting the performance of an action in public and (ii) prohibiting the action *simpliciter,* the relatively small amount of suffering given in case (i) being outweighed by the resulting diminution of offence, while the much larger amount of suffering caused by prohibiting certain actions entirely in case (ii) is not nearly counterbalanced by the good of removing the offence to others.

The primary difficulty here is that it very often is not true that if an action is prohibited in public, one is left "at liberty to do the same thing in private. . . ." For in many cases it is highly inconvenient or virtually impossible to perform the same action in private, and more importantly, in other cases, the very point or rationale of the action disappears if one is restricted to privacy. As an example of the former, consider a man whose waist-length hair is found offensive. He could, of course, wear a close-cropped wig in public, but the inconvenience involved is a nearly prohibitive infringement of his liberty. In the case of a flowing beard, disguise problems become so great as to make it virtually impossible to show the beard in private but not in public.

Not only is there inconvenience involved in such cases, but presumably the very point of having long hair or a beard is to "go about looking that way." The same is true of a woman wearing a mini-skirt, or a very brief bikini, or only the bottom half of the bikini, or no bikini at all. One can be nude in private, but again, the point of so doing (a feeling of freedom in the supermarket, or whatever) may be lost, just as it is if it is demanded that one wear a beard-cover in public.

A crucially important example of this is inter-racial marriage. For a significant number of people, few things are as offensive as the sight of a racially mixed couple. Now it is perhaps possible to be married entirely privately, i.e., to have ceremonies performed far from one's domicile, never to be seen together in public, etc. But surely no one would maintain that these restrictions are compatible with the aims of marriage as conceived of by relatively mature persons. So a large part of the point of marriage is lost if the couple is restricted to private "inter-action" (what remains is comparable with the clandestine keeping of a mistress). In no significant sense can it be said that "the offender is at liberty to do the same thing in private," and it cannot be denied that crucially important means to personal happiness are being withheld by prohibiting publicity. (The same considerations apply to bigamous or homosexual marriages. Notice also that in claiming that marriage is not a wholly private matter, I do not mean simply that some of its aspects are public—openly living in the same domicile, publicly holding hands, etc. It is true that there are such purely public aspects, but even the "essentially private" aspects, ranging from dinner conversation to sexual intercourse, derive much of their significance from the public life that persons live together.) There are, then, important cases in which prohibiting an action from being performed in public is virtually equivalent to prohibiting it entirely, and so this rationale for the public–private distinction fails.

IV

Nothing has been said so far about the most intuitively plausible way of distinguishing between public and private actions. That is that in the public cases, and only in public cases, observers have *foisted* upon them something they dislike seeing; they are *forced* to see what they find unpleasant or disgusting; they cannot avoid what they wish to avoid. The distinction is, it may be urged, simple, clear and powerful when put in these terms. And, it may be added, surely this is the basis that Hart must have in mind in making his distinction.

There are, however, two immediate reasons for rejecting this as being a part of any argument intended by Hart. First, and most simply, nothing that he says even hints at such a claim. (Still, it might be said, the point is so obvious that it is one which could be presumed rather than stated.) Second, the major case in which he uses the public–private distinction is that of bigamy, and the way in which he uses it there seems incompatible with construing public cases as essentially involving foisting something on to an unwilling "outside party":

> Perhaps most who . . . wish to retain the prohibition of bigamy would urge that in a country where deep religious significance is attached to monogamous marriage and to the act of solemnizing it, the law against bigamy should be accepted as an attempt to protect religious feelings from offence by a public act desecrating the ceremony. . . . It is important to see that if, in the case of bigamy, the law intervenes in order to protect religious sensibilities from outrage by a public act, the bigamist is punished neither as irreligious nor as immoral but as a nuisance. For the law is then concerned with the offensiveness to others of his public conduct, not with the immorality of his private conduct, which in most countries, it leaves altogether unpunished.[13]

Lord Devlin's comment on this point is clear and quite on target:

> Bigamy violates neither good manners nor decency. . . . A variety of reasons for leaving the law as it is have been put forward, but the one selected by Professor Hart seems to me to wound Mill's doctrine more sharply than any other. A marriage in a registry office is only in form a public act. Mill's exception is grounded not upon a formal distinction between public and private but upon the right of society not to have obnoxious conduct forced on its attention. No one with deep religious feelings is likely to attend in the registry office. . . .[14]

13 Hart, pp. 40–41.

14 Devlin, op. cit., p. 138. I am not nearly as certain as Devlin seems to be about what Mill does intend.

This needs little elaboration. Whatever sense of "public" Hart is operating with here, it surely cannot be one which involves "foisting one's conduct on the unwilling non-participant," since a quiet marriage ceremony is certainly no more public in this sense than is living out of wedlock with more than one "wife."

At this point, we must look more closely at the rationale behind this way of making the public–private distinction. There is, I think, an ambiguity in what is being said which may be partially responsible for its intuitive appeal. There are two basically different ways of spelling out the claim.

(a) In the case of private (but not public) actions, the action is not forced upon anyone's attention. Therefore, anyone who is offended *consents* to be offended.

(b) In the case of private (but not public) actions, the action is not forced upon anyone's attention. Therefore, no one will be offended by the action (since anyone who finds the action obnoxious will avoid being present at its performance).

Alternative (a) might be an option for Mill, but Hart cannot accept it because he explicitly embraces paternalism.[15] A person may not be the best judge of his own interest; hence, society does have the right to prevent him from harming himself, and therefore from "offending himself" since offence is here being counted as harm. (This position is certainly peculiar at best, but it does seem to be one to which Hart is, perhaps unintentionally, committed. It is so peculiar that it might be taken as a *reductio* of the attempt to hold both that paternalism is acceptable and that offence may count as harm.)

At any rate, the "foisting claim," whether construed as (a) or (b), is not nearly as plausible as it seems intuitively to be. Notice, first, that part of this intuitive plausibility derives from the fact that many of us are likely initially to misconceive the over-all situation. When we hear the distinction formulated we are likely to have in mind that in the case of public actions there will be unwilling observers, whereas, in the case of private ones (e.g., unforced sexual intercourse), all participants are willing and undeceived. In short, we tend to think that in public cases there are unwilling parties to the action, while in private cases there are none. But this description of the over-all situation is quite misleading. For, if we are to take into account *all* of those who may be affected by the action, we must consider the participants, the observers, and those who are affected by simply *knowing of* the action (the latter two groups will be referred to as "non-participants"). Now, if a participant is unwilling (as in the case of rape), whether the action is public or private is irrelevant. So the question at hand is actually whether public actions can be construed as involving foisting offensive actions on to non-participants while private actions cannot be so construed, i.e., whether the public–private distinction coincides with the unwillingness–willingness of the non-participants to be adversely affected.

Surely it is clear, once the "affected parties" are so specified, that they do not coincide. We might say, at first, that public offensive actions need not be thought of as foisting anything at all on the unwilling, since it is always at least possible for the bystander to close his eyes or look the other way, or to avoid being in the area in which the offenders are at work or play. This account of the situation has the virtue of emphasizing that public indecency cannot be said to force offence on to others in anything like the way in which harm is inflicted on the unwilling in cases of murder, robbery, or rape.

Yet the account seems artificial when considered in a practical light. For the unwilling observer may often not be able to avoid certain sights (he has no way of knowing what is going on "around the next corner"); in any case, being able to avoid seeing certain actions only by avoiding certain places is a significant infringement of a man's liberty, and may make it practically impossible for him to avoid seeing them (since, for instance, he may be able to reach his place of employment only by going through the undesired areas). Considered in this way, it appears that public actions do force offence on the unwilling.

So there are grounds both for and against saying that some public actions *force* offence on to others. Which way one decides to describe the situation, however, is not of much importance here. For the question at issue is whether a distinction can be made between public and private actions, and the situation (whichever way it is described) is not very different from what it is in the case of private actions. In fact, it may be more difficult to avoid the offence resulting from merely being aware of private immorality. For instance, the person greatly offended by the mere fact that homosexuals inhabit the house three doors away and there nightly indulge in their "abominable practices" may be virtually incapable of ridding himself of such thoughts. There is no equivalent here to shutting one's eyes or looking the other way. So this person is at least as much, if not more, the unwilling victim as is the potential spectator of a public act. It does not appear that a public–private distinction can be based on the claim that only public actions are forced to the attention of the unwilling non-participant.[16]

V

We have not found a satisfactory way of drawing a public–private distinction, but there could, of course, still be some as yet unconsidered

---

[16] It may be objected that the person offended at the mere knowledge of homosexuals in the community is the victim of his own psyche rather than of any other person, that his offence is "his own fault," rather than the fault of others. But we can also say to a person offended by the public spectacle of a nude person that it is *his* own fault that he finds this offensive.

way of doing so. Instead of continuing to search for tenable grounds for the distinction, however, we should ask a logically prior question: is this a distinction which we really want to draw? The answer may seem to be, obviously, yes, but this is because we tend to think only of those public actions which we classify as cases of public *indecency*. Hart's public–private distinction, however, would allow for the prohibition of any public action which others find offensive, and if we take this implication seriously, the appeal of his position is greatly diminished. (Perhaps Lord Devlin sees this; his argument on p. 120, quoted above, p. 135 [p. 87, Ed.], may mean that the prohibition of *indecency*, rather than the far more inclusive prohibition of *offensiveness*, can only be accounted for if the former is understood as enforcing morality.)

I shall try to bring this out by means of three considerations: first, apparently in relation only to private actions, Hart objects to people being punished "simply because others object to what they do." [17] Such punishment would clearly be incompatible with any sort of libertarian principle. But to punish someone for a *public* action simply because others dislike it is no less contrary to liberal intuitions. Consider, for instance, wearing an orange and pink outfit, picking one's nose, or ostentatiously enjoying eating raw ("slimy") oysters or ("stringy") okra at a sidewalk restaurant; wearing a star of David or a peace symbol in certain areas of the country; a racially mixed couple holding hands in a public park, or a black man simply being far better dressed than any of the white persons in the town can afford to be.[18] These, and many more cases we could think of, are quite likely to be offensive to a portion of the population. But if some should want to prohibit such actions on that ground, the appropriate reply surely would be to tell, "with considerable peremptoriness . . . these intrusively pious members of society to mind their own business." [19]

This "argument" is, I suppose, nothing more than an appeal to intuitions concerning what should and what should not be the concern of society. But there is nothing wrong with such an appeal in its proper place (and I think, although I do not know how to show it, that this is its proper place). In this case, however, we may wonder just whose intuitions are being appealed to; even if we restrict the appeal to "decent men" (whatever that may mean), it is not clear that we can expect the sort of universal agreement on, "you have a right to wear a peace symbol in public even though others are offended," that we can expect on, "you should not break a solemn promise just to save yourself a bit of effort." To whose intuitions am I appealing on these public matters? The intuitions of those who do not believe that private immorality should be subject to prohibition. For there would appear to be a pattern to intui-

17 Hart, p. 47 (quoted in context, p. 138 above [p. 89, Ed.]).

18 Cf. Mill, pp. 106–107. My example differs from his only in that in mine it is a black man who gives the "appearance of a more showy or costly style of living than [others] can hope to rival."

19 Mill, p. 106.

tions (which suggests that they are not really just "intuitions" at all), and I think that Hart can find only a very small audience which would hold both that all public actions that happen to offend are subject to regulation and that no private immoral actions are so subject. In practical political terms (at least in the United States), "liberals" would tend to hold that neither private homosexuality nor publicly wearing a peace sign (or a swastika) is the business of society; "conservatives" would often hold that both are. If liberals, generally, tend to say that they agree with Hart this is because they have not taken seriously the extent of the restrictiveness of his position on public actions. So, if I have correctly spelled out the implications of Hart's view, virtually everyone will find that view either too restrictive (any public act that offends may be prohibited) or too permissive (private immorality may never be prohibited). His compromise is altogether too uneasy.

But perhaps I misrepresent Hart's intentions on p. 47. I have represented him as saying, in effect, "it would be highly counter-intuitive to hold that private disliked actions should be subject to regulation," whereas he actually says that if we allow these actions to be prohibited, we have left only the "liberty to do those things to which no one seriously objects. such liberty plainly is quite nugatory." He is not claiming that allowing the prohibition of some particular private and offensive actions is counter-intuitive, but that the sheer quantity of actions which could not be regulated on a principle that would allow private disliked actions to be regulated is so small as to be "nugatory," that the principle could hardly be called "a principle of liberty," and would not be worth defending.

But (and this is my second point) the principle which Hart defends, while not nugatory, leaves so little in the class of actions which are not "society's business" that one wonders whether *it* is worth the effort of a serious defence. That the principle would protect an extremely narrow class of actions is evident when we realize that not only are essentially public ones left unprotected, but many which we may think of as private are impossible or insignificant if their public "manifestations" are prohibited.[20] If our interest is of a fairly practical nature, and if we are concerned only with this very narrow class of purely private actions, it would appear to be more expedient to argue that the actions in question should not be prohibited because the laws would not be evenly enforceable.[21]

Third, we can easily generate an *ad hominem* argument, directed specifically toward those who were happy to see Hart's "defence of Mill" because they find the latter's defence of individuality persuasive. My claim here is that Hart's position is so far removed from Mill's that it

[20] See Section III above.

[21] For this and other practical "difficulties and evils" in attempting to enforce laws against private immorality, see Louis B. Schwartz, "Morals and the Model Penal Code," in Richard A. Wasserstrom, *Morality and the Law* (Belmont: Wadsworth Publishing Co., 1971), p. 95.

cannot be said to be a defence of it. Mill's conception of individuality is not one of freedom for the individual to act in unusual ways only in private, to perform clandestine actions behind closed doors.[22] Mill is defending the right to *be* different, to *live* differently—the right openly to live at variance with the prevailing religion,[23] to become intoxicated provided only that this does not result in physical violence to another,[24] to engage in public amusements ("music, dancing, public games . . .") even though a majority may disapprove of them,[25] to be married to more than one spouse [26]—and if this offends those who "at heart, think they can do very well without it," [27] so much the worse for those who are so offended. There is a much wider gap between Hart's principle and the position that Mill is defending than Hart apparently realizes.

VI

If the foregoing arguments are acceptable, we have two basic alternatives: we can, with Lord Devlin, decide what actions are fit subjects for regulation by society on the basis of society's evaluation of their moral character. Since Hart has not shown that we can decide, in non-moral terms, what may be regulated, this is the obvious alternative.

On the other hand, the "extreme libertarian" may reason in this way: "Our intuitions are not completely consistent. There are no morally relevant differences between the possible regulation of private immorality, public 'indecency' (nudity, intercourse, etc.), and public actions which are offensive but not 'indecent' (oyster-eating, inter-racial hand-holding, etc.). We insist that the first and last cases should be no business of society (and are not prepared to give up this conviction), and so to be consistent we must set aside our prejudices and admit that nudity, intercourse, etc., even in public, are none of the business of society.[28] What we demand, in the cases in which our intuitions are in favour of non-interference, is that it be shown that actual harm would result if we allow individuals to do what they wish. But we tend to forget this requirement when indecency is in question. Surely, though, our procedure in the non-indecency cases is the correct one: the burden of proof is

22 With the exception of the notorious passage on p. 119.

23 Mill, passim.

24 Mill, p. 119.

25 Mill, pp. 105–106.

26 Mill, pp. 111–113.

27 Mill, p. 79.

28 Cf. Wilson, op. cit., p. 158. "Indecent exposure is analogous to wearing pink shoes or having blue hair. . . . If somebody wanted a law against pink shoes or blue hair, on the grounds that they 'interfered' with his Sunday walk, we should tell him to look the other way or forget about it; and it is significant that we are not prepared to take this line with 'indecent exposure.' "

always on those who would prohibit an action, and what must be shown is the real possibility of actual *harm*. This is the minimum required of any 'principle of freedom' that deserves that title."

As I suppose is obvious by now, my own sympathies lie with the hypothetical "extreme libertarian." I do not claim, however, to have presented a real elucidation and defence of his position. At most, I have shown that that position is consistent even if it is too liberal,[29] while Hart's position is both inconsistent and too repressive. Lord Devlin's principles remain possibilities (I have not directly argued against them) but not for those who, with Mill, would deny the right of society to impress its will upon individuals in the name of moral rectitude.[30]

[29] There are many problems which have nothing to do with public indecency which arise for the "extreme libertarian." Among the more obvious is the possibility of adopting a principle that would prohibit the regulation of such obnoxious sights as automobile "graveyards," odours which may flow from industrial complexes, and the sounds which come from one's neighbour practising his trumpet at three a.m. My inclination is to think that none of these creates an insuperable problem for the "extreme libertarian," but I am not now prepared to argue this. And even if I were, it would not be appropriate to do so within the confines of the present paper, the point of which is not that the "extreme libertarian" is right, but that Hart is wrong.

[30] I should like to thank my colleagues James Doyle, Robert Gordon, and, particularly, Henry Shapiro for comments on earlier drafts of this paper.

The Legal Duty
to Render Aid

The central question of this section is whether the law should be used to ensure that those who are in need of vital assistance receive that assistance from those who can provide it. The issues here touch upon those of the preceding sections. We shall be looking once again at the subject of negligence as we did in the first section. And, as in the second section, we will be considering the enforcement of what many consider a particularly important moral obligation. Again we will have to deliberate about the legitimacy of using legal means to realize some values at the expense of other values.

The rule in Anglo-American jurisprudence has long been that there is no general legal duty to intervene to save the life of another—even where this may be done with little or no inconvenience to the rescuer. Thus, in the criminal law, it is no offense if a mere bystander, with a life ring and line in hand, simply watches as another person drowns a few feet away. And the same rule applies in the law of torts. Generally, the law of torts serves to provide a legal remedy to persons (plaintiffs) who have been injured in some way (other than by breach of contract) and who sue the party responsible for the injury. Typically, the remedy takes the form of damages which must be paid by the defendant in the case. Although some torts are also crimes (e.g., assault), tortfeasors are not the same as criminals and they are not subject to punishment as are criminals. But in tort law, as in criminal law, bystanders are typically not liable for injuries that they could have easily prevented. Before one can be found to be liable for injuries suffered by another as a result of one's inaction, it must be shown that one was under a legal duty to perform actions that would have prevented the injuries. There is no general legal duty to perform such actions.

Jones v. *United States* is an example of the application of this rule in the criminal law. The defendant in that case had "ample means" to provide the food and medical care that the infant, Anthony Lee Green, needed. Moreover, the defendant admitted that a doctor had recommended to her that the child be hospitalized. But whether the death of the child from malnutrition was manslaughter or not depends upon whether the duty neglected was a "legal duty and not a mere moral obligation." Justice Wright lists four situations in which an omission may constitute "breach of a legal duty."

The shocking facts of such cases have prompted some commentators to urge the adoption of law creating a general legal duty to render vital aid. One such attempt is that of Antony M. Honoré in his "Law, Morals and Rescue." After discussing the dimensions of the moral duty to rescue and the ways in which the law might encourage rescue by compensating and rewarding the rescuer, Honoré goes on to discuss the "enforcement" of a legal duty to rescue. This, he says, might be accomplished either by making nonrescuers liable for damage suffered as a result of their inaction or by subjecting them to some kind of criminal penalty. In supporting a legal duty to rescue he alludes to the advantages of such a law and to the "layman's sense of shock" at a legal system which has fallen short of his expectations. But Honoré maintains that more than this is required for such a law to be justified. "The mere fact that the majority is shocked at certain conduct does not, in my view, justify them in imposing civil or criminal liability unless there is also a balance of advantage in doing so." Honoré sketches the calculations which must be made and does not conceal his condemnation for the present state of the law on the question of the duty to rescue.

The approach which Honoré uses here—calculating the balance of advantage—is comparable to a currently popular economic approach to questions of tort liability. Richard A. Epstein's "A Theory of Strict Liability," which is excerpted in this section, is critical of this approach. He presents a spirited defense of the traditional position on the duty to rescue. After contrasting his own "strict liability" approach * with the more generally favored "negligence" approaches, Epstein criticizes both economic and moral negligence theories and indicates how his approach displays the good sense of the common-law position with regard to the good Samaritan. In the course of criticizing a proposed rule that would create a duty to rescue, Epstein discusses (a) the way the rule fails the economic test, (b) the difficulty of determining the application of the rule, (c) the consonancy of the traditional position with Western ethics, (d) the problems in making the required "interpersonal comparisons of utility," (e) the new incentives created by the proposed rule, and (f) the importance to the law of torts of defining "the boundaries of individual liberty." In the end, Epstein opts for legal principles which do not require the potential rescuer to "take into account the welfare" of the victim who could be saved. The conduct of the nonrescuer may be out-

---

* Note that strict liability here, in tort law, is not the same as strict liability in criminal law.

rageous but his liberty should not be restricted, because he does not cause harm to another.

John Harris' paper, "The Marxist Conception of Violence," is an argument for a "drastic revision of our views about agency and responsibility." While Epstein looks to the "ordinary use of causal language" to establish his claims about causation, Harris begins by marshaling examples which recognize (as Epstein does not) "the causal efficacy of omissions." Harris then goes on to examine three recent attempts to "give an adequate account of when a failure to act has consequences" and then tries to develop a theory of "negative action" which is more adequate than the other views. Finally, building on his theory of negative action, Harris offers a justification for the view that the failure to prevent harm is violence just as are rape, murder and the other familiar examples.

JONES V. UNITED STATES

United States Court of Appeals
District of Columbia Circuit

Wright, Circuit Judge.

Appellant, together with one Shirley Green, was tried on a three-count indictment charging them jointly with (1) abusing and maltreating Robert Lee Green, (2) abusing and maltreating Anthony Lee Green,[1] and (3) involuntary manslaughter through failure to perform their legal duty of care for Anthony Lee Green, which failure resulted in his death.[2] At the close of evidence, after trial to a jury, the first two counts were dismissed as to both defendants. On the third count, appellant was convicted of involuntary manslaughter. Shirely Green was found not guilty.

Appellant urges several grounds for reversal. We need consider but two. First, appellant argues that there was insufficient evidence as a matter of law to warrant a jury finding of breach of duty in the care she rendered Anthony Lee. Alternatively, appellant argues that the trial court committed plain error [3] in failing to instruct the jury that it must first find that appellant was under a legal obligation to provide food and necessities to Anthony Lee before finding her guilty of manslaughter

308 F.2d 307 (1962)

[1] Counts 1 and 2 were laid under D.C. Code § 22–901.

[2] D.C. Code § 22–2405.

[3] Rule 52(b), F.R.Cr.P. 18 U.S.C.A.

in failing to provide them. The first argument is without merit. Upon the latter we reverse.

A summary of the evidence, which is in conflict upon almost every significant issue, is necessary for the disposition of both arguments.[4] In late 1957, Shirley Green became pregnant, out of wedlock, with a child, Robert Lee, subsequently born August 17, 1958. Apparently to avoid the embarrassment of the presence of the child in the Green home, it was arranged that appellant, a family friend, would take the child to her home after birth. Appellant did so, and the child remained there continuously until removed by the police on August 5, 1960. Initially appellant made some motions toward the adoption of Robert Lee, but these came to nought, and shortly thereafter it was agreed that Shirley Green was to pay appellant $72 a month for his care. According to appellant, these payments were made for only five months. According to Shirley Green, they were made up to July, 1960.

Early in 1959 Shirley Green again became pregnant, this time with the child Anthony Lee, whose death is the basis of appellant's conviction. This child was born October 21, 1959. Soon after birth, Anthony Lee developed a mild jaundice condition, attributed to a blood incompatability with his mother. The jaundice resulted in his retention in the hospital for three days beyond the usual time, or until October 26, 1959, when, on authorization signed by Shirley Green, Anthony Lee was released by the hospital to appellant's custody. Shirley Green, after a two or three day stay in the hospital, also lived with appellant for three weeks, after which she returned to her parents' home, leaving the children with appellant. She testified she did not see them again, except for one visit in March, until August 5, 1960. Consequently, though there does not seem to have been any specific monetary agreement with Shirley Green covering Anthony Lee's support,[5] appellant had complete custody of both children until they were rescued by the police.

With regard to medical care, the evidence is undisputed. In March, 1960, appellant called a Dr. Turner to her home to treat Anthony Lee for a bronchial condition. Appellant also telephoned the doctor at various times to consult with him concerning Anthony Lee's diet and health. In early July, 1960, appellant took Anthony Lee to Dr. Turner's office where he was treated for "simple diarrhea." At this time the doctor noted the "wizened" appearance of the child and told appellant to tell the mother of the child that he should be taken to a hospital. This was not done.

On August 2, 1960, two collectors for the local gas company had

---

[4] The verdict of a jury in a criminal case must be sustained when there is substantial evidence to support it, taking the view most favorable to the Government. . . .

[5] It was uncontested that during the entire period the children were in appellant's home, appellant had ample means to provide food and medical care.

occasion to go to the basement of appellant's home, and there saw the two children. Robert Lee and Anthony Lee at this time were age two years and ten months respectively. Robert Lee was in a "crib" consisting of a framework of wood, covered with a fine wire screening, including the top which was hinged. The "crib" was lined with newspaper, which was stained, apparently with feces, and crawling with roaches. Anthony Lee was lying in a bassinet and was described as having the appearance of a "small baby monkey." One collector testified to seeing roaches on Anthony Lee.

On August 5, 1960, the collectors returned to appellant's home in the company of several police officers and personnel of the Women's Bureau. At this time, Anthony Lee was upstairs in the dining room in the bassinet, but Robert Lee was still downstairs in his "crib." The officers removed the chldiren to the D. C. General Hospital where Anthony Lee was diagnosed as suffering from severe malnutrition and lesions over large portions of his body, apparently caused by severe diaper rash. Following admission, he was fed repeatedly, apparently with no difficulty, and was described as being very hungry. His death, 34 hours after admission, was attributed without dispute to malnutrition. At birth, Anthony Lee weighed six pounds, fifteen ounces—at death at age ten months, he weighed seven pounds, thirteen ounces. Normal weight at this age would have been approximately 14 pounds.

Appellant argues that nothing in the evidence establishes that she failed to provide food to Anthony Lee. She cites her own testimony and the testimony of a lodger, Mr. Wills, that she did in fact feed the baby regularly. At trial, the defense made repeated attempts to extract from the medical witnesses opinions that the jaundice, or the condition which caused it, might have prevented the baby from assimilating food. The doctors conceded this was possible but not probable since the autopsy revealed no condition which would support the defense theory. It was also shown by the disinterested medical witnesses that the child had no difficulty in ingesting food immediately after birth, and that Anthony Lee, in the last hours before his death, was able to take several bottles, apparently without difficulty, and seemed very hungry. This evidence, combined with the absence of any physical cause for nonassimilation, taken in the context of the condition in which these children were kept, presents a jury question on the feeding issue.

Moreover, there is substantial evidence from which the jury could have found that appellant failed to obtain proper medical care for the child. Appellant relies upon the evidence showing that on one occasion she summoned a doctor for the child, on another took the child to the doctor's office, and that she telephoned the doctor on several occasions about the baby's formula. However, the last time a doctor saw the child was a month before his death, and appellant admitted that on that occasion the doctor recommended hospitalization. Appellant did not hospitalize the child, nor did she take any other steps to obtain medical care in the last crucial month. Thus there was sufficient evidence to go to the jury on the issue of medical care, as well as failure to feed.[6]

Appellant also takes exception to the failure of the trial court to charge that the jury must find beyond a reasonable doubt, as an element of the crime, that appellant was under legal duty to supply food and necessities to Anthony Lee. Appellant's attorney did not object to the failure to give this instruction, but urges here the application of Rule 52(b).

The problem of establishing the duty to take action which would preserve the life of another has not often arisen in the case law of this country.[7] The most commonly cited statement of the rule is found in *People* v. *Beardsley*, 150 Mich. 206, 113 N.W. 1128, 1129, 13 L.R.A. N.S., 1020:

> The law recognizes that under some circumstances the omission of a duty owed by one individual to another, where such omission results in the death of the one to whom the duty is owing, will make the other chargeable with manslaughter. . . . This rule of law is always based upon the proposition that the duty neglected must be a legal duty, and not a mere moral obligation. It must be a duty imposed by law or by contract, and the omission to perform the duty must be the immediate and direct cause of death. . . .

There are at least four situations in which the failure to act may constitute breach of a legal duty. One can be held criminally liable: first, where a statute imposes a duty to care for another;[8] second, where one stands in a certain status relationship to another;[9] third, where one has assumed a contractual duty to care for another;[10] and fourth, where one has voluntarily assumed the care of another and so secluded the helpless person as to prevent others from rendering aid.[11]

It is the contention of the Government that either the third or the fourth ground is applicable here. However, it is obvious that in any of

---

[6] Compare *State* v. *Beach*, Mo.Sup.Ct., 329 S.W.2d 712, and *Rex* v. *Ellen Jones*, 19 Cox Crim. Cas. 678.

[7] The problem has evoked considerable study. See, e.g., Holmes, The Common Law, p. 278 (1881); Moreland, A Rationale of Criminal Negligence, ch. 10 (1944); Hughes, Criminal Omissions, 67 Yale L.J. 590, 620-626 (1958); Annot., 10 A.L.R. 1137 (1921).

[8] See e.g., D.C.Code § 22-902; *Craig* v. *State*, 220 Md. 590, 155 A.2d 684.

[9] A.L.R. Annot., *supra*, Note 7 (parent to child); *Territory* v. *Manton*, 8 Mont. 95, 19 P. 387 (husband to wife); *Regina* v. *Smith*, 8 Carr. & P. 153 (Eng. 1837) (master to apprentice); *United States* v. *Knowles*, 26 Fed.Cas. 800 (No. 15,540) (ship's master to crew and passengers); cf. *State* v. *Reitze*, 86 N.J.L. 407, 92 A. 576 (innkeeper to inebriated customers).

[10] *Regina* v. *Smith, supra*, Note 9; *Rex* v. *Ellen Jones, supra*, Note 6; *People* v. *Montecino*, 66 Cal.App.2d 85, 152 P. 2d 5.

[11] *Reg.* v. *Nicholls*, 13 Cox Crim.Cas. 75; *Rex* v. *Ellen Jones, supra*. Note 6; 1 Wharton, Criminal Law, § 455 (12th Ed.). Cf. *Rex.* v. *Gibbins and Proctor*, 13 Crim. App.R. 134 (Eng.1918); *State* v. *Noakes*, 70 Vt. 247, 40 A. 249.

the four situations, there are critical issues of fact which must be passed on by the jury—specifically in this case, whether appellant had entered into a contract with the mother for the care of Anthony Lee or, alternatively, whether she assumed the care of the child and secluded him from the care of his mother, his natural protector. On both of these issues, the evidence is in direct conflict, appellant insisting that the mother was actually living with appellant and Anthony Lee, and hence should have been taking care of the child herself, while Shirley Green testified she was living with her parents and was paying appellant to care for both children.

In spite of this conflict, the instructions given in the case failed even to suggest the necessity for finding a legal duty of care. The only reference to duty in the instructions was the reading of the indictment which charged, inter alia, that the defendants "failed to perform their legal duty." A finding of legal duty is the critical element of the crime charged and failure to instruct the jury concerning it was plain error. . . .

Reversed and remanded.

LAW, MORALS AND RESCUE

Antony M. Honoré

A woman, viciously attacked, lies bleeding in the street. Fifty people pass by on the other side. A man destroys his barn to prevent a fire spreading to his neighbor's property. The neighbor refuses to compensate him. A young potholer foolishly becomes trapped below ground. A more experienced man, coming to his aid, breaks a leg. When we contemplate facts such as these, three questions seem to confront us concerning law, morals, and their interrelation. The first is about the shared morality of our society. Is there in modern industrial society, which is the only one most of us know, a shared attitude of praise or condemnation, encouragement, or dissuasion about helping those in peril? If so, two further points arise. Should the law, with its mechanisms of inducement, rewards, and compensation, be used to encourage what the shared morality treats as laudable and discourage what it reprobates? Should the law, thirdly, go further and, by the use of threats and penalties, "enforce" morality, as the saying goes? These, it seems, are the main issues. In part they concern matters which, in England at least, have lately stirred up a passionate debate.[1] Is it justifiable to use the mechanism of criminal law to "enforce" the shared morality, for instance in matters of sex? Greeks and Trojans have sallied forth and the clash of arms has rung out. Our concern, however, is with something wider and different: not sex, not only "enforcement," not only crime. I shall have a word, later on, to say in criticism of the use of the word "enforce" in this context. If we pass it for the moment, it yet remains true that "enforcement" is only part of what the law can do in the Good Samaritan situation. Apart from criminal sanctions, the law can encourage or discourage compliance with the shared morality by the use of techniques drawn from tort, contract, and restitution. Even "enforcement" is not confined to criminal law, because tort law, too, can be used to impose an obligation to aid others.

Our concern is not only wider but different from that of the jurists by whose brilliant and elevated jousting we have been entertained. They have debated whether some parts of the law which coincide with common morality should be scrapped. We, on the other hand, wish to know whether parts of morality, at present outside the law, should be incorporated in it. (I mean here Anglo-American law and not those systems in which this has already come about.) Some people feel that the intrusion of law into the private sphere of sex is indecent and outrageous. Others feel outraged by the failure of the law to intrude in relation to rescue and rescuers. Is the refusal to "enforce" the moral obligation to help others itself a moral offense, of which lawyers and legislators have been guilty in the English-speaking world this hundred years? Does the affront of this refusal bring the law and lawyers into disrepute? Should the law encourage or even insist on Do-Goodery? Or would this be an intrusion into yet another private sphere, not of sex, but of conscience?

Clearly we have a moral issue on our hands, and one which is concerned not with the "enforcement" of morals but with its non-enforcement. A number of writers, following Bentham [2] and Mill,[3] have advocated a legal obligation to rescue. Ames [4] and Bohlen [5] put forward an

---

[1] P. Devlin, *The Enforcement of Morals* (Maccabaean Lecture, 1958), reprinted in *The Enforcement of Morals* (Oxford U. P., 1965); W. Friedmann in 4 *Natural Law Forum* (1964), 151; H. L. A. Hart, *Law, Liberty, and Morality* (Oxford U. P., 1963); L. Henkin in 63 *Col. L. Rev.* (1963) 393; G. Hughes in 71 *Yale L. J.* (1961) 622; M. Ginsberg in 1964 *British Journal of Criminology*, 283; A. W. Mewett in 14 *Toronto L. J.* (1962) 213; E. Rostow in 1960 *Cambridge L. J.* 174 reprinted in *The Sovereign Prerogative* (Yale U. P., 1962); N. St. John-Stevas, *Life, Death and the Law* (1961); R S. Summers in 38 *New York U. L. Rev* (1963), 1201; B. Wootton, *Crime and the Criminal Law* (Stevens, 1963), 41.

[2] J. Bentham, *Principles of Morals and Legislation*, 323 ("Who is there that in any of these cases would think punishment misapplied?").

[3] J. S. Mill, *On Liberty*, Introduction ("There are also many positive acts for the benefit of others, which he may rightfully be compelled to perform . . . such as saving a fellow-creature's life").

[4] J. B. Ames, *Law and Morals*, . . . [in *The Good Samaritan and the Law*, ed. James M. Ratcliffe (New York: Doubleday & Co., 1966)], pp. 1–21.

[5] F. Bohlen, *The Moral Duty to Aid Others As a Basis of Liability*, 56 *U. Pa. L. Rev.* (1908) 215, 316.

earnest plea to the same effect. But, though they mentioned, they did not closely analyze the moral issues. It is with these that I shall be principally concerned.

I THE SHARED MORALITY IN MATTERS OF RESCUE

An essential preliminary to the survey of the larger vistas of law and morals is to clear our minds about our moral views in the matter of aid to those in peril. By "our moral views" I mean the shared or common morality. Obviously this is not the same as the statement of what people actually do in a given society—the common practice of mankind. Their actions may fall short of their moral ideals and pretensions. Nor is it the same as that which an individual may accept for himself as morally obligatory. There is a distinction between that which the individual accepts for himself and that which he regards as being of general application. A man may think he has higher ideals, a stricter sense of obligation or duty, than the ordinary run of men could well be expected to entertain. This cherished personal morality, it seems to me, is no part or ingredient of the shared morality, though it may come, in time, to spread to others and so to influence the shared morality.

The shared morality consists, rather, of those moral ideals and duties or obligations which the bulk of the community regard as applying to persons generally. But is the notion, defined, anything more than a figment? Ought we to refrain from speculating about its content until social surveys have determined whether it really exists? I think one must frankly concede that the results of properly conducted surveys would be far more authoritative than the guesses of moralists or lawyers. The survey by which Messrs. Cohen, Robson, and Bates sought to ascertain the moral sense of the Nebraska community on parent-child relations [6] is, no doubt, a forerunner of what will, in time, become common practice. The shared morality of which I am speaking is not, however, quite what the Nebraska inquiry was attempting to ascertain. In that inquiry "community values" were defined as the "choices, expressed verbally, which members of the community feel the law-making authorities ought to make if confronted with alternative courses of action in specified circumstances." [7] These choices surely represent opinion as to legislation on moral issues rather than the shared morality itself. They tell us what people think legislators should do, not what they think ordinary citizens should do. No doubt there is a close, even a very close, connection between the two. Our view of what the law should be will be powerfully shaped by our notions of right and wrong, of what is desirable and what objectionable, but surely the two cannot without more be identified. It

---

[6] J. Cohen, R. A. H. Robson, and A. Bates, *Ascertaining the Moral Sense of the Community*, 8 *Journal of Legal Education* (1955–56) 137.

[7] Ibid.

must *a priori* be an open question whether people who share moral ideas also think that these should be mirrored in the law. If they do, that is also a fact susceptible of and demanding confirmation by a properly conducted survey.

It remains doubtful, therefore, whether a suitable technique has yet been evolved for testing the existence and content of the shared morality of a community. Certainly the results are not yet to hand in a usable form. In the meantime, life does not stand still. Decisions must be reached with the aid of such information and intuition as we may possess. We cannot shirk the question of what our shared morality says about rescues and rescuers on the excuse that one day, we hope, a truly reliable answer will be available.

It is unwise in thinking about the shared morality to treat morality as an undifferentiated mass. For instance, there is a distinction between moral ideals and moral duties.[8] This is not the same as the previous distinction between a man's personal morality and the morality which he regards as of general application. Of course, a connection exists. A person may accept as an obligation for himself what he thinks of merely as an ideal for others. Broadly speaking, moral ideals concern patterns of conduct which are admired but not required. To live up to them is praiseworthy but not exigible. Moral duties, on the other hand, concern conduct which is required but not admired. With an important exception, to which I shall come, merely to do one's duty evokes no comment. Moral duties are pitched at a point where the conformity of the ordinary man can reasonably be expected. As a corollary, while it is tolerable, if deplorable, to fall short of the highest ideals, it is not permissible to neglect one's duties.

Certain virtues, notably altruism and generosity, depend on absence of obligation. It is not altruistic to pay one's debts, or generous to support one's parents (in the latter case the duty may in Anglo-American law be merely moral, but this makes no difference). Other virtues seem to hover between the status of ideals and duties. Is this, perhaps, true of the "neighborliness" which the parable of the Good Samaritan is meant both to illustrate and to inculcate? According to Matthew [9] and Mark,[10] the precept "love your neighbor as yourself" expresses a "commandment" and presumably imposes an obligation. Luke,[11] in contrast, treats it as pointing the way to perfection or "eternal life," a moral ideal. It may be that giving aid to those in peril is sometimes an ideal, sometimes a duty. At least three situations demand separate treatment:

1. The first is the rescue undertaken by one who has a professional or quasi-professional duty to undertake rescues. A fireman or life-saver is a professional rescuer. Doctors, nurses, and other members of the medical

8 E. Cahn, *The Moral Decision* (1956), 39.
9 Matthew 22:34.
10 Mark 12:28.
11 Luke 10:25.

profession have a duty to save life, which, at times, demands that they should give help in an emergency. A priest must comfort the dying, a policeman must stop acts of violence. Besides these true professionals, there are what one may call devoted amateurs; for instance, experienced mountaineers or potholers, who hold themselves out as ready to effect rescues and, I am told, often welcome the chance to display their skills. Strictly speaking, none of these are "volunteers." They are only doing what they are bound by their calling or public profession to do. A doctor is not praised for coming promptly to the scene of an accident; that is only what we expect. He would be blamed if he delayed or refused to come. But this morally neutral reaction is appropriate only when the rescuer acts without risk or serious inconvenience to himself. If the fireman, policeman, or life-saver risks life or limb to help the imperiled, he deserves and receives praise, because there is an element of self-sacrifice or even heroism in his conduct, though what he does is clearly his duty. Heroism and self-sacrifice, unlike altruism, can be evinced both by those who do their duty and those who have no duty to do.

2. The second is the rescue undertaken by one who has special ties with the person imperiled. Family links, employment, and other associative ties may generate a duty to come to the help of a class of persons more limited than those whom the professional or professed rescuer is bound to assist. It is a parent's duty to snatch his child from the path of an oncoming automobile, an employer's to rescue the workman who has been trapped in the factory machine. It may well be their duty to risk their own safety should that prove necessary. Like the professional rescuer, they can expect no encomium merely for helping, but if they risk themselves they merit commendation.

3. The third situation is that of a person not bound by his profession or by special links with the person imperiled to come to his aid. Even in this case, common opinion would, perhaps, see a limited duty to assist when this is possible without risk or grave inconvenience to the rescuer. "It is undoubtedly the moral duty," an American judge has said, "of every person to extend to others assistance when in danger, to throw, for instance, a plank or rope to the drowning man or make other efforts for his rescue, and if such efforts should be omitted by anyone when they could be made without imperilling his own life, he would, by his conduct, draw upon himself the censure and reproach of good men." [12] Common humanity, then, forges between us a link, but a weak one. The duty stops short at the brink of danger. Samaritans, it is held, must be good, but need not be moral athletes.

It is in this third situation alone, when the rescuer, bound by no professional duty or special tie to the person imperiled, exposes himself to danger, that we really call him a "volunteer." I appreciate that in Anglo-American law the notion of the "volunteer" has been at times twisted beyond recall. In order to deny the rescuer a remedy, the doc-

[12] *U.S.* v. *Knowles* (1864) 26 Fed. Cas. 801.

trine of voluntary assumption of risk has sometimes been extended to bar those who were merely doing their duty or responding to an appeal for help.[13] Conversely, in order to afford the rescuer a remedy, courts have at other times treated the altruist as if he were simply doing his plain duty and concluded that his action was a necessary consequence of the hazard and so of the fault of the person who created it.[14] But this is just legal fiction.

If this moral morphology is reasonably accurate, we have four types of rescuer and non-rescuer to contend with. The first is the priest or Levite who passes by on the other side. The second, in ascending order of excellence, is the man who does no more than he is bound to do, whether his duty arises from his profession, from some special link with the person imperiled, or from common humanity. The third is he who, in doing his duty, exposes himself to risk: possibly a hero. The fourth is the true volunteer altruistically exposing himself to danger to help those to whom he is bound by no special tie: perhaps a hero, too.

What should the law have to say to them?

II THE MYTH OF NON-INTERVENTION

First, should the law encourage or discourage the rescuer, or should it remain neutral? Members of my generation remember non-intervention as the name of a policy which, during the Spanish Civil War, ensured the victory of the side which cheated most. It was called by Talleyrand a metaphysical conception, which means very much the same thing as intervention. So with the intervention of law in the sphere of morals. There is no neutrality. If the law does not encourage rescue, it is sure to discourage it. If it does not compensate, it will indirectly penalize. If the rescuer who suffers injury or incurs expense or simply expends his skill goes without compensation, the law, so far as it influences conduct at all, is discouraging rescue.

Perhaps one day sociology will devise means of discovering whether people are really influenced in what they do by the thought of legal remedies. In the meantime, it would be altogether too facile to assume that they are not. A doctor living near a dangerous crossroads is continually called to minister to the victims of the road. The injured are unconscious or, if conscious, are in no mood to contract or to fill in National Health cards. Will the doctor come more readily and care for them more thoroughly if he knows he will be paid? If so, he is a man, not an angel. A mountain guide with a hungry family is called to rescue a foolish climber trapped on the north face of the Eiger. Does anyone

---

[13] *Cutler* v. *United Dairies* (1933) 2 K.B. 297.

[14] Pollock, *Torts* (15th ed.), 370; *Haynes* v. *Harwood* (1953) 1 K.B. at 163; *Morgan* v. *Aylen* (1942) 1 All E.R. 489; *Baker* v. *Hopkins* (1959) 1 W.L.R. 966.

imagine him to be indifferent to the question how his family will be kept if he is killed?

The law cannot stay out of the fight and, if it cannot, there is surely a strong case for compensating the rescuer. To do so will be in the interests of those who might be saved. The community applauds the Good Samaritan. So the law, if it encourages rescue, is helping to satisfy the interests of individuals and the wants of the community. If we think of law as being, among other things, a social service designed to maximize welfare and happiness, this is exactly what the law ought to do. One department of the law's service to society will be its moral service, which it performs by encouraging with the appropriate technical remedies whatever is morally approved and discouraging what is condemned.

Unquestionably there are limits to this function of the law. I will deal with only three. The most obvious is the limit set by oppression. If the encouragement of the shared morality and the discouragement of its breach would be a hardship to some without sufficient corresponding benefit to them or to others, the law should not endorse it. The fact that racial prejudice is approved in a given community does not mean that the courts must hold leases to Negroes in white residential areas void. But the encouragement of rescue will oppress neither rescuer nor rescued. The rescued benefits from being saved, and even if he is compelled to compensate the rescuer he will be, by and large, better off. It is true that compensation may be burdensome and I should not care to argue that civil remedies are necessarily less harsh than punishment. If an uninsured person has to pay heavy damages, he is worse off than if he were fined, for the fine, unlike the damages, is geared to his means. But this fact depends on the rules about assessment of damages in Anglo-American law, and these might be changed. It would be no hardship to suggest that the rescuer should receive compensation, if necessary, from the person imperiled, in accordance with the latter's means: *in id quod facere potest*, as the Roman formula ran.

Another limit or supposed limit may be set by the principle that virtue should be its own reward. Strictly speaking, I doubt if this applies to proposals for compensation as opposed to rewards. Still, the doctor's claim to be paid for his ministrations to the unconscious victim of a road accident may be called a claim for reward. Would it be an inroad on his virtue that he was entitled to be paid? Surely the argument is obtuse. No one is compelled to claim a reward he does not want. The doctor, like the finder of lost property, can preserve immaculate his moral idealism if he wishes. No one can be compelled to be compensated.

A third limit concerns the border line between altruism and meddling. Of course we do not want our next-door neighbor to rescue the baby every time he screams or to interrupt our family quarrels. But this merely shows that the received morality draws the line at officiousness. The test of what is officious will usually be whether the intending rescuer would reasonably suppose that his help will be welcome. If the victim objects or would be expected to object, the rescuer should abstain. But this can hardly apply to those victims who are too young or too deranged to know their own interests, and one might justify the rescue of a person attempting suicide (in a jurisdiction in which suicide is not a crime) on the ground that those who attempt it often lack a settled determination in the matter.

The line will be difficult to draw exactly, but lawyers are professional line-drawers. The relevant factors are easy enough to list: the gravity of the peril, the chances of successful intervention, the attitude of the victim, and the likelihood that another better-qualified rescuer will act.

None of the three limits mentioned seems to alter the proposition that the law would be a poor thing if it did not in general encourage rescue. The means available to do this are essentially the compensation of the rescuer for expenses and injury and the rewarding of his services. It is convenient to take these separately.

1. *Injury*. No immediate difficulty is felt if the rescuer is covered by a personal accident policy or an insurance scheme connected with his employment, as would usually be true of firemen and other professional rescuers. There will still remain the question whether the insurer should be entitled to shift the loss to the person responsible for the peril. Certainly it makes for simplicity if he cannot.

When there is no insurance cover the problem is: where should the compensation come from? Most people would be inclined to place it in the first instance on the person through whose fault the peril arose, whether the person imperiled or another. In order to justify making the person imperiled liable when he had been at fault, Bohlen argued that the basis of liability was the tendency of the defendant's conduct to cause the rescuer to take the risk involved in the attempted rescue.[15] If "cause" is to be taken seriously, this suggests that the rescuer who acts under a sense of obligation would recover for his injury, while the pure altruist would not, because the latter's act is a fresh cause. Yet altruism is not less but more worthy of the law's encouragement than the conscientious performance of one's duty. If in *Carnea* v. *Buyea* [16] the plaintiff who snatched the defendant from the path of the runaway automobile had been unrelated to the defendant, could that reasonably have been a ground for denying him a recovery? Surely the remedy should not be confined to cases where the peril "causes" the rescue, but should extend to those in which it merely prompts the rescuer.

Other writers and courts rely on foreseeability as the ground of liability. This, too, is open to objection. Suppose an intrepid but foolhardy explorer is stranded in an area where rescue is atrociously difficult and rescuers scarce. By the heroism of a James Bond he is saved. Surely the fact that rescue could not be foreseen makes no difference to Bond's claim for compensation? Is not the real basis of liability the twofold fact

15 F. Bohlen, *Studies in the Law of Tort*, 569 n. 33.
16 271 App. Div. 338. 65 N.Y.S. 2d 902 (1946).

that the person imperiled has created a risk from which he wishes to be saved (whether he thinks rescue likely or not) and that his peril has prompted another to come to his aid (whether it has "caused" him to do so or not).

I have been dealing with the rationale of the imperiled person's duty to compensate the rescuer when the former is at fault. Legally speaking, this is the case that has evoked discussion, because it said that the person in peril owes himself no duty. When the peril is created by a third person, the objection is inapplicable. If the third person is at fault, he should be liable to compensate the rescuer for the reasons already given. If no one is at fault, it still remains a question whether compensation should be payable by either the person imperiled or the state. A remedy against the innocent person in peril can be justified either, if he is saved, on the ground that he has benefited at the rescuer's expense and should not take the benefit without paying the cost of its procurement or (whether he is saved or not) on the ground of unauthorized agency. The guiding notion of this (the Roman *negotiorum gestio* and the French *gestion d'affaire*) is that the agent, acting without the principal's authority, nevertheless does what the principal might be presumed to want done, when it is impracticable to obtain his consent. (If there is actual consent, for instance, if the person in peril calls for help, so much the easier, legally speaking, to justify giving a remedy.) [17]

Anglo-American law, in contrast with civil systems, is impregnated with the maxim, "Mind your own business," though recently there have been signs of a change. If we outflank the maxim by asserting that, to a limited extent, the peril of one is the business of all, it seems fair to make the person imperiled, though free from fault, indemnify the rescuer albeit only so far as his means reasonably permit.

None of the headings so far mentioned may afford an adequate remedy to the rescuer. In that case a state compensation scheme might well fill the gap. If the state is to compensate the victims of crimes of violence, as is now done in England,[18] why not compensate the equal heroism of those who suffer injury in effecting rescues?

2. *Expenses.* In principle the same rules should apply to expenses incurred by the rescuer as to injuries received by him. Two points may be noted. One is that the expense of organizing a rescue may nowadays be enormous. Suppose the Air Force presents the lost mariner with a bill for gasoline, maintenance of aircraft, wages of crew, and so on, perhaps incurred over several days of search. The crushing liability must be mitigated by having regard for the mariner's probably slender means. The other point is that in Anglo-American law there is a traditional reluctance to grant tort actions for negligence when the loss suffered is merely pecuniary. The rescuer who incurs expense but suffers no physical injury may thus find the way barred. It seems that courts will have to extend the

---

[17] *Brugh* v. *Bigelow* (1944) 16 N.Y.S. 2d 902 (1946).

[18] Assessed by the Criminal Injuries Compensation Board (1964).

bounds of the tort of negligence and the law of restitution if adequate remedies are to be supplied without legislative intervention. There are already some signs that this is happening.[19]

3. *Rewards.* The moral objections to rewarding altruism, we saw, are misconceived. But is there a positive case to be made in favor of rewarding rescuers? In practice, outstanding acts of courage in effecting rescue are marked by the award of medals and decorations. Many persons saved from danger would think themselves morally bound to offer something to their rescuers. But a legal claim to be paid is usually voiced only by the professional rescuer, especially the self-employed, who may spend much time and energy in this way. Take our friend the doctor who lives near an accident black spot. It is mere fiction to say that the unconscious victim impliedly contracts to pay for treatment.[20] Two other theories are possible: one, that payment is less a true reward than compensation for loss of profitable time; the other, that the person in peril, if he could have been consulted, would have agreed to pay for the treatment because medical services are normally paid for. The second theory, unlike the first, has a narrow range, because it does not extend to a rescuer whose services are normally given free.

III A LEGAL DUTY TO AID THOSE IN PERIL?

My third question raises an issue concerning what is usually called the "enforcement" of morals. The use of this word is, I think, apt to mislead. Literally speaking, the law cannot force citizens to do anything, but only to submit to deprivation of freedom, or to having their money taken from them. Even if "enforcement" is taken, as it normally is, in an extended sense, the notion that morality is enforced by law carries with it the false implication that it is not enforced apart from law. Yet the chief agent for enforcing morality is public opinion. If the approval or disapproval of family and friends is not visited on those who conform or rebel, the conduct in question is not part of the shared morality. Few people, I imagine, would rather incur the censure of family and friends than pay a sum of damages or a fine. This should lead us to suspect that the law, when it imposes a duty to do what the shared morality already requires, is not enforcing but *reflecting, reinforcing,* and *specifying* morality.

There are strong reasons, I think, why the law should reflect, reinforce, and specify, at least that segment of the shared morality which consists in moral duties owed to others. The first is the advantage to those who stand to benefit. It is true that legal incentives probably influ-

---

[19] *Hadley Byrne* v. *Heller* (1964) A.C. 465.

[20] *Cotnam* v. *Wisdom* 83 Ark. 601, 104 S.W. 164. 119 Am. St. R. 157 (1907); *Greenspan* v. *Slate* 12 N.J. 426, 97 Atl. 2d 390 (1953).

ence no more than a tiny minority, but they certainly influence some. A driver sees the victim of a highway accident bleeding by the roadside. He knows he ought to stop, but is tempted to drive on in order to keep an assignment. The thought that there is a law requiring him to stop may pull him up short.

Even if the impact of the law is confined to a few, there is a special reason for reinforcing the duty to aid persons in peril. Peril means danger of death or serious injury or, at the least, of grave damage to property. The more serious the harm to be averted, the more worth-while it is to save even a handful of those who would otherwise suffer irretrievable injury or death.

Secondly, there are some reasons for holding that the law ought in general to mirror moral obligations. In doing so, it ministers to an expectation entertained by the majority of citizens. The lawyer is, perhaps, so used to rules which permit men to flout their moral duties that he is at times benumbed. Promises made without consideration are not binding. A promisor can normally not be compelled to perform his promise but only to pay damage. Children need not support their parents. Samaritans need not be good. When we first learned these rules in law school, I daresay we were a little shocked, but the shock has worn off. It has not worn off the layman.

There are several elements in the sense of shock which laymen feel at the permissive state of the law in regard to moral duties. First, there is the "sense of injustice" of which Edmund Cahn has spoken.[21] If the law permits others to do with impunity that which I am tempted to do, but resist, what is the point of my resistance to temptation? The moral-breaker, like the unpunished lawbreaker, secures an unjust advantage at my expense.

A second element in the layman's sense of shock is the feeling that the law, like an overpermissive father, has set its standard too low. Just as a child loses respect for a father who allows him to back out of his promises, so the community will fail to respect the law which does likewise. It is, I imagine, another of those indubitable and unprovable commonplaces which are the very meat of jurisprudence that people's attitudes to particular laws often depend on their reverence for the law as a whole. If so, the failure of the law to reflect and reinforce moral duties undermines other, quite distinct laws. It may not be sensible for people to think of law in this way as a single, personified whole, but apparently they do.

A third element in the layman's sense of shock is the feeling that the guiding hand has failed. People to some degree expect a lead from the law, not merely threats and incentives. Rules of law which mirror moral duties have, among other things, an educative function. They formulate, in a way which, though not infallible, is yet in a sense authoritative, the content of the shared morality. They specify morality by

---

[21] E. Cahn, *The Sense of Injustice* (1949); *The Moral Decision* (1956).

marking, with more precision than the diffused sense of the people can manage, the minimum that can be tolerated.

The law cannot make men good, but it can, in the sphere of duty at least, encourage and help them to do good. It not only can but should reinforce the sanctions of public opinion, for the reasons given, unless it would be oppressive or impracticable to do so. I need say little of the practicability of imposing a duty to aid those in peril. France, Germany, and other countries have tried it out and found that it works reasonably well. But would it be oppressive? The mere fact that the majority is shocked at certain conduct does not, in my view, justify them in imposing civil or criminal liability unless there is also a balance of advantage in doing so. Difficult as it may be to strike a balance, we have in the case of rescue to add to the evils of injustice, disrespect, and want of guidance (should the law impose no duty to act) the possible benefit to those in peril if such duty is imposed. Then we must subtract the hardship of making people conform to accepted standards of neighborliness or suffer penalties. If the balance is positive, the law not merely may, but should, intervene. It has been urged that there is something peculiarly irksome in requiring people to take positive action as opposed to subjecting them to mere prohibitions. Why this should be so is a mystery. Perhaps we have a picture of Joe lounging in an armchair. It is more effort for him to get up than to stay where he is. But this is not how the law operates. Prohibitions are usually imposed because there is a strong urge or temptation to disregard them. To control the violent impulses of our nature is surely more arduous than to overcome the temptation selfishly to leave others in the lurch. Certainly there are important spheres, for instance, taxation and military service, where the law does not shrink from demanding positive action. Why should it do so in the law of rescue?

If it is argued that to require aid to be given to those in peril saps the roots of altruism by diminishing the opportunities for its exercise, the reply would be that the proposal is merely to impose a legal duty in situations where morality already sees one. Those who go beyond their moral duty will also be going beyond their legal duty. They lose no occasion for displaying altruism, merely because the law reflects a situation which *de facto* already exists.

The apparent objections to the introduction of a legal duty to rescue hardly withstand scrutiny. Perhaps the most substantial of them, in Anglo-American law, is simply tradition. Self-reliance, the outlook epitomized in the words, "Thank you, Jack, I'm all right," an irrational conviction that because law and morals do not always coincide there is some virtue in their being different,[22] all combine to frustrate the promptings of moral sensibility. One cannot but sense in some judicial utterances a certain pride in the irrational, incalculable depravity of the law, as if this

---

[22] Historicus (Sir W. Harcourt), *Some Questions of International Law* (1863), 76, cited in R. Pound, *Law and Morals* (1924), 40. The argument that there is value in moral experiments does not apply to experiments in leaving others in the lurch.

demonstrated its status as an esoteric science, inaccessible to the common run of mankind. As the Russians said of Stalin: a monster, but ours. I will quote one or two.

"The only duty arising under such circumstance [i.e., when one's employee catches her hand and wrist in a mangle] is one of humanity and for a breach thereof the law does not, so far as we are informed, impose any liability." [23] Hence, there is no need to help her to free her hand. "With purely moral obligations the law does not deal. For example, the priest and the Levite who passed by on the other side were not, it is supposed, liable at law for the continued suffering of the man who fell among thieves, which they might and morally ought to have prevented or relieved." [24] In the case from which the quotation is taken, it was held to be no legal wrong for a mill owner to allow a boy of eight to meddle with dangerous machinery, in which his hand was crushed. Indeed, the boy was guilty of committing a trespass when he touched the machinery.

Two thousand years ago a Jewish lawyer demanded a definition of the term "neighbor." This makes him, I suppose, an analytical jurist. Whether the tale of the Samaritan answered his perplexities we cannot say. But he would surely have been astonished had he been informed that there were two answers to his question, one if he was asking as a lawyer, another if he was asking as a layman. To him, neighbor was neighbor and duty, duty. Perhaps this ancient lawyer's tale has a moral for law and lawyers today.

A THEORY OF STRICT LIABILITY

RICHARD A. EPSTEIN

INTRODUCTION

Torts is at once one of the simplest and one of the most complex areas of the law. It is simple because it concerns itself with fact patterns that can be understood and appreciated without the benefit of formal legal instruction. Almost everyone has some opinions, often strong even if unformed, about his rights and responsibilities towards his fellow man;

23 *Allen* v. *Hixson* 36 S.E. 810 (1900).

24 *Buch* v. *Amory Manufacturing Co.* 69 N.H. 247; 44 Atl. 809 (1897).

From *Journal of Legal Studies* 2 (1973), 151–204. Copyright 1973 by the University of Chicago. Reprinted by permission of *The Journal of Legal Studies*.

and almost everyone has had occasion in contexts apart from the judicial process to apply his beliefs to the question of responsibility for some mishap that has come to pass. Indeed, the language of the law of tort, in sharp contrast, say, to that of civil procedure, reveals at every turn its origins in ordinary thought.

But the simplicity of torts based upon its use of ordinary language is deceptive. Even if ordinary language contains most of the concepts that bear on questions of personal responsibility, it often uses them in loose, inexact, and ambiguous ways: witness, for example, the confusion that surrounds the use of "malice." While an intuitive appreciation of the persistent features of ordinary language may help decide easy cases, more is required for the solution of those difficult cases where the use of ordinary language pulls in different directions at the same time. There is need for a systematic inquiry which refines, but which does not abandon, the shared impressions of everyday life. The task is to develop a normative theory of torts that takes into account common sense notions of individual responsibility. Such a theory no doubt must come to grips with the central concerns of the common law of torts. But it need not (though it well may) embrace the common law solution to any particular problem.

This common sense approach to torts as a branch of common law stands in sharp opposition to much of the recent scholarship on the subject because it does not regard economic theory as the primary means to establish the rules of legal responsibility. A knowledge of the economic consequences of alternative legal arrangements can be of great importance, but even among those who analyze tort in economic terms there is acknowledgment of certain questions of "justice" or "fairness" rooted in common sense beliefs that cannot be explicated in terms of economic theory.[1] Even if they cannot provide satisfactory answers to fairness questions, the advocates of economic analysis in the law still insist that their work is of primary importance because it reduces the area in which fairness arguments must be judged in order to reach a decision in a particular case. But once it is admitted that there are questions of fairness as between the parties that are not answerable in economic terms, the exact role of economic argument in the solution of legal question becomes impossible to determine. It may well be that an acceptable theory of fairness can be reconciled with the dictates of economic theory in a manner that leaves ample room for the use of economic thought. But that judgment presupposes that some theory of fairness has been spelled out, which, once completed, may leave no room for economic considerations of any sort.

---

[1] See Guido Calabresi & A. Douglas Melamed, Property Rules, Liability Rules, and Inalienability: One View of the Cathedral, 85 Harv. L. Rev. 1089, 1102-05 (1972). But see Richard A. Posner, A Theory of Negligence, 1 J. Leg. Studies 29 (1972).

In order to raise these fairness questions in the context of traditional legal doctrine, I shall focus on the conflict that has persisted in the common law between theories of negligence and theories of strict liability. The first section of this paper argues that neither the moral nor economic accounts of negligence justify its dominance in the law of tort. The second section analyzes the different contexts in which it is appropriate to assert that "*A* caused *B* harm," and argues that this proposition, when properly understood, provides a suitable justification for the imposition of liability in tort. The third section of the paper applies both the theories of negligence and of strict liability to the troublesome problem of the good Samaritan.

I. A CRITIQUE OF NEGLIGENCE

The development of the common law of tort has been marked by the opposition between two major theories. The first holds that a plaintiff should be entitled, prima facie, to recover from a defendant who has caused him harm only if the defendant intended to harm the plaintiff or failed to take reasonable steps to avoid inflicting the harm. The alternative theory, that of strict liability, holds the defendant prima facie liable for the harm caused whether or not either of the two further conditions relating to negligence and intent is satisfied.

It is most likely that theories of strict liability were dominant during the formative years of the common law. But during the nineteenth century, both in England and this country, there was a decided and express shift towards the theories of negligence.[2] For the most part the impulses that supported the thrust towards a system of negligence liability were grounded on moral rather than on explicitly economic considerations. Indeed, the phrase "no liability without fault" was used to summarize the opposition to a system of strict liability on moral grounds.[3] At the turn of the century Ames described the transition from the early

---

2 The extent of the shift can be overstated; for *Rylands* v. *Fletcher*, L. R. 3 H.L. 330 (1868), was a case which, whatever its precise scope, accepted the principle of strict liability in at least some situations. The problem is that nowhere have the courts decided precisely where the principles of negligence should dominate and where they should not. For example, why should principles of strict liability dominate in products liability cases when automobile cases are decided, in general, in accordance with negligence principles? See Marc A. Franklin, Replacing the Negligence Lottery: Compensation and Selective Reimbursement, 53 Va. L. Rev. 774, 793 (1967). See also Harry Kalven, Jr., Torts: The Quest for Appropriate Standards, 53 Calif. L. Rev. 189, 205–06 (1965).

3 Salmond, an influential writer at the turn of the century, often spoke of "*mens rea*" in the law of tort, even though he conceded that the term had a narrower meaning in the criminal law. See John Salmond, The Law of Torts 11 (7th ed. 1928).

theories of strict liability to the modern theories of negligence in these
confident terms:

> The early law asked simply, "Did the defendant do the physical act which
> damaged the plaintiff?" The law of today, except in certain cases based
> upon public policy, asks the further question, "Was the act blameworthy?"
> The ethical standard of reasonable conduct has replaced the unmoral
> standard of acting at one's peril.[4]

But the law of negligence never did conform in full to the requisites
of the "moral" system of personal responsibility invoked in its behalf.
In particular, the standard of the reasonable man, developed in order to
insure injured plaintiffs a fair measure of protection against their fellow
citizens, could require a given person to make recompense even where
no amount of effort could have enabled *him* to act in accordance with
the standard of conduct imposed by the law. Certain defenses like insanity were never accepted as part of the law of negligence, even though
an insane person is not regarded as morally responsible for his actions.
But if Ames' original premise were correct, then it should follow from
the "modern ethical doctrine" that a lunatic unable to appreciate the
nature or consequences of his act ought not to be responsible for the
damage he has inflicted upon another.[5]

Even if these exceptions to the general rule of negligence affect only
a few of the cases to be decided, they do indicate a theoretical weakness
that helps to explain efforts to find alternative justifications for the law
of negligence couched in economic rather than moral terms. Thus, it was
suggested that a defendant should be regarded as negligent if he did not
take the precautions an economically prudent man would take in his
own affairs, and, conversely, that where the defendant *did* conduct himself in an economically prudent manner, he could successfully defend
himself in an action brought by another person whom he injured.

Although positions of this sort had been suggested from the beginning of this century,[6] they received their most famous exposition in the
opinion of Learned Hand in *United States* v. *Carroll Towing Co.*[7] The
narrow point for decision in *Carroll Towing* was whether the *owner* of a
barge owed to others a duty to keep a bargee or attendant on board while
his barge was moored inside a harbor. In his analysis of the duty question, Hand notes that no general answer has been given to the question,
and in his view for good reason:

---

[4] James Barr Ames, Law and Morals, 22 Harv. L. Rev. 97, 99 (1908).

[5] "[I]f insanity of a pronounced type exists, manifestly incapacitating the suf-
ferer from complying with the rule which has been broken, good sense would require
it to be admitted as an excuse." O. W. Holmes, Jr., The Common Law 109 (1881). See
also James Barr Ames, *supra* note 4, at 99–100.

[6] See, e.g., Henry T. Terry, Negligence, 29 Harv. L. Rev. 40 (1915).

[7] 159 F. 2d 169 (2d Cir. 1947).

It becomes apparent why there can be no such general rule, when we consider the grounds for such a liability. Since there are occasions when every vessel will break from her moorings, and since, if she does, she becomes a menace to those about her . . . the owner's duty, as in other similar situations, to provide against resulting injuries is a function of three variables: (1) The probability that she will break away; (2) the gravity of the resulting injury, if she does; (3) the burden of adequate precautions.[8]

Hand expresses his conclusion in mathematical terms in order to demonstrate its applicability to the entire law of tort:

if the probability be called P; the injury, L; and the burden, B; liability depends upon whether B is less than L multiplied by P: i.e., whether B [is less than] PL.[9]

Despite this implicitly economic ("cost-benefit") formulation of the concept of negligence, it does not appear that Hand in his analysis of the case has broken completely from the traditional view of negligence. True, he does note, consistent with the formula, that

Applied to the situation at bar, the likelihood that a barge will break from her fasts and the damage she will do, vary with the place and time; for example, if a storm threatens, the danger is greater; so it is, if she is in a crowded harbor where moored barges are constantly being shifted about.[10].

But after these general observations, there is a marked shift in the style and logic of opinion, which suggests that after all he is more concerned with the traditional questions of "reasonableness" than with the systematic application of his economic formula:

On the other hand, the barge must not be the bargee's prison, even though he lives aboard; he must go ashore at times. We need not say whether, even in such crowded waters as New York Harbor, a bargee must be aboard at night at all.[11]

The concern he expresses is unfounded. The duty imposed is a duty on the owner of the ship and not upon the bargee himself. There is no reason to assume that the owner could employ at most one bargee. The owner could have employed three bargees, each for eight hours, to protect

8 Id. at 173.

9 Ibid. The case for an economic interpretation of the Hand formula, as well as many of the subsidiary rules of negligence liability and damages, is argued in Richard A. Posner, *supra* note 1.

10 159 F.2d at 173.

11 Ibid.

the other ships in the harbor and still insure that his barge would not be a prison for any of his employees.

But having limited himself to a rule requiring only one bargee, Hand proceeds to examine the conduct, not of the owner, but of the bargee and in the traditional manner so often used to decide the "reasonableness" of the defendant's conduct in negligence cases. The evidence showed that the bargee had been off the ship for a period in excess of twenty-one hours before the accident took place. Moreover, all he had to offer to explain his absence was some "fabricated" tale.[12] There was "no excuse for his absence," and it followed:

> In such circumstances we hold—and it is all that we do hold—that it was a fair requirement that the Conners Company should have a bargee aboard (unless he had some excuse for his absence), during the working hours of daylight.[13]

The use of the concept of "excuse" in Hand's formulation of the particular grounds for decision suggests that some of the elements material to determining "blameworthiness" in the moral sense are applicable with full force even after the statement of the general economic formula. But it is unclear what counts for Hand as an appropriate excuse within the framework of the law of tort. If the bargee left the ship in order to attend some emergency within the harbor, then presumably his absence would be "excused," but if so, no concept of excuse need be invoked. The formula itself covers this case because the defendant could show that the costs of prevention were high when measured against the alternative uses of the bargee's time.

Nor are other possible applications of the term clear. Suppose that the bargee was excused as a matter of contract because his employer allowed him to visit his family for the twenty-one hour period of his absence. In these circumstances the bargee could no doubt plead the release as a valid excuse to any action brought by his employer on the contract. But it is doubtful whether the excuse of the bargee would be available to his employer in a separate action in tort brought against him by the injured party. If the employer released the bargee from his job for the day, presumably he would be under an obligation to hire a substitute, for the same reasons that he was under a duty to provide a bargee in the first instance. Finally, if the provision for "excuses" in Hand's opinion is designed to take into account good faith, insanity, mistake of fact and the like, then it serves to introduce into the back door the very problems that were confronted (even if not solved) by the theory of negligence based upon notions of personal blameworthiness. Thus, although Hand alludes to some noneconomic concept of excuse,

[12] Id. at 173–74.
[13] Id. at 174.

both its specific content and its relationship to the economic concept of negligence remain unclear.[14]

But even if the notion of "excuse" is put to one side, Hand's formula is still not free from difficulty. It is difficult to decide how to apply the formula when there is need for but a single precaution which one party is no better suited to take than the other. If, for example, there were two boats in a harbor, and need for but a single bargee, what result is appropriate if the two boats collide when both are unmanned? Is there negligence, or contributory negligence, or both? The formula is silent on the question of *which* ship should be manned. Yet that is the very question which must be answered, since in economic terms no bargee provides too little accident protection while two bargees provide too much.[15] . . .

II. AN ANALYSIS OF CAUSATION

Implicit in the development of the prior arguments is the assumption that the term causation has a content which permits its use in a principled manner to help solve particular cases. In order to make good on these arguments that concept must be explicated and shown to be a suitable basis for the assignment of responsibility. Those two ends can be achieved only if much of the standard rhetoric on causation in negligence cases is first put to one side.

Under the orthodox view of negligence, the question of causation is resolved by a two-step process. The first part of the inquiry concerns the "cause in fact" of the plaintiff's injury. The usual test to determine whether or not the plaintiff's injury was in fact caused by the negligence of the defendant is to ask whether, "but for the negligence of the defendant, the plaintiff would not have been injured." But this complex proposition is not in any sense the semantic equivalent of the assertion that the defendant caused the injury to the plaintiff. The former expression is in counterfactual form and requires an examination of what

14 Indeed, it is precisely the relationship between the economic tests for responsibility and the notion of excuse that troubles Calabresi in his recent article, because a theory of fairness is required to admit "excuses" into a system of liability rules. See Guido Calabresi & A. Douglas Melamed, *supra* note 2, at 1102-05. Moreover, the need to take excuses into account explains why the concept of the "reasonable man" remains part of the law of negligence even after *Carroll Towing.*

15 For a similar treatment of this same problem in the context of the English cases and the doctrine of reasonable foreseeability see Abraham Harari, The Place of Negligence in the Law of Torts (1962). In particular, Harari argues that the law of negligence must develop some set of rules to *coordinate* the activities of several persons to decide which is under a duty to take precautions when each of them as a prudent man could reasonably foresee the prospect of danger. Id. at 105-24. See part III, *infra,* for a discussion of affirmative duties in the law of tort.

would have been the case if things had been otherwise.[16] The second expression simply asks in direct indicative form what in fact *did* happen. The change in mood suggests the difference between the two concepts.

The "but for" test does not provide a satisfactory account of the concept of causation if the words "in fact" are taken seriously. *A* carelessly sets his alarm one hour early. When he wakes up the next morning he has ample time before work and decides to take an early morning drive in the country. While on the road he is spotted by *B*, an old college roommate, who becomes so excited that he runs off the road and hurts *C*. But for the negligence of *A*, *C* would never have been injured, because *B* doubtless would have continued along his uneventful way. Nonetheless, it is common ground that *A*, even if negligent, is in no way responsible for the injury to *C*, caused by *B*.

Its affinity for absurd hypotheticals should suggest that the "but for" test should be abandoned as even a tentative account of the concept of causation. But there has been no such abandonment. Instead it has been argued that the "but for" test provides a "philosophical" test for the concept of causation which shows that the "consequences" of any act (or at least any negligent act) extend indefinitely into the future.[17] But there is no merit, philosophic or otherwise, to an account of any concept which cannot handle the simplest of cases, and only a mistaken view of philosophic inquiry demands an acceptance of an account of causation that conflicts so utterly with ordinary usage.

Once the "philosophical" account of causation was accepted, it could not be applied in legal contexts without modification because of the unacceptable results that it required. The concept of "cause in law" or "proximate" cause [18] became necessary to confine the concept within

---

[16] The expression "things had been otherwise" is used because at this point in the analysis, it is not clear that the negligence in question refers to the doing of things that ought not to be done, or the failure to do those things that should be done, or both. The consequences that flow from the distinction are discussed at length in part III.

[17] "Everybody is now in accord that *logically* there is no escape from the doctrine of the equivalence of conditions, according to which a defendant's conduct must be held to have caused damage if but for that conduct, however remotely connected with it, it would not have occurred: and that everything that ensues from it to the bitter end is its consequences." F. H. Lawson, Negligence in the Civil Law 53 (1950) (emphasis added). "In a philosophical sense, the consequences of an act go forward to eternity, and the causes of an event go back to the discovery of America and beyond." William L. Prosser, Handbook on the Law of Torts 236 (4th ed. 1971).

[18] The term proximate cause comes from one of Bacon's maxims. "In jure non remota causa sed proxima spectatur." (In law not the remote but only the proximate cause is looked to.) In many discussions, however, the term "legal" cause is used in the hope that it will be less misleading than "proximate cause." See Robert E. Keeton, Legal Cause in the Law of Tort, viii (1963). But the use of the term "legal" serves to establish a false opposition between its technical and its ordinary use, which again hampers the development of a theory that is both intuitively sensible and technically sound.

acceptable limits.[19] In the earlier literature there was an attempt to work out in great detail specifications of the kinds of events and acts which would serve to break the causal connection between the conduct of the defendant and the harm suffered by the plaintiff.* That inquiry is indeed a necessary one in some cases, although it need not be tied to the concept of "but for" causation. In recent years, the inquiry has been continued and refined by Hart and Honoré in their classic work, *Causation in the Law*.[20] Hart and Honoré do not accept the "but for" account of causation, but instead define causation in a manner which recognizes the kinds of intervening acts and events that are to be taken into account before it can be shown that the conduct of the defendant was the cause of the plaintiff's harm; thus they argue that "an act is the cause of harm if it is an intervention in the course of affairs which is sufficient to produce the harm without the cooperation of the voluntary acts of others or abnormal conjunctions of events." [21] This definition, and its careful explication, however, have been rejected for the most part in the legal literature on the ground that they require courts to confront "the never-ending and insoluble problems of causation," [22] "together with the subtleties of *novus actus interveniens.*" [23] In its stead, the question of proximate cause has been said to reduce itself to the question whether the conduct of the defendant is a "substantial factor" [24] contributing to the loss of the plaintiff, or whether the harm suffered was "reasonably foreseeable." [25] But these formulations of the test of proximate cause do

[19] In a separate but related development, the concept of "duty of care" was in the alternative invoked to limit the concept of "but for" causation. See *Palsgraf* v. *Long Is. R.R.* 248 N.Y. 339, 162 N.E. 99 (1928). "The nightmare of unlimited liability [on causal grounds] possessed most judges and most legal writers. To meet this doctrinal crisis the *duty* concept has been developed and where accepted has greatly cleared the jungle of negligence law." Leon Green, Foreseeability in Negligence Law, 61 Colum. L. Rev. 1401, 1408 (1961). Although the reason for the introduction of the concept is clear, its place in the tort law is not, once "but for" is abandoned as an account of causation.

* Original footnote omitted.—Ed.

[20] H. L. A. Hart & A. M. Honoré, Causation in the Law (1959).

[21] Id. at 426.

[22] *Overseas Tankship (U.K.) Ltd.* v. *Morts Dock & Engineering Co. Ltd.* (The Wagon Mound), [1961] A. C. 388, 423 (N.S.W.).

[23] Glanville Williams, The Risk Principle, 77 L.Q. Rev. 179 (1961).

[24] Restatement of Torts 2d § 431, § 433, § 435 (1965); Clarence Morris, Studies in the Law of Torts 256–57 (1952).

[25] "Prima facie at least, the reasons for creating liability should limit it." Warren A. Seavey, Mr. Justice Cardozo and the Law of Torts, 52 Harv. L. Rev. 372, 386; 48 Yale L.J. 390, 404; 39 Colum. L. Rev. 20, 34 (1939). If negligence is accepted as a necessary precondition for liability in torts, then the argument has some appeal, because the defendant is regarded as negligent only if he has created a "reasonably foreseeable" risk of harm to another. Those who favored "directness" as the test for remoteness of damages within a negligence framework have always had to concede that reasonable foresight was the test for liability.

not give much guidance for the solution of particular cases.[26] One might think that this would be treated as a defect in an account of a concept like causation, but in large measure it has been thought to be its strength. Once it is decided that there is no hard content to the term causation, the courts are free to decide particular lawsuits in accordance with the principles of "social policy" under the guise of the proximate-cause doctrine.

But it is false to argue that systems of law that use the principles of causation to decide cases must stand in opposition to those systems that use principles of social policy to achieve that same end. As Hart and Honoré have pointed out, the major premise of most legal systems (until perhaps the recent past) is that causation provides, *as a matter of policy,* the reason to decide cases in one way rather than the other.[27] Moreover, they properly observe that:

> It is fatally easy and has become increasingly common to make the transition from the exhilarating discovery that complex words like 'cause' cannot be simply defined and have no 'one true meaning' to the mistaken conclusion that they have no meaning worth bothering about at all, but are used as a mere disguise for arbitrary decision or judicial policy. This is blinding error, and legal language and reasoning will never develop while it persists.[28]

But for all their force these remarks have not received general acceptance. . . .

The presence or absence of reasonable anticipation of damage determines the legal quality of the act as negligent or innocent. If it be thus determined to be negligent, then the question whether particular damages are recoverable depends only on the answer to the question whether they are the direct consequence of the act.
In re Polemis, [1921] 3 K.B. 560, 574 (C.A.). But once negligence is rejected as the basis for civil liability in tort, the argument of symmetry works in the opposite direction. If foresight (and negligence) are no longer treated as material on the question of liability, then they should be immaterial on the question of remoteness of damage. There is no need to worry about endless liability because "but for" is never used as the test of causation, as it is in the conventional negligence analysis. Robert E. Keeton, *supra* note 18 at viii (1963).

[26] Under the foresight test the distinction between the "general kind" of damages and "its precise details," becomes crucial. See Glanville Williams, *supra* note 32, at 183-85. But the application of that distinction presupposes that we have already selected the *description* of the events in question to which that distinction is applied. But without a standard means to select the unique description, it cannot be determined whether the unforeseeable aspects of the case fall on one side of the line or the others. This is the dilemma: Foresight is not psychologically irrelevant to the solution to problems of remoteness and often affects the judgment of those who try them. Yet foresight cannot function as a test until the facts of the case are described, and since the facts are nearly always susceptible of differing descriptions which will vary the result, a foresight criterion cannot function in a true testing process. Clarence Morris, *supra* note 24, at 260.

[27] H. L. A. Hart & A. M. Honoré, *supra* note 20, at 58-64.
[28] Id. at 3.

. . . The pages that follow are designed to show that the concept of causation, as it applies to cases of physical injury, can be analyzed in a manner that both renders it internally coherent and relevant to the ultimate question who shall bear the loss.

There will be no attempt to give a single semantic equivalent to the concept of causation. Instead, the paper will consider in succession each of four distinct paradigm cases covered by the proposition "*A* caused *B* harm." These paradigms are not the only way in which we can talk about torts cases. They do, however, provide modes of description which best capture the ordinary use of causal language. Briefly put, they are based upon notions of force, fright, compulsion and dangerous conditions. The first of them will be the simplest to analyze. Each of the subsequent paradigms will introduce further problems to be resolved before the judgment on the causal issue can be made. Nonetheless, despite the internal differences, it can, I believe, be demonstrated that each of these paradigms, when understood, exhibits the features that render it relevant to the question of legal responsibility. . . .*

III. THE PROBLEM OF THE GOOD SAMARITAN

The first two portions of this paper have compared the common law rules of negligence with those of strict liability in cases where the defendant has harmed the plaintiff's person or property. If that analysis is sound, then the rules of liability should be based upon the harm in fact caused and not upon any subsequent determination of the reasonableness of the defendant's conduct. The question of liability is thereby severed from both general cost-benefit analysis of the defendant's conduct and a moral examination of his individual worth. In the cases of affirmative action, the rules of strict liability avoid both the unfairness and

---

* I have deleted Epstein's lengthy discussion of his four paradigm cases of causation. In the second article in his three-part series on strict liability, "Defenses and Subsequent Pleas in a System of Strict Liability," *Journal of Legal Studies* 3 (1974): 168, he summarizes this discussion as follows: "In an attempt to dispel some of the confusion that surrounds the use of causal notions, I then isolated the four most common causal paradigms used in both ordinary speech and legal analysis. The first of these rests on the simple notion of the use of force and is captured in the proposition, *A* hit *B*, with its simple transitive structure. The second paradigm, *A* frightened *B*, has much the same grammatical structure as the first, but requires us to take into account *B*'s response to *A*'s actions in order to complete the causal chain. The third paradigm, *A* made *B* hit *C*, states a connection between *A* and *C* only through the acts of *B* which *A* compelled, and thus requires us to take into account the behavior of a third party. The last of these paradigms, *A* created a dangerous condition that resulted in *B*'s harm, demands a detailed analysis of, first, the kinds of conditions that should be regarded as dangerous, and, second, the impact of the actions or events that intervene between *A*'s conduct and *B*'s harm. For all of their internal differences, each of these paradigms reveals a domination of *A*, the author of the action, over *B*, its object, that prima facie calls for redress by the law of torts."—ED.

complications created when negligence, in either its economic or moral sense, is accepted as the basis of the tort law.

The purpose of this section is to show that these conclusions are capable of extension to areas in which the law has traditionally not allowed recovery. The theories of strict liability explain and justify, as the rules of reasonableness cannot, the common law's refusal to extend liability in tort to cases where the defendant has not harmed the plaintiff by his affirmative action.[29] The problem arises in its starkest form in the case of the good Samaritan. *A* finds himself in a perilous situation which was not created by *B,* as when *A* is overwhelmed by cramps while swimming alone in a surging sea. *B,* moreover, is in a position where he could, without any danger of injury to himself, come to *A*'s assistance with some simple and well-nigh costless steps, such as throwing a rope to the plaintiff. The traditional common law position has been that there is no cause of action against *B* solely because *B,* in effect, permitted *A* to drown.

It is important to note the manner in which such cases should be decided under a negligence system. In the verbal formulation of the law of negligence, little attention is paid to the distinction between those cases in which the defendant acted and those cases in which he did not act, failed to act, or omitted to act. "Negligence is the *omission* to do something which a reasonable man guided upon those considerations which ordinarily regulate the conduct of human affairs, would do, or doing something which a prudent and reasonable man would not do." [30] The distinction between acts and omissions is of no consequence to the economic analysis of negligence contained in cases like *Carroll Towing,* for there the emphasis is placed in part upon those precautions which a defendant should have taken (but did not take) in order to prevent those instrumentalities which he owns (here the boat in the harbor) from causing harm to other persons.

Thus, if one considers the low costs of prevention to *B* of rescuing *A,* and the serious, if not deadly, harm that *A* will suffer if *B* chooses not to rescue him, there is no reason why the *Carroll Towing* formula or the general rules of negligence should not require, under pain of liability, the defendant to come to the aid of the plaintiff. Nonetheless, the good Samaritan problem receives special treatment even under the modern law of torts. The reasons for the special position of this problem are clear once the theories of strict liability are systematically applied. Under these rules, the act requirement has to be satisfied in order to show that the defendant in a given lawsuit caused harm to the plaintiff. Once that is done, the private predicament of the defendant, his ability

---

[29] I put aside here all those cases in which there are special relationships between the plaintiff and the defendants: parent and child, invitor and invitee, and the like.

[30] *Blyth* v. *Birmingham Waterworks,* 11 Exch. 781, 784, 156 Eng. Rep. 1047, 1049 (1856) (emphasis added).

to take precautions against the given risk, and the general economic rationality of his conduct are all beside the point.[31] Only the issue of causation, of what *the defendant did,* is material to the statement of the prima facie case. The theory is not utilitarian.[32] It looks not to the consequences of alternate courses of conduct but to what was done. When that theory with its justification is applied to the problem of the good Samaritan, it follows in the case just put that *A* should not be able to recover from *B* for his injuries. No matter how the facts are manipulated, it is not possible to argue that *B* caused *A* harm in any of the senses of causation which were developed in the earlier portions of this article when he failed to render assistance to *A* in his time of need. In typical negligence cases, all the talk of avoidance and reasonable care may shift attention from the causation requirement, which the general "but for" test distorts beyond recognition. But its importance is revealed by its absence in the good Samaritan cases where the presence of all those elements immaterial to tortious liability cannot, even in combination, persuade judges who accept the negligence theory to apply it in the decisive case. . . .

The common law position on the good Samaritan question does not appeal to our highest sense of benevolence and charity, and it is not at all surprising that there have been many proposals for its alteration or abolition. Let us here examine but one of these proposals. After concluding that the then (1908) current position of the law led to intolerable results, James Barr Ames argued that the appropriate rule should be that:

> One who fails to interfere to save another from impending death or great bodily harm, when he might do so with little or no inconvenience to himself, and the death or great bodily harm follows as a consequence of his inaction, shall be punished criminally and shall make compensation to the party injured or to his widow and children in case of death.[33]

---

31 Whatever the historical motivation behind the rule, its validity does not rest on the assumption that "the individual [is] competent to protect himself if not interfered with from without." Francis H. Bohlen, Studies in the Law of Torts 295 (1926). If that were the basis of the rule, it could not apply to infants or lunatics about whom the assumption of "competence" has never been made.

32 But see James Barr Ames, Law and Morals, *supra* note 4, at 110: "The law is utilitarian. It exists for the realization of the reasonable needs of the community. If the interest of an individual runs counter to this chief object of the law, it must be sacrificed."

33 James Barr Ames, *supra* note 4, at 113. See also Wallace M. Rudolph, The Duty to Act: A Proposed Rule, 44 Neb. L. Rev. 499 (1965), for a more complicated rule which states:

A person has a duty to act whenever:

1. The harm or loss is imminent and there is apparently no other practical alternative to avoid the threatened harm or loss except his own action;

2. Failure to act would result in substantial harm or damage to another person

Even this solution, however, does not satisfy the *Carroll Towing* formula. The general use of the cost-benefit analysis required under the economic interpretation of negligence does not permit a person to act on the assumption that he may as of right attach special weight and importance to his own welfare. Under Ames' good Samaritan rule, a defendant in cases of affirmative acts would be required to take only those steps that can be done "with little or no inconvenience." But if the distinction between causing harm and not preventing harm is to be disregarded, why should the difference in standards between the two cases survive the reform of the law? The only explanation is that the two situations are regarded at bottom as raising totally different issues, even for those who insist upon the immateriality of this distinction. Even those who argue, as Ames does, that the law is utilitarian must in the end find some special place for the claims of egoism which are an inseparable byproduct of the belief that individual autonomy—individual liberty—is a good in itself not explainable in terms of its purported social worth. It is one thing to *allow* people to act as they please in the belief that the "invisible hand" will provide the happy congruence of the individual and the social good. Such a theory, however, at bottom must regard individual autonomy as but a means to some social end. It takes a great deal more to assert that men are *entitled* to act as they choose (within the limits of strict liability) even though it is certain that there will be cases where individual welfare will be in conflict with the social good.[34] Only then is it clear that even freedom has its costs: costs revealed in the acceptance of the good Samaritan doctrine.

But are the alternatives more attractive? Once one decides that as a matter of statutory or common law duty, an individual is required under some circumstances to act at his own cost for the exclusive benefit of another, then it is very hard to set out in a principled manner the limits of social interference with individual liberty. Suppose one claims, as Ames does, that his proposed rule applies only in the "obvious" cases

---

    or his property and the effort, risk, or cost of acting is disproportionately less than the harm or damage avoided; and

    3. The circumstances placing the person in a position to act are purely fortuitous.

Id. at 509. The first and second conditions are open to the same sorts of objections as Ames' rule, but the third seeks to limit the scope of its application. Nonetheless, its effect does not appear to be too great, for Rudolph says: "Thus though condition three protects the classic rich from being obligated to the classic poor, it does allow, under limited circumstances, a person of means who is temporarily without funds to require someone else to lend him money, if the resources to be saved by lending the money exceed substantially the risk of losing the money." Id. at 510. See p. 131, *infra,* for a discussion of forced exchanges.

    34 "Each person possesses an inviolability founded on justice that even the welfare of society as a whole cannot override. For this reason justice denies that the loss of freedom for some is made right by a greater good shared by others. It does not allow that the sacrifices imposed on a few are outweighed by the larger sum of advantages enjoyed by many." John Rawls, A Theory of Justice 3-4 (1971).

where everyone (or almost everyone) would admit that the duty was appropriate: to the case of the man upon the bridge who refuses to throw a rope to a stranger drowning in the waters below. Even if the rule starts out with such modest ambitions, it is difficult to confine it to those limits. Take a simple case first. X as a representative of a private charity asks you for $10 in order to save the life of some starving child in a country ravaged by war. There are other donors available but the number of needy children exceeds that number. The money means "nothing" to you. Are you under a legal obligation to give the $10? Or to lend it interest-free? Does $10 amount to a substantial cost or inconvenience within the meaning of Ames' rule? It is true that the relationship between the gift to charity and the survival of an unidentified child is not so apparent as is the relationship between the man upon the bridge and the swimmer caught in the swirling seas. But lest the physical imagery govern, it is clear in both cases that someone will die as a consequence of your inaction in both cases. Is there a duty to give, or is the contribution a matter of charity?

Consider yet another example where services, not cash, are in issue. Ames insists that his rule would not require the only surgeon in India capable of saving the life of a person with a given affliction to travel across the subcontinent to perform an operation, presumably because the inconvenience and cost would be substantial.[35] But how would he treat the case if some third person were willing to pay him for all of his efforts? If the payment is sufficient to induce the surgeon to act, then there is no need for the good Samaritan doctrine at all. But if it is not, then it is again necessary to compare the costs of the physician with the benefits to his prospective patient. It is hard to know whether Ames would require the forced exchange under these circumstances. But it is at least arguable that under his theory forced exchanges should be required, since the payment might reduce the surgeon's net inconvenience to the point where it was trivial.

Once forced exchanges, regardless of the levels of payment, are accepted, it will no longer be possible to delineate the sphere of activities in which contracts (or charity) will be required in order to procure desired benefits and the sphere of activity in which those benefits can be procured as of right. Where tests of "reasonableness"—stated with such confidence, and applied with such difficulty—dominate the law of tort, it becomes impossible to tell where liberty ends and obligation begins; where contract ends, and tort begins. In each case, it will be possible for some judge or jury to decide that there was something else which the defendant should have done, and he will decide that on the strength of some cost-benefit formula that is difficult indeed to apply. These remarks are conclusive, I think, against the adoption of Ames' rule by judicial

---

[35] For an extended discussion of the duties of a professional physician see Wallace M. Rudolph, *supra* note 33, at 512–19, whose proposed rule indeed requires a high standard of conduct.

innovation, and they bear heavily on the desirability of the abandonment of the good Samaritan rule by legislation as well. It is not surprising that the law has, in the midst of all the clamor for reform, remained unmoved in the end, given the inability to form alternatives to the current position.[36]

But the defense of the common law rule on the good Samaritan does not rest solely upon a criticism of its alternatives. Strong arguments can be advanced to show that the common law position on the good Samaritan problem is in the end consistent with both moral and economic principles.

The history of Western ethics has been marked by the development of two lines of belief. One line of moral thought emphasizes the importance of freedom of the will. It is the intention (or motive) that determines the worth of the act; and no act can be moral unless it is performed free from external compulsion.[37] Hence the expansion of the scope of positive law could only reduce the moral worth of human action. Even if positive law could insure conformity to the appropriate external standards of conduct, it, like other forms of external constraints, destroys the moral worth of the act. Hence the elimination of the positive law becomes a minimum condition for moral conduct, even if it means that persons entitled to benefits (in accordance with some theory of entitlements respected but not enforced) will not receive them if their fellow men are immoral.

On the other hand there are those theories that concern themselves not with the freedom of the will, but with the external effects of individual behavior. There is no room for error, because each act which does not further the stated goals (usually, of the maximization of welfare) is in terms of these theories a bad act. Thus a system of laws must either require the individual to act, regardless of motive, in the socially desired manner, or create incentives for him to so behave. Acceptance of this kind of theory has as its corollary the acceptance, if necessary, of an elaborate system of legal rules to insure compliance with the stated goals of maximization even if individual liberty (which now only counts as a kind of satisfaction) is sacrificed in the effort.

At a common sense level, neither of these views is accepted in its pure form. The strength of each theory lays bare the weaknesses of the other. Preoccupation with the moral freedom of a given actor ignores the effects of his conduct upon other persons. Undue emphasis upon the

---

[36] "Such decisions are revolting to any moral sense. They have been denounced with vigor by legal writers. Thus far the difficulties of setting any standards of unselfish service to fellow men, and of making any workable rule to cover possible situations where fifty people might fail to rescue one, has limited any tendency to depart from the rule to cases where some special relation between the parties has afforded a justification for the creation of a duty, without any question of setting up a rule of universal application." William L. Prosser, *supra* note 25, at 341 (3d ed.).

[37] See, e.g., James Street Fulton, The Free Person and Legal Authority, in Responsibility in Law and in Morals 1–11 (Arthur L. Harding ed. 1960).

conformity to external standards of behavior entails a loss of liberty. Hence, most systems of conventional morality try to distinguish between those circumstances in which a person should be compelled to act for the benefit of his fellow man, and those cases where he should be allowed to do so only if prompted by the appropriate motives. To put the point in other terms, the distinction is taken between that conduct which is required and that which, so to speak, is beyond the call of duty. If that distinction is accepted as part of a common morality, then the argument in favor of the good Samaritan rule is that it, better than any possible alternatives, serves to mark off the first class of activities from the second. Compensation for harm caused can be demanded in accordance with the principles of strict liability. Failure to aid those in need can invoke at most moral censure on the ground that the person so accused did not voluntarily conform his conduct to some "universal" principle of justice. The rules of causation, which create liability in the first case, deny it in the second. It may well be that the conduct of individuals who do not aid fellow men is under some circumstances outrageous, but it does not follow that a legal system that does not enforce a duty to aid is outrageous as well.

The defense of the good Samaritan rule in economic terms takes the same qualified form. The cost-benefit analysis has in recent literature been regarded as the best means for the solution of all problems of social organization in those cases where market transactions are infeasible. On that view, the basic principles of economics become a most powerful instrument for the achievement of social justice. But there is another strand of economic thought—more skeptical in its conclusions—which emphasizes the limitations of economic theory for the solution of legal problems.

Most economics textbooks accept that the premises of economic theory do not permit so-called interpersonal comparisons of utility. Thus Kenneth Arrow states: "The viewpoint will be taken here that interpersonal comparison of utilities has no meaning and, in fact, that there is no meaning relevant to welfare comparisons in the measurability of individual utility." [38] In effect, all attempts to compare costs and benefits between different persons require in the end some noneconomic assumption to measure trade-offs in utility between them. Where no noneconomic assumptions are made, it follows that, in strict theory, an economist can make utility comparisons between alternative social arrangements only under a very restricted set of conditions. One social arrangement can be pronounced superior to a second alternative only if (1) it can be shown that everybody is at least as well off under the first alternative as he is under the second, and (2) at least one person is better off under the first system than he is under the second. If these conditions are respected, then no strictly economic judgment can be made between alternative social states where one person under the allegedly preferred state is worse off than he is under the next best alternative. Yet it is

[38] Kenneth Arrow, Social Choice and Individual Values 9 (2d ed. 1963).

precisely that kind of situation that is involved whenever there is a legal dispute. In economic terms, the resolution of every dispute requires a trade-off between the parties, for no one has yet found a way in which both parties could win a lawsuit. In order to decide the case of the good Samaritan, therefore, we must make the very kind of interpersonal comparisons of utility which economic theory cannot make in its own terms.

There is one possible escape from this problem. It could be argued that the defendant should be held liable because if the parties had the opportunity to contract between themselves, they doubtless would have agreed that the defendant should assume the obligation to save the plaintiff in his time of distress. Thus one could argue that (in the absence of externalities) an agreement between two persons can only have favorable welfare effects since each person will be better off on account of the voluntary exchange. On this view the function of the law of tort is to anticipate those contractual arrangements which parties would have made had the transactions costs been low enough to permit direct negotiations.

This position, however, is subject to objections. The courts have struggled for years to determine the content of incomplete and ambiguous contracts which were actually negotiated by the parties. There at least they could look to, among other things, the language of the relevant documents, the custom of the trade, and the history of the prior negotiations. In the good Samaritan context, there are no documents, no customs, and no prior negotiations. The courts have only the observation that the parties would have contracted to advance their mutual interests. Given the infinite variation in terms (what price? what services?) that we could expect to find in such contracts, it is difficult to believe that that theoretical observation could enable us to determine or even approximate any bargain which the parties might have made if circumstances had permitted. It is for good reason that the courts have always refused to make contracts for the parties.

But there is a further point. We are concerned with the enforcement of a contract by private action when one of the parties objects to its performance. It no longer seems possible to argue that both parties are better off on account of the contract since one party has indicated his desire to repudiate it. Even though the theory of the underlying action is shifted from tort to some extended form of contract, the difficulties raised by the rule that forbids interpersonal comparison of utilities still remain. At the time of the enforcement, one party argues not for an *exchange* which makes both parties better off but for a *transfer* of wealth which makes him better off. Again we must find some way—some theory of fairness—which can explain which of them is to be made better off. Welfare economics cannot provide the answer because it cannot accommodate the trade-offs which are part and parcel of legal decisions.

Even after these arguments are made many people will be concerned with the social costs of a system of rules which does not purport to have an economic base. But in a social sense it should be clear that people will act in a manner to minimize their losses, regardless of the legal rules adopted. Once people know that others are not obliged to assist them in their time of peril, they will on their own take steps to keep from being placed in a position where they will need assistance where none may be had. These precautions may not eliminate losses in the individual case, but they should reduce the number of cases in which such losses should occur.

In addition, the incentive effects created by the absence of a good Samaritan rule must be examined in the context of other rules of substantive law. Thus it is critical to ask about the incentives which are created by rules which permit a rescuer to bring an action against the person he saved on quasi-contractual theories. It is also important to ask what modifications of behavior could be expected if the scope of this kind of action were expanded, and important, too, to know about the possible effects of systems of public honors and awards for good Samaritans. None of these arguments is designed to show that the common law approach can be justified on economic grounds, but they do show how perilous it is to attempt to justify legal rules by the incentives that they create.

The same kinds of observations apply to the maxim that a tortfeasor must take his victim as he finds him. It is true that the rule reduces the plaintiff's incentives to take care of himself even where he is able to do so efficiently. But it is a mistake to think that any legal rule on this question can create strong incentives. Indeed, it seems far more likely that few plaintiffs will be prepared to take unnecessary risks of personal injury even if they know that they will be able to recover in full for the injuries from a defendant who caused them. Damages in tort still do not permit a plaintiff to make a profit; and in some cases it is arguable that they do not permit recovery of adequate compensation. Some men may be moved to guide their conduct by general statements of substantive law, but in most cases any incentives created by the selection of one legal rule in preference to another will be masked by the fear of injury which is shared by defendants and plaintiffs alike.

But it is a mistake to dwell too long upon questions of cost, for they should not be decisive in the analysis of the individual cases. Instead it is better to see the law of torts in terms of what might be called its political function. The arguments made here suggest that the first task of the law of torts is to define the boundaries of individual liberty. To this question the rules of strict liability based upon the twin notions of causation and volition provide a better answer than the alternative theories based upon the notion of negligence, whether explicated in moral or economic terms. In effect, the principles of strict liability say that the liberty of one person ends when he causes harm to another. Until that point he is free to act as he chooses, and need not take into account the welfare of others.

But the law of tort does not end with the recognition of individual liberty. Once a man causes harm to another, he has brought himself within the boundaries of the law of tort. It does not follow, however, that he will be held liable in each and every case in which it can be showed that he caused harm, for it may still be possible for him to escape liability, not by an insistence upon his freedom of action, but upon a specific showing that his conduct was either excused or justified. Thus far in this paper we have only made occasional and unsystematic references to the problems raised by both pleas of excuses and justification. Their systematic explication remains crucial to the further development of the law of tort. That task, however, is large enough to deserve special attention of its own.

THE MARXIST CONCEPTION OF VIOLENCE

JOHN HARRIS

The idea that if we are able to change things, to elect not to do so is also to determine what will happen in the world, is very old indeed. For obvious reasons, the idea is only employed when the things that happen are of some significance. The importance of the idea and its history stem from those cases where harm occurs which might have been averted or in which harm will occur unless it is averted. In such cases, many men have found it natural not only to blame those who could have prevented the harm, but did not do so, but also to think of such men as having brought the harm about, as being its cause.

I do not know when this idea first occurred. Plutarch makes use of it; John Bromyard, a fourteenth-century Chancellor of Cambridge, gives it most eloquent expression; and it is, of course, one of the main themes of Shakespeare's *Measure for Measure*. In modern times it has been associated most strongly with Marx, Engels, and Marxist thinkers. In their hands it has been used as a weapon in the controversy about "violence." Marxists have argued that deaths caused by the indifference and neglect of society or its rulers must be seen as being as much a part of human violence as the violent acts of revolutionaries.

In this paper I will defend two theses. The first is the idea that men are causally responsible for harm they could have prevented. The second is the view that such harm may properly be regarded as a form of violence. It is characteristic of those I shall loosely call "Marxists" to combine both theses. I shall therefore, for convenience, call this combined view "the Marxist conception of violence." This loose use of the

From *Philosophy and Public Affairs* **3** (1974): 192-220. Copyright 1974 by Princeton University Press. Reprinted by permission of Princeton University Press.

term "Marxist" is, I think, justified on the grounds that the ideas with which I here associate it are to be found in the writings of both Marx and Engels, and because such ideas are characteristic of thinkers who either consider themselves to be, in some broad sense, followers of Marx, or who are called "Marxists" by their opponents.

In Part I of this essay I shall give a number of examples of the Marxist conception of violence. I have chosen so many examples for three reasons: for their intrinsic interest, because they illustrate both the force and the character of the Marxist view, and finally because their number and variety help to defend the view from the charge that it violates ordinary usage or "turns the language upside down." Part II is devoted to a defense of the first thesis, and Part III to a defense of the second.

I

What I call "the Marxist conception of violence" is probably as old as any thinking on responsibility. Plutarch, for example, makes the point that a man who fails to protect another from a death he was able to prevent, is just as guilty of that man's death as if he had wielded the sword himself. Talking of the revenge of the Triumvirs in his life of Mark Antony, Plutarch states: "At the end of all this bartering of one death for another, they [the Triumvirs] were just as guilty of the deaths of those whom they abandoned as of those whom they seized." [1]

In his guide for preachers, John Bromyard imagines the last judgment:

> On the left, before the supreme Judge's throne stand "the harsh lords, who plundered the people of God with grievous fines, amercements and exactions, . . . the wicked ecclesiastics, who failed to nourish the poor with the goods of Christ . . . as they should have done. . . . Then the oppressed bring a fearful indictment against their oppressors. . . ." We hungered and thirsted and were afflicted with cold and nakedness. And those robbers yonder gave not our own goods to us when we were in want, neither did they feed and clothe us out of them. But their hounds and horses and apes, the rich, the powerful, the abounding, the gluttons, the drunkards and their prostitutes they fed and clothed with them, and allowed us to languish in want. . . .
>
> "O just God, mighty judge, the game was not fairly divided between them and us. Their satiety was our famine; their merriment was our wretchedness; their jousts and tournaments were our torments. . . . Their feasts, delectations, pomps, vanities, excesses and superfluities were our fastings, penalties, wants, calamities and spoilation. The love-ditties and

[1] Plutarch, *Life of Mark Antony*, trans. Ian Scott-Kilvert (Harmondsworth, 1965), p. 287.

laughter of their dances were our mockery, our groanings and remonstra-
tions. They used to sing—'well enough! well enough!'—and we groaned,
saying—'Woe to us! Woe to us!' . . ." [2]

The most compelling and coherent statement of the Marxist view
occurs in Engels's book *The Condition of the Working Class in England*.
It is worth quoting at some length:

> If one individual inflicts a bodily injury upon another which leads to the
> death of the person attacked we call it manslaughter; on the other hand,
> if the attacker knows beforehand that the blow will be fatal we call it
> murder. Murder has also been committed if society places hundreds of
> workers in such a position that they inevitably come to premature and
> unnatural ends. Their death is as violent as if they had been stabbed or
> shot. Murder has been committed if thousands of workers have been de-
> prived of the necessities of life or if they have been forced into a situation
> in which it is impossible for them to survive. Murder has been committed
> if the workers have been forced by the strong arm of the law to go on
> living under such conditions until death inevitably releases them. Murder
> has been committed if society knows perfectly well that thousands of
> workers cannot avoid being sacrificed so long as these conditions are al-
> lowed to continue. Murder of this sort is just as culpable as the murder
> committed by an individual. But if society murders a worker it is a
> treacherous stab in the back against which a worker cannot defend him-
> self. At first sight it does not appear to be murder at all because respon-
> sibility for the death of the victim cannot be pinned on any individual
> assailant. Everyone is responsible and yet no one is responsible, because
> it appears as if the victim has died from natural causes. If a worker dies
> no one places the responsibility for his death on society, though some
> would realise that society has failed to take steps to prevent the victim
> from dying. But it is murder all the same.[3]

Christopher Caudwell, writing in 1938, makes use of a similar
analysis of social relations:

> Thus, just as much as in slave-owning society, bourgeois society turns out
> to be a society built on violent coercion of men by men, the more violent
> in that while the master must feed and protect his slave, whether he works
> or not, the bourgeois employer owes no obligation to the free labourer.[4]

Caudwell concludes, in agreement with Engels, that the absence of
an individual assailant cannot affect responsibility.

The fact that one participates passively in bourgeois economy, that one

---

[2] Quoted in Norman Cohn, *The Pursuit of the Millennium* (London, 1957; repr.
1970), p. 202.

[3] Frederick Engels, *The Condition of the Working Class in England*, trans. and
ed. Henderson and Chaloner (Oxford, 1958), p. 108.

[4] Christopher Caudwell, *Studies in a Dying Culture* (London, 1938), p. 102.

does not oneself wield the bludgeon or fire the cannon, so far from being a defence really makes one's position more disgusting. . . .[5]

Ten years later Harold Orlans summed up his experience of conditions in an American mental hospital, in which he had worked as a conscientious objector during the Second World War, as follows:

It is in the murder by neglect of decrepit old men that I believe the closest analogy is to be found with the death camp murders. The asylum murders are passive; the Auschwitz murders active . . . but otherwise their logic is the same.[6]

Barrington Moore, Jr., warned that the death toll of the French revolutionary terror must be seen as a response to "the prevailing social order," which "always grinds out its toll of unnecessary death year after year." "It would be enlightening," Moore continues, "to calculate the death rate of the *ancien régime* from such factors as preventable starvation and injustice." Moore's point is that "to dwell on the horrors of revolutionary violence while forgetting that of 'normal' times is merely partisan hypocrisy." [7]

Marx himself gives repeated examples of the injury, shame, degradation, and death suffered every day by the working class and directly caused by the capitalist economy. In the chapter entitled "Machinery and Modern Industry" in volume I of *Capital* [8] he spends most of his time pointing out the "antagonistic and murderous side" of modern manufacture. "One of the most shameful, the most dirty, and the worst paid kinds of labour" is that of the rag-sorters who "are the medium for the spread of small-pox and other infectious diseases and are themselves the first victims." We learn that "it is impossible for a child to pass through the purgatory of a tile field without great moral degradation." We are shown how the increase in the incidence of consumption among lace makers rose from one in forty-five in 1852 to one in eight in 1860, and that the "fearful increase in death from starvation during the last ten years in London runs parallel with the extension of machine-sewing." "In one scutching mill at Kildinan, near Cork," we are told, "there occurred between 1852 and 1856, six fatal accidents and sixty mutilations; every one of which might have been prevented by the simplest appliances, at the cost of a few shillings." These mutilations "are of the most fearful nature. In many cases a quarter of the body is torn from the trunk, and either involves death, or a future of wretched incapacity and suffering."

5 Ibid., p. 116.

6 Harold Orlans, "An American Death Camp," in Rosenberg, Gerver, and Howton, eds., *Mass Society in Crisis: Social Problems and Social Pathology* (New York, 1964).

7 Barrington Moore, Jr., *The Social Origins of Dictatorship and Democracy* (Boston, 1966; repr. 1969), p. 103.

8 Karl Marx, *Capital* I, ed. Engels, trans. Moore and Aveling (London, 1887; repr. 1957), chap. xv, sec. 8.c., pp. 466ff.

Marx's emphasis is on the harm caused to human beings by their being forced to work in injurious conditions and by the failure of the employers or society generally to prevent suffering and death that could easily and at little cost be prevented. Whenever harm comes to workers in any way connected with their employment or the conditions of their lives that their work or lack of work forces upon them, the employers and society at large treat the harm as a natural calamity about which it is impossible to do anything. Marx believes that where human intervention could prevent this harm, then failure to prevent the harm must be seen as a cause:

> Wherever there is a working day without restriction as to length, wherever there is night work and unrestricted waste of human life, there the slight-est obstacle presented by the nature of the work to a change for the better is soon looked upon as an everlasting barrier erected by Nature. No poison kills vermin with more certainty than the Factory Act removes such everlasting barriers. No one made a greater outcry over "impossi-bilities" than our friends the earthenware manufacturers. In 1864 how-ever they were brought under the Act, and within sixteen months every "impossibility" had vanished.[9]

Finally, I should like to cite the brief statement of an anonymous witness to a contemporary tragedy. Michael Elkins, broadcasting from Jerusalem for B.B.C. Radio News, reported that an eyewitness to the suicide squad massacre at Jerusalem airport said: "Don't tell me any-one searched the suitcases of those men—whoever let those men on the plane is also guilty of murder." I do not, of course, know whether this witness was a Marxist, even of any kind.

The Marxists emphasize both that the "normal" conditions of society are vicious and injurious and that responsibility rests as much with those who allow such states of affairs to continue as with those who brought them about. It will be obvious that all these examples depend at some point on recognition of the causal efficacy of omissions: workers are murdered because conditions in which they cannot survive are "allowed to continue," one "participates passively" in violent coercion, decrepit old man are murdered "by neglect," the *ancien régime* has a high death rate because of "preventable starvation and injustice," death and mutilation "might have been prevented by the simplest appliances at the cost of a few shillings." I shall next concentrate on the problem of how far we are causally responsible for harm we could have prevented, for if the Marxist claims about causal responsibility for such harm can be made out, then not only does their conception of violence move from rhetoric towards reality (because, of course, one of the essential elements of acts of violence is that there should be an agent), but a radical revision of our views about responsibility becomes imperative.

[9] Ibid., p. 480.

II

Jeremy Bentham called omissions which have consequences "negative actions," presumably because, like Engels, he was impressed by the fact that a failure to act can be as effective a way of doing something as an action traditionally understood. The great problem with omissions is to give an account of when a failure to act has consequences, and when it does not. Bentham obviously experienced this difficulty when he stated that "to strike is a positive act; not to strike on a certain occasion a negative one," [10] but failed to give any account of how to distinguish the occasions on which not to strike is a negative action from those on which it is not.

Since Bentham's time, several attempts have been made to give an adequate account of when a failure to act has consequences, and when it does not. In what follows, I shall consider three of the most influential of such attempts and argue that their deficiencies point the way to a more satisfactory account of negative actions, an account, moreover, which is clearly the one upon which the Marxist conception of violence relies.

The crucial question is: In what circumstances is it appropriate to say that Y is a consequence of not doing X? Eric D'Arcy asks this question, and answers that Y is called a consequence of A's not doing X only when:

(1) Doing X is a standard way of preventing Y.
(2) A is in some way expected to do X.
(3) X is required of A in order that something such as Y should not happen.[11]

D'Arcy makes it clear that A may be expected to do X, in the requisite sense of "expected," if either, (*a*) "X is something that A usually does, or people usually do, in the situation in question," or (*b*) "X is required of him by some rule with which he is expected to comply." "This may of course be some moral rule, precept, or principle; but it will often be a non-moral rule." The rule which requires X of A will often be, on D'Arcy's account, a catch-all Benthamite duty of beneficence which will cover "things which we should, or ought to do or not do to others, even when they are not required by virtue of office, voluntary undertaking, or special relationship."

---

10 Jeremy Bentham, *Introduction to the Principles of Morals and Legislation*, ed. Harrison (Oxford 1947; repr. 1967), chap. viii, par. 8.

11 Eric D'Arcy, *Human Acts* (Oxford, 1963), pp. 47–49, 55.

D'Arcy explains his set of conditions under which Y will be a consequence of A's not doing X, as follows:

> A can . . . be held responsible for Y only to the extent that some relationship of cause and consequence exists between them; the only such relationship is that which exists by virtue of the connexion of each with X; and, by hypothesis, X connects them only to this extent, that X is enjoined upon A in order that something such as Y should not happen.[12]

And he concludes that "in moral investigations, at least, the charge that A did not do X with the result that Y happened will . . . be successfully rebutted if it can be shown, not only that doing X was something which was not required of A: but even that it was not required of him in order that things such as Y might not happen."[13]

On D'Arcy's view, before we can say that A's failure to do X caused any result whatsoever, it must *already* be the case that X is expected or required of A. For if A is not already connected with X by some duty, then when X is not performed with the consequence that Y happens, A will not be connected to X, and therefore not to Y either.

D'Arcy has put his model together back-to-front, for his condition that "X is required of A in order that something such as Y should not happen" would be pointless if it did not exploit our understanding of the causal connection between the failure of X and the occurrence of Y. D'Arcy's own explication of the notion of beneficence confirms this. Beneficence it will be remembered, covers "things which we should, or ought to, do or not do to others." One of D'Arcy's examples (derived from Bentham) of the exercise of this duty is the following: "if a drunkard falls face downwards into a puddle, and is in danger of drowning, a bystander has a duty at least to lift his head a little to one side and so save him." But our duty is not to go around lifting the heads of drunks, *and so save them,* our duty *is* to save them if we can. And we have this duty, because to fail to save someone we could save would be the death of him. It would not be the death of him because we have the duty; it would be the death of him because we fail to save him. His death results from our failure, whether we have a duty to save him or not (we might have a duty to kill this particular man and discharge it by failing to save him). It is not the existence of the duty that makes the death of the drunk a consequence of our failure to save him, rather it is the fact that unless we save him he will die that makes it our duty to save him.

If ever the duty of beneficence was owed, it was owed surely to the man who fell among thieves on the Jericho road. The thieves left him half dead, and he would perhaps have perished had the Samaritan followed the priest and the Levite and left him untended. The probable

---

12 Ibid., p. 49.
13 Ibid., p. 50.

consequence of passing by on the other side would be the death of the man. To see this is to see a causal connection between the failure to tend the man and his death. And it is because we understand this connection that we see the point of the parable, that we realize why it is that the priest and the Levite ought to have tended the man. We do not need to postulate a duty of beneficence to explain how the neglect of the passersby might well have resulted in the man's death, rather we need to understand the causal connection between *neglect and death* to see why anyone might be required to tend to him.

John Casey, in a recent discussion of this problem, notes that "the introduction of a statement which claims to give the *cause* of some event presupposes a pattern of normal expectations such that what will count as the cause of the event is, as it were, an intrusion into the pattern of expectations." [14] Casey goes on to state the conditions under which failure to act can have causal status in terms similar to D'Arcy's. "If a man does not do X, we cannot properly say that his not doing X is the cause of some result Y unless, in the normal course of events, he could have been expected to do X." Casey then argues that a man can be held "personally responsible" for something (and Casey means by this term of art roughly what Hart means by his term "moral liability-responsibility," namely, that the person is responsible in some way for which he may appropriately be praised or blamed) if (and only if):

(a) His actions (or omissions) are causally responsible for it.
(b) The outcome has some importance in terms of what he might be expected to do; in general, that is, in terms of a pattern of role responsibilities, in the context of which he acts.
(c) Normal conditions (i.e., no excusing conditions).[15]

Casey notes that "the correctness of saying that condition (a) is satisfied rests on a rule of conversational propriety which is equivalent to the assertion of condition (b)." This note is necessary because, if "the introduction of a statement which claims to give the *cause* of some event presupposes a pattern of normal expectations such that what will count as the cause of the event is . . . an intrusion into the pattern of expectation," we must have some idea of what our normal expectations are. And if a failure to act is to be identified and given causal status, the normal conditions in the light of which it is a *failure* to act must be known. In knowing what a man is expected to do, we know the normal conditions; when a man fails to do what is expected of him, we can see that the failure is an intrusion into the pattern of normal expectations, and we are then able to say that certain events are the *results* of his failure. Furthermore, Casey believes that what he calls "a man's role" defines

---

[14] John Casey, "Actions and Consequences," in *Morality and Moral Reasoning*, ed. John Casey (London, 1971), p. 180.
[15] Ibid., p. 187.

what sort of agent he is, and what are his responsibilities and obligations, *prior* to any particular case. This is, of course, sometimes true. The cultivation of his own garden is, if he does not employ a gardener, part of a man's "role responsibilities" in the broad sense in which Casey uses the term. If the garden grows to seed and becomes possessed by things rank and gross in nature, the owner is responsible, and we know this prior to the deterioration of the garden, because we know who is responsible for its upkeep. But sometimes we know what a man's responsibilities and obligations are only *because* we see that failure to act in a certain way will result in the occurrence of the sort of thing that we expect or require people to prevent. And where this is so, Casey's notion of a man's role will fail to provide a way of specifying what a man's obligations are which is independent of the consequences of his not fulfilling them. In these cases it is not the fact that X is expected of a man that allows us to say that his not doing X makes him causally responsible for Y, but rather, the fact that we see him to be causally responsible for Y shows us that X was expected of him.

In their book *Causation in the Law,* Hart and Honoré deal extensively with the question of the causal status of omissions.[16] Their account relies heavily on some idea of normalcy. "When things go wrong and we ask the cause, we ask this on the assumption that the environment persists unchanged, and something has 'made the difference' between what normally happens in it and what has happened on this occasion." On their account, when an omission has causal status, it has that status because it constitutes a departure from what normally happens.

> What is taken as normal for the purpose of the distinction between cause and mere conditions is very often an artefact of human habit, custom and convention. This is so because men have discovered that nature is not only sometimes harmful *if* we intervene, but is also sometimes harmful unless we intervene, and have developed customary techniques, procedures and routines to counteract such harm. These have become a second 'nature' and so a second 'norm.' The effect of drought is regularly neutralized by government precautions in preserving water or food; disease is neutralized by inoculation; rain by the use of umbrellas. When such manmade normal conditions are established, deviation from them will be regarded as exceptional and so rank as the cause of harm.

Hart and Honoré emphasize that deviation from customary techniques will rank as a cause, not because harm always results from such deviation, but because the "omitted precaution would have arrested the harm." This is certainly so, and it is an important point, but must the techniques have become *customary,* the procedures and routines *normal,* the method of prevention *standard,* before we can say that their omission caused some outcome?

[16] H. L. A. Hart and A. M. Honoré, *Causation in the Law* (Oxford, 1959), pp. 34–35, 37.

At what point does the failure to neutralize the harmful effects of disease come to rank as the cause of those harmful effects? On the Hart-Honoré view this happens only when the practice of inoculation has become "a second 'nature' and so a second 'norm.' " Let us suppose that a vaccine against cancer is developed, tried, and tested at a university or by a drug manufacturer, that its discovery is made known by the firm which developed it, but that no one takes steps to make it generally available or to provide money for its mass production. Are we not entitled, indeed required, to conclude that a government, for example, or a drug company, which continues to allow people to die of cancer, when they could so easily be saved, is causally responsible for their deaths? And are we not entitled to say this even though no customary practice of vaccination against cancer has become second nature to the society in question? Hart and Honoré might reply that while vaccination against cancer has not become customary, the practice of inoculation is a standard method of prevention of disease, and that it is this practice which makes it possible to say that the failure to make available any new vaccine may involve causal responsibility for the continuing prevalence of the disease.

But we can push our inquiry further back and ask whether, when it had become clear that Jenner's vaccine was successful in preventing smallpox, it would have been necessary to wait until the practice of inoculation had become standard *before* it would be correct to cite failure to vaccinate as a cause, perhaps the most significant cause, of an epidemic.[17]

When in 1939 Howard Florey and his team concentrated and purified Fleming's antibiotic penicillin and demonstrated its curative properties, it would surely have been ludicrous to suggest that it was necessary to wait until its use had become standard before anyone was in a position to realize that any failure to put it into mass production would cost thousands of lives. Indeed, its use could not become standard until it was put into mass production, and there would be no reason to put it into mass production and thus make its use standard, if it were not already obvious that to fail to do so would *cost* lives.

When is it true to say that Y is a consequence of A's not doing X? The idea that a prerequisite of our saying that A's failure to do X caused Y is that X be somehow expected of A, which is employed by Hart and Honoré, D'Arcy and Casey, is probably correct for the majority of negative actions. The fact that someone normally does X, or that it is expected for some other reason that someone will do X, makes the nonoccurrence of X on a particular occasion something that calls for explanation. Or again, if A is required to do X, we have a reason for

[17] This is not perhaps the best example since it did not become clear that vaccination against smallpox was effective until the practice had become reasonably widespread. But with the modern practice of clinical trials we can easily imagine cases in which a completely new method of preventing or curing disease might be developed and proved effective before their use was at all general, let alone a second nature.

wanting to know if X has happened, and if it has not happened, for wondering why not. In either case, we first expect X of A, and whatever reason we have for so doing also shows why the nonoccurrence of X calls for an explanation at all, and indicates the direction in which to look for an answer. If we know it is the porter's job to raise the college flag at daybreak and at noon the college flagstaff is naked, we may want to know why the flag has not been raised, and the somnolence of the porter satisfies our curiosity. But the nakedness of flagpoles is unproblematic unless, *because* we know the porter's duties, we have some reason for expecting to see them clothed in flags. Where harm to human beings is concerned, however, our interest needs no special occasion. We are always interested in the causes of harm to ourselves and our fellow men.

The discussion of the theories of Hart and Honoré, D'Arcy, and Casey seems to indicate that the moment we realize that harm to human beings could be prevented, we are entitled to see the failure to prevent it as a cause of harm. As it stands, this statement seems too comprehensive in scope. We do not usually think of the man who fails to give money to save the victims of famine abroad as causing the deaths of some of the victims, even though we know that even a small donation would save lives. Still less, perhaps, do we think of society as guilty of massive carnage because it continues to allow the use of motor vehicles, although we know that were motor vehicles, or most of them, to be banned, thousands of lives would be saved each year. That we do not usually speak of causes in these cases seems to show that there is something wrong with saying that the moment we realize that harm could be avoided, we are entitled to see the failure to prevent it as a cause of the harm. What appears to be wrong with the statement, and certainly the criticism that Hart and Honoré would level at it, is that it involves a confusion between causes and mere conditions. Wherever there is a possibility of preventing harm, its nonprevention is a necessary condition of the harm's occurring, but is something more required for a necessary condition to become a cause?

Hart and Honoré give a detailed account of just what more this is. They distinguish "mere conditions" from "causes" properly so called. Mere conditions are "just those [factors] which are present alike both in the case where such accidents occur and in the cases where they do not, and it is this consideration that leads us to reject them as the cause of the accident, even though it is true that without them the accident would not have occurred." It is plain, of course, that to cite factors which are present both in the case of disaster and of normal functioning would explain nothing; such factors do not "make the difference" between disaster and normal functioning. Hart and Honoré emphasize that what is or is not normal functioning can be relative to the context of any given enquiry in two ways: either because some feature which pervades most contexts has been specifically excluded in a particular case, or because "in one and the same case . . . the distinction between cause and condition can be drawn in different ways. The cause of a great famine in India may be identified by the Indian peasant as the drought, but the World Food Authority may identify the Indian government's failure to build up reserves as the cause and the drought as a mere condition." Hart and Honore suppose that what we want to know, when we ask for a causal explanation in cases like this, is what made *these* people die of starvation when normally *they* would have lived? And the answer given is that one can say that what made this difference was the Indian government's failure to build up reserves—"an abnormal failure of a normal condition."

But what if normal functioning is always a disaster? Every year, just like clockwork, the poor and the jobless, the aged and the infirm, suffer terribly, and many of them die. What is the cause? The myopic view is that they die because they are poor and jobless, aged and infirm, that this is what distinguishes them from those who do not suffer, from those who do not die. But the "World Moral Authority" may identify the neglect of other members of society or of the government as the cause, and the other features as mere conditions. And surely the "World Moral Authority's" causal explanation is not upset by the discovery that this society normally neglects its weakest members, that there is no difference between what they did this year and what they always do, that caring for their needy is by no means an established procedure with them. Of course, Hart and Honoré can retreat to a second line of defense which their account prudently affords. They can say that, while this society may be callous, provision for the needy is none the less a well-established procedure among men, and it is this that allows us to cite neglect as the cause of suffering in the case; or in the case of the Indian famine, that building up reserves is a technique for preventing famine established at least since the time of Moses. This can only be a temporary line of defense, because there was a time when these precautions against harm were not the normal practice, and at that time, when men were wondering what was the cause of all the misery they saw about them, they did not ask themselves: why are these people suffering when *normally* they would not suffer? but, why are these people suffering *when they could have been spared* their suffering?

When we are seeking a causal explanation of the disasters that overtake human beings, we are often not seeking to explain why a disaster occurred on this occasion when normally it would not have occurred, but why it occurred on this occasion when it need not have done. Human life is often such a chapter of disasters that what we want explained is why these disasters happen when they could have been prevented. In these cases the question that interests us and the question that must interest anyone who wishes to explain why human beings so often needlessly come to grief, is not: *what made the difference,* but, *what might have made the difference?* In the case of the Indian famine the "mere" conditions will be the drought, the failure of the crops, and so on; the cause will be the failure of the Indian government to build up reserves or perhaps the failure of other governments to send speedy and sufficient aid. When we are looking for what might make the difference between harm's occurring and its not occurring, anything that could have been done to prevent the harm in question is a likely candidate for causal status.

So far, we have been interested in the question of when a failure to act has consequences and when it doesn't, in when Y is a consequence of A's failure to do X and when it isn't. Our interest has been quite undiscriminating between the circumstances in which it is correct to say that Y is a *consequence* of A's actions or omissions and those in which one can say that A *caused* Y or that A is *responsible* for Y. But when we say that someone was the cause of harm to human beings, we are singling him out as the author of the harm (or at least as *one of* the authors), we are saying that he is responsible for it and probably that he is to blame (or if, for some reason, we feel that the harm was well-deserved, those responsible might be praised). Praise or blame is usually appropriate where harm to human beings is knowingly caused. If we think that a particular method of preventing a particular harm is for some reason ineligible, then we are unlikely to blame people for not using it, and if it is the only way that the harm could have been averted, we are unlikely to cite the failure to use the method as a *cause* of the harm, even though the fact that the harm occurred is, of course, a *consequence* of the failure to prevent it.

But what do these facts about the words we usually choose in different situations indicate about negative causation? If we think that a possible method of preventing harm is ineligible, that its use is for some reason completely out of the question, then we are unlikely to see it as something that might have made the difference (or that made the difference) between the harm's occurring and its not occurring. We just do not think of it as something that "could have been done" to avert the disaster.

But people are likely to differ crucially about just how viable options of saving others are. Suffering people are likely to see the possibility of their sufferings being relieved as highly eligible, but those who would have to make sacrifices to bring relief are likely to think differently, especially if they have interests which would be permanently prejudiced by any change in the status quo.

Of course, if someone claims out of the blue that people who fail to do something that has hitherto been almost universally judged to be quite out of the question are causally responsible for the deaths of human beings, then some explanation at least is owed. But the legitimacy of claiming that a failure to exercise a particular option is causing death does not depend on our agreeing that the option should be, or should have been, exercised.

I have suggested that where Y involves harm to human beings, then Y will be a consequence of A's not doing X simply where X would have prevented Y and A could have done X. Where the doing of X is considered to be out of the question, we tend to act and talk as though the condition that A could have done X is not satisfied. People will differ as to just how "impossible" the doing of X really is, different principles and interests will pull in different directions: what is out of the question for A, B will do without a second thought. If a doctor believes that he must never deliberately take life and so refuses to perform an abortion, even though the mother will die if the abortion is not performed, he does not see himself as causing the mother's death, rather he believes himself to have no choice. It is significant that such a man is often described as following the dictates of the divine law, or of his conscience, "whatever the consequences," and that discussions of the problems raised by such dilemmas are discussions of whether absolutist moral principles which ignore consequences can be justified. The point is not that one has to be a consequentialist, but that the adoption of principles or values, or even ways of life or ways of organizing society, which makes the prevention of certain sorts of harm by certain means "out of the question," does not prevent the harm being a consequence of the maintenance of those principles or that way of life. If we decide that preventing particular harm by particular means is "out of the question," we are unlikely to talk as though the harm were a consequence of our failure to prevent it. But the occurrence of such harm is the price we pay for the maintenance of our principles or of our way of life. Maybe it's worth it, maybe it isn't; that is another question. We can never rule out the possibility of hungry people in the third world, or even the victims of motor accidents in our own society claiming, with justice, that we are causally responsible for their plight because we decline to arrange things so that they may be preserved from harm.

To sum up, we must emphasize a distinction that has been implicit in the foregoing discussion: that between A causing Y by his failure to do X and his bringing about of Y by his failure to do X. That is, the distinction between *negative causation* and *negative action*. We can state formally the difference between the two as follows:

(a) Negative Causation: *A's failure to do X caused Y where A could have done X and X would have prevented Y, and where either: X is somehow expected or required of A, or Y involves harm to human beings.*

As many thinkers have observed, it seems inappropriate, even silly, to talk of a man being causally responsible for everything and anything he might have made different. There must be some reason for his interference, some point to it. There must be some feature of the situation that raises the issue of A's preventing Y by doing X. This feature, whatever it is, will make it appropriate to talk both of A's failure to do X, and of A's thereby causing Y. And this will be so even where we neither expect nor require A to do X, nor to prevent Y. Thus either our expecting or requiring A to do X, or the fact that Y involves harm to human beings, are features of a situation that make it appropriate to talk of A's failure to prevent Y by doing X, as his causing Y. I don't intend this to be an exhaustive list of the conditions under which A's failure to do X can be said to cause Y. There may be situations in which quite different features may give reasons for interference and so make talk of causes appropriate.

(*b*) Negative action: *A's failure to do X with the result Y will make the bringing about of Y a negative action of A's, only where A's doing X would have prevented Y and A knew or ought reasonably to have known this, and where A could have done X and knew, or ought reasonably to have known, this.*

We must here again note the distinction (pointed out by H. L. A. Hart) [18] between causal responsibility and "moral liability-responsibility"; that is, between causing some outcome and being liable, accountable in some way that makes praise or blame appropriate. We are usually accountable for some outcome because we are causally responsible for it, but not simply because we are. It is only if the bringing about of Y is a negative action of A's that his causal responsibility for Y will raise the question of whether or not he might also be morally responsible for Y. And of course, whether A is morally responsible, whether he is to be held to account for bringing about Y, will depend on a number of other considerations, as indeed it would if he had brought Y about by positive actions.

If the argument so far is right, it presents us with a choice between only two consistent views about negative causation. We can deny that anyone is ever responsible for things he could have prevented or changed. This would go against many of our intuitions and common-sense judgments, and would deny a whole realm of discourse long established and firmly entrenched both in our practice and in our habits of speech. The second alternative will be even less attractive to many, for if we admit the concept of negative causation, if we allow that anyone is ever responsible for something he could have prevented or changed, then we must accept a drastic revision of our views about agency and responsibility.

In this section I have concentrated on showing that the Marxist conception of violence depends upon some theory of negative action. I have attempted to show that the accepted views about the causal efficacy of omissions are inadequate and to provide a consistent theory which not only accounts for the cases covered by the accepted view, but has the additional merit of explaining and underpinning the claims that Marxists and others wish to make about our responsibility for what happens in the world. This theory shows that the claims of the Marxists are not merely empty rhetoric, but are based on a solid and defensible theory of action.

I will conclude by trying very briefly to indicate the extent to which

18 H. L. A. Hart, "Postscript: Responsibility and Punishment," in *Punishment and Responsibility* (Oxford, 1968), pp. 212-230.

we are, I believe, morally responsible for our negative actions, and so make clearer why the theory of negative action developed in this section forces on us a radical revision of our views about responsibility.

If we take what is possibly the most generally recognized duty, that of refraining from killing, injuring or otherwise inflicting suffering on our fellow men, we see that this duty has both a positive and a negative form. We have the *duty not to injure anyone by performing harmful actions we could avoid.* This is the active voice of the duty which may be expressed in passive voice as the *duty not to injure anyone by failing to perform actions which we could perform and which, if performed, would prevent the injury from occurring.* If we sometimes take comfort from the reflection that no man is an island, we may sometimes also ponder just how, or how far, we are involved in mankind. If we accept the prohibition against killing or injuring other people, the theory of negative actions developed in this section shows us that, whereas we may have thought that whatever we do to allay the sufferings of others is mere charity, we are in most cases bound to help by the strongest of obligations. What possible basis could there be for distinguishing between active and passive forms of the duty not to injure others on moral, or any other grounds, that would make one form of the duty less binding than the other? If we have a duty not to kill others, it would be strange indeed if the duty not to kill by positive actions was somehow stronger than the duty not to kill by negative actions. I do not see how we can escape the conclusion that in whatever sense we are morally responsible for our positive actions, in that same sense we are morally responsible for our negative actions. And the corollary of this is, of course, that whatever considerations mitigate our moral responsibility for particular positive acts, considerations of equal moral force are needed to mitigate our responsibility for negative acts with the same consequences.

The morality to which our equal responsibility for positive and negative acts with the same consequences would commit us is clearly a very demanding one, but I think equally clearly a more moral one than is current. It would oblige us to work actively and, in the present state of the world, unremittingly for the relief and prevention of suffering. Whether or not all of us whose negative actions make us responsible for harm to others should be blamed, I am not sure. One should not perhaps blame people too severely for not rising much above the standards of their time. But whether or not we choose to blame people for all the harmful consequences of their negative actions, does not affect the question of their blameworthiness, and it does not affect their moral responsibility for their actions. We might have to accept for some while a discrepancy between most people's practice and the standards set by this morality.[19] I am sure, however, that we should recognize that this is a

---

[19] This way of dealing charitably with the problem of blame I owe to Jonathan Glover.

morality towards which we ought to work, and one of the ways to do this is to make people aware of what they are *doing*.

The view that to bring about harmful consequences through negative actions is every bit as bad as to do so through positive actions, has of course been challenged, particularly in the debates about the moral difference between killing and letting die. To defend this view against all the attacks that have been or might be leveled against it and to show how it would apply to some of the most controversial or paradoxical cases would require more space than I have here, and is therefore a task for another day.[20] We must now return to the question of violence. If the claims that the Marxists make about violence can be made out, it looks as though those who condemn violence are committed to oppose more than they imagine. I will now try to show that this is so.

III

The Marxists are pointing out that much of the harm that has been thought to be part of the natural hazards of life is not at all natural, and that if we ask why this harm is occurring when it might have been prevented, we will find that it is in fact attributable to the machinations of men. Far from being the result of the operation of gratuitous and impersonal forces, much harm must be seen as the work of assignable agents. Now what is the justification for calling the infliction of such harm "violence"? Well, what is the objection?

The argument against the Marxist view goes roughly like this: The Marxists are attempting to call any harm caused by men to one another "violence," but violence is just one of the ways of doing harm—not all of them. Moreover, the Marxist view would obscure or collapse the traditional distinction between violence and nonviolence. We can, and do, tell the difference between clubbing a man to death and peacefully enjoying a good meal while he starves to death outside, or between burning down a man's house and evicting him. The distinction between violent and nonviolent ways of doing things is clear and useful for evaluating actions, and it allows us to try to understand and explain just what it is about violence that makes it such a fearful thing, so fearful a thing, indeed, that many men have been led to renounce violence absolutely (or at least as much as is convenient). The maintenance of the violent-nonviolent distinction, so far from begging any questions, as Marxists sometimes argue, leaves open all questions as to whether violent means are, for example, better or worse than nonviolent means. The distinction

---

20 My paper "The Survival Lottery," shortly to appear in *Philosophy* [50 (1975): 81-87, Ed.], argues for this view by examining in detail one such case.

merely allows us to reserve the name of violence for those fearful acts upon which the traditional abhorrence of violence is founded.

This objection to the Marxist view is twofold. The claim is first that the Marxists simply use the concept of violence inappropriately, that they stretch its meaning beyond the breaking point and use it in a way which ignores distinctions that are ordinarily made. The second objection is more subtle. It is that the Marxists wish to claim that the distinction between positive and negative ways of contributing to some-one else's injury is a morally insignificant distinction, and that they support the point by applying the word violence to both types of case. The objection, then, is that to apply the word violence to both types of case is self-defeating, for it concedes the moral importance of the distinc-tion, in relying on the rhetorical force the word violence has because it standardly describes a certain kind of positive direct action.

To take the second point first: it is, of course, true that violence gets its rhetorical force from the sorts of cases which spring to mind when the word is mentioned. But just what are the cases from which violence derives its rhetorical potency? They are, surely, the cases which come closest to what we might call the rape, murder, fire, and sword paradigm, the terrible cases of violent infliction of death or serious in-jury. Of course, sack and pillage are not exactly everyday events, and even murder and grievous bodily harm make up only a small proportion of human violence. Much, perhaps most, of the violence which the anti-Marxists are willing to recognize is of a minor, even trivial nature; e.g., petty assaults, punch-ups outside bars, incidents in football crowds and on the field, and scuffles in demonstrations, breakings of windows and minor damage to property. Clearly the rhetorical force of "violence" does not derive from these! And the Marxists do not rely on the fact that violence standardly describes certain types of positive direct action. They do rely on violence conjuring up pictures of tragic death, mutilation, or other serious injury. But there seems to be no compelling reason why these should have been inflicted only by positive direct rather than nega-tive or indirect actions. The point is that it would be absurd to suppose that the moral importance of the distinction between acts of violence and acts which do not involve violence consists solely or even principally in their being positive rather than negative. Of course, the Marxists are relying on the rhetorical force the word violence has because of the cases with which it is standardly associated, but what is it about these cases which they rely on? Not, certainly, on the trivial contingency that they involve positive actions, but surely on the vital fact that they involve serious injury attributable to assignable agents.

So, the Marxist conception of violence cannot be regarded as self-defeating. It does not concede the moral importance of a distinction it wishes to demolish when it makes use of the rhetorical force of the word violence, nor does it rely on that distinction. Rather, the Marxists rely on the fact that the word violence derives its rhetorical force from its conjuring up pictures of the fearful injuries inflicted on men by men, and the Marxists claim that in this respect the cases they wish to call violence are isomorphic with those the anti-Marxists recognize.

Now, what of the claim that, whether or not the Marxist conception of violence is self-defeating, it none the less involves a mistake, the simple conceptual error of confusing violent methods of harming people with methods which are not violent? But how, in fact, do we distinguish violent methods from those which are not violent, and acts of violence from acts that are not acts of violence? The first thing to note is that there is an important difference between these two ways of posing the distinction. "Violent" is an adjective, and a violent act an act appropriately qualified by that adjective. An act of violence, on the other hand, is an act belonging to a particular category or class of actions not co-extensive with violent acts.

We can state the distinction between violent acts and acts of violence in this way: Almost any action a human being can perform can be performed violently. Mr. Wilson slicing viciously into a bunker, or Mr. Gladstone denuding the countryside of trees, are both performing violent acts. Even a cup of tea may be stirred violently. For those who dislike the circularity of saying that a violent act is an act performed violently, we can say simply that a violent act is any act appropriately characterized by the following sorts of words taken from the "violence" entry in *Roget's Thesaurus*: "inclemency, vehemence, might, impetuosity, boisterousness, turbulence, bluster, uproar, riot, row, rumpus, fury, brute force, outrage, shock, explosion. . . ." The considerations which lead us to classify acts as acts of violence are clearly of a different sort. When trying, for example, to assess the prevalence and the causes of violence in human affairs we are clearly not concerned with a well-hit golf ball; we might say that what concerns us here is what is left when we subtract a violent act from an act of violence. It is important to note that the words "violent" and "violence" and the phrases "act of violence" and "violent act" are often used indiscriminately between the two senses I have distinguished. In each case, the context must make clear whether the descriptive or classificatory sense of the term is intended.

What principles then determine the classification of acts as acts of violence for those who regard the Marxist view as conceptually confused?

To define with any sort of clarity the concept of violence upon which the anti-Marxists rely is no easy matter. Clearly they have in mind the rape, murder, fire and sword paradigm which involves the sudden forceful, and perhaps unexpected, infliction of painful physical injury upon an unwilling victim. Nowadays terrorists who machine-gun or bomb their victims are the classic case. But if the terrorists poison the water supply or gas their victims while they sleep, or brick them up in their houses to die of starvation or suffocation, we would not, I think, regard it as mistaken or confused if people continued to speak of "terrorist violence." And the terrorists could hardly claim to have renounced violence if they adopted such methods. If it is not inapposite to talk of violence in these cases, the door is already open to the Marxists.

We were told recently that children in Belfast adopt the following tactic against British soldiers.[21] Here is one of the children describing the method: "That's the street right? These are the lamp-posts and that's the Army Land-Rover coming up the street. You tie your cheese-wire between two of the lamp-posts about six feet up. There's always a soldier standing on the back of the jeep; even with the search lights he can't see the wire in the dark. It's just at the right height to catch his throat." No violent act on the part of the child, but clearly an act of violence. So long as such tactics are employed no one would call Belfast a violence-free city.

If a man is stabbed to death, we do not doubt that he has been the victim of a violent assault. Would we have to alter our judgment if we later learn that the stiletto slid between his ribs as easily as you please? This stiletto point is the thin end of the wedge. For if we are interested in the question of the prevalence of violence in human affairs, or in comparing the scale of violence in different societies, in different eras, or in assessing the violence of opposing factions, it would be absurd to ignore or exclude methods men find of killing or injuring their fellows that do not happen to involve vigorous direct actions.

If, for example, instead of bombs and guns, poison, nerve gas, and exposure to radiation became standard ways of eliminating our fellow men, we would not, I think, be inclined to claim that men had become less violent in their dealings with each other even though such methods do not involve physical assault or violent actions of any kind. If we are interested in the question of whether a particular society does or does not use violence as a method of settling differences or resolving disputes, we would certainly not ignore the fact that the society eliminated an opposition group or an unpopular minority by herding them into ghettos where they were left to die of starvation or disease. While such things go on, the claim that mankind is becoming less violent will be viewed with skepticism.

The questions that interest us about violence—questions about its prevalence, its causes, its prevention, questions about when it should be used and why, about whether or not it has been used in particular cases, whether it is on the increase, whether some societies or periods are or were more violent than others—would be trivial questions if all that they are about is whether or not actions of a particular description are used. Trivial also because much of our interest in these questions stems from our concern to solve the problem of violence, to minimize its use or even remove it entirely from human affairs, and this we might succeed in doing and yet leave intact all the features of the problem of violence that make a solution desirable. Death, injury and

[21] Morris Fraser, "Children of Violence," *Sunday Times Weekly Review,* 29 April 1973, p. 33.

suffering might be just as common as before, only the characteristic complex of actions by which they are inflicted would have changed.

Surely our interest in all these questions about violence reflects a concern with the phenomenon of men inflicting injury, suffering, or death on one another? We are not so much interested in the particular methods men use to do this, or in the look, the physical character of the actions they use. We are interested in violence because it is a particular kind of activity—the activity in which men cause each other injury and suffering.

The point of contention between the Marxists and those who object to their conception of violence concerns what feature is constitutive of the concept. The Marxists claim that violence is the phenomenon of men inflicting injury on one another. The anti-Marxists might concede that this is part of the concept, but would insist that it is a necessary condition that those injuries be inflicted by vigorous, direct action. The question then arises as to whether the Marxists and their opponents are pointing to different forms of the same activity or to different activities. Are they using different conceptions of the same concept or different concepts? This question forces us to answer the question with which we started: what is the justification for calling the infliction of harm by negative actions "violence"?

We have seen that a distinction must be made in our use of the terms violent and violence between what I have called the purely descriptive use of violence and its classificatory sense. I have shown that the classificatory sense of violence cannot be made parasitic on the descriptive sense without trivializing all the questions that most interest us. The justification for calling the infliction of harm by negative actions "violence" is that when we classify an act as an act of violence we are saying that it is part of a single phenomenon, that all men who use violence are involved, in some sense, in the same activity. If we ask what this activity is, the answer that forces itself upon us is that it must be the infliction of injury or suffering upon others. It is this that makes the Marxist conception of violence one conception of the same concept which captures the rape, murder, fire, and sword paradigm.

For Thomas Hobbes, the first and fundamental reason for establishing the state was to protect men from the disasters of the war of every man against every man. Man's natural propensity to violence caused the worst features of this war, which were "continual fear and danger of violent death, and the life of man solitary, poor, nasty, brutish and short." [22] The Marxists did not need to create a fictional state of nature to see men in this condition, they just looked around. At the sight of men causing others to lead lives in fear and danger, poor, nasty, brutish and short, the Marxists naturally spoke of violence, for they were faced with an activity of essentially the same kind as that which

[22] Thomas Hobbes, *Leviathan*, pt. 1, chap. 13.

Hobbes most feared. For Hobbes the remedy was the social contract; for the Marxists, the social revolution.

I have been concerned in this section to defend a particular use of a particular word against the charge that it is conceptually confused, self-defeating and likely to lead to ambiguity and equivocation. Defense, I think, must be the best form of attack, for it shows a way to turn the tables on this form of criticism and argue that it, in turn, is based on a confusion—that of failing to distinguish acts of violence and violent acts. One would then say that it is this confusion that has tempted a number of philosophers to criticize certain definitions of violence on the grounds that they class actions as acts of violence which do not involve violent acts.

Amidst all this confusion it would be very easy to miss the point, which is, surely, that the differences between the followers of what I have called the Marxist conception of violence and their critics are not due to confusion of any kind. The Marxists are not unaware of the many different sorts of harm that human beings can suffer, nor are their critics necessarily ignorant of the fact that vigorous direct action is not a sufficient condition of violence. The dispute between Marxists and their opponents over the definition of violence is not to be explained by reference to the conceptual confusion of the protagonists.

The extreme intractability of the controversy over this definition is, of course, in part the result of the unwillingness of the various parties to renounce the right to use one of the most powerful terms of political rhetoric. But there are other things at stake. When we remember that violence is commonly thought of as a problem of world proportions requiring urgent solution, we uncover another motive for defining violence in a particular way. For to define violence is, in a sense, to determine the scope of this problem. In disputes over which features are constitutive of the concept of violence both political and philosophical motives play a part, and it may be that there is no final answer, no definitive analysis. Different features of the phenomenon of violence will loom larger as the form of the phenomenon varies, or as the political perspective of the theorists changes. Where muggings and violent demonstrations are the fear and the theorists speak for the fearful, vigorous direct actions will seem the most important features of violence. Where the streets are quiet, but people who could be saved are left to die of neglect or cold or hunger, or are crippled or killed by their living or working conditions, a different group of people may suffer, and other theorists may see their suffering as attributable to human agency, and so class it as part of man's violence to man.

If I am right that when we talk of violence we are not simply interested in the means whereby particular harm is inflicted, but rather in some characteristic activity or phenomenon, then there may be different distinctive features which are the hallmark of this activity, and

reasonable men may differ as to what those features are. In this paper
I have shown that the Marxist conception of violence isolates a feature
of violence which, on any account must be central, and which is shared
by the paradigm cases. I have argued that this conception in fact captures the activity which is constitutive of the concept of violence. About
this, of course, there may be argument, but I believe that I have said
enough to establish the Marxist conception of violence, at the very least,
as one coherent conception of violence.

The Prosecution of
the Conscientious Violator

That the demands of legal authority can conflict with the claims of morality has been clear for thousands of years. In classical literature, both *Antigone,* Sophocles' play, and the *Apology,* Plato's representation of Socrates' defense before an Athenian court of law, still make contributions to contemporary understanding of this conflict. Indeed, the history of the United States of America begins in a sense with a document—the Declaration of Independence—which recognizes that certain circumstances may justify the setting aside of allegiance in favor of principled activity done in disregard of established law. (England, in fact, declared the signing of the document to be high treason, punishable by death.) American history contains many examples of persons who, rightly or wrongly, placed conscience above the law: Henry David Thoreau, those who operated the "Underground Railroad," those who were involved, like Martin Luther King, in the civil-rights struggles of the fifties and sixties, and many who opposed the war in Vietnam.

Examples such as these have provoked several types of philosophical inquiry. They have stimulated investigation into the sources of our obligation to the law. Further, they have prodded philosophers and jurists to define the concept of civil disobedience, to determine whether it is ever justified and, if so, when. But there is a further question which may still have to be answered even after these others are settled. This question arises when we look at the conscientious violator of the law from the point of view of the judge, the prosecutor, or the legislator: Should some allowance be made for the person who disobeys the law out of conscience?

To a small but significant degree, the American legal system has recognized certain scruples as justifying exemption from the usual reach of the law. The use of the drug peyote, normally a criminal offense, has been permitted in certain religious contexts: this is one example of such recognition. And the well-known exemption from military combat duty of those conscientiously opposed to war on religious grounds is another. These exceptions (and several others like them) are created out of a concern to avoid burdening those who cannot adhere to the law without violating their religious convictions, a concern which is found in the "establishment" and "free exercise" clauses of the First Amendment: "Congress shall make no law respecting an establishment of religion, or prohibiting the free exercise thereof. . . ." On the other hand, it is important to note that not every religious practice receives such protection. The conviction of a Mormon for polygamy was upheld by the Supreme Court even when his church imposed a duty upon him to practice it.

In the legal opinion which begins this section, *United States* v. *Sisson,* Judge Charles Wyzanski is faced with "a clash between law and morality" in which the defendant, a draftee, "is not in a formal sense a religious conscientious objector." On April 17, 1968, John Sisson had refused to accept induction into the armed forces. The issue considered in the opinion is "whether the government can constitutionally require combat service in Vietnam of a person who is conscientiously opposed to American military activities in Vietnam because he believes them to be immoral and unjust, that belief resting, not upon formal religion but upon the deepest convictions and ethical commitments, apart from formal religion, of which a man is capable." Judge Wyzanski assumes that "a conscientious objector, religious or otherwise, may be conscripted for some kinds of service in peace or in war." But he determines that the question of whether Congress may "draft conscientious objectors for combat duty in a distant conflict not pursuant to a declared war" is a separate issue. This issue, he finds, is one which can be decided by balancing, with "reference to the Constitution as a whole," the competing claims of public and private interests in two areas: individual liberty and national defense. Judge Wyzanski also considers the weight which should be given to conscientious scruples that are not rooted in religious belief, the problem of distinguishing the sincere conscientious objector from the hypocrite, and the importance of limiting the legal immunization of those whose acts are "dictated by religious or conscientious scruple." Holding in favor of Sisson, Judge Wyzanski comments: "When the law treats a reasonable, conscientious act as a crime it subverts its own power. It invites civil disobedience. It impairs the very habits which nourish and preserve the law."

On April 16, 1968, the day before John Sisson refused induction, and only a few days after the assassination of Martin Luther King precipitated riots in more than one hundred American cities, the Solicitor General of the United States delivered an address to the Tulane University School of Law on the occasion of the Third Annual George Abel Dreyfous Lectures on Civil Liberties. Erwin N. Griswold's talk is the second piece in this section. His main concern is that "our society has become increasingly tolerant of the mischievous attempts to excuse deliberate violations of the law committed in furtherance of what the actor personally regards as a lofty cause." Regarding "Civil Order" as the "very foundation of civilized society itself" and effective self-government as the "greatest achievement of mankind," Griswold is nevertheless quite ready to abide many forms of dissent and protest, especially those that play a role in the search for truth and wisdom. He expresses doubts, however, about forms of protest which are "reflexive rather than cerebral," which are offensive, which contribute more heat than light. He is concerned that we may not have "psychologically caught up with" the enlarged role of dissent made possible by increased literacy and enhanced means of communication. But Griswold clearly draws the line where dissent and protest involve the violation of valid laws. If there ever were a moral right to violate "a rule ordained by constituted government," Griswold suggests that the exercise of that right would have to be understood as a charming but foredoomed attempt "to abdicate membership in society." And, as a violation of a valid law, even morally justified disobedience would have to be punished: "In determining whether and when to exercise the moral right to disobey the dictates of the law it must also be recognized that society not only does not but cannot recognize this determination as entitled to legal privilege." As Griswold puts it: "it is of the essence of law that it is equally applied to all, that it binds all alike, irrespective of personal motive."

Just a few months after the speech at Tulane (but before Judge Wyzanski decided *Sisson*) Ronald Dworkin replied to Griswold in the pages of the *New York Review of Books*. Dworkin notes that the validity of a law may be in doubt even after the Supreme Court has decided, and he tries to show that this is especially likely to be true where "a significant number of people" are tempted to disobey it on moral grounds, our constitution incorporating a good deal of our conventional political morality. Where it is reasonable to believe that a law is invalid, the provision of some legal protection for the conscientious violator will help, in the end, to settle questions of validity and to insure that the laws measure up to our standards of fairness and justice. Moreover, good citizenship may properly involve disobedience of doubtful law and the government should endeavor, as much as possible, to accommodate itself to the good citizen's conscientious disobedience: "it cannot be unfair not to punish him if he is acting as, given his opinions, we think he should." Dworkin maintains that there are many cases in which we properly choose not to enforce criminal laws (or to soften their effect) and the case of the conscientious violator may well be one of them.

UNITED STATES V. SISSON

United States District Court of Massachusetts

Wyzanski, Chief Judge.

A. INTRODUCTION

March 21, 1969, in the United States District Court sitting in Boston, a jury returned a verdict that John Heffron Sisson, Jr., was guilty of unlawfully, knowingly, and wilfully having refused to comply with the order of Local Board No. 114 to submit to induction into the armed forces of the United States, in violation of the Military Selective Service Act of 1967. Title 50, Appendix, United States Code, Section 462. 32 Code of Federal Regulations 1632.14.

Pursuant to Rule 34 of the Rules of Criminal Procedure, Sisson on March 28, 1969, filed an amended motion in arrest of judgment. Adequate reference is made to earlier contentions. A new point is also raised: that the judicial power vested in this court by Article III of the United States Constitution does not give jurisdiction to adjudicate the merits of a criminal case in which the court is precluded, by the doctrine of so-called "political questions" or otherwise, from deciding relevant constitutional, domestic, and international law questions raised by defendant. It is said that a trial designed to exclude relevant issues violates the "due process" clause of the Fifth Amendment.

Important as is the new issue, defendant indicated both before and during the trial that he also intended to preserve his older contention that no offense is charged in the indictment because it is laid under a statute, which, as applied to him, violates the provision of the First Amendment that "Congress shall make no law respecting an establishment of religion, or prohibiting the free exercise thereof" and the "due process" clause of the Fifth Amendment.

It would have been better practice to make in the motion in arrest of judgment a more detailed reference to, and repetition of, that earlier contention. But, of course, at every stage the court is required to bear in mind constitutional and jurisdictional issues which have been raised and remain of vital consequence. Furthermore, this court on March 26

297 F.Supp. 902 (1969).

provided that until April 3 defendant could file a motion in arrest. No doubt, defendant will seasonably make his motion in arrest even clearer.

This court in this opinion addresses itself not to the new point but to a further consideration of the never-abandoned issue whether the government can constitutionally require combat service in Vietnam of a person who is conscientiously opposed to American military activities in Vietnam because he believes them immoral and unjust, that belief resting not upon formal religion but upon the deepest convictions and ethical commitments, apart from formal religion, of which a man is capable.

While Sisson has raised and not abandoned other issues, most of them have already been disposed of by earlier rulings in this case, *United States* v. *Sisson*, 294 F.Supp. 511, 515, 520 (D. Mass., 1968). Out of an abundance of caution this court repeats the following rulings already made, of which the first is peculiarly pertinent.

November 25, 1968 this court's opinion held that *under present circumstances,* described in that opinion, *Sisson has the necessary standing to raise the issues he tenders.* See 294 F.Supp. 511, 512-513.

The same opinion held that this court has no jurisdiction to decide the "political question" whether the military actions of the United States in Vietnam require as a constitutional basis a declaration of war by Congress.

November 26, 1968 in a second opinion this court held it has no jurisdiction to decide the "political question" whether American military operations in Vietnam violate international law. The holding is expanded and clarified in this court's order of December 3, 1968.

That order also ruled that if the Government should prove defendant intentionally refused to comply with a duly authorized order of his draft board to submit to induction then under the act it would not be open to defendant to offer as a statutory excuse that he regarded the war as illegal, immoral, or unjust.

B. THE FACTS

From the transcript of the jury trial and the exhibits then admitted, the facts appear virtually without dispute. Indeed in substance the case arises upon an agreed statement of facts.

The usual preliminaries having been completed, Local Board No. 114, Middlesex County, Massachusetts, on Form 252, executed and mailed to Sisson March 18, 1968 an order to report for induction on April 17, 1968. Sisson received the order. On the scheduled day he reported to the local board and from there went to the Boston induction center, as required. At the Boston center, Sisson, after the officer in charge had painstakingly warned him of the consequences, deliberately refused to take the step forward which is, as he understood, the symbolic act of accepting induction.

The evidence shows that the proceedings were in every respect regular. Sisson has never made complaint that there was any error with respect to his registration, the chronological order in which he was called, his physical, mental, and moral examinations, or any other procedural step.

Sisson does not now and never did claim that he is or was in the narrow statutory sense a religious conscientious objector.

Sisson graduated in 1963 from the Phillips Exeter Academy and in 1967 from Harvard College. He enlisted in the Peace Corps in July 1967, but after training he was, for reasons that have no moral connotations, "deselected" in September 1967. In January 1968 he went to work as a reporter for The Southern Courier, published in Montgomery, Alabama. That paper assigned him to work in Mississippi, where he was when he received the induction order.

The first formal indication in the record that Sisson had conscientious scruples is a letter of February 29, 1968 in which he notified Local Board No. 114 that "I find myself to be conscientiously opposed to service in the Armed Forces. Would you please send me SSS Form No. 150 so that I might make my claim as a conscientious objector." On receiving the form, Sisson concluded that his objection not being religious, within the administrative and statutory definitions incorporated in that form, he was not entitled to have the benefit of the form. He, therefore, did not execute it.

But, although the record shows no earlier formal indication of conscientious objection, Sisson's attitude as a non-religious conscientious objector has had a long history. Sisson himself referred to his moral development, his educational training, his extensive reading of reports about and comments on the Vietnam situation, and the degree to which he had familiarized himself with the U.N. Charter, the charter and judgments of the Nuremberg Tribunal, and other domestic and international matters bearing upon the American involvement in Vietnam.

On the stand Sisson was diffident, perhaps beyond the requirements of modesty. But he revealed sensitiveness, not arrogance or obstinacy. His answers lacked the sharpness that sometimes reflects a prepared mind. He was entirely without eloquence. No line he spoke remains etched in memory. But he fearlessly used his own words, not mouthing formulae from court cases or manuals for draft avoidance.

There is not the slightest basis for impugning Sisson's courage. His attempt to serve in the Peace Corps, and the assignment he took on a Southern newspaper were not acts of cowardice or evasion. Those actions were assumptions of social obligations. They were in the pattern of many conscientious young men who have recently come of age. From his education Sisson knows that his claim of conscientious objection may cost him dearly. Some will misunderstand his motives. Some will be reluctant to employ him.

Nor was Sisson motivated by purely political considerations. Of course if "political" means that the area of decision involves a judgment as to the conduct of a state, then any decision as to any war is not without some political aspects. But Sisson's table of ultimate values is moral and ethical. It reflects quite as real, pervasive, durable, and commendable a marshalling of priorities as a formal religion. It is just as much a residue of culture, early training, and beliefs shared by companions and family. What another derives from the discipline of a church, Sisson derives from the discipline of conscience.

Thus, Sisson bore the burden of proving by objective evidence that he was sincere. He was as genuinely and profoundly governed by his conscience as would have been a martyr obedient to an orthodox religion.

Sisson's views are not only sincere, but without necessarily being right, are reasonable. Similar views are held by reasonable men who are qualified experts. The testimony of Professor Richard Falk of Princeton University and Professor Howard Zinn of Boston University is sufficient proof. See also Ralph B. Potter, New Problems for Conscience in War, American Society for Christian Ethics, January 19, 1968; War and Moral Discourse, John Knox Press, 1969.

C. LIMITATION OF ISSUES

The facts found by the jury and recited above raise many points of law, some presented early in this case, others raised explicitly or inferentially in the amended motion filed in arrest of judgment.

If any one of those points is incontrovertibly sound, the court should so state and probably not give rulings on others. Such additional rulings would be gratuitous and violative of the canon of avoidance of unnecessary constitutional adjudications. Hence if this court were a court of last resort, this court would adopt the prudential principle of striking for the jugular alone.

But this inferior court cannot say that any of the issues is clear. It cannot by ruling on one surely make the others moot. This court's ruling is appealable. Hence any constitutional issue whatsoever which defendant here alleged as a ground for having judgment arrested remains open in an appellate court.

More significantly at least all those issues which are raised under the First Amendment are so interlocked textually and substantively, that one of those issues cannot properly be considered apart from the others. Sound interpretation of any phrase of the Amendment requires reconciliation both with every other phrase of that Amendment and with the Constitution as a whole.

Therefore, it is meet for this opinion to consider both the broad contention, growing principally out of "the free exercise of" religion phrase, that no statute can require combat service of a conscientious objector whose principles are either religious or akin thereto, and the narrower contention growing principally out of "the establishment" of religion phrase, that the 1967 draft act invalidly discriminates in favor of certain types of religious objectors to the prejudice of Sisson. An appellate court might find it suitable to render its judgment solely on the latter issue. This inferior court, as already explained, is not so conveniently situated. In candor it must be added that this court found its understanding of the narrow issue much clarified by first analyzing, as will be seen, the broad issue.

While this court believes it cannot escape a full survey of the First Amendment issues, the court does not now deem it necessary to address itself to the new contentions in the amended motion, filed March 28 in arrest of judgment. Those contentions as to the judicial power of the United States Courts are of the most serious nature. If defendant's other grounds for his amended motion in arrest of judgment do not prevail in the Supreme Court, that court no doubt will have to rule upon the new contentions with respect to judicial power, or to remand the case to this court for a ruling. But that bridge need not be crossed if this opinion has effectively found another way of crossing the stream.

D. EXHAUSTION OF ADMINISTRATIVE REMEDIES

The First Amendment issues are open to Sisson in this and other courts even though Sisson did not raise them before the draft board or in any other step in the administrative process. What Sisson is here doing is challenging the constitutionality of the 1967 Act as applied to him. There was no realistic opportunity to make such a challenge until now. Whatever may be academic theory, no administrative agency, such as a draft board, believes it has power or, practically, would exercise power, to declare unconstitutional the statute under which it operates. Maybe a day will come when an administrative agency's right and duty not to apply an unconstitutional statutory provision are generally acknowledged, practiced and approved. Under present practice the first time a contention of unconstitutionality of a statutory provision may effectively be made is in a court.

Sisson waited until the administrative process was over because he had no choice. Cf. *Clark* v. *Gabriel*, 393 U.S. 256, 259, 89 S.Ct. 424, 21 L.Ed.2d 418 (1968).

This court waited until the jury had given a guilty verdict because only then did the judge have no choice.

In Sisson's case the judges have become the first and the last before whom the constitutional issues can be effectively raised as a matter of law.

E. THE CONSTITUTIONAL POWER OF CONGRESS TO DRAFT CONSCIENTIOUS OBJECTORS FOR COMBAT DUTY IN A DISTANT CONFLICT NOT PURSUANT TO A DECLARED WAR

Indubitably Congress has constitutional power to conscript the generality of persons for military service in time of war. Selective Draft Law Cases, 245 U.S. 366, 38 S.Ct. 159, 62 L.Ed. 349 (1918). That is, there is not a constitutional gap, nor a defect of power to conscript in time of war, any more than there is a defect of power to raise an army of volunteers. Daniel Webster's contrary views have been superseded. See *Holmes* v. *United States,* 391 U.S. 936, 940 note 3, 88 S.Ct. 1835, 20 L.Ed.2d 856 (1968). His historical reading of the past was better than of the future.

Whether this constitutional power exists in time of peace has been thought by some justices of the Supreme Court to be an open question. See *Holmes* v. *United States,* 391 U.S. 936, 938–949, 88 S.Ct. 1835 (1968); *Hart* v. *United States,* 391 U.S. 956, 88 S.Ct. 1851, 20 L.Ed.2d 871 (1968); *McArthur* v. *Clifford,* 393 U.S. 1002, 89 S.Ct. 487, 21 L.Ed.2d 466 (1968). However, this court, until otherwise authoritatively instructed, assumes that Congressional power to conscript for war embraces Congressional power in time of peace to conscript for later possible war service. But the assumption is not fully supported despite what this court indicated in 294 F.Supp. at p. 513, by *Hamilton* v. *Regents of University of California,* 293 U.S. 245, 55 S.Ct. 197, 79 L.Ed. 343 (1934). *Hamilton* goes on the narrow ground that the Fourteenth Amendment does not confer "the right to be students in the State University free from the obligation to take military training as one of the conditions of attendance," Thomas Reed Powell, Conscience and the Constitution in William T. Hutchinson, Editor, Democracy and National Unity, The University of Chicago Press, 1941, p. 15 of the reprint. The opinion of Justice Butler, it is true, proceeded on the premise that the conscription power was the same in peace as in war. But, Justice Cardozo, speaking for himself, Justice Brandeis, and Justice Stone, observed that "There is no occasion at this time to mark the limits of governmental power in the exaction of military service when the nation is at peace." (P. 265, 55 S.Ct. p. 205)

This court's assumption that Congress has the general power to conscript in time of peace is not dispositive of the specific question whether that general power is subject to some exception or immunity available to a draftee because of a constitutional restriction in favor of individual liberty. See Powell, above, at pp. 6, 18.

However, some have supposed the specific question is foreclosed. At the head of the procession is Judge Learned Hand who a decade ago, before the Vietnam conflict sharpened our focus, announced in the Oliver Wendell Holmes Lectures on The Bill of Rights, Harvard University Press, (1958), p. 64 (same book republished with same pagination, Athenaeum Press, 1964), without pausing for a footnote, that "We could, though we do not, lawfully require all citizens to do military service regardless of their religious principles."

No doubt Judge Learned Hand recalled the argument Mr. John W. Davis made in *United States* v. *Macintosh,* 283 U.S. 605, 51 S.Ct. 570, 75 L.Ed. 1302 (1931), that it is a "fixed principle of our Constitution . . . that a citizen cannot be forced and need not bear arms in a war if he has conscientious religious scruples against doing so." (P. 623, 51 S.Ct. p. 575). Judge Hand remembered that the argument of Mr. Davis had been rejected by Justice Sutherland, 283 U.S. at pages 623–624, 51 S.Ct. 570, in language quoted by Justice Butler at p. 264 of 293 U.S., at p. 205 of 55 S.Ct. in *Hamilton:*

> The conscientious objector is relieved from the obligation to bear arms in obedience to no constitutional provision, express or implied; but because, and only because, it has accorded with the policy of Congress thus to relieve him. . . . [T]he war powers . . . include . . . the power, *in the last extremity,* to compel the armed service of any citizen in the land, without regard to his objections or his views in respect of the justice or morality of the particular war or of war in general. (Emphasis added.)

Sweeping as the foregoing quotation seems to be, there are restrictive implications inherent in the use of the phrase "in the last extremity." And while Justice Sutherland does use the comprehensive words "to compel the armed service of any citizen," it is arguable that he was not seeking prematurely to answer a question which a few years later Thomas Reed Powell treated as still undecided, that is "whether a conscientious objector could constitutionally be required to kill." Powell at p. 17.

The sum of the matter is that a careful scholar would conclude in 1969, as Professor Powell did in 1941, that "Notwithstanding all judicial declarations, it has not been actually decided that a conscientious objector, not within any group exempted by Congress, can be put into the front-line trenches or put into the army where certain refusals to obey orders may be punished by death." See Powell, above, at p. 18.

Yet, open as the issue may be, *this Court in the following discussion assumes that a conscientious objector, religious or otherwise, may be conscripted for some kinds of service in peace or in war. This Court further assumes that in time of declared war or in the defense of the homeland against invasion, all persons may be conscripted even for combat service.*

But the precise inquiry this Court cannot avoid is whether now Sisson may be compelled to submit to non-justiciable military orders which may require him to render combat service in Vietnam. Cf. *In re Jenison*, 375 U.S. 14, 84 S.Ct. 63, 11 L.Ed.2d 39 (1963); same case on remand 267 Minn. 136, 125 N.W.2d 588, 2 A.L.R.3d 1389 (1964).

Implicit is the problem whether in deciding the issue as to the constitutional claim of a conscientious objector to be exempt from combat service circumstances alter cases. (See the admittedly distinguishable case of jury duty. *In re Jenison* above.)

This is not an area of constitutional absolutism. It is an area in which competing claims must be explored, examined, and marshalled with reference to the Constitution as a whole.

There are two main categories of conflicting claims. First, there are both public and private interests in the common defense. Second, there are both public and private interests in individual liberty.

Every man, not least the conscientious objector, has an interest in the security of the nation. Dissent is possible only in a society strong enough to repel attack. The conscientious will to resist springs from moral principles. It is likely to seek a new order in the same society, not anarchy or submission to a hostile power. Thus conscience rarely wholly disassociates itself from the defense of the ordered society within which it functions and which it seeks to reform, not to reduce to rubble.

In parallel fashion, every man shares and society as a whole shares an interest in the liberty of the conscientious objector, religious or not. The freedom of all depends on the freedom of each. Free men exist only in free societies. Society's own stability and growth, its physical and spiritual prosperity are responsive to the liberties of its citizens, to their deepest insights, to their free choices—"That which opposes, also fits."

Those rival categories of claims cannot be mathematically graded. There is no table of weights and measures. Yet there is no insuperable difficulty in distinguishing orders of magnitude.

The sincerely conscientious man, whose principles flow from reflection, education, practice, sensitivity to competing claims, and a search for a meaningful life, always brings impressive credentials. When he honestly believes that he will act wrongly if he kills, his claim obviously has great magnitude. That magnitude is not appreciably lessened if his belief relates not to war in general, but to a particular war or to a particular type of war. Indeed a selective conscientious objector might reflect a more discriminating study of the problem, a more sensitive conscience, and a deeper spiritual understanding.

It is equally plain that when a nation is fighting for its very existence there are public and private interests of great magnitude in conscripting for the common defense all available resources, including manpower for combat.

But a campaign fought with limited forces for limited objects with no likelihood of a battlefront within this country and without a declaration of war is not a claim of comparable magnitude.

Nor is there any suggestion that in present circumstances there is a national need for combat service from Sisson as distinguished from other forms of service by him. The want of magnitude in the national demand for combat service is reflected in the nation's lack of calls for sacrifice in any serious way by civilians.

Before adding up the accounts and striking a balance there are other items deserving notice.

Sisson is not in a formal sense a religious conscientious objector. His claim may seem less weighty than that of one who embraces a creed which recognizes a Supreme Being, and which has as part of its training and discipline opposition to war in any form. It may even seem that the Constitution itself marks a difference because in the First Amendment reference is made to the "free exercise of" "religion," not to the free exercise of conscience. Moreover, Sisson does not meet the 1967 congressional definition of religion. Nor does he meet the dictionary definition of religion.

But that is not the end of the matter. The opinions in *United States* v. *Seeger,* 380 U.S. 163, 85 S.Ct. 850, 13 L.Ed.2d 733 (1965) disclosed wide vistas. The court purported to look only at a particular statute. It piously disclaimed any intent to interpret the Constitution or to examine the limitations which the First and Fifth Amendments place upon Congress. But commentators have not forgotten the Latin tag *pari passu.* See Note, The Conscientious Objector and The First Amendment: There but for the Grace of God, 34 U.Chi.L.Rev. 79 (1966); James B. White, Processing Conscientious Objector Claims: A Constitutional Inquiry, 56 Cal.L.Rev. 652 (1968); Hugh C. Macgill, Selective Conscientious Objection: Divine Will and Legislative Grace, 54 Va.L.Rev. 1355 (1968); John Mansfield, Conscientious Objection—1964 Term, 1965 Religion and the Public Order 1.

The rationale by which Seeger and his companions on appeal were exempted from combat service under the statute is quite sufficient for Sisson to lay valid claim to be constitutionally exempted from combat service in the Vietnam type of situation.

Duty once commonly appeared as the "stern daughter of the voice of God." Today to many she appears as the stern daughter of the voice of conscience. It is not the ancestry but the authenticity of the sense of duty which creates constitutional legitimacy.

Some suppose that the only reliable conscience is one responsive to a formal religious community of memory and hope. But in Religion In The Making, Alfred North Whitehead taught us that "religion is what the individual does with his own solitariness." pp. 16, 47, 58.

Others fear that recognition of individual conscience will make it too easy for the individual to perpetuate a fraud. His own word will so often enable him to sustain his burden of proof. Cross-examination will not easily discover his insincerity.

Seeger cut the ground from under that argument. So does experience. Often it is harder to detect a fraudulent adherent to a religious creed than to recognize a sincere moral protestant. See Justice Jackson's dissent in *United States* v. *Ballard,* 322 U.S. 78, 92–95, 64 S.Ct. 882, 88

L.Ed. 1148 (1944). We all can discern Thoreau's integrity more quickly than we might detect some churchman's hypocrisy.

The suggestion that courts cannot tell a sincere from an insincere conscientious objector underestimates what the judicial process performs every day. Ever since, in *Edginton* v. *Fitzmaurice* (1882) L.R. 29 Ch. Div. 359, Bowen L. J. quipped that "the state of a man's mind is as much a fact as the state of his digestion," each day courts have applied laws, criminal and civil, which make sincerity the test of liability.

There have been suggestions that to read the Constitution as granting an exemption from combat duty in a foreign campaign will immunize from public regulation all acts or refusals to act dictated by religious or conscientious scruple. Such suggestions fail to note that there is no need to treat, and this court does not treat, religious liberty as an absolute. The most sincere religious or conscientious believer may be validly punished even if in strict pursuance of his creed or principles, he fanatically as-sassinates an opponent, or practices polygamy, *Reynolds* v. *United States,* 98 U.S. 145, 154, 25 L.Ed. 244 (1878), or employs child labor, *Prince* v. *Massachusetts,* 321 U.S. 158, 64 S.Ct. 438, 88 L.Ed. 645 (1944). Religious liberty and liberty of conscience have limits in the face of social demands of a community of fellow citizens. There are, for example, important rival claims of safety, order, health, and decency.

Nor is it true that to recognize liberty of conscience and religious liberty will set up some magic line between nonfeasance and misfeasance. A religiously motivated failure to discharge a public obligation may be as serious a crime as a religiously motivated action in violation of law. We may, argumentatively, assume that one who out of religious or conscientious scruple refuses to pay a general income or property tax, assessed without reference to any particular kind of contemplated expenditure, is civilly and criminally liable, regardless of his sincere belief that he is responding to a divine command not to support the government.

Most important, it does not follow from a judicial decision that Sisson cannot be conscripted to kill in Vietnam that he cannot be conscripted for non-combat service there or elsewhere.

It would be a poor court indeed that could not discern the small constitutional magnitude of the interest that a person has in avoiding all helpful service whatsoever or in avoiding paying all general taxes whatsoever. His objections, of course, may be sincere. But some sincere objections have greater constitutional magnitude than others.

There are many tasks, technologically or economically related to the prosecution of a war, to which a religious or conscientious objector might be constitutionally assigned. As Justice Cardozo wrote "Never in our history has the notion been accepted, or even, it is believed, advanced, that acts thus indirectly related to service in the camp or field are so tied to the practice of religion as to be exempt, in law or in morals, from regulation by the state." *Hamilton* v. *Regents of University of California,* 293 U.S. 245, 267, 55 S.Ct. 197, 206, 79 L.Ed. 343 (1934).

Sisson's case being limited to a claim of conscientious objection to combat service in a foreign campaign, this court holds that the free exercise of religion clause in the First Amendment and the due process clause of the Fifth Amendment prohibit the application of the 1967 draft act to Sisson to require him to render combat service in Vietnam.

The chief reason for reaching this conclusion after examining the competing interests is the magnitude of Sisson's interest in not killing in the Vietnam conflict as against the want of magnitude in the country's present need for him to be so employed.

The statute as here applied creates a clash between law and morality for which no exigency exists, and before, in Justice Sutherland's words, "the last extremity" or anything close to that dire predicament has been glimpsed, or even predicted, or reasonably feared.

When the state through its laws seeks to override reasonable moral commitments it makes a dangerously uncharacteristic choice. The law grows from the deposits of morality. Law and morality are, in turn, debtors and creditors of each other. The law cannot be adequately enforced by the courts alone, or by courts supported merely by the police and the military. The true secret of legal might lies in the habits of conscientious men disciplining themselves to obey the law they respect without the necessity of judicial and administrative orders. When the law treats a reasonable, conscientious act as a crime it subverts its own power. It invites civil disobedience. It impairs the very habits which nourish and preserve the law.

F. THE CONSTITUTIONAL POWER OF CONGRESS TO DISCRIMINATE AS IT DID IN THE 1967 DRAFT ACT BETWEEN THE DRAFT STATUS OF SISSON AS A CONSCIENTIOUS OBJECTOR AND THE DRAFT STATUS OF ADHERENTS TO CERTAIN TYPES OF RELIGIONS

The Supreme Court may not address itself to the broad issue just decided. Being a court of last resort, it, unlike an inferior court, can confidently rest its judgment upon a narrow issue. Indeed *Seeger* foreshadows exactly that process. So it is incumbent on this court to consider the narrow issue, whether the 1967 Act invalidly discriminates against Sisson as a non-religious conscientious objector.

The draft act now limits "exemption from combat training and service" to one "who, by reason of religious training and belief, is conscientiously opposed to participation in war in any form" 50 U.S.C.App. Section 456(j), commonly cited as Section 6(j) of the Act as amended.

A Quaker, for example, is covered if he claims belief in the ultimate implications of William Penn's teaching.

Persons trained in and believing in other religious ways may or may not be covered. A Roman Catholic obedient to the teaching of

Thomas Aquinas and Pope John XXIII might distinguish between a just war in which he would fight and an unjust war in which he would not fight. Those who administer the Selective Service System opine that Congress has not allowed exemption to those whose conscientious objection rests on such a distinction. See Lt. Gen. Lewis B. Hershey, Legal Aspects of Selective Service, U.S. Gov. Printing Office, January 1, 1969, pp. 13-14. This court has a more open mind.

However, the administrators and this court both agree that Congress has not provided a conscientious objector status for a person whose claim is admittedly not formally religious.

In this situation Sisson claims that even if the Constitution might not otherwise preclude Congress from drafting him for combat service in Vietnam, the Constitution does preclude Congress from drafting him under the 1967 Act. The reason is that this Act grants conscientious objector status solely to religious conscientious objectors but not to non-religious objectors.

Earlier this opinion noted that it is practical to accord the same status to non-religious conscientious objectors as to religious objectors. Moreover, it is difficult to imagine any ground for a statutory distinction except religious prejudice. In short, in the draft act Congress unconstitutionally discriminated against atheists, agnostics, and men, like Sisson, who, whether they be religious or not, are motivated in their objection to the draft by profound moral beliefs which constitute the central convictions of their beings.

This Court, therefore, concludes that in granting to the religious conscientious objector but not to Sisson a special conscientious objector status, the Act, as applied to Sisson, violates the provision of the First Amendment that "Congress shall make no law respecting an establishment of religion or prohibiting the free exercise thereof." *Torcaso* v. *Watkins*, 367 U.S. 488, 81 S.Ct. 1680, 6 L.Ed.2d 982 (1961). Cf. *Sherbert* v. *Verner*, 374 U.S. 398, 404, 83 S.Ct. 1790, 10 L.Ed.2d 965 (1963); *Everson* v. *Board of Education*, 330 U.S. 1, 15-16, 67 S.Ct. 504, 91 L.Ed. 711 (1947).

In the words of Rule 34, the indictment of Sisson "does not charge an offense."

This court's "decision arresting a judgment of conviction for insufficiency of the indictment . . . is based upon the invalidity . . . of the statute upon which the indictment . . . is founded" within the meaning of those phrases as used in 18 U.S.C. Section 3731. *United States* v. *Green*, 350 U.S. 415, 416, 76 S.Ct. 522, 100 L.Ed. 494 (1956); *United States* v. *Bramblett*, 348 U.S. 503, 504, 75 S.Ct. 504, 99 L.Ed. 594 (1955). Therefore, "an appeal may be taken by and on behalf of the United States . . . direct to the Supreme Court of the United States."

To guard against misunderstanding, this Court has *not* ruled that:

(1) The Government has no right to conduct Vietnam Operations; or
(2) The Government is using unlawful methods in Vietnam; or

(3) The Government has no power to conscript the generality of men for combat service; or

(4) The Government in a defense of the homeland has no power to conscript for combat service anyone it sees fit; or

(5) The Government has no power to conscript conscientious objectors for non-combat service.

Indeed the Court assumes without deciding that each one of those propositions states the exact reverse of the law.

All that this Court decides is that as a sincere conscientious objector Sisson cannot constitutionally be subjected to military orders (not reviewable in a United States constitutional Court) which may require him to kill in the Vietnam conflict.

Enter forthwith this decision and this court's order granting defendant Sisson's motion in arrest of judgment.

DISSENT—1968

Erwin N. Griswold *

"Preserving civil peace is the first responsibility of government." [1]

"Unfortunately, since the populace has been sluggish and complacent, occasional violence seems to be advantageous to wake people up. . . ." [2]

When I first accepted the invitation to deliver this year's Dreyfous Lecture, it was my intention to discuss, in a rather abstract way, some of the changes that have taken place in the modes of dissent over the years. The sad events of the past ten days, however, have led me to revise my emphasis somewhat. Rather than recite the changes of the past, I wish to speak to you tonight about some fundamental postulates of our democratic society, principles which I believe must be kept in vivid focus and which must be meaningfully communicated to the com-

From the *Tulane Law Review*, 17 (1968): 725-739. Copyright 1968 by the Tulane Law Review Association. Reprinted by permission of the author and the publisher.

* I wish to express my sincere thanks to my associate, Philip A. Lacovara, LL.B. Columbia, 1966, for assistance in the preparation of this lecture.

[1] Report of the National Advisory Commission on Civil Disorders 171 (March 1, 1968).

[2] Goodman, "The Resisters Support U.S. Traditions and Interests" in *On Civil Disobedience, 1967*, N.Y. Times Magazine, November 26, 1967, at 124.

munity as a whole if true freedom—not frenetic license—is to endure.

Let me begin by confessing that I am aware that between the polar extremes which I shall discuss there are confusing overlays of principle and policy and there will remain very substantial areas where the conscientious judgment of the informed individual is the only operative standard. But for the individual to make a rational choice, he must be aware of the values and consequences at stake when he forms his conscience and determines to follow it, and it is in hope that it will encourage reflective appreciation of what is truly involved in "civil disobedience"— which has become the most pervasive contemporary aspect of civil liberties—that I submit these remarks for your attention.

I

Ambassador Sol M. Linowitz touched on the core of the problem in his address last month before a conference organized by the American Assembly and the American Bar Association when he suggested that in recent years there has been a material change in the public attitude toward law. He observed that law is now too often viewed "not as the living model for a free society, but rather as a mode of callous repression, or—no less disturbingly—as a collection of precatory suggestions which can be flouted or ignored." [3]

The focus of these remarks, just as with the Ambassador's observation, is not professional crime engaged in by those who are indifferent to legal obstacles to their own enrichment. What is of more concern is that our society has become increasingly tolerant of the mischievous attempts to excuse deliberate violations of the law committed in furtherance of what the actor personally regards as a lofty cause. I shall advert later on to justifiable examples of civil disobedience, but what I suggest is that the intellectual and practical consequence of indiscriminate civil disobedience is the "Legitimation of violence" of which we have seen too much in America. I borrow this phrase from the recent Presidential Riot Commission, which listed this sorry fact of American society as one of the basic causes of riots. The Commission's conclusion, under this heading is as follows: [4]

> A climate that tends toward the approval and encouragement of violence as a form of protest has been created by white terrorism directed against nonviolent protest, including instances of abuse and even murder of some civil rights workers in the South, by the open defiance of law and Federal authority by state and local officials resisting desegregation, and

[3] Linowitz, *Our Changing Society: The Lawyers Challenge*, 54 A.B.A.J. 445, 448 (1968).

[4] Report of the National Advisory Commission on Civil Disorders 92 (March 1, 1968).

by some protest groups engaging in civil disobedience who turn their backs on nonviolence, go beyond constitutionally protected rights of petition and free assembly and resort to violence to attempt to compel alteration of laws and policies with which they disagree. This condition has been re-enforced by a general erosion of respect for authority in American society and the reduced effectiveness of social standards and community restraints on violence and crime.

The ink is not yet dry on the latest confirmation of this conclusion. The almost inevitable retaliation that the Commission spoke of was not long in coming, and over a hundred cities have been wracked by the manifestation of grim, mindless destruction. To argue that massive retaliation against society at large is both unjustifiable and self-defeating [5] —while unquestionably correct—misses the point that our national temperament has become too much acclimated to violence as a method of social protest.

Perhaps you may interject that no one who champions the right of protest in general, or the privilege of civil disobedience in particular, would seek to justify either political assassinations or riots. Of course I would not dispute this caveat, but the troubling circumstances I have sketched have both a logical and a practical relevance to issues of protest and dissent. They are logically related to our focus because they represent the ultimate mode of dissent—rejection not merely of the position of the majority but of the very foundation of civilized society itself: Civil Order. They have a practical impact on our topic too, for these extreme acts I have adverted to are in a sense the product of the same undiscriminating and uncritical attitude toward individual choice about the binding nature of law that underlies less dramatic but similarly irresponsible forms of protest.

II

We Americans have always taken a considerable measure of pride in our personal independence and right to nonconformity. But in my view, effective self-government is nevertheless the greatest achievement of mankind. I trust that most Americans share the conclusion that Government is not merely inevitable but highly desirable. And from this axiom, certain corollaries flow.

The *first* of these is, I think, that civil disobedience differs quite radically in important respects from ordinary modes of protest and dissent. The crucial attribute of civil disobedience is that it is expressed through deliberate violation of the law.[6] Read in the context of its

---

[5] E.g., Leibman, *Civil Disobedience: A Threat to Our Law Society*, 51 A.B.A.J. 645, 646 (1965).

[6] One of the more thoughtful analyses of this topic is that given by Dean Francis Allen in *Civil Disobedience and the Legal Order*, 36 U. Cin. L. Rev. 1, 175 (1967).

origin, the first amendment not only creates a right to dissent but in a very real sense encourages the exercise of this prerogative. That is why we are concerned about "chilling" first amendment freedoms. But our law and custom have long been clear that the right to differ with society and to reject its code of behavior has limits, and the first amendment will not do service to sanction every sort of activity that is sought to be justified as an expression of non-conformity.

Second, equally important and sometimes profoundly troubling, our political tradition has long recognized that a man's abiding duty to his conscience transcends his obligation to the State. Chief Justice Hughes once put it this way: [7]

> Much has been said of the paramount duty to the State, a duty to be recognized, it is urged, even though it conflicts with convictions of duty to God. Undoubtedly that duty to the State exists within the domain of power, for government may enforce obedience to laws regardless of scruples. When one's belief collides with the power of the State, the latter is Supreme within its sphere and submission or punishment follows. But, in the forum of conscience, duty to a moral power higher than the State has always been maintained.

Third, in a democracy such as ours, each individual shares both a political and a moral duty "actively to participate—to some degree, at least—in the processes of government and law-making." I am quoting the words of my friend, Professor J. N. D. Anderson of the University of London.[8] He continues: "In a democracy, indeed, every citizen bears a measure of personal responsibility for misgovernment, bad laws, or wrong policies, unless he has played his full part in trying to get a better government into power, better laws on the statute book, and better policies adopted."

As my *fourth* corollary, and here perhaps I will meet with slightly less universal agreement, I suggest that what we have been classically concerned about protecting is the dissemination of ideas—protecting the individual's access to the intellectual market-place where he may offer his conception of the ills and remedies for social or political problems. Thus, historically, our motivation and our objective have been the attempt to encourage the search for truth or wisdom, or both. To quote Chief Justice Hughes again: [9]

> The maintenance of the opportunity for free political discussion to the end that government may be responsive to the will of the people and that changes may be obtained by lawful means, an opportunity essential

7 *United States* v. *Macintosh,* 283 U.S. 605, 633 (1931) (Hughes, C.J., and Holmes, Brandeis, and Stone, JJ., dissenting).

8 J. Anderson, Into the World—the Need and Limits of Christian Involvement 41 (London 1968).

9 *Stromberg* v. *California,* 283 U.S. 359, 369 (1931).

to the security of the Republic, is a fundamental principle of our constitutional system.

Given these principles, which I regard as not merely orthodox but sound, let me turn to the forms of dissent and protest which are currently the vogue so that we may proceed to consider some of the problems of dissent and in particular of civil disobedience.

III

Toward the end of the last century, Justice Holmes observed that on the basis of his experience, "Behind every scheme to make the world over, lies the question, What kind of world do you want?" [10] It may well have been true in those times that dissent and protest and agitation —for women's suffrage, or prohibition, or socialism, or anarchism, or whatever—had a more or less conscious and systematic design for the objective which was sought to be achieved. But today, much protest seems reflexive rather than cerebral, motivated more by the desire to reject established positions and policies than by deliberate preference for some alternatives. Perhaps I am not perceptive enough to discern the latent wisdom and goals of movements that seek the elevation of dirty words on campus, or that exalt the virtues of "flower power," or that conduct a "strip-in" in a public park. The message, if there is one, escapes me.

We have in this country, of course, recognized that the display of symbols as an expression of some dissenting position is entitled to constitutional protection. That was settled as long ago at least as the "Red Flag" case.[11] But all this presupposes that there is some intelligible and definable nexus between the form of the protest and what is being protested. Thus, when a prominent New York couple several years ago decided to express their indignation at increased municipal taxes by stringing clotheslines draped with rags and tattered uniforms in their front yard, the state courts found this "bizarre" manner of symbolic dissent unprotected, with Judge Stanley Fuld writing that it was clear that the "value of their 'protest' lay not in its message but in its offensiveness." [12] And the Supreme Court summarily ruled that their claims of "free speech" were in the circumstances clearly frivolous.

I have similar difficulty with other popular forms of modern "dissent." Have we reached the point in this country where anything is

[10] The Occasional Speeches of Justice Oliver Wendell Holmes 75 (Howe ed. 1962).

[11] *Stromberg* v. *California*, 283 U.S. 359 (1931). Compare *West Virginia State Board of Education* v. *Barnette*, 319 U.S. 624 (1943).

[12] *People* v. *Stover*, 12 N.Y.2d 462, 470, 240 N.Y.S.2d 734, 740, 191 N.E.2d 272, 277 (1963), *appeal dismissed*, 375 U.S. 42 (1963).

contributed to our shared desire for progress and achievement by "writing dirty words on a fence about the President of the country? Or calling members of his Administration names?" [13] No less prominent a spokesman for dissent than Bayard Rustin has expressed his "puzzlement" at the tactics employed by some young people in proclaiming their disenchantment with present conditions. He remarks rather pointedly that he is "concerned about their believing that you can educate people on the basis of simplistic slogans . . . rather than on the basis of a concrete program of concrete recommendations." [14] While satire and sharp rapier-thrusts have long been among the accepted and effective modes of social and politcial criticism, I doubt that personal ridicule or broad-gauge contumely has ever produced light rather than heat, or constructively contributed to the resolution of major questions.

I do not question the constitutional right to be irrelevant or intemperate or even unfair. Our jurisprudence has made it clear that it is a prerogative of American citizenship "to criticize public men and measures—and that means not only informed and responsible criticism but the freedom to speak foolishly and without moderation." [15] In part this is the consequence of the assumption of our democratic system that the people can be trusted to test competing ideas and proposals, after free discussion, and "to withstand ideas that are wrong." [16] And in part it reflects our policy that even damaging and false assertions, and those unrelated to alternative programs, must be suffered lest the submission of important and constructive suggestions be deterred.[17]

IV

There is a contemporary aspect of the problem to which, I think, too little attention has been given.

When our basic notions of freedom of speech, and of the right to dissent, were developed—largely in the eighteenth century—communication was very different from what it is now. There were fewer people—only three million in the United States. Most of them were close to the soil, and many were not unduly literate. The market place for political ideas was more limited than it is now.

Perhaps of even greater importance, though, was the fact that the

[13] Farrell, "Today's Disobedience is Uncivil," in *On Civil Disobedience, 1967,* N.Y. Times Magazine, November 26, 1967, at 29.

[14] Rustin, in *Civil Disobedience* 10 (Center for the Study of Democratic Institutions 1966).

[15] *Baumgartner* v. *United States,* 322 U.S. 665, 673-674 (1944). See also *Bridges* v. *California,* 314 U.S. 252 (1941).

[16] *Barenblatt* v. *United States,* 360 U.S. 109, 146 (1959) (Black, J. dissenting).

[17] See generally *New York Times Co.* v. *Sullivan,* 376 U.S. 254 (1964).

speed of communication of ideas was very slow. Freedom of speech and press meant freedom for Thomas Paine to publish "Common Sense," or for John Adams to write an article for a newspaper and for the newspaper to publish it. When these and other things were printed, they were read in the privacy of the home, with few other persons around. Ideas had an opportunity to percolate, to be examined and considered, and to be refined and reformed in the thoughts of the people.

Of course, there was speech making, too. But one person's voice could reach perhaps a thousand people, perhaps somewhat more under very special circumstances. The speech could, of course, be printed, but it would be the next day before it was read in the same community, and days or weeks before it was read elsewhere. Almost always, there was time for thoughtful consideration. Moreover, the volume of material which was communicated, in print or by speech, was very limited. There was adequate opportunity for thoughtful people to comprehend, to absorb, and digest. In the modern world, though, this has been changed completely. The change has been developing over the years, with the telegraph and telephone, and the speed of transportation. With the coming of the radio, it was possible for President Roosevelt to address fifty or one hundred million people at once, with an impact that had never been known before.

In recent years, the facilities of communication have continued to develop until our situation is utterly different from what it was even a generation ago. In older days, a person who had an idea to express— whether of dissent, or otherwise, had some difficulty in bringing this about. To publish it in a book or pamphlet might be beyond his means. There were few newspapers, and these did not have much space. Unless the idea was extremely good, or well expressed, it was not likely that a newspaper could be found to publish it.

Today, however, the news media are avid for news. Television stations are putting out news through all the hours of the day, and they are always seeking something new or different, something that will attract viewers to their station. Almost anyone who wants to do something bizarre on a public street can find his way on television, and be seen by millions or tens of millions of people all over the country, and, indeed, through much of the world.

Because the newspapers are in competition with the television stations, they have to present the same news. Thus, there has been an enormous increase in the opportunity to express dissent, and, perhaps even more important, an even greater increase in the immediacy of dissent and the impact which it can make. There may be real room to question whether we have psychologically caught up with the developments in communications' speed and distribution, whether we are capable of absorbing and evaluating all of the materials which are now communicated daily to hundreds of millions of people.

I do not mean to suggest that the communications agencies have acted irresponsibly. They, too, have had to learn their power while the public was beginning to become aware of it. There are clear signs that television and newspapers are aware of their responsibilities in these areas, and are accepting them. There is a hard line for them to follow. For they must serve the ideals of a free press. Yet, all of the problems are enormously magnified, and the essential nature of responsibility in the exercise of a free press stands out more clearly as the magnification increases. The power of communication, through press, radio and television, has become an awesome power. Its use is essential to the preservation of a free society. Only time will tell, I suppose, whether our system can adequately adjust itself to the impact of modern communications methods. I am only trying to point out here the importance of the exercise of responsibility in the expression of dissent in the modern world.

V

We must draw two fundamental distinctions when we speak of dissent; the first involves primarily legal and moral variables and divides permissible from impermissible dissent; the second presupposes that the dissent is tolerable but involves the social and political considerations of whether, or when or how the protest *should* be made. The latter is not a question of right, but of judgment and morals, even of taste, and a proper sense of restraint and responsibility, qualities which are or should be inherent in the very concept of civil liberties.

We must begin any analysis of these questions with the undoubted fact that we live in a society, an imperfect and struggling one, no doubt, but one where Government and order are not only a necessity, but are the preference of an overwhelming majority of the citizenry. The rules that society has developed to organize and order itself are found in a body of law which has not been imposed from outside, but has been slowly built up from experience expressed through the consent of the governed, and now pervades all aspects of human activity. Inevitably there are occasions when individuals or groups will chafe under a particular legal bond, or will bridle in opposition to a particular governmental policy, and the question presents itself, what can be done?

Vocal objection, of course—even slanderous or inane—is permissible. But the fact that one is a dissenter with a right to express his opposition entitles him to no special license. Thus, in expressing views that are themselves wholly immune to official strictures he gains no roving commission to ignore the rules and underlying assumptions of society that relate in a neutral way to activity rather than to the maintenance or expression of idea. Thus, I submit that one cannot rightly engage in conduct which is otherwise unlawful merely because he intends that either that conduct or the idea he wishes to express in the course of the conduct is intended to manifest his dissent from some government policy. I cannot distinguish in principle the legal quality of the determination to halt a troop train to protest the Vietnam war or to block workmen from entering a segregated job site to protest employment discrimination, from the determination to fire shots into a civil rights leader's home to protest integration. The right to disagree—and to manifest disagreement —which the constitution allows to the individuals in those situations— does not authorize them to carry on their campaign of education and persuasion at the expense of someone else's liberty, or in violation of some laws whose independent validity is unquestionable.

This distinction runs deep in our history, but has too frequently been ignored in this decade. But the line is a clear one, and we should reestablish it in the thinking and understanding of our people. While I share Professor Harry Kalven's assessment that the "generosity and empathy with which [public streets and parks] are made available [as a "public forum"] is an index of freedom," [18] I regard as unassailable the limitation that the mere fact that a person wishes to make a public point does not sanction any method he chooses to use to make it. Yet there seems to be currently a considerable tendency to ignore if not to reject this limitation. Certainly many of the modern forms of dissent, including those I have just mentioned, proceed on the basis of the contrary proposition. Only last Term, the Supreme Court was asked to sustain the right of demonstrators active in a cause that most of us here and the Court itself no doubt regarded as laudable, to lodge their demand for an end to segregation on the grounds of a city jail where, it seemed, biased treatment was being accorded prisoners. The argument was made that a demonstration at that site was "particularly appropriate," irrespective of the consequences. Speaking for the Court, Justice Black rejected this rationale, explaining that [19]

> Such an argument has as its major unarticulated premise the assumption that people who want to propagandize protests or views have a constitutional right to do so whenever and however and wherever they please.

That notion the Court expressly "vigorously and forthrightly rejected."

Another form of protest that can never, in my view, be excused or tolerated, is that which assumes the posture of a violent and forcible assault on public order, whatever the motivation. The interests at stake in such a situation must transcend the validity of the particular cause and the permissibility of adhering to it. Violent opposition to law—any law—or forcible disregard of another's freedom to disagree falls beyond the pale of legitimate dissent or even of civil disobedience, properly understood; it is nothing short of rebellion.

The utter indefensibility of violent opposition to law is that it proceeds on the foolhardy and immoral principle that might makes

---

[18] Kalven, *The Concept of the Public Forum: Cox v. Louisiana,* 1965 Supreme Court Review 1, 12.

[19] *Adderley* v. *Florida,* 385 U.S. 39, 47-48 (1966).

right. Centuries ago Rousseau rejected this approach as a viable political alternative: [20]

> For, if force creates right, the effect changes with the cause: every force that is greater than the first succeeds to its right. As soon as it is possible to disobey with impunity, disobedience is legitimate; and, the strongest being always in the right, the only thing that matters is to act so as to become the strongest. But what kind of right is that which perishes when force fails?

To permit factions the resort to force when they feel—however correctly—that a particular law or policy is wrong would be to renounce our own experience and that of the Founders. In support of this view, I offer two sentences written by Justice Frankfurter: "Law alone saves a society from being rent by internecine strife or ruled by mere brute power however disguised." [21] And "Violent resistance to law cannot be made a legal reason for its suspension without loosening the fabric of our society." [22]

What is at stake is not mere order but also the lessons of history. True freedom and substantial justice come not from violent altercations or incendiary dissent. "No mob has ever protected any liberty, even its own." [23] While the first amendment embodies a distrust of the collective conscience of the majority in areas of fundamental liberty, it no more intended to leave the limits of freedom to the judgment of coercive dissenters. "Civil government cannot let any group ride rough-shod over others simply because their 'consciences' tell them to do so." [24]

VI

These reflections have dealt with the question when law and government may tolerate dissent, or dissent manifested in certain ways, and I have suggested that it is illicit to violate otherwise valid laws either as a symbol of protest or in the course of protest, and secondly that I regard it as indefensible to attempt to promote a viewpoint either by flagrant violence or by organized coercion. Now I will turn finally to the second distinction to which I referred earlier in this lecture. That is, assuming a legal or moral right to protest, what considerations of prudence and responsibility should infuse the determination to exercise these rights?

First, you will note that I imply that a line may be drawn between

[20] The Social Contract, Bk. I, Ch. 3.
[21] *United States* v. *United Mine Workers,* 330 U.S. 258, 308 (1947).
[22] *Cooper* v. *Aaron,* 358 U.S. 1, 22 (1958).
[23] *Terminiello* v. *Chicago,* 337 U.S. 1, 32 (1949) (Jackson, J., dissenting).
[24] *Douglas* v. *City of Jeannette,* 319 U.S. 157, 179 (1943) (opinion of Jackson, J.).

legal and moral rights to dissent. I am not now referring to what I accept as the genuine possibility that one may exercise his constitutional right to dissent in a way that, because of recklessness or unfairness, makes his conduct ethically improper. I mention this distinction, however, because I believe awareness and evaluation of it should always be taken into account in considering an exercise of the right to dissent. But for the present, I mean to concentrate on the converse of this distinction, that there may be a moral right to dissent without a corresponding legal privilege to do so. It is in this context that "civil disobedience" must be viewed.

Earlier, I observed that our system contemplates that there may be a moral right to "civil disobedience" (properly understood) that exists notwithstanding a "legal" duty to obey. I also referred to the source of this moral right: the ultimate sanctity of a man's own conscience, as the intellectual and volitional composite that governs his conception of his relation to Eternal Truth. I wish now to emphasize the considerations which, in my view, condition the existence and exercise of this moral right, because I believe the current rhetoric which sometimes seems to consecrate "civil disobedience" as the noblest response in the pantheon of virtues has obscured the nature and consequence of this activity. To define my term—I mean by "civil disobedience" the deliberate violation of a rule ordained by constituted government because of a conscientious conviction that the law is so unjust that it cannot morally be observed by the individual.

The most important point to be stressed is that this decision is one that should be made only after the most painful and introspective reflection, and only when the firm conclusion is reached that obedience offends the most fundamental personal values. It is self-evident that routine or random non-compliance with the law for transient or superficial reasons would negate the first principles of civilized behavior. Unless society can safely assume that *almost* without exception individuals will accept the will of the majority even when to do so is grudging and distasteful, the foundation of secure liberty will rather rapidly erode. John Locke, who in his profound *Letter Concerning Toleration* analyzed and defended the right of obedience to conscience over civil law in case of severe conflict, thereafter cautioned in his essay *Concerning Civil Government:* [25]

> May [the sovereign] be resisted, as often as any one shall find himself aggrieved, and but imagine he has not right done him? This will unhinge and overturn all polities, and instead of government and order, leave nothing but anarchy and confusion.

Last year, in delivering this Lecture, Arthur Goodhart observed, "Thus, it has been correctly said that obedience to the law is a major

[25] Ch. XVIII, para. 203.

part of patriotism." [26] He meant this not as a castigation of dissent or as an outburst of flag-waving chauvinism, but rather as a formulation of a central political truth: That if human society is to enjoy freedom, it cannot tolerate license. Henry David Thoreau is generally regarded as the most notable American exponent of civil disobedience, and all of us share admiration for his determination. But we must not ignore the vital aspect of Thoreau's non-conformity—his passionate attempt to dissociate himself from society. He was, as Harry Kalven has put it, "a man who does not see himself as belonging very intensely to the community in which he was raised," [27] and who sought constantly but futilely to reject the society to which he had not voluntarily adhered.

Thoreau's poignant attitude was charming enough in mid-nineteenth century America. But it was, essentially, an effort to withdraw from the realities of life, and it was, I suggest, myopic even then, for it was painfully inconsistent with the fact that man is a part of society by nature, by geography, and by citizenship. Unlike a member of a purely artificial group, like a bar association or country club, a citizen cannot resign from the "social compact" because he protests policies of the regime. Now in the last third of the Twentieth Century, we must be even more cognizant that there is nothing noble or salutary about foredoomed attempts to abdicate membership in society. Complex problems demand rational attention that can come only from personal focus on solutions and never from stubbornly turning one's back on harsh and unpleasant realities.

This is precisely what non-conformity as a way of life is. It is the essential irrationality of the "hippie movement"—a mass endeavor to drop out of life. It is a protest of sorts, of course, but one that can bear no fruit, because it takes issue with what is not only inevitable, but more importantly, indispensable—social regulation of individual behavior.

Stretched to its logical extreme, this also is civil disobedience, and for this reason I urge that before any man embarks upon a unilateral nullification of any law he must appreciate that his judgment has not merely a personal significance but also portends grave consequences for his fellows.

In determining whether and when to exercise the moral right to disobey the dictates of the law it must also be recognized that society not only does not but cannot recognize this determination as entitled to legal privilege. It is part of the Gandhian tradition of civil disobedience that the sincerity of the individual's conscience presupposes that the law will punish this assertion of personal principle. In the very formation of our country, in the Federalist Papers, Hamilton explained the

[26] Goodhart, *Recognition of the Binding Nature of Law,* 41 Tul. L. Rev. 769, 773 (1967).
[27] "On Thoreau" in *Civil Disobedience* 25, 28 (Center for the Study of Democratic Institutions 1966).

reason why government cannot compromise its authority by offering a dispensation for individual conscience: [28]

> Government implies the power of making laws. It is essential to the idea of a law, that it be attended with a sanction; or, in other words, a penalty or punishment for disobedience. If there be no penalty annexed to disobedience, the resolutions or commands which pretend to be laws will, in fact, amount to nothing more than advice or recommendation.

Thus, it is of the essence of law that it is equally applied to all, that it binds all alike, irrespective of personal motive. For this reason, one who contemplates civil disobedience out of moral conviction should not be surprised and must not be bitter if a criminal conviction ensues. And he must accept the fact that organized society cannot endure on any other basis. His hope is that he may aid in getting the law changed. But if he does not succeed in that, he cannot complain if the law is applied to him.

VII

Though I speak with seriousness about civil disobedience, I hope that my remarks are not misunderstood. I endeavored to make it plain in my opening analysis that a proper recognition of the rights of conscience is one of the basic assumptions of our society. The problem, of course, is to determine what is "proper." Like all questions worth discussing, it is inevitably one of degree.

In considering this question, it is well to examine not only *whether* civil disobedience is appropriate in a particular situation, but also *how* it is to be carried out. We have a vivid illustration of this in the experience of this generation. We are all aware of the fact that for many long years the legal structure was often used to perpetuate deprivations which were at odds with the most basic constitutional and moral values. During this time, conditions of political, social, and economic inequality made ineffective meaningful attempts to change these regulations and policies by petition within the customary channels of reform. In this situation, the only realistic recourse was deliberate refusal to abide by the restrictions any longer. Lunch-counter sit-ins and freedom rides are among the most dramatic examples of the techniques that were used to expose the injustices that were perpetrated under the banner of law. In many of these cases, these actions were not, indeed, illegal, since the restrictive laws were plainly invalid if one had the time, energy and money to take them up to higher courts. In other cases, though, the line was not clear and sometimes the actions taken were undoubtedly illegal. We cannot

---

[28] The Federalist, Number 15 (Hamilton).

fail to recognize the fact that it was these tactics which succeeded in putting the basic issues squarely before the courts and the public. And it was in this way that the law was clarified in the courts and the legislative changes were brought about.

There are great lessons to be learned from this experience. Perhaps the greatest of these is that what mattered was not merely the moral fervor of the demonstrators, or the justice of their cause, but also the way in which they conducted themselves. They and their leaders were aware of the moral dimensions of their cause and they knew that this required an equal adherence to morality in the means by which they sought to indicate their cause. Because of this, rigid adherence to the philosophy of nonviolence was sought and widely achieved. In retrospect, I am sure that our Nation will point with pride not only to the courage of those who risked punishment in order to challenge injustice, but also to the morality of their actions in scrupulously avoiding violence, even in reaction to the force which was exerted on them. The affirmation of the close relation between morality and non-violence will be one of the many monuments of the Rev. Martin Luther King, Jr.

As this experience shows, the ultimate legal success as well as the intrinsic moral quality of civil disobedience turns on the restraint with which it is exercised. This is an extremely hard line to draw, but is one which must be earnestly sought out. Unfortunately, some of those who claim this mantle today do not appreciate the moral quality of thought and action which made their predecessors worthy to wear it.

Of course, it has not been my intention to disparage the objectives of any individual or group, or to discourage the honest and forthright and candid prophylaxis and therapy that are the legacy of reflective and constructive criticism. My only concern has been that some contemporary forms and philosophies of protest may in fact unwillingly retard the improvements in society which we all seek. I hope the ideas I have sought to present here may contribute to the thoughtful consideration of critical issues with which we must all deal in the creative evolution of our cherished land.

ON NOT PROSECUTING CIVIL DISOBEDIENCE

Ronald Dworkin

How should the government deal with those who disobey the draft laws out of conscience? Many people think the answer is obvious: the

From the *New York Review of Books,* 10 (June 6, 1968): 14-21. Copyright 1968 the New York Review. Reprinted with permission of the *New York Review of Books* and the author.

government must prosecute the dissenters, and if they are convicted it must punish them. Some people reach this conclusion easily, because they hold the mindless view that conscientious disobedience is the same as lawlessness. They think that the dissenters are anarchists who must be punished before their corruption spreads. Many lawyers and intellectuals come to the same conclusion, however, on what looks like a more sophisticated argument. They recognize that disobedience to law may be *morally* justified, but they insist that it cannot be *legally* justified, and they think that it follows from this truism that the law must be enforced. Erwin Griswold, the Solicitor General of the United States, and the former dean of the Harvard Law School, appears to have adopted this view in a recent statement. "[It] is of the essence of law," he said, "that it is equally applied to all, that it binds all alike, irrespective of personal motive. For this reason, one who contemplates civil disobedience out of moral conviction should not be surprised and must not be bitter if a criminal conviction ensues. And he must accept the fact that organized society cannot endure on any other basis."

The New York Times applauded that statement. A thousand faculty members of several universities had signed a *Times* advertisement calling on the Justice Department to quash the indictments of the Rev. William Sloane Coffin, Dr. Benjamin Spock, Marcus Raskin, Mitchell Goodman, and Michael Ferber, for conspiring to counsel various draft offenses. The *Times* said that the request to quash the indictments "confused moral rights with legal responsibilities."

But the argument that, because the government believes a man has committed a crime, it must prosecute him is much weaker than it seems. Society "cannot endure" if it tolerates all disobedience; it does not follow, however, nor is there evidence, that it will collapse if it tolerates some. In the United States prosecutors have discretion whether to enforce criminal laws in particular cases. A prosecutor may properly decide not to press charges if the lawbreaker is young, or inexperienced, or the sole support of a family, or is repentant, or turns state's evidence, or if the law is unpopular or unworkable or generally disobeyed, or if the courts are clogged with more important cases, or for dozens of other reasons. This discretion is not license—we expect prosecutors to have good reasons for exercising it—but there are, at least *prima facie,* some good reasons for not prosecuting those who disobey the draft laws out of conscience. One is the obvious reason that they act out of better motives than those who break the law out of greed or a desire to subvert government. Another is the practical reason that our society suffers a loss if it punishes a group that includes—as the group of draft dissenters does—some of its most thoughtful and loyal citizens. Jailing such men solidifies their alienation from society, and alienates many like them who are deterred by the threat.

Those who think that conscientious draft offenders should always be punished must show that these are not good reasons for exercising discretion, or they must find contrary reasons that outweigh them. What

arguments might they produce? There are practical reasons for enforcing the draft laws, and I shall consider some of these later. But Dean
Griswold and those who agree with him seem to rely on a fundamental
moral argument that it would be unfair, not merely impractical, to let
the dissenters go unpunished. They think it would be unfair, I gather,
because society could not function if everyone disobeyed laws he disapproved of or found disadvantageous. If the government tolerates those
few who will not "play the game," it allows them to secure the benefits
of everyone else's deference to law, without shouldering the burdens,
such as the burden of the draft.

This argument is a serious one. It cannot be answered simply by
saying that the dissenter would allow everyone else the privilege of
disobeying a law he believed immoral. In fact, few draft dissenters
would accept a changed society in which sincere segregationists were
free to break civil rights laws they hated. The majority want no such
change, in any event, because they think that society would be worse
off for it; until they are shown this is wrong, they will expect their
officials to punish anyone who assumes a privilege which they, for the
general benefit, do not assume.

There is, however, a flaw in the argument. The reasoning contains
a hidden assumption that makes it almost entirely irrelevant to the draft
cases, and indeed to any serious case of civil disobedience in the United
States. The argument assumes that the dissenters know that they are
breaking a valid law, and that the privilege they assert is the privilege
to do that. Of course, almost everyone who discusses civil disobedience
recognizes that in America a law may be invalid because it is unconstitutional. But the critics handle this complexity by arguing on separate
hypotheses: If the law is invalid, then no crime is committed, and
society may not punish. If the law is valid, then a crime has been committed, and society must punish. This reasoning hides the crucial fact
that the validity of the law may be doubtful. The officials and judges
may believe that the law is valid, the dissenters may disagree, and both
sides may have plausible arguments for their positions. If so, then the
issues are different from what they would be if the law were clearly valid
or clearly invalid, and the argument of fairness, designed for these alternatives, is irrelevant.

Doubtful law is by no means special or exotic in cases of civil
disobedience. On the contrary. In the United States, at least, almost any
law which a significant number of people would be tempted to disobey
on moral grounds would be doubtful—if not clearly invalid—on constitutional grounds as well. The constitution makes our conventional
political morality relevant to the question of validity; any statute that
appears to compromise that morality raises constitutional questions, and
if the compromise is serious, the constitutional doubts are serious also.

The connection between moral and legal issues is especially clear
in the current draft cases. Dissent has largely been based on the following
moral objections: (*a*) The United States is using immoral weapons and

tactics in Vietnam. (*b*) The war has never been endorsed by deliberate, considered, and open vote of the peoples' representatives. (*c*) The United States has no interest at stake in Vietnam remotely strong enough to justify forcing a segment of its citizens to risk death there. (*d*) If an army is to be raised to fight that war, it is immoral to raise it by a draft that defers or exempts college students, and thus discriminates against the economically underprivileged. (*e*) The draft exempts those who object to all wars on religious grounds, but not those who object to particular wars on moral grounds; there is no relevant difference between these positions, and so the draft, by making the distinction, implies that the second group is less worthy of the nation's respect than the first. (*f*) The law that makes it a crime to counsel draft resistance stifles those who oppose the war, because it is morally impossible to argue that the war is profoundly immoral, without encouraging and assisting those who refuse to fight it.

Lawyers will recognize that these moral positions, if we accept them, provide the basis for the following constitutional arguments: (*a*) The constitution makes treaties part of the law of the land, and the United States is a party to international conventions and covenants that make illegal the acts of war the dissenters charge the nation with committing. (*b*) The constitution provides that Congress must declare war; the legal issue of whether our action in Vietnam is a "war" and whether the Tonkin Bay Resolution was a "declaration" is the heart of the moral issue of whether the government has made a deliberate and open decision. (*c*) Both the due process clause of the Fifth and Fourteenth Amendments and the equal protection clause of the Fourteenth Amendment condemn special burdens placed on a selected class of citizens when the burden or the classification is not reasonable; the burden is unreasonable when it patently does not serve the public interest, or when it is vastly disproportionate to the interest served. If our military action in Vietnam is frivolous or perverse, as the dissenters claim, then the burden we place on men of draft age is unreasonable and unconstitutional. (*d*) In any event, the discrimination in favor of college students denies to the poor the equal protection of the law that is guaranteed by the constitution. (*e*) If there is no pertinent difference between religious objection to all wars and moral objection to some wars, then the classification the draft makes is arbitrary and unreasonable, and unconstitutional on that ground. The "establishment of religion" clause of the First Amendment forbids governmental pressure in favor of organized religion; if the draft's distinction coerces men in this direction, it is invalid on that count also. (*f*) The First Amendment also condemns invasions of freedom of speech. If the draft law's prohibition on counseling does inhibit expression of a range of views on the war, it abridges free speech.

The principal counterargument, supporting the view that the courts ought not to hold the draft unconstitutional, also involves moral issues. Under the so-called "political question" doctrine, the courts deny their own jurisdiction to pass on matters—such as foreign or military policy—

whose resolution is best assigned to other branches of the government. The Boston court trying the Coffin, Spock case has already declared, on the basis of this doctrine, that it will not hear arguments about the legality of the war. But the Supreme Court has shown itself (in the reapportionment cases, for example) reluctant to refuse jurisdiction when it believed that the gravest issues of political morality were at stake and that no remedy was available through the political process. If the dissenters are right, and the war and the draft are state crimes of profound injustice to a group of citizens, then the argument that the courts must refuse jurisdiction is considerably weakened.

We cannot conclude from these arguments that the draft (or any part of it) is unconstitutional. If the Supreme Court is called upon to rule on the question, it will probably reject some of them, and refuse to consider the others on grounds that they are political. The majority of lawyers would probably agree with this result. But the arguments of unconstitutionality are at least plausible, and a reasonable and competent lawyer might well think that they present a stronger case, on balance, than the counterarguments. If he does, he will consider that the draft is not constitutional, and there will be no way of proving that he is wrong.

Therefore we cannot assume, in judging what to do with the draft dissenters, that they are asserting a privilege to disobey valid laws. We cannot decide that fairness demands their punishment until we try to answer the further question: What should a citizen do when the law is unclear, and when he thinks it allows what others think it does not? I do not mean to ask, of course, what it is *legally* proper for him to do, or what his *legal* rights are— that would be begging the question, because it depends upon whether he is right or they are right. I mean to ask what his proper course is as a citizen, what in other words, we would consider to be "playing the game." That is a crucial question, because it cannot be wrong not to punish him if he is acting as, given his opinions, we think he should.[1]

There is no obvious answer on which most citizens would readily agree, and that is itself significant. If we examine our legal institutions and practices, however, we shall discover some relevant underlying principles and policies. I shall set out three possible answers to the question, and then try to show which of these best fits our practices and expectations. The three possibilities I want to consider are these:

(1) If the law is doubtful, and it is therefore unclear whether it permits someone to do what he wants, he should assume the worst, and act on the assumption that it does not. He should obey the executive

---

[1] I do not mean to imply that the government should always punish a man who deliberately breaks a law he knows is valid. There may be reasons of fairness or practicality, like those I listed in the third paragraph, for not prosecuting such men. But cases like the draft cases present special arguments for tolerance; I want to concentrate on these arguments and therefore have isolated these cases.

authorities who command him, even though he thinks they are wrong, while using the political process, if he can, to change the law.

(2) If the law is doubtful, he may follow his own judgment, that is, he may do what he wants if he believes that the case that the law permits this is stronger than the case that it does not. But he may follow his own judgment only until an authoritative institution, like a court, decides the other way in a case involving him or someone else. Once an institutional decision has been reached, he must abide by that decision, even though he thinks that it was wrong. (There are, in theory, many subdivisions of this second possibility. We may say that the individual's choice is foreclosed by the contrary decision of any court, including the lowest court in the system if the case is not appealed. Or we may require a decision of some particular court or institution. I shall discuss this second possibility in its most liberal form, namely that the individual may properly follow his own judgment until a contrary decision of the highest court competent to pass on the issue, which, in the case of the draft, is the United States Supreme Court.)

(3) If the law is doubtful, he may follow his own judgment, even after a contrary decision by the highest competent court. Of course, he must take the contrary decision of any court into account in making his judgment of what the law requires. Otherwise the judgment would not be an honest or reasonable one, because the doctrine of precedent, which is an established part of our legal system, has the effect of allowing the decision of the courts to *change* the law. Suppose, for example, that a taxpayer believes that he is not required to pay tax on certain forms of income. If the Supreme Court decides to the contrary, he should, taking into account the practice of according great weight to the decisions of the Supreme Court on tax matters, decide that the Court's decision has itself tipped the balance, and that the law now requires him to pay the tax.

Someone might think that this qualification erases the difference between the third and the second models, but it does not. The doctrine of precedent gives different weights to the decisions of different courts, and greatest weight to the decisions of the Supreme Court, but it does not make the decision of any court conclusive. Sometimes, even after a contrary Supreme Court decision, an individual may still reasonably believe that the law is on his side; such cases are rare, but they are most likely in disputes over constitutional law when civil disobedience is involved. The Court has shown itself more likely to overrule its past decisions if these have limited important personal or political rights, and it is just these decisions that a dissenter might want to challenge.

We cannot assume, in other words, that the Constitution is always what the Supreme Court says it is. Oliver Wendell Holmes, for example, did not follow such a rule in his famous dissent in the *Gitlow* case. A few years before, in *Abrams*, he had lost his battle to persuade the court that the First Amendment protected an anarchist who had been urging general strikes against the government. A similar issue was presented in *Gitlow*, and Holmes once again dissented. "It is true," he said, "that in my opinion this criterion was departed from in [Abrams] but the convictions that I expressed in that case are too deep for it to be possible for me as yet to believe that it . . . settled the law." Holmes voted for acquitting Gitlow, on the ground that what Gitlow had done was no crime, even though the Supreme Court had recently held that it was.

Here then are three possible models for the behavior of dissenters who disagree with the executive authorities when the law is doubtful. Which of them best fits our legal and social practices?

I think it plain that we do not follow the first of these models, that is, that we do not expect citizens to assume the worst. If no court has decided the issue, and a man thinks, on balance, that the law is on his side, most of our lawyers and critics think it perfectly proper for him to follow his own judgment. Even when many disapprove of what he does—such as peddling pornography—they do not think he must desist just because its legality is subject to doubt.

It is worth pausing a moment to consider what society would lose if it did follow the first model or, to put the matter the other way, what society gains when people follow their own judgment in cases like this. When the law is uncertain, in the sense that lawyers can reasonably disagree on what a court ought to decide, the reason usually is that different legal principles and policies have collided, and it is unclear how best to accommodate these conflicting principles and policies.

Our practice, in which different parties are encouraged to pursue their own understanding, provides a means of testing relevant hypotheses. If the question is whether a particular rule would have certain undesirable consequences, or whether these consequences would have limited or broad ramifications, then, before the issue is decided, it is useful to know what does in fact take place when some people proceed on that rule. (Much anti-trust and business regulation law has developed through this kind of testing.) If the question is whether and to what degree a particular solution would offend principles of justice or fair play deeply respected by the community, it is useful, again, to experiment by testing the community's response. The extent of community indifference to anti-contraception laws, for example, would never have become established had not some organizations deliberately flouted those laws in Connecticut.

If the first model were followed, we would lose the advantages of these tests. The law would suffer, particularly if this model were applied to constitutional issues. When the validity of a criminal statute is in doubt, the statute will almost always strike some people as being unfair or unjust, because it will infringe some principle of liberty or justice or fairness which they take to be built into the Constitution. If our practice were that whenever a law is doubtful on these grounds, one must act as if it were valid, then the chief vehicle we have for challenging the law on moral grounds would be lost, and over time the law we obeyed would certainly become less fair and just, and the liberty of our citizens would certainly be diminished.

We would lose almost as much if we used a variation of the first model, that a citizen must assume the worst unless he can anticipate that the courts will agree with his view of the law. If everyone deferred to his guess of what the courts would do, society and its law would be poorer. Our assumption in rejecting the first model was that the record a citizen makes in following his own judgment, together with the arguments he makes supporting that judgment when he has the opportunity, are helpful in creating the best judicial decision possible. This remains true even when, at the time the citizen acts, the odds are against his success in court. We must remember, too, that the value of the citizen's example is not exhausted once the decision has been made. Our practices require that the decision be criticized, by the legal profession and the law schools, and the record of dissent may be invaluable here.

Of course a man must consider what the courts will do when he decides whether it would be *prudent* to follow his own judgment. He may have to face jail, bankruptcy, or opprobrium if he does. But it is essential that we separate the calculation of prudence from the question of what, as a good citizen, he may properly do. We are investigating how society ought to treat him when its courts believe that he judged wrong; therefore we must ask what he is justified in doing when his judgment differs from others. We beg the question if we assume that what he may properly do depends on his guess as to how society will treat him.

We must also reject the second model, that if the law is unclear a citizen may properly follow his own judgment until the highest court has ruled that he is wrong. This fails to take into account the fact that any court, including the Supreme Court, may overrule itself. In 1940 the Court decided that a West Virginia law requiring students to salute the Flag was constitutional. In 1943 it reversed itself, and decided that such a statute was unconstitutional after all. What was the duty, as citizens, of those people who in 1941 and 1942 objected to saluting the Flag on grounds of conscience, and thought that the Court's 1940 decision was wrong? We can hardly say that their duty was to follow the first decision. They believed that saluting the Flag was unconscionable, and they believed, reasonably, that no valid law required them to do so. The Supreme Court later decided that in this they were right. The Court did not simply hold that after the second decision failing to salute would not be a crime; it held (as in a case like this it almost always would) that it was no crime after the first decision either.

Some will say that the flag-salute dissenters should have obeyed the Court's first decision, while they worked in the legislatures to have the law repealed, and tried in the courts to find some way to challenge the law again without actually violating it. That would be, perhaps, a plausible recommendation if conscience were not involved, because it would then be arguable that the gain in orderly procedure was worth the personal sacrifice of patience. But conscience was involved, and if the dissenters had obeyed the law while biding their time, they would have suffered the irreparable injury of having done what their conscience forbade them to do. It is one thing to say that an individual must sometimes violate his conscience when he knows that the law commands him to do it. It is quite another to say that he must violate his conscience even when he reasonably believes that the law does not require it, because it would inconvenience his fellow citizens if he took the most direct, and perhaps the only, method of attempting to show that he is right and they are wrong.

Since a court may overrule itself, the same reasons we listed for rejecting the first model count against the second as well. If we did not have the pressure of dissent, we would not have a dramatic statement of the degree to which a court decision against the dissenter is felt to be wrong, a demonstration that is surely pertinent to the question of whether it was right. We would increase the chance of being governed by rules that offend the principles we claim to serve.

These considerations force us, I think, from the second model, but some will want to substitute a variation of it. They will argue that once the Supreme Court has decided that a criminal law is valid, then citizens have a duty to abide by that decision until they have a reasonable belief, not merely that the decision is bad law, but that the Supreme Court is likely to overrule it. Under this view the West Virginia dissenters who refused to salute the Flag in 1942 were acting properly, because they might reasonably have anticipated that the Court would change its mind. But if the Court were to hold the draft laws constitutional, it would be improper to continue to challenge these laws, because there would be no great likelihood that the Court would soon change its mind. This suggestion must also be rejected, however. For once we say that a citizen may properly follow his own judgment of the law, in spite of his judgment that the courts will probably find against him, there is no plausible reason why he should act differently because a contrary decision is already on the books.

Thus the third model, or something close to it, seems to be the fairest statement of a man's social duty in our community. A citizen's allegiance is to the law, not to any particular person's view of what the law is, and he does not behave improperly or unfairly so long as he proceeds on his own considered and reasonable view of what the law requires. Let me repeat (because it is crucial) that this is not the same as saying that an individual may disregard what the courts have said. The doctrine of precedent lies near the core of our legal system, and no one can make a reasonable effort to follow the law unless he grants the courts the general power to alter it by their decisions. But if the issue is one touching fundamental personal or political rights, and it is arguable that the Supreme Court has made a mistake, a man is within his social rights in refusing to accept that decision as conclusive.

One large question remains before we can apply these observations to the problems of draft resistance. I have been talking about the case of a man who believes that the law is not what other people think, or what the courts have held. This description may fit some of those who disobey the draft laws out of conscience, but it does not fit most of them. Most of the dissenters are not lawyers or political philosophers; they believe that the laws on the books are immoral, and inconsistent with their country's legal ideals, but they have not considered the question of whether they may be invalid as well. Of what relevance to their situation, then, is the proposition that one may properly follow one's own view of the law?

To answer this, I shall have to return to the point I made earlier. The Constitution, through the due process clause, the equal protection clause, the First Amendment, and the other provisions I mentioned, injects an extraordinary amount of our political morality into the issue of whether a law is valid. The statement that most draft dissenters are unaware that the law is invalid therefore needs qualification. They hold beliefs that, if true, strongly support the view that the law is on their side; the fact that they have not reached that further conclusion can be traced, in at least most cases, to their lack of legal sophistication. If we believe that when the law is doubtful people who follow their own judgment of the law may be acting properly, it would seem wrong not to extend that view to those dissenters whose judgments come to the same thing. No part of the case that I made for the third model would entitle us to distinguish them from their more knowledgeable colleagues.

We can draw several tentative conclusions from the argument so far: When the law is uncertain, in the sense that a plausible case can be made on both sides, then a citizen who follows his own judgment is not behaving unfairly. Our practices permit and encourage him to follow his own judgment in such cases. For that reason, our government has a special responsibility to try to protect him, and soften his predicament, whenever it can do so without great damage to other policies. It does not follow that the government can guarantee him immunity—it cannot adopt the rule that it will prosecute no one who acts out of conscience, or convict no one who reasonably disagrees with the courts. That would paralyze the government's ability to carry out its policies; it would, moreover, throw away the most important benefit of following the third model. If the state never prosecuted, then the courts could not act on the experience and the arguments the dissent has generated. But it does follow from the government's responsibility that when the practical reasons for prosecuting are relatively weak in a particular case, or can be met in other ways, the path of fairness may lie in tolerance. The popular view that the law is the law and must always be enforced refuses to distinguish the man who acts on his own judgment of a doubtful law, and thus behaves as our practices provide, from the common criminal. I know of no reason, short of moral blindness, for not drawing a distinction in principle between the two cases.

I anticipate a philosophical objection to these conclusions: that I am treating law as a "brooding omnipresence in the sky." I have spoken of people making judgments about what the law requires, even in cases in which the law is unclear and undemonstrable. I have spoken of cases in which a man might think that the law requires one thing, even though the Supreme Court has said that it requires another, and even when it was not likely that the Supreme Court would soon change its mind. I will therefore be charged with the view that there is always a "right answer" to a legal problem to be found in natural law or locked up in some transcendental strongbox.

The strongbox theory of law is, of course, nonsense. When I say that people hold views on the law when the law is doubtful, and that these views are not merely predictions of what the courts will hold, I intend no such metaphysics. I mean only to summarize as accurately as I can many of the practices that are part of our legal process.

Lawyers and judges make statements of legal right and duty, even when they know these are not demonstrable, and support them with arguments even when they know that these arguments will not appeal to everyone. They make these arguments to one another, in the professional journals, in the classroom, and in the courts. They respond to these arguments, when others make them, by judging them good or bad or mediocre. In so doing they assume that some arguments for a given doubtful position are better than others. They also assume that the case on one side of a doubtful proposition may be stronger than the case on the other, which is what I take a claim of law in a doubtful case to mean. They distinguish, without too much difficulty, these arguments from predictions of what the courts will decide.

These practices are poorly represented by the theory that judgments of law on doubtful issues are nonsense, or are merely predictions of what the courts will do. Those who hold such theories cannot deny the fact of these practices; perhaps these theorists mean that the practices are not sensible, because they are based on suppositions that do not hold, or for some other reason. But this makes their objection mysterious, because they never specify what they take the purposes underlying these practices to be; and unless these goals are specified, one cannot decide whether the practices are sensible. I understand these underlying purposes to be those I described earlier: the development and testing of the law through experimentation by citizens and through the adversary process.

Our legal system pursues these goals by inviting citizens to decide the strengths and weaknesses of legal arguments for themselves, or through their own counsel, and to act on these judgments, although that permission is qualified by the limited threat that they may suffer if the courts do not agree. Success in this strategy depends on whether there is sufficient agreement within the community on what counts as a good or bad argument, so that, although different people will reach different judgments, these differences will be neither so profound nor so frequent as to make the system unworkable, or dangerous for those who act by their own lights. I believe there is sufficient agreement on the criteria of the argument to avoid these traps, although one of the main tasks of legal philosophy is to exhibit and clarify these criteria. In any event, the practices I have described have not yet been shown to be misguided; they therefore must count in determining whether it is just and fair to be lenient to those who break what others think is the law.

I have said that the government has a special responsibility to those who act on a reasonable judgment that a law is invalid. It should make accommodation for them as far as possible, when this is consistent with other policies. It may be difficult to decide what the government ought to do, in the name of that responsibility, in particular cases. The decision will be a matter of balance, and flat rules will not help. Still, some principles can be set out.

I shall start with the prosecutor's decision whether to press charges. He must balance both his responsibility to be lenient and the risk that convictions will rend the society, against the damage to the law's policy that may follow if he leaves the dissenters alone. In making his calculation he must consider not only the extent to which others will be harmed, but also how the law evaluates that harm; and he must therefore make the following distinction. Every rule of law is supported, and presumably justified, by a set of policies it is supposed to advance and principles it is supposed to respect. Some rules (the laws prohibiting murder and theft, for example) are supported by the proposition that the individuals protected have a moral right to be free from the harm proscribed. Other rules (the more technical anti-trust rules, for example) are not supported by any supposition of an underlying right; their support comes chiefly from the alleged utility of the economic and social policies they promote. These may be supplemented with moral principles (like the view that it is a harsh business practice to undercut a weak competitor's prices) but these fall short of recognizing a moral right against the harm in question.

The point of the distinction here is this: The judgment that someone has a moral right to be free from certain injuries is a very strong form of moral judgment, because a moral right, once acknowledged, outweighs competing claims of utility or virtue. When a law rests on such a judgment, that is a powerful argument against tolerating violations which inflict those injuries—for example, violations that involve personal injury or the destruction of property. The prosecutor may respect the dissenter's view that the law is invalid, but unless he agrees, he must honor the law's judgment that others have an overriding claim of right.

It may be controversial, of course, whether a law rests on the assumption of a right. One must study the background and administration of the law, and reflect on whether any social practices of right and obligation support it. We may take one example in which the judgment is relatively easy. There are many sincere and ardent segregationists who believe that the civil rights laws and decisions are unconstitutional, because they compromise principles of local government and of freedom of association. This is an arguable, though not a persuasive, view. But the constitutional provisions that support these laws clearly embody the view that Negroes, as individuals, have a right not to be segregated. They do not rest simply on the judgment that national policies are best pursued by preventing their segregation. If we take no action against the man who blocks the school house door, therefore, we violate the rights, confirmed by law, of the schoolgirl he blocks. The responsibility of leniency cannot go this far.

The schoolgirl's position is different, however, from that of the draftee who may be called up sooner or given a more dangerous post if draft offenders are not punished. The draft laws do not reflect a judgment that a man has a social or moral right to be drafted only after certain other men or groups have been called. The draft classifications, and the order-of-call according to age within classifications, are arranged for social and administrative convenience. They also reflect considerations of fairness, like the proposition that a mother who has lost one of two sons in war ought not to be made to risk losing the other. But they presuppose no fixed rights. The draft boards are given considerable discretion in the classification process, and the army, of course, has almost complete discretion in assigning dangerous posts. If the prosecutor tolerates draft offenders, he makes small shifts in the law's calculations of fairness and utility. These may cause disadvantage to others in the pool of draftees but that is a different matter from contradicting their social or moral rights.

It is wrong therefore to analyze draft cases and segregation cases in the same way, as many critics do when considering whether tolerance is justified. I do not mean that fairness to others is irrelevant in draft cases; it must be taken into account, and balanced against fairness to dissenters and the long-term benefit to society. But it does not play the commanding role here that it does in segregation cases, and in other cases when rights are at stake.

Where, then, does the balance of fairness and utility lie in the case of those who counsel draft resistance? If these men had encouraged violence or otherwise trespassed on the rights of others, then there would be a strong case for prosecution. But in the absence of such actions, the balance of fairness and utility seems to me to lie the other way, and I therefore think that the decision to prosecute Coffin, Spock, Raskin, Goodman, and Ferber was wrong. It may be argued that if those who counsel draft resistance are free from prosecution, the number who resist induction will increase; but it will not, I think, increase much beyond the number of those who would resist in any event.

If I am wrong, and there is much greater resistance, then a sense of this residual discontent is of importance to policy makers, and it ought not to be hidden under a ban on speech. Conscience is deeply involved— it is hard to believe that many who counsel resistance do so on any other grounds. The case is strong that the laws making counseling a crime are unconstitutional; even those who do not find the case persuasive will admit that its arguments have substance. The harm to potential draftees, both those who may be persuaded to resist and those who may be called earlier because others have been persuaded, is remote and speculative.

The cases of men who refuse induction when drafted are more complicated. The crucial question is whether a failure to prosecute will lead to wholesale refusals to serve. It may not—there are social pressures, including the threat of career disadvantages, that would force many young Americans to serve if drafted, even if they knew they would not go to jail if they refused. If the number would not much increase, then the state should leave the dissenters alone, and I see no great harm in delaying any prosecution until the effect of that policy becomes clearer. If the number of those who refuse induction turns out to be large, this would argue for prosecution. But it would also make the problem academic, because if there were sufficient dissent to bring us to that pass, it would be most difficult to pursue the war in any event, except under a near-totalitarian regime.

There may seem to be a paradox in these conclusions. I argued earlier that when the law is unclear citizens have the right to follow their own judgment, partly on the grounds that this practice helps to shape issues for adjudication; now I propose a course that eliminates or postpones adjudication. But the contradiction is only apparent. It does not follow from the fact that our practice facilitates adjudication, and renders it more useful in developing the law, that a trial should follow whenever citizens do act by their own lights. The question arises in each case whether the issues are ripe for adjudication, and whether adjudication would settle these issues in a manner that would decrease the chance of, or remove the grounds for, further dissent.

In the draft cases, the answer to both these questions is negative: There is much ambivalence about the war just now, and uncertainty and ignorance about the scope of the moral issues involved in the draft. It is far from the best time for a court to pass on these issues, and tolerating dissent for a time is one way of allowing the debate to continue until it has produced something clearer. Moreover, it is plain that an adjudication of the constitutional issues now will not settle the law. Those who have doubts whether the draft is constitutional will have the same doubts even if the Supreme Court says that it is. This is one of those cases, touching fundamental rights, in which our practices of precedent will encourage these doubts. Certainly this will be so if, as seems likely, the Supreme Court appeals to the political question doctrine, and refuses to pass on the more serious constitutional issues.

Even if the prosecutor does not act, however, the underlying problem will be only temporarily relieved. So long as the law appears to make acts of dissent criminal, a man of conscience will face danger. What can Congress, which shares the responsibility of leniency, do to lessen this danger?

Congress can review the laws in question to see how much accommodation can be given the dissenters. Every program a legislature adopts is a mixture of policies and restraining principles. We accept loss of efficiency in crime detection and urban renewal, for example, so that we can respect the rights of accused criminals and compensate property owners for their damages. Congress may properly defer to its responsibility toward the dissenters by adjusting or compromising other policies. The relevant questions are these: What means can be found for allowing the greatest possible tolerance of conscientious dissent while minimizing its impact on policy? How strong is the government's responsibility for leniency in this case—how deeply is conscience involved, and how strong is the case that the law is invalid after all? How important is the policy in question—is interference with that policy too great a price to pay? These questions are no doubt too simple, but they suggest the heart of the choices that must be made.

For the same reasons that those who counsel resistance should not be prosecuted, I think that the law that makes this a crime should be repealed. The case is strong that this law abridges free speech. It certainly coerces conscience, and it probably serves no beneficial effect. If counseling would persuade only a few to resist who otherwise would not, the value of the restraint is small; if counseling would persuade many, that is an important political fact that should be known.

The issues are more complex, again, in the case of draft resistance itself. Those who believe that the war in Vietnam is itself a grotesque blunder will favor any change in the law that makes peace more likely. But if we take the position of those who think the war is necessary, then we must admit that a policy that continues the draft but wholly exempts dissenters would be unwise. Two less drastic alternatives might be considered, however: a volunteer army, and an expanded conscientious objector category that includes those who find this war immoral. There is much to be said against both proposals, but once the requirement of respect for dissent is recognized, the balance of principle may be tipped in their favor.

So the case for not prosecuting conscientious draft offenders, and for changing the laws in their favor, is a strong one. It would be unrealistic to expect this policy to prevail, however, for political pressures now oppose it. Relatively few of those who have refused induction have been indicted so far, but the pace of prosecution is quickening, and many more indictments are expected if the resistance many college seniors have pledged does in fact develop. The Coffin, Spock trial continues, although when the present steps toward peace negotiation were announced, many lawyers had hoped it would be dropped or delayed. There is no sign of any movement to amend the draft laws in the way I have suggested.

We must consider, therefore, what the courts can and should now do. A court might, of course, uphold the arguments that the draft laws are in some way unconstitutional, in general or as applied to the defendants in the case at hand. Or it may acquit the defendants because the facts necessary for conviction are not proved. I shall not argue the constitutional issues, or the facts of any particular case. I want instead to suggest that a court ought not to convict, at least in some circumstances, even if it sustains the statutes and finds the facts as charged. The Supreme Court has not ruled on the chief arguments that the present draft is unconstitutional, nor has it held that these arguments raise political questions that are not relevant to its jurisdiction. If the alleged violations take place before the Supreme Court has decided these issues, and the case reaches that Court, there are strong reasons why the Court should acquit even if it does then sustain the draft. It ought to acquit on the ground that before its decision the validity of the draft was doubtful, and it is unfair to punish men for disobeying a doubtful law.

There would be precedent for a decision along these lines. The Court has several times reversed criminal convictions, on due process grounds, because the law in question was too vague. (It has overturned convictions, for example, under laws that made it a crime to charge "unreasonable prices" or to be a member of a "gang.") Conviction under a vague criminal law offends the moral and political ideals of due process in two ways. First, it places a citizen in the unfair position of either acting at his peril or accepting a more stringent restriction on his life than the legislature may have authorized: As I argued earlier, it is not acceptable, as a model of social behavior, that in such cases he ought to assume the worst. Second, it gives power to the prosecutor and the courts to make criminal law, by opting for one or the other possible interpretations after the event. This would be a delegation of authority by the legislature that is inconsistent with our scheme of separation of powers.

Conviction under a criminal law whose terms are not vague, but whose constitutional validity is doubtful, offends due process in the first of these ways. It forces a citizen to assume the worst, or act at his peril. It offends due process in something like the second way as well. Most citizens would be deterred by a doubtful statute if they were to risk jail by violating it. Congress, and not the courts, would then be the effective voice in deciding the constitutionality of criminal enactments, and this also violates the separation of powers.

If acts of dissent continue to occur after the Supreme Court has ruled that the laws are valid, or that the political question doctrine applies, then acquittal on the grounds I have described is no longer appropriate. The Court's decision will not have finally settled the law, for the reasons given earlier, but the Court will have done all that can be done to settle it. The courts may still exercise their sentencing discretion, however, and impose minimal or suspended sentences as a mark of respect for the dissenters' position.

Some lawyers will be shocked by my general conclusion that we have a responsibility toward those who disobey the draft laws out of conscience, and that we may be required not to prosecute them, but rather to change our laws or adjust our sentencing procedures to accommodate them. The simple Draconian propositions, that crime must be punished, and that he who misjudges the law must take the consequences, have an extraordinary hold on the professional as well as the popular imagination. But the rule of law is more complex and more intelligent than that and it is important that it survive.

SECTION FIVE

Preferential Treatment

It is now generally conceded that in America certain groups have historically been the victims of injustices so substantial and so widespread as to diminish the life prospects of the members of those groups. There have been pervasive practices which are captured in terms like "racism," "sexism," and "ageism," and which are expressed in the dozens of familiar words used to slur the members of certain groups. These practices have existed in employment, in housing, in education, in public accommodations, and they have made it difficult and often impossible for the members of some groups to realize values which, otherwise, would have been within reach. Most important, we have passed laws which have enforced these practices in some cases and permitted them in others. It must be added, however, that increased awareness of the ways in which our laws have perpetuated injustice—for example see *Brown* v. *Board of Education,* 347 U.S. 483—has led to attempts to change these laws in both the courts and the legislatures.

The Fourteenth Amendment of the United States Constitution has provided the primary basis for the legal attack which has been made upon discriminatory legislation. The relevant portion reads: "No state shall . . . deny to any person within its jurisdiction the equal protection of the laws." Generally the "rational basis" test is applied in the evaluation of state-created classifications which are under Fourteenth Amendment review. That is, in determining whether a classification is in violation of the "equal protection" clause, the court asks whether the classification is "reasonably related to a legitimate public purpose." We have already seen this procedure in Justice Douglas's opinion in *Belle Terre.* However, where a "suspect" classification (or a fundamental interest) is involved, a stricter scrutiny is required. The classification will then not "pass constitutional muster" unless it is "necessary to the accomplishment of a compelling state interest." Race has been held to be a suspect classification. At this writing only a minority of the Court has held sex to be a suspect classification—see *Frontiero* v. *Richardson,* 411 U.S. 677—but should an Equal Rights Amendment be adopted, this would be changed.

Now it is one thing simply to repeal or overturn state-created classifications which invidiously discriminate against the members of certain groups. But it may seem that more is required than this, that something ought to be done "to eliminate the continued effects of past segregation and discrimination." And if such efforts are undertaken, it may be that the same classifications which were associated with invidious discrimination in the first place, will reappear at some point in the attempt to undo the effects of past wrongs. Some will say that such "preferential treatment" is as much an evil as the discrimination it is aimed at overcoming. Others will argue that it is importantly different from invidious discrimination and may be justified by the circumstances. Seldom has a philosophical issue in law evoked as much controversy as the issue of preferential treatment. And seldom has a case which the Supreme Court refused to decide, attracted as much attention as *DeFunis* v. *Odegaard,* the case which begins this section.

On August 2, 1971, Marco DeFunis, who was neither Black, Chicano, American Indian nor Filipino, was rejected by the University of Washington School of Law. Had Marco DeFunis been a member of one of these groups (other things being equal), his application would have been processed differently and it is unlikely that he would have been rejected. DeFunis sued various parties associated with the University of Washington, claiming that there had been discrimination against him in violation of the Fourteenth Amendment. Winning his case in the lower court, DeFunis was admitted to the law school in the fall of 1971. The defendants in the case then brought it before the Supreme Court of Washington where they won. But DeFunis remained in the law school while his case proceeded to the Supreme Court of the United States for final resolution. However, on April 23, 1974, when the Supreme Court finally issued an opinion on the case, it appeared to the majority of the Court that, because DeFunis was in his final quarter of law school, he was entitled to complete his legal education regardless of any decision that they might make. Accordingly, with Brennan and Douglas dissenting, the Court held that the case had become moot, and so they did not reach the equal protection question.

The equal protection question was, however, reached in the majority opinion of the Supreme Court of Washington (which I have excerpted), in two dissents from that opinion (I have included portions of one of these), and in the dissent of Justice Douglas to the majority opinion of the Supreme Court (which is also excerpted). The facts of the case are set out in the majority opinion of the Washington Supreme Court. The issue to them is "whether the law school may, in consonance with the equal protection provisions of the state and federal constitutions, consider the racial or ethnic backgrounds of applicants as one factor in the selection of students." In holding that neither the admissions policy of the law school nor the denial of admission to DeFunis violate equal protection, the Court makes three separate points. The first is that some racial classifications—for example those that do not "stigmatize a racial group with the stamp of inferiority," those that merely deny "benefits," those in which "color is not used per se," and those that are "used in a compensatory way to promote integration"—may not be in violation of the Fourteenth Amendment. The second point is that racial classifications must be subjected to "the most rigid scrutiny"; it must be established that such classifications are "necessary to the accomplishment of a compelling state interest." And third, the racial classifications at issue in the admission procedures withstand such scrutiny; they do so in the light of the necessity of racial classifications to the accomplishment of compelling and overriding state interests. These interests lie in "eliminating racial imbalance within public education," "in providing *all* law students with a legal education that will adequately prepare them to deal with societal problems which will confront them upon graduation," and in overcoming the serious underrepresentation of minorities within the legal profession. Dissenting strongly from this reasoning, Chief Justice Hale wonders how we can "achieve the goal of equal opportunity for all if, in the process, we deny equal opportunity for some."

The dissenting opinion of Justice William O. Douglas in the Supreme Court case points out the imprecision of the conventional procedures used in law school admissions, procedures involving grade point averages and the Law School Admission Test (the LSAT). Further, he calls attention to the way in which uniform treatment of all applicants, regardless of cultural background, can militate against minorities: "a test sensitively tuned for most applicants would be wide of the mark for many minorities." Douglas rejects the view, however, that "state-sponsored preference to one race over another" is permissible under the equal protection clause; he fears that if such preference were permissible, our constitutional guarantees would "acquire an accordionlike quality." It is not clear to Justice Douglas that the University of Washington Law School admissions procedure invidiously discriminated against DeFunis. Rather, it seems plain to him that the standard admissions procedure, involving the LSAT, is questionable on constitutional grounds. A new trial is required to determine whether LSATs "should be eliminated so far as minorities are concerned." "The key to the problem is consideration of each application *in a racially neutral way*." This may require separate treatment "to make more certain that racial factors do not militate *against an applicant or on his behalf*." But preferential treatment is not permitted.

In the selections that follow the legal materials, four philosophers examine the issue of preferential treatment. James W. Nickel's piece, "Classification by Race in Compensatory Programs," is a discussion of two replies to the charge that those who favor preferential treatment for blacks in the light of past injustice, but condemn discrimination of the ordinary disreputable sort, are guilty of an inconsistency: they both affirm and deny that race is a relevant consideration. One reply, which Nickel calls the "different-characteristics reply," denies that race is relevant in compensatory programs: "The reason for providing compensatory programs for blacks is not their race but the fact that they have been victimized by slavery and discrimination." Race may, however, serve as the "administrative basis" in compensatory programs provided that justice and efficiency are best served through the use of such a classification. A second reply is that while race is irrelevant in allocating penalties or losses, it may be relevant when people are being helped. Nickel points out several serious problems with this second reply and eventually rejects it.

In "Reverse Discrimination as Unjustified," Lisa H. Newton distinguishes between the Aristotelian notion of justice in the root political sense, a fragile condition in which free men stand as citizens, equal within the rule of law, and the more modern notion of justice as a moral ideal, calling for the extension of the circle of equal citizenship to include all persons. Taking the moral ideal of justice as logically distinct from and parasitic upon the political virtue of justice, Newton argues that any program of discrimination, "reverse or otherwise," moves us toward the destruction of justice in the political sense and, further, undermines the moral ideal of justice, "for it has content only where justice obtains, and by destroying justice we render the ideal meaningless." Newton sees difficulties in specifying the groups which are to be the beneficiaries of reverse discrimination and in specifying the degree to which reverse discrimination is required. Moreover, because "primary human rights" (as opposed to "rights under the law"), cannot provide a basis for restitution, restitution is not possible for a disadvantaged minority "whose grievance is that there was no law to protect them."

While Newton argues that "all discrimination is wrong prima facie because it violates justice," Judith Jarvis Thomson holds that, when I am distributing benefits which are mine to dispose of, "I can give to whom I like, on any ground I please, and in so doing, I violate no one's *rights,* I treat no one unjustly." Thomson seems to doubt that race should be a qualification in the hiring of university teachers, the case with which she is concerned. But she believes that it is legitimate to sidestep this question by grounding her argument on the principle that "no perfect stranger has a right to be given a benefit which is yours to dispose of." The principle applies to Thomson when she is giving away her apples, to eating clubs when they are hiring a cook, and, with qualifications that Thomson makes, to private universities when they are choosing among applicants for teaching positions. Things are somewhat more complicated in the case of public universities and, more generally, in cases where clubs or communities—Thomson refers to these entities as "Persons"—are distributing benefits to their participants. In these cases, owners or members have a right to an equal share in or an equal chance at the benefits generated by the "Person" in which they are participants. However, according to Thomson, this right to an equal chance or an equal share may be overridden by a number of considerations. It may be that, in the light of the rights of others, only those participants who are qualified in a certain way should be considered. The rights of students in a public university will surely require that hiring officers not give an equal chance to those who are unqualified to teach. It may be that certain participants are owed a debt of gratitude. Thomson considers here the preference given to veterans. Finally, it may be that some participants have been wronged and, as a result, justice may call for making amends. Thus, the wrongs done to blacks and women may justify favoring them over equally qualified white males in university hiring. In this case, however, young white males who did not participate in the wrongdoings (but who have benefited from them) will be required to bear the burden "of the community's amends-making." Thomson suggests that other beneficiaries of the community's wrongdoing—"the older white male, now comfortably tenured"—should take up some of this burden.

In her article entitled " 'It's Mine,' " Gertrude Ezorsky takes issue with Thomson's claim that "wholly private employers have a moral right to hire whomever they please." Ezorsky argues that in failing to distinguish carefully between morally rightful ownership and legally rightful ownership, Thomson has committed what Ezorsky calls the legalist fallacy, "committed whenever one infers that an individual who possesses a legal right, thereby has some moral right." In consequence, the argument that Thomson advances for her claim is invalid. Moreover, to show that Thomson's claim is false, Ezorsky applies a generalization argument against discriminatory hiring. In this context Ezorsky points out that we have a fundamental interest in avoiding the suffering brought about when we neglect the consequences of our collective activity. "Given the familiar propensity to familiar kinds of prejudice, we may reasonably expect that if employers were to engage in discriminatory hiring for . . . jobs, whenever so inclined, the consequences would be bad indeed." Applying the generalization argument, it follows that employers have no right to engage in such conduct. Ezorsky concludes with a suggestion that what is needed is a "comprehensive theory of moral ownership rights."

DEFUNIS V. ODEGAARD

Supreme Court of Washington

Defendants, who include the members of the Board of Regents of the University of Washington, the president of the university, and the

82 Wn. 2d 11, 507 P.2d 1169 (1973)
Locations of deleted citations marked with double asterisk (**), Ed.

dean and certain members of the Admissions Committee of the University of Washington School of Law, appeal from a judgment ordering them to admit plaintiff Marco DeFunis, Jr., as a first-year student to the University of Washington School of Law, as of September 22, 1971.

Broadly phrased, the major question presented herein is whether the law school may, in consonance with the equal protection provisions of the state and federal constitutions, consider the racial or ethnic background of applicants as one factor in the selection of students.

Marco DeFunis, Jr. (hereinafter plaintiff), his wife, and his parents commenced an action in the superior court, alleging that plaintiff, an applicant for admission to the University of Washington School of Law (hereinafter law school) for the class commencing September 1971, had been wrongfully denied admission in that . . . persons were admitted to the law school with lesser qualifications than those of plaintiff. The complaint asked that the court order the defendants to admit and enroll plaintiff in the law school in the fall of 1971 . . .

. . . After a nonjury trial, the court ruled that in denying plaintiff admission to the law school, the University of Washington had discriminated against him in violation of the equal protection of the laws guaranteed by the fourteenth amendment to the United States Constitution.

Law school admissions pose a complex problem, and require a sensitive balancing of diverse factors. To gain insight into the complicated process of selecting first-year law students, and to better appreciate the essence of plaintiff's complaint against the law school, we turn first to the circumstances and operative facts—as delineated by the record—from which this litigation arises.

Under RCW 28B.20.130(3), the Board of Regents of the University of Washington has the power and duty to establish entrance requirements for students seeking admission to the university. The dean and faculty of the law school, pursuant to the authority delegated to them by the Board of Regents and the president of the university, have established a committee on admissions and readmissions to determine who shall be admitted to the law school. For the academic year September 15, 1970, to June 15, 1971, the committee was composed of five faculty members and two student members; on June 7, 1971, the faculty of the law school expanded the membership of the committee to six faculty members and three student members. The chairman estimated that the committee spent over 1,300 hours in the selection process for the 1971-72 first-year class.

The number of qualified applicants to the law school has increased dramatically in recent years. In 1967, the law school received 618 applications; in 1968, 704; in 1969, 860; and in 1970, 1,026 applications were received. The law school received 1,601 applications for admission to the first-year class beginning September, 1971. Under the university's enrollment limitation there were only 445 positions allotted to the law school, and of these the number available for the first-year class was between 145 and 150. The chairman of the admissions committee stated that most of these applicants would be regarded as qualified by admissions standards at this and other comparable law schools in recent years. Hence, the task of selection is difficult, time-consuming and requires the exercise of careful and informed discretion, based on the evidence appearing in the application files. While many applicants are relatively easy to select for admission because of very outstanding qualifications, and others are relatively easy to reject, the middle group of candidates is much more difficult to assess. Plaintiff was in this latter category.

Applicants for admission to the law school must have earned an undergraduate degree and taken the Law School Admission Test (LSAT) administered by the Educational Testing Service of Princeton, New Jersey. They must also submit with their written application a copy of transcripts from all schools and colleges which they have attended prior to application for admission, together with statements from their undergraduate dean of students and letters of recommendation from faculty members in their major field of study. They may submit additional letters of recommendation and statements. The application for admission gives the applicant the option to indicate his "dominant" ethnic origin. The admissions process does not include personal interviews and does not reveal whether applicants are poor or affluent.

The committee's basic criteria for selecting students are expressed in the "Guide for Applicants," a copy of which plaintiff received with his 1971 application:

> We below describe the process we applied to determine the class that entered the University of Washington School of Law in September 1970. We anticipate that the same process will be applied in determining membership in the class of 1971. . . .
>
> In assessing applications, we began by trying to identify applicants who had the potential for outstanding performance in law school. We attempted to select applicants for admission from that group on the basis of their ability to make significant contributions to law school classes and to the community at large.

For the purpose of a preliminary ranking of the applicants for the class of 1974, the junior-senior undergraduate grade point average and the Law School Admissions Test scores [1] for each applicant were combined through a formula to yield a predicted first-year of law school grade average for the applicant. This preliminary index number is called the Predicted First-Year Average (PFYA). The relative weight of grades and test scores in this formula was determined on the basis of past experience at the law school. The same formula is used for all applicants in a given year. If an applicant has taken the LSAT more than once in the

---

[1] The Law School Admissions Test yields two scores for each candidate, a general law aptitude score and a writing ability score.

past 3 years, the average score is employed rather than the latest score; this is done to offset a learning effect which statistical studies by the Educational Testing Service indicate occurs as the result of the multiple taking of the test.

Plaintiff's PFYA as determined by the law school, was 76.23. . . . Applicants with PFYAs above 77 were reviewed and decided by the full committee as they came in, in order to reach an early decision as to the acceptance of such students. Each of these files was assigned to a committee member for thorough review and for presentation to the committee.

Applicants with PFYAs below 74.5 were reviewed by the chairman of the committee, and were either rejected by him, or placed in a group for later review by the full committee. The decision of rejection or committee review of an application was based on the chairman's judgment derived from information in the applicant's file indicating whether the applicant had a significantly better potential for law study than the relatively low predicted first-year average tended to indicate. Cases of doubt were to be resolved in favor of deferring judgment until committee review could be undertaken.

Two exceptions were made in regard to applicants with PFYAs below 74.5. First, the law school had established a policy that persons who had been previously admitted but who were unable to enter, or forced to withdraw from, the law school because of induction into the military service, had a right to reenroll if they reapplied immediately upon honorable completion of their tour of duty. Second, all files of "minority" applicants (which the committee defined for this purpose as including Black Americans, Chicano Americans, American Indians and Philippine Americans [2]) were considered by the full committee as warranting their attention, regardless of the PFYA of the individual applicant. . . .

In considering minority applicants, the committee was guided by a university-wide policy which sought to eliminate the continued effects of past segregation and discrimination against Blacks, Chicanos, American Indians and other disadvantaged racial and ethnic minority groups. At trial, the President of the University of Washington testified as to the origin of this policy:

> More and more it became evident to us that just an open door, as it were, at the point of entry to the University, somehow or other seemed insufficient to deal with what was emerging as the greatest internal problem of the United States of America, a problem which obviously could not be resolved without some kind of contribution being made not only

---

[2] The chairman of the admissions committee testified that Asian Americans, e.g., were not treated as "minority" applicants for admissions purposes, since a significant number could be admitted on the same basis as general applicants. As used herein, the term "minority" refers to and includes only Black Americans, Chicano Americans, American Indians and Philippine Americans.

by the schools, but obviously, also, by the colleges in the University and the University of Washington, in particular, given the racial distribution of this state. . . .

So that was the beginning of a growing awareness that just an open-door sheer equality in view of the cultural circumstances that produced something other than equality, was not enough; that some more positive contribution had to be made to the resolution of this problem in American life, and something had to be done by the University of Washington.

Thus, the university sought to achieve a reasonable representation within the student body of persons from these groups which have been historically suppressed by encouraging their enrollment within the various programs offered at the university. Policies for admission of minorities throughout the university recognized that the conventional "mechanical" credentializing system does not always produce good indicators of the full potential of such culturally separated or deprived individuals, and that to rely solely on such formal credentials could well result in unfairly denying to qualified minority persons the chance to pursue the educational opportunities available at the university.

The law school sought to carry forward this university policy in its admission program, not only to obtain a reasonable representation from minorities within its classes, but to increase participation within the legal profession by persons from racial and ethnic groups which have been historically denied access to the profession and which, consequently, are grossly underrepresented within the legal system. In doing so, the admissions committee followed certain procedures which are the crux of plaintiff's claimed denial of equal protection of the laws.

First, in reviewing the files of minority applicants, the committee attached less weight to the PFYA in making a total judgmental evaluation as to the relative ability of the particular applicant to succeed in law school. Also, the chairman testified that although the same standard was applied to all applicants (i.e., the relative probability of the individual succeeding in law school), minority applicants were directly compared to one another, but were not compared to applicants outside of the minority group. The committee sought to identify, within the minority category, those persons who had the highest probability of succeeding in law school. Thus, the law school included within its admitted group minority applicants whose PFYAs were lower than those of some other applicants, but whose entire record showed the committee that they were capable of successfully completing the law school program.

As a result of this process, the committee admitted a group of minority applicants, placed a group of such applicants on a waiting list, and rejected other minority applications. The dean of the law school testified that the law school has no fixed admissions quota for minority students, but that the committee sought a reasonable representation of such groups in the law school. He added that the law school has accepted no unqualified minority applicants, but only those whose records indicated that they were capable of successfully completing the law school program. . . .

Plaintiff was . . . notified on August 2, 1971, that he was neither admitted nor any longer on the waiting list. As of August 1, 1971, 275 students were admitted to the freshman law school class and 55 students remained on the waiting list, making a total of 330 students. . . .

Because of the judgmental factors in the admissions process, as outlined, the ultimate determination of applicants to whom admission was offered did not follow exactly the relative ranking of PFYAs. Of those invited, 74 had lower PFYAs than plaintiff; 36 of these were minority applicants, 22 were returning from military service, and 16 were applicants judged by the committee as deserving invitations on the basis of other information contained in their files. Twenty-nine applicants with higher PFYAs than plaintiff's were denied admission. Of the 36 minority group students invited 18 actually enrolled in the first-year class.

The trial court found that some minority applicants with college grades and LSAT scores so low that had they been of the white race their applications would have been summarily denied were given invitations for admission; that some such students were admitted instead of plaintiff; that since no more than 150 applicants were to be admitted to the law school, the admission of less qualified students resulted in a denial of places to those better qualified; and that plaintiff had better "qualifications" than many of the students admitted by the committee. The trial court also found that plaintiff was and is fully qualified and capable of satisfactorily attending the law school.

The trial court concluded . . . that, in denying plaintiff admission to the law school, the University of Washington discriminated against him and did not accord to him equal protection of the laws as guaranteed by the fourteenth amendment to the United States Constitution; and therefore, that plaintiff should be admitted to the law school for the class of 1974, beginning September 22, 1971.[3] . . .

The essence of plaintiff's Fourteenth Amendment argument is that the law school violated his right to equal protection of the laws by denying him admission, yet accepting certain minority applicants with lower PFYAs than plaintiff who, but for their minority status, would not have been admitted.[4]

---

[3] At time of oral argument in this court it was stated that plaintiff had actually been admitted to the law school in September, 1971, and was still in attendance. Due to the conditions under which plaintiff was admitted and the great public interest in the continuing issues raised by this appeal, we do not consider the case to be moot.

[4] Our review is specifically limited to a consideration of the alleged constitutional infirmities in the law school's admissions policy and procedures. Beyond question, it would be inappropriate for this court to determine the actual composition of the first-year class through an independent evaluation of each applicant's file, substituting our criteria and judgment for those of the admissions committee. In regard to the scope of judicial review in this area, the United States Supreme Court has stated that: "In

To answer this contention we consider three implicit, subordinate questions: (A) whether race can ever be considered as one factor in the admissions policy of a state law school or whether racial classifications are *per se* unconstitutional because the equal protection of the laws requires that law school admissions be "color-blind"; (B) if consideration of race is not *per se* unconstitutional, what is the appropriate standard of review to be applied in determining the constitutionality of such a classification; and (C) when the appropriate standard is applied does the specific minority admissions policy employed by the law school pass constitutional muster? [5]

A.

Relying solely on *Brown* v. *Board of Educ.*, 347 U.S. 483,** (1954), the trial court held that a state law school can never consider race as one criterion in its selection of first-year students. In holding that all such racial classifications are *per se* unconstitutional, the trial court stated in its oral opinion:

> Since no more than 150 applicants were to be admitted the admission of less qualified resulted in a denial of places to those otherwise qualified. The plaintiff and others in this group have not, in my opinion, been accorded equal protection of the laws guaranteed by the Fourteenth Amendment.
>
> In 1954 the United States Supreme Court decided that public education must be equally available to all regardless of race.
>
> After that decision the Fourteenth Amendment could no longer be stretched to accommodate the needs of any race. Policies of discrimination will inevitably lead to reprisals. In my opinion the only safe rule is to treat all races alike, and I feel that is what is required under the equal protection clause.

In *Brown* v. *Board of Educ., supra,* the Supreme Court addressed a question of primary importance at page 493:

---

seeking to define even in broad and general terms how far this remedial power extends it is important to remember that judicial powers may be exercised only on the basis of a constitutional violation. Remedial judicial authority does not put judges automatically in the shoes of school authorities whose powers are plenary. Judicial authority enters only when local authority defaults." *Swann* v. *Charlotte-Mecklenburg Bd. of Educ.*, 402 U.S. 1, 16 (1971).**

[5] Considering the statutory delegation of power to establish entrance requirements for students to the university, no serious question is raised as to whether the action of the law school here complained of constitutes "state action" within the meaning of the Fourteenth Amendment.

Does segregation of children in public schools solely on the basis of race, even though the physical facilities and other "tangible" factors may be equal, deprive the children of the minority group of equal educational opportunities? We believe that it does.

The court in *Brown* held the equal protection clause of the Fourteenth Amendment prohibits state law from requiring the operation of racially segregated, dual school systems of public education and requires that the system be converted into a unitary, nonracially segregated system. In so holding, the court noted that segregation inevitably stigmatizes Black children:

> To separate them from others of similar age and qualifications solely because of their race generates a feeling of inferiority as to their status in the community that may affect their hearts and minds in a way unlikely ever to be undone.

Brown v. *Board of Educ., supra* at 494. Moreover, "The impact is greater when it has the sanction of the law; for the policy of separating the races is usually interpreted as denoting the inferiority of the negro group." *Brown* at 494.

Brown did not hold that all racial classifications are *per se* unconstitutional; rather, it held that invidious racial classifications—i.e., those that stigmatize a racial group with the stamp of inferiority—are unconstitutional. Even viewed in a light most favorable to plaintiff, the "preferential" minority admissions policy administered by the law school is clearly not a form of invidious discrimination. The goal of this policy is not to separate the races, but to bring them together. And, as has been observed,

> Preferential admissions do not represent a covert attempt to stigmatize the majority race as inferior; nor is it reasonable to expect that a possible effect of the extension of educational preferences to certain disadvantaged racial minorities will be to stigmatize whites.

O'Neil, *Preferential Admissions: Equalizing the Access of Minority Groups to Higher Education,* 80 Yale L.J. 699, 713 (1971).

While *Brown* v. *Board of Educ., supra,* certainly provides a starting point for our analysis of the instant case, we do not agree with the trial court that *Brown* is dispositive here. Subsequent decisions of the United States Supreme Court have made it clear that in some circumstances a racial criterion *may* be used—and indeed in some circumstances *must* be used—by public educational institutions in bringing about racial balance. School systems which were formerly segregated de jure [6] now have an affirmative duty to remedy racial imbalance.

---

[6] "De jure" segregation generally refers to "segregation directly intended or mandated by law or otherwise issuing from an official racial classification," *Hobson* v. *Hansen,* 269 F.Supp. 401, 492 (D.D.C. 1967), or, in other words, to segregation which

In *Green* v. *County School Bd.*, 391 U.S. 430 (1968)**, the Supreme Court considered a school board's adoption of a "freedom-of-choice" plan which allowed a student to choose his own public school. No student was assigned or admitted to school on the basis of race. In holding that, on the facts presented, the plan did not satisfy the board's duty to create a unitary, nonracial system, the court stated at pages 437–40:

> In the context of the state-imposed segregated pattern of long standing, the fact that in 1965 the Board opened the doors of the former "white" school to Negro children and of the "Negro" school to white children merely begins, not ends, our inquiry whether the Board has taken steps adequate to abolish its dual, segregated system. . . . The burden on a school board today is to come forward with a plan that promises realistically to work, and promises realistically to work *now*. . . . As Judge Soboloff has put it, " 'Freedom of choice' is not a sacred talisman; it is only a means to a constitutionally required end—the abolition of the system of segregation and its effects. If the means prove effective, it is acceptable, but if it fails to undo segregation, other means must be used to achieve this end. The school officials have the continuing duty to take whatever action may be necessary to create a 'unitary, nonracial system.' " *Bowman* v. *County School Board*, 382 F.2d 326, 333 (C.A. 4th Cir. 1967) (concurring opinion).

Pursuing this principle further, the Supreme Court in *Swan* v. *Charlotte-Mecklenburg Bd. of Educ.*, (concurring opinion), 402 U.S. 1, 16 (1971),** unanimously held that school authorities, in seeking to achieve a unitary, nonracial system of public education, need not be "color-blind," but may consider race a valid criterion when considering admissions and producing a student body:

> School authorities are traditionally charged with broad power to formulate and implement educational policy and might well conclude, for example, that in order to prepare students to live in a pluralistic society each school should have a prescribed ratio of Negro to white students reflecting the proportion for the district as a whole. To do this as an educational policy is within the broad discretionary powers of school

---

has, or had, the sanction of law. In the context of public education the United States Supreme Court has expanded the meaning of the term "de jure segregation" "[T]o comprehend any situation in which the activities of school authorities have had a racially discriminatory impact contributing to the establishment or continuation [of racial imbalance]. . . ." *State ex-rel. Citizens Against Mandatory Bussing* v. *Brooks*, 80 Wn.2d 121, 130, 492 P.2d 536 (1972).

Where the segregation is inadvertent and without the assistance or collusion of school authorities, and is not caused by any "state action," but rather by social, economic and other determinants, it will be referred to as "de facto" herein. *See* Fiss, *Racial Imbalance in the Public Schools: the Constitutional Concepts*, 78 Harv. L. Rev. 564, 565-66, 584, 598 (1965).

authorities; absent a finding of a constitutional violation, however, that would not be within the authority of a federal court.

The Supreme Court then approved the district court's opinion requiring the school authorities to consider race in determining the composition of individual schools:

> As we said in *Green,* a school authority's remedial plan or a district court's remedial decree is to be judged by its effectiveness. Awareness of the racial composition of the whole school system is likely to be a useful starting point in shaping a remedy to correct past constitutional violations.

Swann v. Charlotte-Mecklenburg Bd. of Educ., supra at 25.

Thus, the constitution is color conscious to prevent the perpetuation of discrimination and to undo the effects of past segregation. In holding invalid North Carolina's anti-bussing law, which flatly forbade assignment of any student on account of race or for the purpose of creating a racial balance or ratio in the schools and which prohibited bussing for such purposes, the court stated:

> [T]he statute exploits an apparently neutral form to control school assignment plans by directing that they be "color blind"; that requirement, against the background of segregation, would render illusory the promise of *Brown v. Board of Education,* 347 U.S. 483 (1954). Just as the race of students must be considered in determining whether a constitutional violation has occurred, so also must race be considered in formulating a remedy. . . .

Clearly, consideration of race by school authorities does not violate the Fourteenth Amendment where the purpose is to bring together, rather than separate, the races. The "minority" admissions policy of the law school, aimed at insuring a reasonable representation of minority persons in the student body, is not invidious. Consideration of race is permissible to carry out the mandate of *Brown,* and, as noted, has been required in some circumstances.

However, plaintiff contends that cases such as *Green v. County School Bd., supra,* and *Swann v. Charlotte-Mecklenburg Bd. of Educ., supra,* are inapposite here since none of the students there involved were deprived of an education by the plan to achieve a unitary school system. It is questionable whether defendants deprived plaintiff of a legal education by denying him admission.[7] But even accepting this contention, arguendo, the denial of a "benefit" on the basis of race is not necessarily a *per se* violation of the Fourteenth Amendment, if the racial classification is used in a compensatory way to promote integration.

---

[7] Plaintiff alleged in his complaint that he had previously applied to and been accepted by the law school at each of the following universities: University of Oregon, University of Idaho, Gonzaga University and Willamette University.

For example, in *Porcelli* v. *Titus,* 431 F.2d 1254 (3d Cir. 1970)**, a group of white teachers alleged that the school board had bypassed them in abolishing the regular promotion schedule and procedure for selecting principals and vice-principals, and had given priority to Black candidates in order to increase the integration of the system's faculty. In upholding the board's judgment to suspend the ordinary promotion system upon racial considerations, the court stated:

> State action based partly on considerations of color, when color is not used per se, and in furtherance of a proper governmental objective, is not necessarily a violation of the Fourteenth Amendment.

Porcelli v. *Titus, supra* at 1257.

Similarly, the eighth circuit concluded that in order to eradicate the effects of past discrimination,

> [I]t would be in order for the district court to mandate that one out of every three persons hired by the [Minneapolis] Fire Department would be a minority individual who qualifies until at least 20 minority persons have been so hired.

Carter v. *Gallagher,* 452 F.2d 315**. Thus, the court ordered the department to hire minority applicants, although in doing so a more qualified nonminority applicant might be bypassed.**

We conclude that the consideration of race as a factor in the admissions policy of a state law school is not a *per se* violation of the equal protection clause of the Fourteenth Amendment. We proceed, therefore, to the question of what standard of review is appropriate to determine the constitutionality of such a classification.

B.

Generally, when reviewing a state-created classification alleged to be in violation of the equal protection clause of the Fourteenth Amendment, the question is whether the classification is reasonably related to a legitimate public purpose. And, in applying this "rational basis" test "[A] discrimination will not be set aside if any state of facts reasonably may be conceived to justify it." **

However, where the classification is based upon race, a heavier burden of justification is imposed upon the state. In overturning Virginia's antimiscegenation law, the Supreme Court explained this stricter standard of review:

> The clear and central purpose of the Fourteenth Amendment was to eliminate all official state sources of invidious racial discrimination in the States. [Citation omitted.]

. . . At the very least, the Equal Protection Clause demands that racial classifications, especially suspect in criminal statutes, be subjected to the "most rigid scrutiny," [citation omitted] and, if they are ever to be upheld, they must be shown to be necessary to the accomplishment of some permissible state objective, independent of the racial discrimination which it was the object of the Fourteenth Amendment to eliminate. . . .

There is patently no legitimate overriding purpose independent of invidious racial discrimination which justifies this classification.

Loving v. *Virginia,* 388 U.S. 1, 10-11.**

It has been suggested that the less strict "rational basis" test should be applied to the consideration of race here, since the racial distinction is being used to redress the effects of past discrimination; thus, because the persons normally stigmatized by racial classifications are being benefited, the action complained of should be considered "benign" and reviewed under the more permissive standard. However, the minority admissions policy is certainly not benign with respect to nonminority students who are displaced by it. *See* O'Neil, *Preferential Admissions: Equalizing the Access of Minority Groups to Higher Education,* 80 Yale L.J. 699, 710 (1971).

The burden is upon the law school to show that its consideration of race in admitting students is necessary to the accomplishment of a compelling state interest.

C.

It can hardly be gainsaid that the minorities have been, and are, grossly underrepresented in the law schools—and consequently in the legal profession—of this state and this nation.[8] We believe the state has an overriding interest in promoting integration in public education in

[8] Report of Black Lawyers and Judges in the United States, 1960–70, 91st Cong., 2d Sess., 116 Cong. Rec. 30786 (1970); U.S. Dep't of Commerce, Bureau of Census, General Population Characteristics of the State of Washington, Tables 17 and 18 (1970); Office of Program Planning and Fiscal Management of the State of Washington, Pocket Data Book (1971); Rosen, *Equalizing Access to Legal Education: Special Programs for Law Students Who Are Not Admissible by Traditional Criteria,* 1970 U. Tol. L. Rev. 321 (1970); Edwards, *A New Role for the Black Law Graduates—A Reality or an Illusion?* 69 Mich. L. Rev. 1407 (1971); Gelhorn, *The Law Schools and the Negro,* 1968 Duke L.J. 1069 (1968); Reynoso, *Laraza, the Law and the Law Schools,* 1970 U. Tol L. Rev. 809 (1970); Toles, *Black Population and Black Judges,* 17 Student Lawyer J. 20 (Feb. 1972); O'Neil, *Preferential Admissions: Equalizing Access to Legal Education,* 1970 U. Tol. L. Rev. 281 (1970); Atwood, *Survey of Black Law Student Enrollment,* 16 Student Lawyer J. 18 (June 1971); Comment, *Selected Bibliography: Minority Group Participation in the Legal Profession,* 1970 U. Tol L. Rev. 935 (1970).

In relying on statistical evidence to establish the underrepresentation of minority groups in the legal profession, defendants are supported by ample precedent. *See,* e.g., *Hobson* v. *Hansen, supra* note 10.

light of the serious underrepresentation of minority groups in the law schools, and considering that minority groups participate on an equal basis in the tax support of the law school, we find the state interest in eliminating racial imbalance within public legal education to be compelling. . . .

Significantly, this case does not present for review a court order imposing a program of desegregation. Rather, the minority admissions policy is a voluntary plan initiated by school authorities. Therefore, the question before us is not whether the Fourteenth Amendment *requires* the law school to take affirmative action to eliminate the continuing effects of de facto segregation; the question is whether the constitution *permits* the law school to remedy racial imbalance through its minority admissions policy. In refusing to enjoin school officials from implementing a plan to eradicate de facto school segregation by the use of explicit racial classifications, the second circuit observed: "That there may be no constitutional duty to act to undo de facto segregation, however, does not mean that such action is unconstitutional." *Offermann* v. *Nitkowski*, 378 F.2d 22, 24 (2d Cir. 1967).

The de jure–de facto distinction is not controlling in determining the constitutionality of the minority admissions policy voluntarily adopted by the law school.[9] Further, we see no reason why the state interest in eradicating the continuing effects of past racial discrimination is less merely because the law school itself may have previously been neutral in the matter.

The state also has an overriding interest in providing *all* law students with a legal education that will adequately prepare them to deal with the societal problems which will confront them upon graduation. As the Supreme Court has observed, this cannot be done through books alone:

> [A]lthough the law is a highly learned profession, we are well aware that it is an intensely practical one. The law school, the proving ground for legal learning and practice, cannot be effective in isolation from the individuals and institutions with which the law interacts. Few students and no one who has practiced law would choose to study in an academic vacuum, removed from the interplay of ideas and the exchange of views with which the law is concerned.

Sweatt v. *Painter*, 339 U.S. 629 (1950)**.

The legal profession plays a critical role in the policy making sector of our society, whether decisions be public or private, state or local. That lawyers, in making and influencing these decisions, should be cognizant of the views, needs and demands of all segments of society

---

[9] We do not, therefore, reach the question of whether there is an inherent cultural bias in the Law School Admission Test, or in the methods of teaching and testing employed by the law school, which perpetuates racial imbalance to such an extent as to constitute de jure segregation.

is a principle beyond dispute. The educational interest of the state in producing a racially balanced student body at the law school is compelling.

Finally, the shortage of minority attorneys—and, consequently, minority prosecutors, judges and public officials—constitutes an undeniably compelling state interest.[10] If minorities are to live within the rule of law, they must enjoy equal representation within our legal system.

Once a constitutionally valid state interest has been established, it remains for the state to show the requisite connection between the racial classification employed and that interest. The consideration of race in the law school admissions policy meets the test of necessity here because racial imbalance in the law school and the legal profession is the evil to be corrected, and it can only be corrected by providing legal education to those minority groups which have been previously deprived.

It has been suggested that the minority admissions policy is not necessary, since the same objective could be accomplished by improving the elementary and secondary education of minority students to a point where they could secure equal representation in law schools through direct competition with nonminority applicants on the basis of the same academic criteria. This would be highly desirable, but 18 years have passed since the decision in *Brown* v. *Board of Educ.,* 347 U.S. 483,** and minority groups are still grossly underrepresented in law schools. If the law school is forbidden from taking affirmative action, this underrepresentation may be perpetuated indefinitely. No less restrictive means would serve the governmental interest here; we believe the minority admissions policy of the law school to be the only feasible "plan that promises realistically to work, and promises realistically to work *now.*" *Green* v. *County School Bd.,* 391 U.S. 430.**

We conclude that defendants have shown the necessity of the racial classification herein to the accomplishment of an overriding state interest, and have thus sustained the heavy burden imposed upon them under the equal protection provision of the Fourteenth Amendment.

There remains a further question as to the scope of the classification. A validly drawn classification is one "which includes all [and only those] persons who are similarly situated with respect to the purpose of the law." Tussman and tenBroek, *The Equal Protection of the Laws,* 37 Calif. L. Rev. 341, 346 (1949). The classification used by defendants does not include all racial minorities, but only four (Blacks, Chicanos, Indians and Philippine Americans). However, the purpose of the racial classification here is to give special consideration to those racial minority groups which are underrepresented in the law schools and legal profession, and which cannot secure proportionate representation if strictly subjected to the standardized mathematical criteria for admission to the law school.

In selecting minority groups for special consideration, the law

---

[10] *See* O'Neil, *Preferential Admissions: Equalizing Access to Legal Education, supra* note 12.

school sought to identify those groups most in need of help. The chairman of the admissions committee testified that Asian Americans, e.g., were not treated as minority applicants for admissions purposes since a significant number could be admitted on the same basis as general applicants. In light of the purpose of the minority admissions policy, the racial classification need not include all racial minority groups.[11] The state may identify and correct the most serious examples of racial imbalance, even though in so doing it does not provide an immediate solution to the entire problem of equal representation within the legal system.

We hold that the minority admissions policy of the law school, and the denial by the law school of admission to plaintiff, violate neither the equal protection clause of the fourteenth amendment to the United States Constitution nor article 1, section 12 of the Washington State Constitution.[12] . . .

The judgment of the trial court is reversed.

The foregoing opinion was prepared by Justice Marshall A. Neill while a member of this court. It is adopted by the undersigned as the opinion of the court.

Finley, Hamilton, Stafford, Wright, and Utter, J. J., and Tuttle, J. Pro Tem.

Hale, C. J. (dissenting)—Racial bigotry, prejudice and intolerance will never be ended by exalting the political rights of one group or class over those of another. The circle of inequality cannot be broken by shifting the inequities from one man to his neighbor. To aggrandize the first will, to the extent of the aggrandizement, diminish the latter. There is no remedy at law except to abolish all class distinctions heretofore existing in law. For that reason, the constitutions are, and ever ought to be, color blind. Now the court says it would hold the constitutions color conscious that they may stay color blind. I do not see how they can be both color blind and color conscious at the same time toward the same persons and on the same issues, so I dissent.

The court, as I see it, upholds palpably discriminatory law school admission practices of the state university mainly because they were initiated for the laudable purpose of enhancing the opportunities of members of what are described as "ethnic minorities." It thus suggests a new rule of constitutional interpretation to be applied here that, if the administrative intentions are adequately noble in purpose, Mr. DeFunis may be deprived of equal protection of the laws and certain special immunities and privileges may be granted to others which, on the same

11 See O'Neil, *Preferential Admissions: Equalizing the Access of Minority Groups to Higher Education,* 80 Yale L.J. 699, 750 (1971).

12 As we have held, the equal protection clause of U.S. Const. amend. 14, and the privileges and immunities clause of Const. art. 1, § 12, have the same import, and we apply them as one. *Markham Adv. Co.* v. *State,* 73 Wn.2d 405, 427, 439 P.2d 248 (1968), *appeal dismissed,* 393 U.S. 316 (1969).

terms, are denied to him. One should keep in mind the wisdom of the old saying that the road to perdition is paved with good intentions.

The court holds that the university law school may give preferential treatment to persons who come from groups "which have been historically suppressed by encouraging their enrollment within the various programs offered at the University." But what seems to me to be a flagrant departure from the constitutions, ignored by the court, is epitomized in the statement that the admission policy was adopted by the law school "to increase participation within the legal profession by persons from racial and ethnic groups which have been historically denied access to the profession and which, consequently, are grossly underrepresented within the legal system." This assertion confesses to prior racial discrimination which I doubt existed, and fails to recognize, in a case where the demand for seats in the law school is much greater than the school's capacity, that the increased minority participation assured by such admission procedures inevitably produces a correlative denial of access to nonminority applicants.

Thus, in keeping with what may be described as the expanding horizons of latter-day constitutional principles in perpetual processes of invention and assertion, the court discovers in an administrative agency of the state the power to determine, first, who, among the applicants, shall be classified as Black Americans, Chicano Americans, American Indians and Philippine Americans and, then, a concomitant power to exclude all other ethnic minorities, including Asian Americans, from the preferred classification. It lets the agency grant preferences—or as they more accurately should be described, indulgences—accordingly. For reasons not clear in the record, Asian Americans and all others of different ethnic derivation than those enumerated are not included among those to receive such preferences or indulgences. . . .

With the possible exception of administering justice, I accept the dicta in *Brown* v. *Board of Educ.*, 347 U.S. 483,** that education is probably the most important function of state and local government. It should not be forgotten, however, that in striking down decisively the separate but equal concept of segregated schools, the rationale of that decision rested on equality of opportunity and the premise that segregation based on race or color amounted categorically to an unconstitutional denial of that equality. In speaking of equality of educational opportunity, the court there said, "Such an opportunity, where the state has undertaken to provide it, is a right which must be made available to all on equal terms." 347 U.S. at 493. . . .

The rationale of *Anderson* v. *San Francisco Unified School Dist.*, 357 F. Supp. 248 (N.D. Cal. 1972), an opinion dated October 30, 1972, filed in the United States District Court, Northern District of California, I think, expresses the principles which should govern the *DeFunis* case. That court held unconstitutional a school district's plan to give preference in employment and promotions to members of ethnic minorities in administrative and supervisory positions, such as principals, assistant

principals, deans and heads of departments—a plan designed to increase
the numerical representation of ethnic minorities in the administration
of the schools. That court, in holding the scheme unconstitutional, said
that "The key issue in this case is whether or not a classification which
is based on race is valid," and answered it with a statement of principles
which ought to control here:

> Preferential treatment under the guise of "affirmative action" is the im-
> position of one form of racial discrimination in place of another. The
> questions that must be asked in this regard are: must an individual
> sacrifice his right to be judged on his own merit by accepting discrimina-
> tion based solely on the color of his skin? How can we achieve the goal
> of equal opportunity for all if, in the process, we deny equal opportunity
> to some?

Mr. DeFunis came before the bar of the Superior Court much as did
petitioners, parents of schoolchildren, in *Brown* v. *Board of Educ.*, 347
U.S. 483,** asking that he not be denied admission to the university law
school because of race or ethnic origin. The trial court properly ordered
his admission. So, too, would I, and, therefore, I would affirm.

DEFUNIS V. ODEGAARD

SUPREME COURT OF THE UNITED STATES

Mr. Justice Douglas, dissenting.

I agree with Mr. Justice Brennan that this case is not moot, and
because of the significance of the issues raised I think it is important to
reach the merits. . . .
There was a time when law schools could follow the advice of
Wigmore, who believed that "the way to find out whether a boy has
the makings of a competent lawyer is to see what he can do in a first
year of law studies." Wigmore, Juristic Psychopoyemetrology—Or, How
to Find Out Whether a Boy Has the Makings of a Lawyer, 24 Ill. L.
Rev. 454, 463–464 (1929). In those days there were enough spaces to
admit every applicant who met minimal credentials, and they all could
be given the opportunity to prove themselves at law school. But by the
1920's many law schools found that they could not admit all minimally

qualified applicants, and some selection process began.[1] The pressure to use some kind of admissions test mounted, and a number of schools instituted them. One early precursor to the modern day LSAT was the Ferson-Stoddard Law Aptitude examination. Wigmore conducted his own study of that test with 50 student volunteers, and concluded that it "had no substantial practical value." Id., at 463. But his conclusions were not accepted, and the harried law schools still sought some kind of admissions test which would simplify the process of judging applicants, and in 1948 the LSAT was born. It has been with us ever since.[2]

The test purports to predict how successful the applicant will be in his first year of law school, and consists of a few hours' worth of multiple-choice questions. But the answers the student can give to a multiple-choice question are limited by the creativity and intelligence of the test-maker; the student with a better or more original understanding of the problem than the test-maker may realize that none of the alternative answers are any good, but there is no way for him to demonstrate his understanding. "It is obvious from the nature of the tests that they do not give the candidate a significant opportunity to express himself. If he is subtle in his choice of answers it will go against him; and yet there is no other way for him to show any individuality. If he is strong-minded, nonconformist, unusual, original, or creative— as so many of the truly important people are—he must stifle his impulses and conform as best he can to the norms that the multiple-choice testers set up in their unimaginative, scientific way. The more profoundly gifted the candidate is, the more his resentment will rise against the mental strait jacket into which the testers would force his mind." B. Hoffmann, The Tyranny of Testing 91–92 (1962).

Those who make the tests and the law schools which use them point, of course, to the high correlations between the test scores and the grades at law school the first year. E.g., Winterbottom, Comments on "A Study of the Criteria for Legal Education and Admission to the Bar," An Article by Dr. Thomas M. Goolsby, Jr., 21 J. Legal Ed. 75 (1968). Certainly the tests do seem to do better than chance. But they do not have the value that their deceptively precise scoring system suggests. The proponents' own data show that, for example, most of those scoring in the bottom 20% on the test do better than that in law school—indeed six of every 100 of them will be in the *top* 20% of their law school class. Id., at 79. And no one knows how many of those who were not admitted because of their test scores would in fact have done well were they given the chance. There are many relevant factors, such as motivation, cul-

---

[1] For a history of gradual acceptance among law schools of standardized tests as an admission tool, see Ramsey, Law School Admissions: Science, Art, or Hunch?, 12 J. Legal Ed. 503 (1960).

[2] For a survey of the use of the LSAT by American law schools as of 1965, see Lunneborg and Radford, The LSAT: A Survey of Actual Practice, 18 J. Legal Ed. 313 (1966).

tural backgrounds of specific minorities that the test cannot measure, and they inevitably must impair its value as a predictor.[3] Of course, the law school that admits only those with the highest test scores finds that on the average they do much better, and thus the test is a convenient tool for the admissions committee. The price is paid by the able student who for unknown reasons did not achieve that high score—perhaps even the minority with a different cultural background. Some tests, at least in the past, have been aimed at eliminating Jews.

The school can safely conclude that the applicant with a score of 750 should be admitted before one with a score of 500. The problem is that in many cases the choice will be between 643 and 602 or 574 and 528. The numbers create an illusion of difference tending to overwhelm other factors. "The wiser testers are well aware of the defects of the multiple-choice format and the danger of placing reliance on any one method of assessment to the exclusion of all others. What is distressing is how little their caveats have impressed the people who succumb to the propaganda of the test-makers and use these tests mechanically as though they were a valid substitute for judgment." Hoffmann, *supra,* at 215.

Of course, the tests are not the only thing considered; here they were combined with the prelaw grades to produce a new number called the Average. The grades have their own problems; one school's A is another school's C. And even to the extent that this formula predicts law school grades, its value is limited. The law student with lower grades may in the long pull of a legal career surpass those at the top of the class. "[L]aw school admissions criteria have operated within a hermetically sealed system; it is now beginning to leak. The traditional combination of LSAT and GPA [undergraduate grade point average] may have provided acceptable predictors of likely performance in law school in the past. . . . [But] [t]here is no clear evidence that the LSAT and GPA provide particularly good evaluators of the intrinsic or enriched ability of an individual to perform as a law student or lawyer in a functioning society undergoing change. Nor is there any clear evidence that grades and other evaluators of law school performance, and the bar examination, are particularly good predicators of competence or success as a lawyer." Rosen, Equalizing Access to Legal Education: Special Programs for Law Students Who Are Not Admissible by Traditional Criteria, 1970 U. Tol. L. Rev. 321, 332–333.

But, by whatever techniques, the law school must make choices. Neither party has challenged the validity of the Average employed here as an admissions tool, and therefore consideration of its possible deficiencies is not presented as an issue. The Law School presented no evidence to show that adjustments in the process employed were used in order validly to compare applicants of different races; instead, it chose to avoid making such comparisons. Finally, although the Committee did consider

---

[3] Rock, Motivation, Moderators, and Test Bias, 1970 U. Tol. L. Rev. 527, 535.

other information in the files of all applicants, the Law School has made no effort to show that it was because of these additional factors that it admitted minority applicants who would otherwise have been rejected. To the contrary, the school appears to have conceded that by its own assessment—taking all factors into account—it admitted minority applicants who would have been rejected had they been white. We have no choice but to evaluate the Law School's case as it has been made.

The Equal Protection Clause did not enact a requirement that Law Schools employ as the sole criterion for admissions a formula based upon the LSAT and undergraduate grades, nor does it prohibit law schools from evaluating an applicant's prior achievements in light of the barriers that he had to overcome. A Black applicant who pulled himself out of the ghetto into a junior college may thereby demonstrate a level of motivation, perseverance and ability that would lead a fair-minded admissions committee to conclude that he shows more promise for law study than the son of a rich alumnus who achieved better grades at Harvard. That applicant would not be offered admission because he is Black, but because as an individual he has shown he has the potential, while the Harvard man may have taken less advantage of the vastly superior opportunities offered him. Because of the weight of the prior handicaps, that Black applicant may not realize his full potential in the first year of law school, or even in the full three years, but in the long pull of a legal career his achievements may far outstrip those of his classmates whose earlier records appeared superior by conventional criteria. There is currently no test available to the Admissions Committee that can predict such possibilities with assurance, but the Committee may nevertheless seek to gauge it as best it can, and weigh this factor in its decisions. Such a policy would not be limited to Blacks, or Chicanos or Filipinos, or American Indians, although undoubtedly groups such as these may in practice be the principal beneficiaries of it. But a poor Appalachian white, or a second generation Chinese in San Francisco, or some other American whose lineage is so diverse as to defy ethnic labels, may demonstrate similar potential and thus be accorded favorable consideration by the committee.

The difference between such a policy and the one presented by this case is that the Committee would be making decisions on the basis of individual attributes, rather than according a preference solely on the basis of race. To be sure, the racial preference here was not absolute—the Committee did not admit all applicants from the four favored groups. But it did accord all such applicants a preference by applying, to an extent not precisely ascertainable from the record, different standards by which to judge their applications, with the result that the Committee admitted minority applicants who, in the school's own judgment, were less promising than other applicants who were rejected. Furthermore, it is apparent that because the Admissions Committee compared minority applicants only with one another, it was necessary to reserve some proportion of the class for them, even if at the outset a precise number of places were not set aside.[4] That proportion, apparently 15% to 20%, was chosen because the school determined it to be "reasonable,"[5] although no explanation is provided as to how that number rather than some other was found appropriate. Without becoming embroiled in a semantic debate over whether this practice constitutes a "quota," it is clear that, given the limitation on the total number of applicants who could be accepted, this policy did reduce the total number of places for which DeFunis could compete—solely on account of his race. Thus, as the Washington Supreme Court concluded, whatever label one wishes to apply to it, "the minority admissions policy is certainly not benign with respect to nonminority students who are displaced by it." 82 Wash. 2d, at 32, 507 P. 2d, at 1182. A finding that the state school employed a racial classification in selecting its students subjects it to the strictest scrutiny under the Equal Protection Clause.

The consideration of race as a measure of an applicant's qualification normally introduces a capricious and irrelevant factor working an invidious discrimination, *Anderson* v. *Martin,* 375 U.S. 399, 402; *Loving* v. *Virginia,* 388 U. S. 1, 10; *Harper* v. *Virginia Board of Elections,* 383 U. S. 663, 668. Once race is a starting point educators and courts are immediately embroiled in competing claims of different racial and ethnic groups that would make difficult manageable standards consistent with the Equal Protection Clause. "The clear and central purpose of the Fourteenth Amendment was to eliminate all official state sources of invidious racial discrimination in the States." *Loving, supra,* at 10. The Law School's admissions policy cannot be reconciled with that purpose, unless cultural standards of a diverse rather than a homogeneous society are taken into account. The reason is that professional persons, particularly lawyers, are not selected for life in a computerized society. The Indian who walks to the beat of Chief Seattle of the Muckleshoot Tribe in Washington[6] has a different culture from examiners at law schools.

The key to the problem is the consideration of each application *in*

---

[4] At the outset the Committee may have chosen only a range, with the precise number to be determined later in the process as the total number of minority applicants, and some tentative assessment of their quality, could be determined. This appears to be the current articulated policy, see Appendix § 6, and we are advised by the respondents that § 6 "represents a more formal statement of the policy which was in effect in 1971 . . . but does not represent any change in policy." Letter to the Court dated March 19, 1974, p. 1. The fact that the Committee did not set a precise number in advance is obviously irrelevant to the legal analysis. Nor does it matter that there is some minimal level of achievement below which the Committee would not reach in order to achieve its stated goal as to the proportion of the class reserved for minority groups, so long as the Committee was willing, in order to achieve that goal, to admit minority applicants who, in the Committee's own judgment, were less qualified than other rejected applicants and who would not otherwise have been admitted.

[5] See [note 4, above]. . . .

[6] Uncommon Controversy, Report Prepared for American Friends Service Committee 29–30 (1970).

a racially neutral way. Since LSAT reflects questions touching on cultural backgrounds, the Admissions Committee acted properly in my view in setting minority applications apart for separate processing. These minorities have cultural backgrounds that are vastly different from the dominant Caucasian. Many Eskimos, American Indians, Filipinos, Chicanos, Asian Indians, Burmese, and Africans come from such disparate backgrounds that a test sensitively tuned for most applicants would be wide of the mark for many minorities.

The melting pot is not designed to homogenize people, making them uniform in consistency. The melting pot as I understand it is a figure of speech that depicts the wide diversities tolerated by the First Amendment under one flag. See 2 S. Morison and H. Commager, The Growth of the American Republic, c. VIII (4th ed. 1950). Minorities in our midst who are to serve actively in our public affairs should be chosen on talent and character alone, not on cultural orientation or leanings.

I do know, coming as I do from Indian country in Washington, that many of the young Indians know little about Adam Smith or Karl Marx but are deeply imbued with the spirit and philosophy of Chief Robert B. Jim of the Yakimas, Chief Seattle of the Muckleshoots, and Chief Joseph of the Nez Perce which offer competitive attitudes towards life, fellow man, and nature.[7]

I do not know the extent to which Blacks in this country are imbued with ideas of African Socialism.[8] Leopold Senghor and Sékou Touré, most articulate of African leaders, have held that modern African political philosophy is not oriented either to Marxism or to capitalism.[9] How far the reintroduction into educational curricula of ancient African art and history has reached the minds of young Afro-Americans I do not know. But at least as respects Indians, Blacks, and Chicanos—as well as those from Asian cultures—I think a separate classification of these applicants is warranted, lest race be a subtle force in eliminating minority members because of cultural differences.

Insofar as LSAT tests reflect the dimensions and orientation of the Organization Man they do a disservice to minorities. I personally know that admissions tests were once used to eliminate Jews. How many other minorities they aim at I do not know. My reaction is that the presence of an LSAT test is sufficient warrant for a school to put racial minorities into a separate class in order better to probe their capacities and potentials.

The merits of the present controversy cannot in my view be resolved on this record. A trial would involve the disclosure of hidden prejudices, if any, against certain minorities and the manner in which substitute measurements of one's talents and character were employed

---

[7] See C. Fee, Chief Joseph, The Biography of a Great Indian (1936).

[8] See F. Brockway, African Socialism (1963); African Socialism (W. Friedland and C. Rosberg ed. 1964).

[9] See L. Senghor, On African Socialism (M. Cook ed. 1964).

in the conventional tests. I could agree with the majority of the Washington Supreme Court only if, on the record, it could be said that the Law School's selection was racially neutral. The case, in my view, should be remanded for a new trial to consider, *inter alia,* whether the established LSAT tests should be eliminated so far as racial minorities are concerned.

This does not mean that a separate LSAT test must be designed for minority racial groups, although that might be a possibility. The reason for the separate treatment of minorities as a class is to make more certain that racial factors do not militate *against an applicant or on his behalf.*[10]

There is no constitutional right for any race to be preferred. The years of slavery did more than retard the progress of Blacks. Even a greater wrong was done the whites by creating arrogance instead of humility and by encouraging the growth of the fiction of a superior race. There is no superior person by constitutional standards. A DeFunis who is white is entitled to no advantage by reason of that fact; nor is he subject to any disability, no matter what his race or color. Whatever his race, he had a constitutional right to have his application considered on its individual merits in a racially neutral manner.

The slate is not entirely clean. First, we have held that *pro rata* representation of the races is not required either on juries, see *Cassell* v. *Texas,* 339 U.S. 282, 286–287, or in public schools, *Swann* v. *Charlotte-Mecklenburg Board of Education,* 402 U.S. 1, 24. Moreover, in *Hughes* v. *Superior Court,* 339 U.S. 460, we reviewed the contempt convictions of pickets who sought by their demonstration to force an employer to prefer Negroes to whites in his hiring of clerks, in order to ensure that 50% of the employees were Negro. In finding that California could constitutionally enjoin the picketing there involved we quoted from the opinion of the California Supreme Court, which noted that the pickets would "make the right to work for Lucky dependent not on fitness for the work nor on an equal right of all, regardless of race, to compete in an open market, but, rather, on membership in a particular race. If petitioners were upheld in their demand then other races, white, yellow,

---

[10] We are not faced here with a situation where barriers are overtly or covertly put in the path of members of one racial group which are not required by others. There was also no showing that the purpose of the school's policy was to eliminate arbitrary and irrelevant barriers to entry by certain racial groups into the legal profession groups. *Griggs* v. *Duke Power Co.,* 401 U.S. 424. In *Swann* v. *Charlotte-Mecklenburg Board of Education,* 402 U.S. 1, 16, we stated that as a matter of educational policy school authorities could, within their broad discretion, specify that each school within its district have a prescribed ratio of Negro to white students reflecting the proportion for the district as a whole, in order to disestablish a dual school system. But there is a crucial difference between the policy suggested in *Swann* and that under consideration here: the *Swann* policy would impinge on no person's constitutional rights, because no one would be excluded from a public school and no one has a right to attend a segregated public school.

brown and red, would have equal rights to demand discriminatory hiring on a racial basis." Id., at 463–464. We then noted that

> [t]o deny to California the right to ban picketing in the circumstances of this case would mean that there could be no prohibition of the pressure of picketing to secure proportional employment on ancestral grounds of Hungarians in Cleveland, of Poles in Buffalo, of Germans in Milwaukee, of Portuguese in New Bedford, of Mexicans in San Antonio, of the numerous minority groups in New York, and so on through the whole gamut of racial and religious concentrations in various cities. Id., at 464.

The reservation of a proportion of the law school class for members of selected minority groups is fraught with similar dangers, for one must immediately determine which groups are to receive such favored treatment and which are to be excluded, the proportions of the class that are to be allocated to each, and even the criteria by which to determine whether an individual is a member of a favored group. There is no assurance that a common agreement can be reached, and first the schools, and then the courts, will be buffeted with the competing claims. The University of Washington included Filipinos, but excluded Chinese and Japanese; another school may limit its program to Blacks, or to Blacks and Chicanos. Once the Court sanctioned racial preferences such as these, it could not then wash its hands of the matter, leaving it entirely in the discretion of the school, for then we would have effectively overruled *Sweatt* v. *Painter*, 339 U. S. 629, and allowed imposition of a "zero" allocation.[11] But what standard is the Court to apply when a rejected applicant of Japanese ancestry brings suit to require the University of Washington to extend the same privileges to his group? The Committee might conclude that the population of Washington is now 2% Japanese, and that Japanese also constitute 2% of the Bar, but that had they not been handicapped by a history of discrimination, Japanese would now constitute 5% of the Bar, or 20%. Or, alternatively, the Court could attempt to assess how grievously each group has suffered from discrimination, and allocate proportions accordingly; if that were the standard the current University of Washington policy would almost surely fall, for there is no Western State which can claim that it has always treated Japanese and Chinese in a fair and evenhanded manner. See e.g., *Yick Wo* v. *Hopkins,* 118 U. S. 356; *Terrace* v. *Thompson,* 263 U. S. 197; *Oyama* v. *California,* 332 U. S. 633. This Court has not sustained a racial

---

11 *Sweatt* held that a State could not justify denying a black admission to its regular law school by creating a new law school for blacks. We held that the new law school did not meet the requirements of "equality" set forth in *Plessy* v. *Ferguson,* 163 U. S. 537.

The student, we said, was entitled to "legal education equivalent to that offered by the State to students of other races. Such education is not available to him in a separate law school as offered by the State." 339 U. S. 629, 635.

classification since the wartime cases of *Korematsu v. United States,* 323 U. S. 214 (1944), and *Hirabayashi v. United States,* 320 U. S. 81 (1943), involving curfews and relocations imposed upon Japanese-Americans.[12]

Nor obviously will the problem be solved if next year the Law School included only Japanese and Chinese, for then Norwegians and Swedes, Poles and Italians, Puerto Ricans and Hungarians, and all other groups which form this diverse Nation would have just complaints.

The key to the problem is consideration of such applications *in a racially neutral way.* Abolition of the LSAT would be a start. The invention of substitute tests might be made to get a measure of an applicant's cultural background, perception, ability to analyze, and his or her relation to groups. They are highly subjective, but unlike the LSAT they are not concealed, but in the open. A law school is not bound by any legal principle to admit students by mechanical criteria which are insensitive to the potential of such an applicant which may be realized in a more hospitable environment. It will be necessary under such an approach to put more effort into assessing each individual than is required when LSAT scores and undergraduate grades dominate the selection process. Interviews with the applicant and others who know him is a time-honored test. Some schools currently run summer programs in which potential students who likely would be bypassed under conventional admissions criteria are given the opportunity to try their hand at law courses,* and certainly their performance in such programs could be weighed heavily. There is, moreover, no bar to considering an individual's prior achievements in light of the racial discrimination that barred his way, as a factor in attempting to assess his true potential for

---

[12] Those cases involved an exercise of the war power, a great leveler of other rights. Our Navy was sunk at Pearl Harbor and no one knew where the Japanese fleet was. We were advised on oral argument that if the Japanese landed troops on our west coast nothing could stop them west of the Rockies. The military judgment was that, to aid in the prospective defense of the west coast, the enclaves of Americans of Japanese ancestry should be moved inland, lest the invaders by donning civilian clothes would wreak even more serious havoc on our western ports. The decisions were extreme and went to the verge of wartime power; and they have been severely criticized. It is, however, easy in retrospect to denounce what was done, as there actually was no attempted Japanese invasion of our country. While our Joint Chiefs of Staff were worrying about Japanese soldiers landing on the west coast, they actually were landing in Burma and at Kota Bharu in Malaya. But those making plans for defense of the Nation had no such knowledge and were planning for the worst. Moreover, the day we decided *Korematsu* we also decided *Ex parte Endo,* 323 U. S. 283, holding that while evacuation of the Americans of Japanese ancestry was allowable under extreme war conditions, their detention after evacuation was not. We said: "A citizen who is concededly loyal presents no problem of espionage or sabotage. Loyalty is a matter of the heart and mind, not of race, creed, or color. He who is loyal is by definition not a spy or a saboteur. When the power to detain is derived from the power to protect the war effort against espionage and sabotage, detention which has no relationship to that objective is unauthorized." Id., at 302.

* Original footnote omitted.—Ed.

a successful legal career. Nor is there any bar to considering on an individual basis, rather than according to racial classifications, the likelihood that a particular candidate will more likely employ his legal skills to service communities that are not now adequately represented than will competing candidates. Not every student benefited by such an expanded admissions program would fall into one of the four racial groups involved here, but it is no drawback that other deserving applicants will also get an opportunity they would otherwise have been denied. Certainly such a program would substantially fulfill the Law School's interest in giving a more diverse group access to the legal profession. Such a program might be less convenient administratively than simply sorting students by race, but we have never held administrative convenience to justify racial discrimination.

The argument is that a "compelling" state interest can easily justify the racial discrimination that is practiced here. To many, "compelling" would give members of one race even more than *pro rata* representation. The public payrolls might then be deluged say with Chicanos because they are as a group the poorest of the poor and need work more than others, leaving desperately poor individual Blacks and whites without employment. By the same token large quotas of blacks or browns could be added to the Bar, waiving examinations required of other groups, so that it would be better racially balanced.[13] The State, however, may not proceed by racial classification to force strict population equivalencies for every group in every occupation, overriding individual preferences. The Equal Protection Clause commands the elimination of racial barriers, not their creation in order to satisfy our theory as to how society ought to be organized. The purpose of the University of Washington cannot be to produce Black lawyers for Blacks, Polish lawyers for Poles, Jewish lawyers for Jews, Irish lawyers for Irish. It should

---

[13] In *Johnson* v. *Committee on Examinations*, 407 U. S. 915, we denied certiorari in a case presenting a similar issue. There the petitioner claimed that the bar examiners reconsidered the papers submitted by failing minority applicants whose scores were close to the cutoff point, with the result that some minority applicants were admitted to the Bar although they initially had examination scores lower than those of white applicants who failed.

As the Arizona Supreme Court denied Johnson admission summarily, in an original proceeding, there were no judicial findings either sustaining or rejecting his factual claims of racial bias, putting the case in an awkward posture for review here. Johnson subsequently brought a civil rights action in Federal District Court, seeking both damages and injunctive relief. The District Court dismissed the action and the Court of Appeals affirmed, holding that the lower federal courts did not have jurisdiction to review the decisions of the Arizona Supreme Court on admissions to the state bar. Johnson then sought review here and we denied his motion for leave to file a petition for mandamus, prohibition and/or certiorari on February 19, 1974. *Johnson* v. *Wilmer*, 415 U. S. 911. Thus in the entire history of the case no court had ever actually sustained Johnson's factual contentions concerning racial bias in the bar examiners' procedures. *DeFunis* thus appears to be the first case here squarely presenting the problem.

be to produce good lawyers for Americans and not to place First Amendment barriers against anyone.[14] That is the point at the heart of all our school desegregation cases, from *Brown* v. *Board of Education,* 347 U.S. 483, through *Swann* v. *Charlotte-Mecklenburg Board of Education,* 402 U.S. 1. A segregated admissions process creates suggestions of stigma and caste no less than a segregated classroom, and in the end it may produce that result despite its contrary intentions. One other assumption must be clearly disapproved, that Blacks or Browns cannot make it on their individual merit. That is a stamp of inferiority that a State is not permitted to place on any lawyer.

If discrimination based on race is constitutionally permissible when those who hold the reins can come up with "compelling" reasons to justify it, then constitutional guarantees acquire an accordionlike quality. Speech is closely brigaded with action when it triggers a fight, *Chaplinsky* v. *New Hampshire,* 315 U.S. 568, as shouting "fire" in a crowded theater triggers a riot. It may well be that racial strains, racial susceptibility to certain diseases, racial sensitiveness to environmental conditions that other races do not experience, may in an extreme situation justify differences in racial treatment that no fairminded person would call "invidious" discrimination. Mental ability is not in that category. All races can compete fairly at all professional levels. So far as race is concerned, any state-sponsored preference to one race over another in that competition is in my view "invidious" and violative of the Equal Protection Clause.

The problem tendered by this case is important and crucial to the operation of our constitutional system; and educators must be given leeway. It may well be that a whole congeries of applicants in the marginal group defy known methods of selection. Conceivably, an admissions committee might conclude that a selection by lot of, say, the last 20 seats is the only fair solution. Courts are not educators; their expertise is limited; and our task ends with the inquiry whether, judged by the main purpose of the Equal Protection Clause—the protection against racial discrimination [15]—there has been an "invidious" discrimination.

---

[14] Underlying all cultural background tests are potential ideological issues that have plagued bar associations and the courts. *In re Summers,* 325 U.S. 561, involved the denial of the practice of law to a man who could not conscientiously bear arms. The vote against him was five to four. *Konigsberg* v. *State Bar,* 353 U.S. 252, followed, after remand, by *Konigsberg* v. *State Bar,* 366 U.S. 36, resulted in barring one from admission to a state bar because of his refusal to answer questions concerning Communist Party membership. He, too, was excluded five to four. The petitioner in *Schware* v. *Board of Bar Examiners,* 353 U.S. 232, was, however, admitted to practice even though he had about 10 years earlier been a member of the Communist Party. But in *In re Anastaplo,* 366 U.S. 82, a five-to-four decision, barred a man from admission to a state bar not because he invoked the Fifth Amendment when asked about membership in the Communist Party, but because he asserted that the First Amendment protected him from that inquiry. *Baird* v. *State Bar of Arizona,* 401 U.S. 1, held by a divided vote that a person could not be kept out of the state bar for refusing to answer whether he had ever been a member of the Communist Party; and see *In re Stolar,* 401 U.S. 23.

[15] See *Slaughter House Cases,* 16 Wall. 36, 81.

We would have a different case if the suit were one to displace the applicant who was chosen in lieu of DeFunis. What the record would show concerning his potentials would have to be considered and weighed. The educational decision, provided proper guidelines were used, would reflect an expertise that courts should honor. The problem is not tendered here because the physical facilities were apparently adequate to take DeFunis in addition to the others. My view is only that I cannot say by the tests used and applied he was invidiously discriminated against because of his race.

I cannot conclude that the admissions procedure of the Law School of the University of Washington that excluded DeFunis is violative of the Equal Protection Clause of the Fourteenth Amendment. The judgment of the Washington Supreme Court should be vacated and the case remanded for a new trial.

CLASSIFICATION BY RACE IN COMPENSATORY PROGRAMS

JAMES W. NICKEL

Suppose that a person who favors compensatory programs for American blacks because of America's history of slavery and discrimination is charged with inconsistency in the following way: "When blacks are denied benefits and given heavier burdens because of race you claim that race is irrelevant and hence claim that discrimination is being practiced.[1] But when racial classifications are used to give preferential treatment to blacks you claim that race is a relevant consideration and deny that this is reverse discrimination." I want to consider two replies that can be made to this charge of inconsistency. The first reply holds that race, the characteristic which is held to be irrelevant when blacks are mistreated, is not the characteristic which is being held to be relevant when compensatory programs are defended. This reply denies that race is the basis for compensation; it claims that the real basis is the wrongs and losses blacks have suffered and the special needs that they have. Hence the characteristic which is held to be relevant in connection with compensa-

From *Ethics* 84 (1974): 146-50. © 1974 by the University of Chicago. Reprinted by permission of the author and the publisher, The University of Chicago Press.

1 There are two senses of "discrimination." One of these is morally neutral and applies to the simple discernment of differences. The other implies moral disapproval and applies to differentiations which involve bias, prejudice, and the use of irrelevant characteristics. My concern here is with "discrimination" in the latter sense.

tory programs is not race but a different characteristic, and there is no inconsistency. I will call this the "different-characteristics reply." The second reply allows that race is the characteristic about which differing relevance claims are made, but it denies that there is any inconsistency since claiming that race is irrelevant to whether someone should be mistreated is not incompatible with claiming that race is relevant to whether someone should be helped. Different issues are involved, and what is relevant to one issue can be irrelevant to another. I will call this the "different-issues reply."

THE DIFFERENT-CHARACTERISTICS REPLY

This reply claims that there is no inconsistency in condemning racial discrimination while favoring compensatory programs for blacks because race, the characteristic which is held to be irrelevant when blacks are mistreated, is not the characteristic which is the basis for providing compensation to blacks. And since race is not the basis for compensatory programs, it need not be claimed that race is relevant in such contexts. The reason for providing compensatory programs for blacks is not their race but the fact that they have been victimized by slavery and discrimination. Not race, but the wrongs that were done, the losses that were suffered, and the special needs resulting from these provide the basis for special treatment now. On this view, race is not held to be relevant in defending compensatory programs, and hence there is no inconsistency with the original claim that race is irrelevant to how people should be treated.[2]

I think this reply is helpful in many cases, but in cases where explicit racial classifications are used by compensatory programs, the person who takes this approach must either claim that such explicit racial classifications are unjustifiable or suggest that they are an unavoidable administrative expediency. To suggest the latter is to suggest that this is a case where the administrative basis for a program (i.e., the characteristic which is used by administrators to decide who is to be served by the program) is different from the justifying basis (i.e., the characteristic which is the reason for having the program). It is not uncommon for these two to differ, although they should overlap substantially. If the justifying basis is a characteristic which occurs in more individuals than the characteristic which is the administrative basis, the latter is underinclusive. And if the justifying basis is a characteristic which occurs in fewer individuals than the characteristic which is the administrative basis, the latter is overinclusive. When resources are limited it is not

---

[2] This is the position that I took in my article, "Discrimination and Morally Relevant Characteristics," *Analysis* 32 (1972): 113-14. Also see J. L. Cowan's reply, "Inverse Discrimination," *Analysis* 33 (1972): 10-12.

uncommon to use an underinclusive administrative basis (e.g., when a poverty program only serves those with an income of less than $2,000 per year), even though this forces the program to ignore deserving cases. And difficulties in identifying those with the characteristic which is the justifying basis may cause the program, for reasons of efficiency, to serve more people than those who have the characteristic which is the justifying basis (e.g., when everyone in a certain county—the administrative basis—is inoculated in order to eliminate a disease—the justifying basis—which 60 percent of the people have but which is difficult to detect except in advanced stages).[3]

The advocate of the "different-characteristics reply" is committed to denying that race is the justifying basis for compensatory programs. But if the justifying basis for such programs is the losses and needs resulting from slavery and discrimination there will be a high correlation between being black and having suffered these losses and having these needs, and because of this the advocate of this reply can allow, without inconsistency, that race can serve as part of the administrative basis for such a program. Efficiency in administering large-scale programs often requires that detailed investigations of individual cases be kept to a minimum, and this means that many allocative decisions will have to be made on the basis of gross but easily discernible characteristics. This may result in a certain degree of unfairness, but it does help to decrease administrative costs so that more resources can be directed to those in need. Programs designed to help victims of discrimination are probably of this sort. Since it is usually quite difficult to determine the extent to which a person has suffered from racial discrimination, it may be necessary simply to take the susceptibility to this discrimination (and perhaps some other gross criterion such as present income) as the basis for allocation. The use of such an administrative basis would result in a certain degree of both over- and underinclusiveness, but in most cases this degree would probably not be an intolerable one from the perspective of fairness and efficiency.

THE DIFFERENT-ISSUES REPLY

This reply to the charge of inconsistency ignores possible differences in the characteristic which is the justifying basis; it presupposes, as does the person making the charge of inconsistency, that race is the justifying basis for compensatory programs. This reply claims that even if race is held to be irrelevant when blacks are being mistreated and relevant when blacks are being helped, there is no inconsistency in this since different issues are involved, and a characteristic which is relevant

---

[3] The distinction between over- and underinclusive classifications is derived from Tussman and tenBroek, "The Equal Protection of the Laws," *California Law Review* 37 (1949): 341.

to one issue is often irrelevant to another. Relevance involves a relation between a characteristic and an issue, C is relevant to I, and because of this "C_1 is relevant to I_1" is not inconsistent with "C_1 is not relevant to I_2."

But for this reply to work it must be shown that there really are two issues here, that the issue of deciding whether to allocate a penalty or loss is a different issue from deciding whether to allocate a benefit. This seems to be what Mark Green is suggesting in his article, "Reparations for Blacks," when he says, "It is a verbal gimmick to elide past prejudice with preferential treatment. A subsidy is obviously dissimilar to a penalty, a beneficiary different from a victim, although both fit under the discrimination rubric." [4] Green seems to hold that the crucial difference is between subsidies and penalties, between helping and harming, and that it is the fact that racial classifications are used in compensatory programs to do good that makes them permissible. Green's view seems to be that it is one thing to use race as a basis for doing harm but quite another to use it as a basis for providing help.

But is there a sufficient difference between deciding to allocate a subsidy and deciding to allocate a penalty or loss to enable us to say that different issues are being decided and that race can be relevant to the former and irrelevant to the latter? The best reason I have been able to discover for thinking that there is a sufficient difference derives from the fact that the allocation of losses and penalties is a much more dangerous enterprise than the allocation of help and benefits. Deciding to impose a penalty or loss involves making a person worse off, whereas deciding not to provide a benefit usually involves merely leaving a person as he is. Since the former decision involves weightier consequences in most cases, we may be inclined to allow that it is a different decision than the latter and to allow that different considerations can be relevant to the two issues. This will be to claim that because of this difference there are and should be tighter moral and legal restriction on grounds that can serve as a basis for distributing penalties and losses, and that even though it is impermissible to use race as the basis for imposing losses and penalties, it is permissible to use race as the basis for distributing benefits.

One problem with putting so much weight on the distinction between distributing benefits and distributing penalties and losses is that in many cases a single distribution does both. If the item which is being allocated is a scarce and important benefit (like a good job), giving it to one person will often be tantamount to denying it to another person with an equally good claim to it, and denying it to this person will often be a considerable loss to him. Here the allocative decision concerns both

---

[4] "Reparations for Blacks," *Commonweal* 90 (June 1969): 359. In saying that both subsidies and penalties "fit under the discrimination rubric," Green seems to overlook the connection between discrimination and the use of an irrelevant characteristic. He seems, that is, to slip into using the morally neutral sense when it is the other sense of "discrimination" that is in question.

providing a benefit and causing a loss, and hence one cannot merely say that race is a permissible basis for the decision because it is a decision about whom to help. If in a situation like this we decide to help Jones because he is black, this may be tantamount to causing Smith to suffer a loss because he is nonblack. Cases like this do exist,[5] and in these cases the "different-issues" approach provides no help.

Leaving this problem aside, there is another difficulty with the "different-issues reply." Even if it is allowed that what is relevant to the distribution of a benefit is sometimes different from what is relevant to the distribution of penalties and losses, it still remains to be shown that race is the justifying basis for programs which provide special help to blacks. If this cannot be shown then one must fall back on the claim that race is only the administrative basis for such programs.

So the question that we must ask is whether race or ancestry as such can serve as a justifying basis for a program which distributes benefits rather than burdens. And I am inclined to think that it cannot. The mere fact that many people in this country are of African ancestry does not in itself provide any justification for a program of benefits to these people—no more than the mere fact that many people in California are of Oklahoman ancestry provides a justifying basis for a program of benefits to them. One's race or ancestry could serve as a justifying basis for special benefits only if having this race or ancestry was, in itself, a special merit which deserved reward or a special lack which required compensation. But unless one is prepared to return to racist and aristocratic principles, one must deny that one's race or ancestry is in itself a matter of special merit or special lack. And hence one must deny that race or ancestry, in itself, can serve as a justifying basis for a program of special benefits.

It might be replied, however, that this overlooks important aspects of the context. In a context where the members of one race have over a long period been subject to discrimination and mistreatment it might be argued that race can be the justifying basis for a program of benefits. I think, however, that as soon as one begins to emphasize the wrongs done to blacks, the losses they have suffered, and the special needs they have now, it becomes clear that these things are the justifying basis for help to blacks and not race per se.

Suppose, however, that the person making this reply continues by asserting that in this period in America so many people think that being black is a special defect or lack that in effect it is a special defect or lack which requires compensation. But again one must insist that it is not race itself that justifies compensation; it is rather the effects of people's misconceptions about race that do this. Race or ancestry in itself constitutes no merit or defect; it is only in combination with people's misconceptions about it that it can aspire to this status. It is the adverse effects of these misconceptions, not race per se, that provide the justifying basis for spe-

[5] See, for example, Bob Kuttner, "White Males and Jews Need Not Apply," *The Village Voice*, August 31, 1972.

cial help programs. Race simply is not plausible as a justifying basis for a program, even for a program of benefits.

If I am right about this the "different-issues reply" turns out not to be helpful since it presupposes that race is the justifying basis for compensatory programs. Unless some other option emerges, the defender of compensatory programs will have to use the "different-characteristics reply" to the charge of inconsistency. This view allows that race can sometimes serve as the administrative basis for programs but makes its use contingent on considerations of fairness and efficiency. Whether race or ancestry can serve as a reasonable administrative basis (or a part of such a basis) for a program designed to provide special benefits to victims of slavery and discrimination will depend on whether among the possible alternatives it is the classification which is most workable and involves the combination of over- and underinclusiveness which is least unfair.

REVERSE DISCRIMINATION AS UNJUSTIFIED

Lisa H. Newton

I have heard it argued that "simple justice" requires that we favor women and blacks in employment and educational opportunities, since women and blacks were "unjustly" excluded from such opportunities for so many years in the not so distant past. It is a strange argument, an example of a possible implication of a true proposition advanced to dispute the proposition itself, like an octopus absent-mindedly slicing off his head with a stray tentacle. A fatal confusion underlies this argument, a confusion fundamentally relevant to our understanding of the notion of the rule of law.

Two senses of justice and equality are involved in this confusion. The root notion of justice, progenitor of the other, is the one that Aristotle (*Nichomachean Ethics* 5. 6; *Politics* 1. 2; 3. 1) assumes to be the foundation and proper virtue of the political association. It is the condition which free men establish among themselves when they "share a common life in order that their association bring them self-sufficiency" —the regulation of their relationship by law, and the establishment, by law, of equality before the law. Rule of law is the name and pattern of this justice; its equality stands against the inequalities—of wealth, talent, etc.—otherwise obtaining among its participants, who by virtue of that equality are called "citizens." It is an achievement—complete, or, more

From *Ethics* 83 (1973): 308-12. © 1973 by the University of Chicago. Reprinted by permission of the author and the publisher, The University of Chicago Press.

frequently, partial—of certain people in certain concrete situations. It is fragile and easily disrupted by powerful individuals who discover that the blind equality of rule of law is inconvenient for their interests. Despite its obvious instability, Aristotle assumed that the establishment of justice in this sense, the creation of citizenship, was a permanent possibility for men and that the resultant association of citizens was the natural home of the species. At levels below the political association, this rule-governed equality is easily found; it is exemplified by any group of children agreeing together to play a game. At the level of the political association, the attainment of this justice is more difficult, simply because the stakes are so much higher for each participant. The equality of citizenship is not something that happens of its own accord, and without the expenditure of a fair amount of effort it will collapse into the rule of a powerful few over an apathetic many. But at least it has been achieved, at some times in some places; it is always worth trying to achieve, and eminently worth trying to maintain, wherever and to whatever degree it has been brought into being.

Aristotle's parochialism is notorious; he really did not imagine that persons other than Greeks could associate freely in justice, and the only form of association he had in mind was the Greek *polis*. With the decline of the *polis* and the shift in the center of political thought, his notion of justice underwent a sea change. To be exact, it ceased to represent a political type and became a moral ideal: the ideal of equality as we know it. This ideal demands that all men be included in citizenship—that one Law govern all equally, that all men regard all other men as fellow citizens, with the same guarantees, rights, and protections. Briefly, it demands that the circle of citizenship achieved by any group be extended to include the entire human race. Properly understood, its effect on our associations can be excellent: it congratulates us on our achievement of rule of law as a process of government but refuses to let us remain complacent until we have expanded the associations to include others within the ambit of the rules, as often and as far as possible. While one man is a slave, none of us may feel truly free. We are constantly prodded by this ideal to look for possible unjustifiable discrimination, for inequalities not absolutely required for the functioning of the society and advantageous to all. And after twenty centuries of pressure, not at all constant, from this ideal, it might be said that some progress has been made. To take the cases in point for this problem, we are now prepared to assert, as Aristotle would never have been, the equality of sexes and of persons of different colors. The ambit of American citizenship, once restricted to white males of property, has been extended to include all adult free men, then all adult males including ex-slaves, then all women. The process of acquisition of full citizenship was for these groups a sporadic trail of half-measures, even now not complete; the steps on the road to full equality are marked by legislation and judicial decisions which are only recently concluded and still often not enforced. But the fact that we can now discuss the possibility of favoring such groups in hiring shows that over the area that concerns us, at least, full equality is presupposed as a basis for discussion. To that extent, they are full citizens, fully protected by the law of the land.

It is important for my argument that the moral ideal of equality be recognized as logically distinct from the condition (or virtue) of justice in the political sense. Justice in this sense exists *among* a citizenry, irrespective of the number of the populace included in that citizenry. Further, the moral ideal is parasitic upon the political virtue, for "equality" is unspecified—it means nothing until we are told in what respect that equality is to be realized. In a political context, "equality" is specified as "equal rights"—equal access to the public realm, public goods and offices, equal treatment under the law—in brief, the equality of citizenship. If citizenship is not a possibility, political equality is unintelligible. The ideal emerges as a generalization of the real condition and refers back to that condition for its content.

Now, if justice (Aristotle's justice in the political sense) is equal treatment under law for all citizens, what is injustice? Clearly, injustice is the violation of that equality, discriminating for or against a group of citizens, favoring them with special immunities and privileges or depriving them of those guaranteed to the others. When the southern employer refuses to hire blacks in white-collar jobs, when Wall Street will only hire women as secretaries with new titles, when Mississippi high schools routinely flunk all black boys above ninth grade, we have examples of injustice, and we work to restore the equality of the public realm by ensuring that equal opportunity will be provided in such cases in the future. But of course, when the employers and the schools *favor* women and blacks, the same injustice is done. Just as the previous discrimination did, this reverse discrimination violates the public equality which defines citizenship and destroys the rule of law for the areas in which these favors are granted. To the extent that we adopt a program of discrimination, reverse or otherwise, justice in the political sense is destroyed, and none of us, specifically affected or not, is a citizen, a bearer of rights—we are all petitioners for favors. And to the same extent, the ideal of equality is undermined, for it has content only where justice obtains, and by destroying justice we render the ideal meaningless. It is, then, an ironic paradox, if not a contradiction in terms, to assert that the ideal of equality justifies the violation of justice; it is as if one should argue, with William Buckley, that an ideal of humanity can justify the destruction of the human race.

Logically, the conclusion is simple enough: all discrimination is wrong prima facie because it violates justice, and that goes for reverse discrimination too. No violation of justice among the citizens may be justified (may overcome the prima facie objection) by appeal to the ideal of equality, for that ideal is logically dependent upon the notion of justice. Reverse discrimination, then, which attempts no other justification than an appeal to equality, is wrong. But let us try to make the conclusion more plausible by suggesting some of the implications of the suggested practice of reverse discrimination in employment and education. My argument will be that the problems raised there are insoluble, not only in practice but in principle.

We may argue, if we like, about what "discrimination" consists of. Do I discriminate against blacks if I admit none to my school when none of the black applicants are qualified by the tests I always give? How far must I go to root out cultural bias from my application forms and tests before I can say that I have not discriminated against those of different cultures? Can I asume that women are not strong enough to be roughnecks on my oil rigs, or must I test them individually? But this controversy, the most popular and well-argued aspect of the issue, is not as fatal as two others which cannot be avoided: if we are regarding the blacks as a "minority" victimized by discrimination, what is a "minority"? And for any group—blacks, women, whatever—that has been discriminated against, what amount of reverse discrimination wipes out the initial discrimination? Let us grant as true that women and blacks were discriminated against, even where laws forbade such discrimination, and grant for the sake of argument that a history of discrimination must be wiped out by reverse discrimination. What follows?

First, are there other groups which have been discriminated against? For they should have the same right of restitution. What about American Indians, Chicanos, Appalachian Mountain whites, Puerto Ricans, Jews, Cajuns, and Orientals? And if these are to be included, the principle according to which we specify a "minority" is simply the criterion of "ethnic (sub) group," and we're stuck with every hyphenated American in the lower-middle class clamoring for special privileges for *his* group —and with equal justification. For be it noted, when we run down the Harvard roster, we find not only a scarcity of blacks (in comparison with the proportion in the population) but an even more striking scarcity of those second-, third-, and fourth-generation ethnics who make up the loudest voice of Middle America. Shouldn't they demand *their* share? And eventually, the WASPs will have to form their own lobby, for they too are a minority. The point is simply this: there is no "majority" in America who will not mind giving up just a bit of their rights to make room for a favored minority. There are only other minorities, each of which is discriminated against by the favoring. The initial injustice is then repeated dozens of times, and if each minority is granted the same right of restitution as the others, an entire area of rule governance is dissolved into a pushing and shoving match between self-interested groups. Each works to catch the public eye and political popularity by whatever means of advertising and power politics lend themselves to the effort, to capitalize as much as possible on temporary popularity until the restless mob picks another group to feel sorry for. Hardly an edifying spectacle, and in the long run no one can benefit: the pie is no larger—it's just that instead of setting up and enforcing rules for getting a piece, we've turned the contest into a free-for-all, requiring much more effort for no larger a reward. It would be in the interests of all the participants to reestablish an objective rule to govern the process, carefully enforced and the same for all.

Second, supposing that we do manage to agree in general that women and blacks (and all the others) have some right of restitution, some right to a privileged place in the structure of opportunities for a while, how will we know when that while is up? How much privilege is enough? When will the guilt be gone, the price paid, the balance restored? What recompense is right for centuries of exclusion? What criterion tells us when we are done? Our experience with the Civil Rights movement shows us that agreement on these terms cannot be presupposed: a process that appears to some to be going at a mad gallop into a black takeover appears to the rest of us to be at a standstill. Should a practice of reverse discrimination be adopted, we may safely predict that just as some of us begin to see "a satisfactory start toward righting the balance," others of us will see that we "have already gone too far in the other direction" and will suggest that the discrimination ought to be reversed again. And such disagreement is inevitable, for the point is that we could not *possibly* have any criteria for evaluating the kind of recompense we have in mind. The context presumed by any discussion of restitution is the context of rule of law: law sets the rights of men and simultaneously sets the method for remedying the violation of those rights. You may exact suffering from others and/or damage payments for yourself if and only if the others have violated your rights; the suffering you have endured is not sufficient reason for them to suffer. And remedial rights exist only where there is law: primary human rights are useful guides to legislation but cannot stand as reasons for awarding remedies for injuries sustained. But then, the context presupposed by any discussion of restitution is the context of preexistent full citizenship. No remedial rights could exist for the excluded; neither in law nor in logic does there exist a right to *sue* for a standing to sue.

From these two considerations, then, the difficulties with reverse discrimination become evident. Restitution for a disadvantaged group whose rights under the law have been violated is possible by legal means, but restitution for a disadvantaged group whose grievance is that there was no law to protect them simply is not. First, outside of the area of justice defined by the law, no sense can be made of "the group's rights," for no law recognizes that group or the individuals in it, qua members, as bearers of rights (hence *any* group can constitute itself as a disadvantaged minority in some sense and demand similar restitution). Second, outside of the area of protection of law, no sense can be made of the violation of rights (hence the amount of the recompense cannot be decided by any objective criterion). For both reasons, the practice of reverse discrimination undermines the foundation of the very ideal in whose name it is advocated; it destroys justice, law, equality, and citizenship itself, and replaces them with power struggles and popularity contests.

PREFERENTIAL HIRING

Judith Jarvis Thomson

Many people are inclined to think preferential hiring an obvious injustice.[1] I should have said "feel" rather than "think": it seems to me the matter has not been carefully thought out, and that what is in question, really, is a gut reaction.

I am going to deal with only a very limited range of preferential hirings: that is, I am concerned with cases in which several candidates present themselves for a job, in which the hiring officer finds, on examination, that all are equally qualified to hold that job, and he then straightway declares for the black, or for the woman, because he or she *is* a black or a woman. And I shall talk only of hiring decisions in the universities, partly because I am most familiar with them, partly because it is in the universities that the most vocal and articulate opposition to preferential hiring is now heard—not surprisingly, perhaps, since no one is more vocal and articulate than a university professor who feels deprived of his rights.

I suspect that some people may say, Oh well, in *that* kind of case it's all right, what we object to is preferring the less qualified to the better qualified. Or again, What we object to is refusing even to consider the qualifications of white males. I shall say nothing at all about these things. I think that the argument I shall give for saying that preferential hiring is not unjust in the cases I do concentrate on can also be appealed to to justify it outside that range of cases. But I won't draw any conclusions about cases outside it. Many people do have that gut reaction I mentioned against preferential hiring in *any* degree or form; and it seems to me worthwhile bringing out that there is good reason to think they are wrong to have it. Nothing I say will be in the

From *Philosophy and Public Affairs* 2, (1973): 364-84. Copyright 1973 by Princeton University Press. Reprinted by permission of Princeton University Press.

[1] This essay is an expanded version of a talk given at the Conference on the Liberation of Female Persons, held at North Carolina State University at Raleigh, on March 26-28, 1973, under a grant from the S & H Foundation. I am indebted to James Thomson and the members of the Society for Ethical and Legal Philosophy for criticism of an earlier draft.

slightest degree novel or original. It will, I hope, be enough to set the relevant issues out clearly.

I

But first, something should be said about qualifications.

I said I would consider only cases in which the several candidates who present themselves for the job are equally qualified to hold it; and there plainly are difficulties in the way of saying precisely how this is to be established, and even what is to be established. Strictly academic qualifications seem at a first glance to be relatively straight-forward: the hiring officer must see if the candidates have done equally well in courses (both courses they took, and any they taught), and if they are recommended equally strongly by their teachers, and if the work they submit for consideration is equally good. There is no denying that even these things are less easy to establish than first appears: for example, you may have a suspicion that Professor Smith is given to exaggeration, and that his "great student" is in fact less strong than Professor Jones's "good student"—but do you *know* that this is so? But there is a more serious difficulty still: as blacks and women have been saying, strictly academic indicators may themselves be skewed by prej-udice. My impression is that women, white and black, may possibly suffer more from this than black males. A black male who is discouraged or down-graded for being black is discouraged or down-graded out of dislike, repulsion, a desire to avoid contact; and I suspect that there are very few teachers nowadays who allow themselves to feel such things, or, if they do feel them, to act on them. A woman who is discouraged or down-graded for being a woman is not discouraged or down-graded out of dislike, but out of a conviction she is not serious, and I suspect that while there are very few teachers nowadays who allow themselves to feel that women generally are not serious, there are many who allow themselves to feel of the particular individual women students they confront that Ah, this one isn't serious, and in fact that one isn't either, nor is that other one—women generally are, of course, one thing, but these particular women, really they're just girls in search of husbands, are quite another. And I suspect that this will be far harder to root out. A teacher could not face himself in the mirror of a morning if he had down-graded anyone out of dislike; but a teacher can well face himself in the mirror if he down-grades someone out of a conviction that that person is not serious: after all, life is serious, and jobs and work, and who can take the unserious seriously? who pays attention to the dilet-tante? So the hiring officer must read very very carefully between the lines in the candidates' dossiers even to assess their strictly academic qualifications.

And then of course there are other qualifications besides the strictly

academic ones. Is one of the candidates exceedingly disagreeable? A
department is not merely a collection of individuals, but a working
unit; and if anyone is going to disrupt that unit, and to make its work
more difficult, then this counts against him—he may be as well qualified
in strictly academic terms, but he is not as well qualified. Again, is one
of the candidates incurably sloppy? Is he going to mess up his records,
is he going to have to be nagged to get his grades in, and worse, is he
going to lose students' papers? This too would count against him: keeping track of students' work, records, and grades, after all, is part of the
job.

What seems to me to be questionable, however, is that a candidate's race or sex is itself a qualification. Many people who favor preferential hiring in the universities seem to think it is; in their view,
if a group of candidates is equally well qualified in respect of those
measures I have already indicated, then if one is of the right race
(black) or of the right sex (female), then that being itself a qualification, it tips the balance, and that one is the best qualified. If so, then
of course no issue of injustice, or indeed of any other impropriety, is
raised if the hiring officer declares for that one of the candidates straightway.

Why does race or sex seem to many to be, itself, a qualification?
There seem to be two claims in back of the view that it is. First, there is
the claim that blacks learn better from a black, women from a woman.
One hears this less often in respect of women; blacks, however, are
often said to mistrust the whites who teach them, with the result that
they simply do not learn as well, or progress as far, as they would if
taught by blacks. Secondly, and this one hears in respect of women
as well as blacks, what is wanted is *role models*. The proportion of
black and women faculty members in the larger universities (particularly
as one moves up the ladder of rank) is very much smaller than the proportion of blacks and women in the society at large—even, in the case
of women, than the proportion of them amongst recipients of Ph.D.
degrees from those very same universities. Black and women students
suffer a constricting of ambition because of this. They need to see members of their race or sex who are accepted, successful, professionals.
They need concrete evidence that those of their race or sex *can* become
accepted, successful professionals.

And perhaps it is thought that it is precisely by virtue of having a
role model right in the classroom that blacks do learn better from a
black, women from a woman.

Now it is obviously essential for a university to staff its classrooms
with people who can teach, and so from whom its students can learn,
and indeed learn as much and as well as possible—teaching, after all,
is, if not the whole of the game, then anyway a very large part of it.
So if the first claim is true, then race and sex *do* seem to be qualifications. It obviously would not follow that a university should continue
to regard them as qualifications indefinitely; I suppose, however, that

it would follow that it should regard them as qualifications at least until the proportion of blacks and women on the faculty matches the proportion of blacks and women among the students.

But in the first place, allowing this kind of consideration to have a bearing on a hiring decision might make for trouble of a kind that blacks and women would not be at all happy with. For suppose it could be made out that white males learn better from white males? (I once, years ago, had a student who said he really felt uncomfortable in a class taught by a woman, it was interfering with his work, and did I mind if he switched to another section?) I suppose we would feel that this was due to prejudice, and that it was precisely to be discouraged, certainly not encouraged by establishing hiring ratios. I don't suppose it is true of white males generally that they learn better from white males; I am concerned only with the way in which we should take the fact, if it were a fact, that they did—and if it would be improper to take it to be reason to think being a white male is a qualification in a teacher, then how shall we take its analogue to be reason to think being black, or being a woman, is a qualification in a teacher?

And in the second place, I must confess that, speaking personally, I do not find the claim we are looking at borne out in experience; I do not think that as a student I learned any better, or any more, from the women who taught me than from the men, and I do not think that my own women students now learn any better or any more from me than they do from my male colleagues. Blacks, of course, may have, and may have had, very different experiences, and I don't presume to speak for them—or even for women generally. But my own experience being what it is, it seems to *me* that any defense of preferential hiring in the universities which takes this first claim as premise is so far not an entirely convincing one.

The second claim, however, does seem to me to be plainly true: black and women students do need role models, they do need concrete evidence that those of their race or sex can become accepted, successful, professionals—plainly, you won't try to become what you don't believe you can become.

But do they need these role models right there in the classroom? Of course it might be argued that they do: that a black learns better from a black teacher, a woman from a woman teacher. But we have already looked at this. And if they are, though needed, not needed in the classroom, then is it the university's job to provide them?

For it must surely be granted that a college, or university, has not the responsibility—or perhaps, if it is supported out of public funds, even the right—to provide just *any* service to its students which it might be good for them, or even which they may need, to be provided with. Sports seem to me plainly a case in point. No doubt it is very good for students to be offered, and perhaps even required to become involved in, a certain amount of physical exercise; but I can see no reason whatever to think that universities should be expected to provide facilities for it, or taxpayers to pay for those facilities. I suspect others may disagree, but my own feeling is that it is the same with medical and psychiatric services: I am sure that at least some students need medical and psychiatric help, but I cannot see why it should be provided for them in the universities, at public expense.

So the further question which would have to be answered is this: granting that black and female students need black and female role models, why should the universities be expected to provide them within their faculties? In the case of publicly supported universities, why should taxpayers be expected to provide them?

I don't say these questions can't be answered. But I do think we need to come at them from a quite different direction. So I shall simply sidestep this ground for preferential hiring in the universities. The defense I give will not turn on anyone's supposing that of two otherwise equally well qualified candidates, one may be better qualified for the job by virtue, simply, of being of the right race or sex.

II

I mentioned several times in the preceding section the obvious fact that it is the taxpayers who support public universities. Not that private universities are wholly private: the public contributes to the support of most of them, for example by allowing them tax-free use of land, and of the dividends and capital gains on investments. But it will be the public universities in which the problem appears most starkly: as I shall suggest, it is the fact of public support that makes preferential hiring in the universities problematic.

For it seems to me that—other things being equal—there is no problem about preferential hiring in the case of a wholly private college or university, that is, one which receives no measure of public support at all, and which lives simply on tuition and (non-tax-deductible) contributions.

The principle here seems to me to be this: no perfect stranger has a right to be given a benefit which is yours to dispose of; no perfect stranger even has a right to be given an equal chance at getting a benefit which is yours to dispose of. You not only needn't give the benefit to the first perfect stranger who walks in and asks for it; you needn't even give him a chance at it, as, e.g., by tossing a coin.

I should stress that I am here talking about *benefits,* that is, things which people would like to have, which would perhaps not merely please them, but improve their lives, but which they don't actually *need.* (I suspect the same holds true of things people do actually need, but many would disagree, and as it is unnecessary to speak here of needs, I shall not discuss them.) If I have extra apples (they're mine: I grew them, on my own land, from my own trees), or extra money, or extra tickets to a series of lectures I am giving on How to Improve Your Life Through Philosophy, and am prepared to give them away, word of this may get around, and people may present themselves as candidate recipients. I do not have to give to the first, or to proceed by letting them all draw straws; if I really do own the things, I can give to whom I like, on any ground I please, and in so doing, I violate no one's *rights,* I treat no one *unjustly.* None of the candidate recipients has a right to the benefit, or even to a chance at it.

There are four caveats. (1) Some grounds for giving or refraining from giving are less respectable than others. Thus, I might give the apples to the first who asks for them simply because he is the first who asks for them. Or again, I might give the apples to the first who asks for them because he is black, and because I am black and feel an interest in and concern for blacks which I do not feel in and for whites. In either case, not merely do I do what it is within my rights to do, but more, my ground for giving them to that person is a not immoral ground for giving them to him. But I might instead give the apples to the sixth who asks, and this because the first five were black and I hate blacks—or because the first five were white and I hate whites. Here I do what I have a right to do (for the apples are *mine*), and I violate no one's rights in doing it, but my ground for disposing of the apples as I did was a bad one; and it might even, more strongly, be said that I ought not have disposed of the apples in the way I did. But it is important to note that it is perfectly consistent, on the one hand, that a man's ground for acting as he did was a bad one, and even that he ought not have done what he did, and, on the other hand, that he had a right to do what he did, that he violated no one's rights in doing it, and that no one can complain he was unjustly treated.

The second caveat (2) is that although I have a right to dispose of my apples as I wish, I have no right to harm, or gratuitously hurt or offend. Thus I am within my rights to refuse to give the apples to the first five because they are black (or because they are white); but I am not within my rights to say to them "I refuse to give you apples because you are black (or white) and because those who are black (or white) are inferior."

And (3) if word of my extra apples, and of my willingness to give them away, got around because I advertised, saying or implying First Come First Served Till Supply Runs Out, then I cannot refuse the first five because they are black, or white. By so advertising I have *given* them a right to a chance at the apples. If they come in one at a time, I must give out apples in order, till the supply runs out; if they come in together, and I have only four apples, then I must either cut up the apples, or give them each an equal chance, as, e.g., by having them draw straws.

And lastly (4), there may be people who would say that I don't really, or don't fully own those apples, even though I grew them on my own land, from my own trees, and therefore that I don't have a right to give them away as I see fit. For after all, I don't own the police who protected my land while those apples were growing, or the sunlight because of which they grew. Or again, wasn't it just a matter of luck for me that I was born with a green thumb?—and why should I profit from a competence that I didn't deserve to have, that I didn't earn? Or perhaps some other reason might be put forward for saying that I don't own those apples. I don't want to take this up here. It seems to me wrong, but I want to let it pass. If anyone thinks that I don't own the apples, or, more generally, that no one really or fully owns anything, he will regard what I shall say in the remainder of this section, in which I talk about what may be done with what is privately owned, as an idle academic exercise. I'll simply ask that anyone who does think this be patient: we will come to what is publicly owned later.

Now what was in question was a job, not apples; and it may be insisted that to give a man a job is not to give him a benefit, but rather something he needs. Well, I am sure that people do need jobs, that it does not fully satisfy people's needs to supply them only with food, shelter, and medical care. Indeed, I am sure that people need, not merely jobs, but jobs that interest them, and that they can therefore get satisfaction from the doing of. But on the other hand, I am not at all sure that any candidate for a job in a university needs a job in a university. One would very much like it if all graduate students who wish it could find jobs teaching in universities; it is in some measure a tragedy that a person should spend three or four years preparing for a career, and then find there is no job available, and that he has in consequence to take work which is less interesting than he had hoped and prepared for. But one thing seems plain: no one *needs* that work which would interest him most in all the whole world of work. Plenty of people have to make do with work they like less than other work—no economy is rich enough to provide everyone with the work he likes best of all—and I should think that this does not mean they lack something they *need*. We are all of us prepared to tax ourselves so that no one shall be in need; but I should imagine that we are not prepared to tax ourselves (to tax barbers, truck drivers, salesclerks, waitresses, and factory workers) in order that everyone who wants a university job, and is competent to fill it, shall have one made available to him.

All the same, if a university job is a benefit rather than something needed, it is anyway not a "pure" benefit (like an apple), but an "impure" one. To give a man a university job is to give him an opportunity to do work which is interesting and satisfying; but he will only *be* interested and satisfied if he actually does the work he is given an opportunity to do, and does it well.

What this should remind us of is that certain cases of preferential hiring might well be utterly irrational. Suppose we have an eating club, and need a new chef; we have two applicants, a qualified French chef, and a Greek who happens to like to cook, though he doesn't do it very well. We are fools if we say to ourselves "We like the Greeks, and dislike the French, so let's hire the Greek." We simply won't eat as well as we could have, and eating, after all, was the point of the club. On the other hand, it's *our* club, and so *our* job. And who shall say it is not within a man's rights to dispose of what really is his in as foolish a way as he likes?

And there is no irrationality, of course, if one imagines that the two applicants are equally qualified French chefs, and one is a cousin of one of our members, the other a perfect stranger. Here if we declare directly for the cousin, we do not act irrationally, we violate no one's rights, and indeed do not have a morally bad ground for making the choice we make. It's not a morally splendid ground, but it isn't a morally bad one either.

Universities differ from eating clubs in one way which is important for present purposes: in an eating club, those who consume what the club serves are the members, and thus the owners of the club themselves—by contrast, if the university is wholly private, those who consume what it serves are not among the owners. This makes a difference: the owners of the university have a responsibility not merely to themselves (as the owners of an eating club do), but also to those who come to buy what it offers. It could, I suppose, make plain in its advertising that it is prepared to allow the owners' racial or religious or other preferences to outweigh academic qualifications in its teachers. But in the absence of that, it must, in light of what a university is normally expected to be and to aim at, provide the best teachers it can afford. It does not merely act irrationally, but indeed violates the rights of its student-customers if it does not.

On the other hand, this leaves it open to the university that in case of a choice between equally qualified candidates, it violates no one's rights if it declares for the black because he is black, or for the white because he is white. To the wholly *private* university, that is, for that is all I have so far been talking of. Other things being equal—that is, given it has not advertised the job in a manner which would entitle applicants to believe that all who are equally qualified will be given an equal chance at it, and given it does not gratuitously give offence to those whom it rejects—the university may choose as it pleases, and violates no one's rights in doing so. Though no doubt its grounds for choosing may be morally bad ones, and we may even wish to say, more strongly, that it ought not choose as it does.

What will have come out in the preceding is that the issue I am concerned with is a moral, and not a legal one. My understanding is that the law does prevent an employer wholly in the private sector from choosing a white rather than a black on ground of that difference alone—though not from choosing a black rather than a white on ground of that difference alone. Now if, as many people say, legal rights (or perhaps, legal rights in a relatively just society) create moral rights, then even a moral investigation should take the law into account; and indeed, if I am not mistaken as to the law, it would have to be concluded that blacks (but not whites) do have rights of the kind I have been denying. I want to sidestep all this. My question can be re-put: would a private employer's choosing a white (or black) rather than a black (or white) on ground of that difference alone be a violation of anyone's rights if there were no law making it illegal. And the answer seems to me to be: it would not.

III

But hardly any college or university in America is purely private. As I said, most enjoy some public support, and the moral issues may be affected by the extent of the burden carried by the public. I shall concentrate on universities which are entirely publicly funded, such as state or city universities, and ignore the complications which might arise in case of partial private funding.

The special problem which arises here, as I see it, is this: where a community pays the bills, the community owns the university.

I said earlier that the members, who are therefore the owners, of a private eating club may declare for whichever chef they wish, even if the man they declare for is not as well qualified for the job as some other; in choosing amongst applicants, they are *not* choosing amongst fellow members of the club who is to get some benefit from the club. But now suppose, by contrast, that two of us who are members arrive at the same time, and there is only one available table. And suppose also that this has never happened before, and that the club has not voted on any policy for handling it when it does happen. What seems to me to be plain is this: the headwaiter cannot indulge in preferential seating, he cannot simply declare for one or the other of us on just any ground he pleases. He must randomize: as it might be, by tossing a coin.

Or again, suppose someone arrives at the dining room with a gift for the club: a large and very splendid apple tart. And suppose that this, too, has never happened before, and that the club has not voted on any policy for handling it when it does happen. What seems to me plain is this: the headwaiter cannot distribute that tart in just any manner, and on any ground he pleases. If the tart won't keep till the next meeting, and it's impossible to convene one now, he must divide the tart amongst us equally.

Consideration of these cases might suggest the following principle: every owner of a jointly owned property has a right to either an equal chance at, or an equal share in, any benefit which that property generates, and which is available for distribution amongst the owners—equal chance rather than equal share if the benefit is indivisible, or for some reason is better left undivided.

Now I have all along been taking it that the members of a club jointly own the club, and therefore jointly own whatever the club owns. It seems to me possible to view a community in the same way: to suppose that its members jointly own it, and therefore jointly own whatever it owns. If a community is properly viewed in this way, and if the principle I set out above is true, then every member of the community is a joint owner of whatever the community owns, and so in particular, a joint owner of its university; and therefore every member of the community has a right to an equal chance at, or equal share in, any benefit which the university generates, which is available for distribution amongst the owners. And that includes university jobs, if, as I argued, a university job is a benefit.

Alternatively, one might view a community as an imaginary Person: one might say that the members of that community are in some sense participants in that Person, but that they do not jointly own what the Person owns. One might in fact say the same of a club: that its members do not jointly own the club or anything which the club owns, but only in some sense participate in the Person which owns the things. And then the cases I mentioned might suggest an analogous principle: every "participant" in a Person (Community-Person, Club-Person) has a right to either an equal chance at, or an equal share in, any benefit which is generated by a property which that Person owns, which is available for distribution amongst the "participants."

On the other hand, if we accept any of this, we have to remember that there are cases in which a member may, without the slightest impropriety, be deprived of this equal chance or equal share. For it is plainly not required that the university's hiring officer decide who gets the available job by randomizing amongst *all* the community members, however well- or ill-qualified, who want it. The university's student-customers, after all, have rights too; and their rights to good teaching are surely more stringent than each member's right (if each has such a right) to an equal chance at the job. I think we do best to reserve the term "violation of a right" for cases in which a man is unjustly deprived of something he has a right to, and speak rather of "overriding a right" in cases in which, though a man is deprived of something he has a right to, it is not unjust to deprive him of it. So here the members' rights to an equal chance (if they have them) would be, not violated, but merely overridden.

It could of course be said that these principles hold only of benefits of a kind I pointed to earlier, and called "pure" benefits (such as apples and apple tarts), and that we should find some other, weaker, principle to cover "impure" benefits (such as jobs).

Or it could be said that a university job is not a benefit which is available for distribution amongst the community members—that although a university job is a benefit, it is, in light of the rights of the students, available for distribution only amongst those members of the community who are best qualified to hold it. And therefore that they alone have a right to an equal chance at it.

It is important to notice, however, that unless *some* such principle as I have set out is true of the publicly owned university, there is no real problem about preferential hiring in it. Unless the white male applicant who is turned away had a right that this should not be done, doing so is quite certainly not violating any of his rights. Perhaps being joint owner of the university (on the first model) or being joint participant in the Person which owns the university (on the second model), do not give him a right to an equal chance at the job; perhaps he is neither joint owner nor joint participant (some third model is preferable), and it is something else which gives him his right to an equal chance at the job. Or perhaps he hasn't a right to an equal chance at the job, but has instead some other right which is violated by declaring for the equally qualified black or woman straightway. It is here that it seems to me it emerges most clearly that opponents of preferential hiring are merely expressing a gut reaction against it: for they have not asked themselves precisely what right is in question, and what it issues from.

Perhaps there is lurking in the background some sense that everyone has a right to "equal treatment," and that it is this which is violated by preferential hiring. But what on earth right is this? Mary surely does not have to decide between Tom and Dick by toss of a coin, if what is in question is marrying. Nor even, as I said earlier, if what is in question is giving out apples, which she grew on her own land, on her own trees.

It could, of course, be argued that declaring for the black or woman straightway isn't a violation of the white male applicant's rights, but is all the same wrong, bad, something which ought not be done. As I said, it is perfectly consistent that one ought not do something which it is, nevertheless, no violation of anyone's rights to do. So perhaps opponents of preferential hiring might say that rights are not in question, and still argue against it on other grounds. I say they *might*, but I think they plainly do better not to. If the white male applicant has no rights which would be violated, and appointing the black or woman indirectly benefits other blacks or women (remember that need for role models), and thereby still more indirectly benefits us all (by widening the available pool of talent), then it is very hard to see how it could come out to be morally objectionable to declare for the black or woman straightway.

I think we should do the best we can for those who oppose preferential hiring: I think we should grant that the white male applicant has a right to an equal chance at the job, and see what happens for preferential hiring if we do. I shall simply leave open whether this right issues from considerations of the kind I drew attention to, and so also whether or not every member of the community, however well- or ill-qualified for the job, has the same right to an equal chance at it.

Now it is, I think, widely believed that we may, without injustice, refuse to grant a man what he has a right to only if *either* someone else has a conflicting and more stringent right, *or* there is some very great benefit to be obtained by doing so—perhaps that a disaster of some kind is thereby averted. If so, then there really is trouble for preferential hiring. For what more stringent right could be thought to override the right of the white male applicant for an equal chance? What great benefit obtained, what disaster averted, by declaring for the black or the woman straightway? I suggested that benefits are obtained, and they are not small ones. But are they large enough to override a right? If these questions cannot be satisfactorily answered, then it looks as if the hiring officer does act unjustly, and does violate the rights of the white males, if he declares for the black or woman straightway.

But in fact there are other ways in which a right may be overridden. Let's go back to that eating club again. Suppose that now it has happened that two of us arrive at the same time when there is only one available table, we think we had better decide on some policy for handling it when it happens. And suppose that we have of late had reason to be especially grateful to one of the members, whom I'll call Smith: Smith has done a series of very great favors for the club. It seems to me we might, out of gratitude to Smith, adopt the following policy: for the next six months, if two members arrive at the same time, and there is only one available table, then Smith gets in first, if he's one of the two; whereas if he's not, then the headwaiter shall toss a coin.

We might even vote that for the next year, if he wants apple tart, he gets more of it than the rest of us.

It seems to me that there would be no impropriety in our taking these actions—by which I mean to include that there would be no injustice in our taking them. Suppose another member, Jones, votes No. Suppose he says "Look. I admit we all benefited from what Smith did for us. But still, I'm a member, and a member in as good standing as Smith is. So I have a right to an equal chance (and equal share), and I demand what I have a right to." I think we may rightly feel that Jones merely shows insensitivity: he does not adequately appreciate what Smith did for us. Jones, like all of us, has a right to an equal chance at such benefits as the club has available for distribution to the members; but there is no injustice in a majority's refusing to grant the members this equal chance, in the name of a debt of gratitude to Smith.

It is worth noticing an important difference between a debt of gratitude and debts owed to a creditor. Suppose the club had borrowed $1000 from Dickenson, and then was left as a legacy, a painting appraised at $1000. If the club has no other saleable assets, and if no member is willing to buy the painting, then I take it that justice would precisely require *not* randomizing amongst the members who is to get that painting, but would instead require our offering it to Dickenson. Jones could not complain that to offer it to Dickenson is to treat him, Jones, unjustly: Dickenson has a right to be paid back, and that right is more stringent than any member's right to an equal chance at the painting. Now Smith, by contrast, did not have a right to be given anything, he did not have a right to our adopting a policy of preferential seating in his favor. If we fail to do anything for Dickenson, we do him an injustice; if we fail to do anything for Smith, we do *him* no injustice—our failing is, not injustice, but ingratitude. There is no harm in speaking of debts of gratitude and in saying that they are owed to a benefactor, by analogy with debts owed to a creditor; but it is important to remember that a creditor has, and a benefactor does not have, a right to repayment.

To move now from clubs to more serious matters, suppose two candidates for a civil service job have equally good test scores, but that there is only one job available. We could decide between them by coin-tossing. But in fact we do allow for declaring for A straightway, where A is a veteran, and B is not.[2] It may be that B is a nonveteran through no fault of his own: perhaps he was refused induction for flat feet, or a heart murmur. That is, those things in virtue of which B is a non-veteran may be things which it was no more in his power to control or change than it is in anyone's power to control or change the color of his skin. Yet the fact is that B is not a veteran and A is. On the assumption that the veteran has served his country,[3] the country owes him something. And it seems plain that giving him preference is a not unjust way in which part of that debt of gratitude can be paid.

And now, finally, we should turn to those debts which are incurred by one who wrongs another. It is here we find what seems to me the most powerful argument for the conclusion that the preferential hiring of blacks and women is not unjust.

I obviously cannot claim any novelty for this argument: it's a very familiar one. Indeed, not merely is it familiar, but so are a battery of objections to it. It may be granted that if we have wronged A, we owe him something: we should make amends, we should compensate him for the wrong done him. It may even be granted that if we have wronged A, we must make amends, that justice requires it, and that a failure to make amends is not merely callousness, but injustice. But (*a*) are the young blacks and women who are amongst the current applicants for university jobs amongst the blacks and women who were wronged? To turn to particular cases, it might happen that the black applicant is middle class, son of professionals, and has had the very best in private schooling; or that the woman applicant is plainly the product of feminist upbringing and encouragement. Is it proper, much less required, that the black or woman be given preference over a white male who grew up in poverty, and has to make his own way and earn his encouragements? Again, (*b*), did we, the current members of the community, wrong any blacks or women? Lots of people once did; but then isn't it for them to do the compensating? That is, if they're still alive. For presumably nobody now alive owned any slaves, and perhaps nobody now alive voted against women's suffrage. And (*c*) what if the white male applicant for the job has never in any degree wronged any blacks or women? If so, *he* doesn't owe any debts to them, so why should *he* make amends to them?

These objections seem to me quite wrong-headed.

[2] To the best of my knowledge, the analogy between veterans' preference and the preferential hiring of blacks has been mentioned in print only by Edward T. Chase, in a Letter to the Editor, *Commentary*, February 1973.

[3] Many people would reject this assumption, or perhaps accept it only selectively, for veterans of this or that particular war. I ignore this. What interests me is what follows if we make the assumption—as, of course, many other people do, more, it seems, than do not.

Obviously the situation for blacks and women is better than it was a hundred and fifty, fifty, twenty-five years ago. But it is absurd to suppose that the young blacks and women now of an age to apply for jobs have not been wronged. Large-scale, blatant, overt wrongs have presumably disappeared; but it is only within the last twenty-five years (perhaps the last ten years in the case of women) that it has become at all widely agreed in this country that blacks and women must be recognized as having, not merely this or that particular right normally recognized as belonging to white males, but all of the rights and respect which go with full membership in the community. Even young blacks and women have lived through down-grading for being black or female: they have not merely not been given that very equal chance at the benefits generated by what the community owns which is so firmly insisted on for white males, they have not until lately even been felt to have a right to it.

And even those who were not themselves down-graded for being black or female have suffered the consequences of the down-grading of other blacks and women: lack of self-confidence, and lack of self-respect. For where a community accepts that a person's being black, or being a woman, are right and proper grounds for denying that person full membership in the community, it can hardly be supposed that any but the most extraordinarily independent black or woman will escape self-doubt. All but the most extraordinarily independent of them have had to work harder—if only against self-doubt—than all but the most deprived white males, in the competition for a place amongst the best qualified.

If any black or woman has been unjustly deprived of what he or she has a right to, then of course justice does call for making amends. But what of the blacks and women who haven't actually been deprived of what they have a right to, but only made to suffer the consequences of injustice to other blacks and women? *Perhaps* justice doesn't require making amends to them as well; but common decency certainly does. To fail, at the very least, to make what counts as public apology to all, and to take positive steps to show that it is sincerely meant, is, if not injustice, then anyway a fault at least as serious as ingratitude.

Opting for a policy of preferential hiring may of course mean that some black or woman is preferred to some white male who as a matter of fact has had a harder life than the black or woman. But so may opting for a policy of veterans' preference mean that a healthy, unscarred, middle class veteran is preferred to a poor, struggling, scarred nonveteran. Indeed, opting for a policy of settling who gets the job by having all equally qualified candidates draw straws may also mean that in a given case the candidate with the hardest life loses out. Opting for any policy other than hard-life preference may have this result.

I have no objection to anyone's arguing that it is precisely hard-life preference that we ought to opt for. If all, or anyway all of the equally qualified, have a right to an equal chance, then the argument would have to draw attention to something sufficiently powerful to override that right. But perhaps this could be done along the lines I followed in the case of blacks and women: perhaps it could be successfully argued that we have wronged those who have had hard lives, and therefore owe it to them to make amends. And then we should have in more extreme form a difficulty already present: how are these preferences to be ranked? shall we place the hard-lifers ahead of blacks? both ahead of women? and what about veterans? I leave these questions aside. My concern has been only to show that the white male applicant's right to an equal chance does not make it unjust to opt for a policy under which blacks and women are given preference. That a white male with a specially hard history may lose out under this policy cannot possibly be any objection to it, in the absence of a showing that hard-life preference is not unjust, and, more important, takes priority over preference for blacks and women.

Lastly, it should be stressed that to opt for such a policy is not to make the young white male applicants themselves make amends for any wrongs done to blacks and women. Under such a policy, no one is asked to give up a job which is already his; the job for which the white male competes isn't his, but is the community's, and it is the hiring officer who gives it to the black or woman in the community's name. Of course the white male is asked to give up his equal chance at the job. But that is not something he pays to the black or woman by way of making amends; it is something the community takes away from him in order that *it* may make amends.

Still, the community does impose a burden on him: it is able to make amends for its wrongs only by taking something away from him, something which, after all, we are supposing he has a right to. And why should *he* pay the cost of the community's amends-making?

If there were some appropriate way in which the community could make amends to its blacks and women, some way which did not require depriving anyone of anything he has a right to, then that would be the best course of action for it to take. Or if there were anyway some way in which the costs could be shared by everyone, and not imposed entirely on the young white male job applicants, then that would be, if not best, then anyway better than opting for a policy of preferential hiring. But in fact the nature of the wrongs done is such as to make jobs the best and most suitable form of compensation. What blacks and women were denied was full membership in the community; and nothing can more appropriately make amends for that wrong than precisely what will make them feel they now finally have it. And that means jobs. Financial compensation (the cost of which could be shared equally) slips through the fingers; having a job, and discovering you do it well, yield—perhaps better than anything else—that very self-respect which blacks and women have had to do without.

But of course choosing this way of making amends means that the costs are imposed on the young white male applicants who are turned away. And so it should be noticed that it is not entirely inappropriate that those applicants should pay the costs. No doubt few, if any, have themselves, individually, done any wrongs to blacks and women. But they have profited from the wrongs the community did. Many may actually have been direct beneficiaries of policies which excluded or down-graded blacks and women—perhaps in school admissions, perhaps in access to financial aid, perhaps elsewhere; and even those who did not directly benefit in this way had, at any rate, the advantage in the competition which comes of confidence in one's full membership, and of one's rights being recognized as a matter of course.

Of course it isn't only the young white male applicant for a university job who has benefited from the exclusion of blacks and women: the older white male, now comfortably tenured, also benefited, and many defenders of preferential hiring feel that he should be asked to share the costs. Well, presumably we can't demand that he give up his job, or share it. But it seems to me in place to expect the occupants of comfortable professorial chairs to contribute in some way, to make some form of return to the young white male who bears the cost, and is turned away. It will have been plain that I find the outcry now heard against preferential hiring in the universities objectionable; it would also be objectionable that those of us who are now securely situated should placidly defend it, with no more than a sigh of regret for the young white male who pays for it.

IV

One final word: "discrimination." I am inclined to think we so use it that if anyone is convicted of discriminating against blacks, women, white males, or what have you, then he is thereby convicted of acting unjustly. If so, and if I am right in thinking that preferential hiring in the restricted range of cases we have been looking at is *not* unjust, then we have two options: (*a*) we can simply reply that to opt for a policy of preferential hiring in those cases is not to opt for a policy of discriminating against white males, or (*b*) we can hope to get usage changed —e.g., by trying to get people to allow that there is discriminating against and discriminating against, and that some is unjust, but some is not.

Best of all, however, would be for that phrase to be avoided altogether. It's at best a blunt tool: there are all sorts of nice moral discriminations [*sic*] which one is unable to make while occupied with it. And that bluntness itself fits it to do harm: blacks and women are hardly likely to see through to what precisely is owed them while they are being accused of welcoming what is unjust.

"IT'S MINE"

Gertrude Ezorsky

Do wholly private employers have a moral right to hire whomever they please? According to Judith Thomson they do.[1] I shall claim, first, that her argument in support of this view is invalid. She commits a fallacy which I shall call the legalist fallacy. Secondly, I shall argue that employers "wholly in the private sector" do not have such hiring rights.

I

Professor Thomson writes:

> There is no problem about preferential hiring in . . . a wholly private college or university [without] public support (p. 249) [or by] . . . (an employer wholly in the private sector [p. 252]) . . . [without] public support. . . . Other things being equal—that is [the employer doesn't gratuitously offend rejected applicants or advertise jobs misleadingly] . . . the university, [as] . . . (a private employer) . . . may choose as it pleases, and violates no one's rights in doing so (pp. 252-253).

> The principle here seems to me to be this: . . . no perfect stranger even has a right to be given an equal chance of getting a benefit which is yours to dispose of (p. 249). . . . if I really do own the things, I can give to whom I like, on any ground I please, and in so doing, I violate no one's *rights,* I treat no one *unjustly.* None of the candidate recipients has the right to the benefit, or even a chance at it (p. 250, emphasis in original).

Thomson restricts her view of ownership rights to "benefits," although she "suspect[s]" it applies also to things people do "actually need." It would be useful first, however, to waive this restriction. Consider the following statement of her claim concerning ownership:

> If one is the full rightful owner of some entity then one has the right of giving it to whomever one pleases.[2]

From *Philosophy and Public Affairs* 3 (1974): 321-30. Copyright 1974 by Princeton University Press. Reprinted by permission of Princeton University Press.

[1] "Preferential Hiring," *Philosophy and Public Affairs* 2, no. 4 (Summer 1973): 364-384. Otherwise unidentified page numbers in the text refer to this article. [Numbers have been changed to refer to pages in this volume.–Ed.]

[2] I assume that in all cases where one has a right to give some entity to any person one pleases, then one has not committed himself otherwise.

At first reading, the statement appears tautologous, i.e., trivially true. Being the full rightful owner of an entity surely means having the right of giving that entity to whomever one pleases. Suppose however that John Jones, by law, is the full rightful owner of a slave and of the community's entire water supply. Surely Jones hasn't the right of giving what he owns to whomever *he* pleases. In that case, the claim concerning ownership is not trivially true, but significant and false.

I suggest that conflicting interpretations of the statement about ownership may be explained as follows:

The notion of a right is ambiguous between a legal and a moral sense. (When a verbal promise to Smith is broken, his moral, but not necessarily, his legal rights are violated.) Similarly the notion of rightful ownership is ambiguous between morally and legally rightful ownership.

Consider the following cases where individuals claim morally rightful ownership. Marxist workers assert that the commodities they produce really belong to them. A long deposed monarch insists that the once royal residence is still his, for he was anointed as its owner. An immoral, but legal government, legally bars all persons of *M*'s sort from any ownership rights. But *M* still regards herself as the real owner of the notebook in which she wrote her personal diary. Marxist, monarch, and diarist are asserting morally rightful ownership against what prevailing law, in fact, makes legally rightful ownership.

Our conflicting interpretations of the ownership statement may now be explained. Where that statement is read as:

> If one is the full *legally* rightful owner of some entity, then one has the *legal* right of giving it to whomever one pleases.

Or as:

> If one is the full *morally* rightful owner of some entity, then one has the *moral* right of giving it to whomever one pleases.

Then the claim is trivially true.[3]

But where that claim is interpreted as:

> If one is the full *legally* rightful owner of some entity, then one has the *moral* right of giving it to whomever one pleases.

Then the claim is significant and false.

The statement on ownership, so interpreted, exemplifies what I

---

[3] I assume the following: Where one has a legal right to give some entity to another person, then the recipient has a legal right to accept it. Where a person has a moral right to give some entity to another person then the recipient has a moral right to accept it.

shall call the legalist fallacy. This fallacy is committed whenever one infers that an individual who possesses a legal right, thereby has some moral right. Among the persons who commit this fallacy is Judith Thomson.

She claims that if a person is the owner of a benefit in the "wholly private" sector, then he has a moral right to give the benefit to whomever he pleases (pp. 249-250) ("in so doing I violate no one's *rights,* I treat no one *unjustly*" [p. 250]). Where such an owner is an employer "wholly in the private sector," then, she argues, he has a moral right to dispense his jobs as he pleases (p. 252). This owner, in the private sector, is indeed a legally rightful owner. But she implicitly infers that in virtue of such *legal* ownership he is the full, morally rightful owner, with the moral right to give what he owns to whomever he pleases. By such inference she commits the legalist fallacy.[4]

Let it be noted however that Thomson does not commit the legalist fallacy where the moral rights of job applicants are involved. She explicitly refuses to infer that job applicants have a moral right to equal opportunity hiring if they have obtained such legal rights:

> . . . the issue I am concerned with is a moral, and not a legal one. . . .
> [I]f . . . a moral investigation should take the law into account, . . .
> blacks . . . do [currently] have rights of the kind I have been denying.
> *I want to side-step all this.* My question can be re-put: would a private
> employer's choosing a white (or black) rather than a black (or white) on
> grounds of that difference alone be a violation of anyone's [moral] rights,
> if there were no law making it illegal. And the answer seems . . . it would
> not (pp. 252–253, emphasis added).

But why not so side-step where the moral rights of employers as well as of job applicants are concerned? Where no equal opportunity law prevails, an owner in the private sector has a legal right to hire whomever he pleases. But (legal rights aside) what *moral* consideration gives an employer the *moral* right to hire anyone *he* pleases? What, morally speaking, justifies his saying of the job he dispenses, "It's really *mine*."

---

[4] Thomson notes that some persons deny that anyone "really or fully owns anything," even that she owns the apples she grew in her garden. They will regard her "talk about what may be done with what is privately owned, as an idle academic exercise" (p. 251). But no one is going to regard her talk about the moral hiring rights of private (legally rightful) owners as "an idle academic exercise." One would regard the following—If a person is the full legally rightful private owner of an entity, then that person has the moral right to give that entity to whomever he pleases—as "an idle academic exercise," only if one believed that there are, in fact, no legally rightful owners. But, to my knowledge, no one holds that belief. Those who, according to Thomson, would deny "anyone really or fully owns anything" are denying morally rightful ownership. They would regard her claim concerning the moral rights of legally rightful private owners as important and false.

II

Thomson makes the following claim concerning the rights of private employers:

> Employers "wholly in the private sector" (hereafter, private employers) have the full moral rights of ownership over the jobs they dispense, i.e., to give such jobs to whomever they please (pp. 249, 252–253).

I have suggested that her reasoning in support of this claim is invalid. I shall, in what follows, argue that her claim concerning the rights of employers is, in fact, false.

But, we recall, Thomson restricted her notion of ownership rights to benefits, although she "suspect[s]" it also applies to what people "actually need." I shall argue that her claim concerning the rights of employers is false for either sort of job.

But how does one distinguish between such jobs? When is something a benefit, rather than actually needed.

Thomson suggests the following:

> *Benefits* . . . [are] things which people would like to have, which would perhaps not merely please them, but improve their lives, but which they don't actually *need* (p. 249, emphasis in original).

She gives three examples of "things . . . people . . . don't actually *need*," which, "if I have . . . I can give to whom I like":

> [my] extra money;
>
> [my] extra home grown apples;
>
> [my] extra tickets to . . . [my] lectures . . . on How to Improve Your Life Through Philosophy.

But the notion that apples, i.e., an item of *food,* and *money,* are, like her lecture tickets, "things . . . people . . . don't actually *need*" is astonishing. Food and money are urgently needed by a very large number of people. (Some apples and a little money were exactly what many Depression relief families were given.) Ex hypothesi, apples and money are among *her* extra items. Hence *she* doesn't need them. But surely, "I have enough of such food or money" does not imply "Other people have enough of such food or money."

Marie Antoinette made a similar error of inference. I suggest that the distinction between things actually needed and benefits be conceived as follows: What is actually needed is the sort of thing a needy person lacks, i.e. necessities such as minimally adequate food, clothing, shelter, medical aid. An actually needed job pays merely enough for such necessities. A benefit is such that if an individual is in need of that sort of thing, he is not therefore needy. A job which is a benefit gives a person more than the bare necessities that needy people need.

Does a private employer have the moral right (hereafter, right) to give either a job which is a benefit (hereafter, a decent job), or a job actually needed (hereafter, a minimum job) to whom he pleases? [5]

If an employer has such rights, then he has the right to engage in what I shall call discriminatory hiring. The general notion of discriminatory hiring may be clarified if we explicate a specific kind of discriminatory hiring, i.e. of whites. An act is an act of discriminatory hiring of whites, by an employer, if and only if:

(1) The employer hires a white candidate, rather than a nonwhite candidate because he prefers white persons.
(2) If the candidates' job performance qualifications are equivalent, the employer hires a white rather than a nonwhite person, but had the candidates' job performance qualifications not been equivalent, the employer would, within some qualification range, have hired a white, rather than a more qualified nonwhite candidate.
(3) If the job candidates' performance qualifications are not equivalent, the employer hires a white candidate, rather than a more qualified nonwhite candidate.

Application of the following generalization argument to discriminatory hiring suffices, I suggest, to show that no employer has discriminatory hiring rights:

> If an individual has a right to act in a given fashion, whenever so inclined, then every person in relevantly similar circumstances has that right.

[5] Concerning the sort of jobs people need, Thomson writes:

> [I]t may be insisted that to give a man a job is not to give him a benefit, but rather something he needs. . . . I am sure that people need, not merely jobs, but jobs that interest them, . . . But . . . I am not at all sure that any candidate for a . . . university (job) . . . needs a job in a university. . . . We are all of us prepared to tax ourselves so that no one shall be in need; but . . . not prepared to tax ourselves (to tax barbers, truck drivers, sales clerks, waitresses and factory workers) in order that everyone . . . (competent) who wants a university job . . . shall have one (p. 251). . . .

According to Thomson, things needed (rather than benefits) are what "all of us" ("barbers, truck drivers," etc.) would, by voluntary taxation, ensure that no one is deprived of. Thus, by her voluntary taxation criterion, the class of things needed approximates the class (as I, too, have conceived it) of necessities (e.g., minimally adequate food) supposedly dispensed by tax-funded public welfare agencies. By her voluntary taxation criterion, decent (rather than minimum) jobs are (as I have also suggested) benefits (rather than things needed), since all of us would not tax ourselves to provide decent jobs for everyone.

Note, however, that Thomson forgets her own voluntary taxation criterion when she writes: "I am sure that people need, not merely jobs, but jobs that interest them." But would "all of us" ("barbers, truck drivers," etc.) tax ourselves so that every qualified candidate for an interesting job shall have one?

> If the consequences of every person in such circumstances so acting would
> be bad, then not everyone in such circumstances has the right to so act.
> If not everyone in such circumstances has the right to so act, then no one
> in those circumstances has the right to so act.

Let us apply our generalization argument to the discriminatory
hiring rights of employers, first, over decent jobs, and second, over minimum jobs.

What would be the consequences if every employer engaged in discriminatory hiring for decent jobs whenever so inclined?

The situation of blacks in this country prior to very recent equal
opportunity laws is instructive in this matter. Employers who dispensed
decent jobs engaged, to the hilt, in discriminatory hiring against blacks.
As a rule, most employed blacks worked at miserable exhausting labor,
paying just enough for bare necessities, and with no hope of anything
better for themselves or their families. How would one of us regard the
prospect of our children spending the whole of their lives in such fashion?
I suggest we would regard that prospect as dreadful. And that sort of life
is dreadful, for anyone. Given the familiar propensity to familiar kinds
of prejudice, we may reasonably expect that if employers were to engage
in discriminatory hiring for decent jobs, whenever so inclined, the consequences would be bad indeed. Thus (following the generalization argument), no employers have such hiring rights. An employer who practices
discriminatory hiring, violates the rights of the candidates, who as a
result of such practice are denied jobs in his enterprise.

Members of groups who have suffered from the denial of such rights
are now protected in small measure by recent equal opportunity employment laws. But before enactment of such measures the power of private
employers to keep blacks in the worst jobs was uncurbed by law. (As many
such owners saw the matter, "niggers" weren't fit to do anything better.)
However, according to Thomson, blacks, barred by these employers, from
"even a chance" at a decent job in their establishments, were not treated
unjustly. Indeed they had no moral right to complain of such treatment.
Now under equal opportunity laws, blacks have a chance to work in
private enterprises, not merely at such minimum jobs as cleaning toilets,
but at decent jobs, e.g., bricklayers, stenographers and sales people. However, according to Thomson, the laws which gave black "even [this] . . .
chance" gave them more than they had any moral right to have (see
pp. 249-253).

Oddly enough, while according to Thomson, a private employer has
a right to deny a black applicant "even a chance" at a decent job, she
denies that the employer has a right to "gratuitously give offence to" the
black applicant by telling him the reason for his rejection (pp. 250, 252).
That would be unjust.

Let us now apply the generalization argument to the right of discriminatory hiring in minimum jobs. What would the consequences be
if every employer engaged in such hiring whenever so inclined?

Again the situation of blacks in this country is instructive. They were, in general, "last to be hired, first to be fired." As a result, most blacks were cast into terrifying poverty. They were imprisoned by such problems as getting warm clothing, medicine, coal, or food. In parts of the country, their children's bodies were deformed by slow starvation. Discriminatory hiring was, of course, not the only cause contributing to their wretchedness. There were others, for example, the fact that private owners refused to let blacks live in *their* buildings, to admit blacks to *their* private hospitals, or to charge blacks fair prices in *their* stores. But it was the place of blacks in the Kingdom of Jobs, the miserable kingdom of minimum jobs, which contributed most of all to their absolute impoverishment.

Given the familiar propensity to familiar kinds of prejudice, we may expect that if all employers engaged in discriminatory hiring, for minimum jobs, whenever so inclined, the consequences would be most harmful. Thus (following the generalization argument) no employers, in fact, have such hiring rights.

I conclude that Thomson's claim concerning the rights of private employers is false, both for decent and minimum jobs.[6]

---

[6] Note that the act of discriminatory hiring, whose consequences, if generally performed (whenever an employer is so inclined), are here assessed, is not specified as being performed by a *wholly private employer*, i.e. *wholly free of government financing*.

Here is why: Suppose we ask, "What would the consequences be if every red-haired employer, with eleven children, engaged in discriminatory hiring, whenever so inclined?" Assume there would be only one act of discriminatory hiring *so specified*. It is quite possible that the consequences of one act of discriminatory hiring would not be bad. (Perhaps this red-haired employer with eleven children went into bankruptcy the following month, while the black applicant he rejected was immediately given a steady job by another employer.) Thus, while the consequences of every employer's engaging in discriminatory hiring (whenever so inclined) would be bad, the consequences of every red-haired employer with eleven children so acting, might not be bad.

But we do not envisage a change in the value of the consequences (from bad to not bad) as being due to the causal functioning of the specifying properties, being red-haired and having eleven children. Consider, however, that in applying the generalization argument we determine the value (bad or not bad) of the consequences, *causally* induced, if the act were generally performed (whenever the agent was so inclined). Thus, only if the specifying properties of acts are causally effective in altering the value of the act's consequences are they eligible for specifying an act of discriminatory hiring in our application of the generalization argument.

Suppose we ask, "What would the consequences be if every *wholly private employer*, i.e. *wholly free of government financing*, engaged in discriminatory hiring, whenever so inclined?" There are not, in fact, currently many employers *wholly* free of government financing. Let us assume that the number of acts of discriminatory hiring, so specified, would be insignificant. In that case, it is possible that the value of the general consequences of acts of discriminatory hiring, when *so specified*, might not be bad.

But we envisage this change in the value of the consequences (from bad to not bad) because, ex hypothesi, the *number* of acts, so specified, would be insignificant, not because the specifying property, being wholly free of government financing, would be causally effective in changing the value of the general consequences from bad to not bad. Thus the specifying property, being performed by a wholly private employer, i.e.,

A last word about the generalization argument. The application of this argument requires that we assess the consequences of a class of persons acting in a given fashion, whenever so inclined. Such assessment depends on causal factors, among which is the extent of such inclination. Suppose we were estimating the consequences of everyone's engaging in charitable actions, whenever so inclined. Surely, such consequences would not be bad. But imagine that everyone desired daily to give away something he needed to someone else who needed it. In that case, unrestricted general indulgence of such desires might lead to bad consequences. ("Possessions" might circulate constantly in chaotic fashion.) Hence, in such circumstances, the generalization argument might show that human beings do not have the right to some kinds of charitable acts, which we now consider praiseworthy.

Consider now our application of the generalization argument to discriminatory hiring. We know already that when employers have, in fact, engaged in discriminatory hiring, whenever so inclined, the consequences were widespread suffering. Hence, I have concluded that employers have no such rights. But whether, given relevantly different causal conditions, employers would have the right of discriminatory hiring, or any ownership rights whatsoever, over jobs, is a question I have not discussed here. That question should however be answered by a comprehensive theory of moral ownership rights.

Why not make a clean Cartesian start? What are the circumstances under which a person has the moral right to say, "It's mine." After such inquiry, Judith Thomson might conclude that, morally speaking, far fewer things are rightfully owned in our society than are dreamt of in her philosophy.

---

wholly free of government financing, is not eligible for specification of an act of discriminatory hiring in our application of the generalization argument. (See David Lyons' *Forms and Limits of Utilitarianism* [New York, 1965], pp. 52-61, for a discussion of this problem. For a disagreement with some of Lyons' conclusions, see my review in the *Journal of Philosophy* 65, no. 18 [September 1968]: pp. 533-544).

SECTION SIX

Plea Bargaining

In the United States, after a suspect has been arrested and charged with a criminal offense, additional procedures must still be applied before it is possible to arrive at an authoritative judgment of guilt and a sentence. Usually when we think about how this is justly to be done, we think about trials. But it would not be inaccurate to say that the plea bargain is presently the standard way in which criminal cases are disposed of, the trial being used in only a small minority of cases.

The trial has traditionally been the most important institution in Anglo-American criminal procedure, embodying and protecting, as it does, a wide range of values. The plea bargain, on the other hand, has only recently received a nod of approval from the Supreme Court and there has been a good deal of concern about its soundness, as well there might be when, as here, the rules governing a central institution are dramatically altered. In a criminal trial the task of the prosecutor is to demonstrate to the jury (or, to the judge, in a bench trial) that the defendant is guilty of the charged offense beyond a reasonable doubt. The attorney for the defense may merely indicate that there is reasonable doubt—the burden of proof is upon the prosecutor. Both attorneys carry out their tasks within an elaborate system of rules which are intended to insure fairness and efficiency in the procedure and which are authoritatively applied by the judge in the case. (However, after the trial either attorney may appeal a decision by the trial judge to a higher court.) Usually, then, we think of the foreperson of the jury pronouncing the verdict of "Guilty" or "Not guilty." In fact, however, often the defendant waives a jury trial and the judge is both the trier of fact and of law. Where there is a guilty verdict the judge passes sentence within the limits specified by the legislature, bearing in mind, presumably, any mitigating or aggravating factors that have been brought forward.

In contrast, plea bargaining involves both the defense attorney and the prosecutor at a stage earlier than that of the trial. The two lawyers negotiate an agreement in which the defendant pleads guilty to an offense (not necessarily the one which was originally charged) in exchange for some concession by the state, usually a guarantee of a minimal sentence. After the agreement has been worked out, the "trial" becomes a formality in which both the defense attorney and the prosecutor have interests in seeing to it that the substance of the agreement passes the scrutiny of the judge. The defendant, who will have approved the deal, pleads guilty, sparing everyone the costs of a trial, and the judge checks to insure that there is a "factual basis for the plea." When the guilty plea is accepted by the judge, that constitutes the conviction and all that remains is the sentencing. Generally the judge is aware of the agreement and will not violate its spirit in passing sentence. It should be noted that, unlike those convicted at trial, those who enter guilty pleas in doing so waive many of their rights to appeal to a higher court.

North Carolina v. *Alford,* the case which begins this section, treats an instance of plea bargaining, illustrates some of the problems which arise within that practice, and shows the extent to which jurists disagree about its propriety. Having been indicted for first-degree murder, a crime punishable by death (under a North Carolina statute which was later declared unconstitutional), the defendant had agreed to plead guilty to a charge of second-degree murder. He did this in order to avoid the probable death penalty: ". . . because they said if I didn't they would gas me for it, and that is all." In his testimony before the judge as he entered his guilty plea, Alford denied that he had committed the offense: ". . . I'm not guilty but I plead guilty."

Having been convicted of second-degree murder and sentenced to 30 years imprisonment, Alford appealed to the Supreme Court, claiming, according to Justice White, that "his plea of guilty was invalid because it was the product of fear and coercion." Writing the opinion for the Court, Justice White holds that the fact that Alford entered his guilty plea to avoid the death penalty does not mean that Alford was compelled to incriminate himself—which, of course, would be in violation of the Fifth Amendment. Alford's plea represented "a voluntary and intelligent choice among the alternative courses of action. . . ." Moreover, a trial judge may accept a guilty plea accompanied by a claim of innocence. This may be allowed when there is a strong factual basis for the plea and when the defendant clearly expresses a desire to enter such a plea despite his contrary belief in his own innocence. Finally, Justice White does not find in either the Fourteenth Amendment or the Bill of Rights any prohibition of the practice of accepting pleas of guilty to lesser offenses.

Dissenting from the opinion of the Court, Justice Brennan writes that when a guilty plea is entered accompanied by a "contemporaneous denial of the acts constituting the crime," that denial is a relevant factor in determining whether the plea was voluntarily and intelligently made.

Moreover, Brennan finds that "the facts set out in the majority opinion demonstrate that Alford was 'so gripped by fear of the death penalty' that his decision to plead guilty was not voluntary but was 'the product of duress as much so as choice reflecting physical constraint.' "

The two selections that follow *Alford*, Arnold Enker's and my own, heighten the conflict that one sees in the differing opinions in that case. In his "Perspectives on Plea Bargaining," Arnold Enker tries "to evaluate the practice and put it in perspective, assess its dangers and implications, and suggest some—admittedly imperfect—approaches toward improving the process." Though there are risks in the practice, some of which may be mitigated by reforms, Enker stresses the significant purposes served by plea bargains: "It eases the administrative burden of crowded court dockets; it preserves the meaningfulness of the trial process for those cases in which there is real basis for dispute; it furnishes defendants a vehicle to mitigate the system's harshness, whether that harshness stems from callous infliction of excessive punishment or from the occasional inequities inherent in a system of law based upon general rules; and it affords the defense some participation in and control over an unreviewable process that often gives the appearance of fiat and arbitrariness." Enker worries about innocent defendants who may be induced to plead guilty by the terms of a bargain, but, in the end, he does not feel that plea bargaining is any less likely to produce intelligent results than the jury trial. Enker discusses the concern that plea bargains may involve involuntary waiver of trial and compelled self-incrimination. However, he finds the term "voluntary" to be "exceedingly ambiguous" and, on balance, does not think it desirable to prohibit plea bargaining.

In my own contribution to this section, I develop the case against the institution of plea bargaining. Following Justice Brennan's remarks in *Alford*, I suggest that plea bargains may well involve something comparable to duress, a well-established defense in contract law which nullifies the legal effects of compelled agreements. I submit that if I am right, we have good reason to suspect that our Fifth Amendment right to be free from compelled self-incrimination has been seriously eroded. Beyond this, I try to show that the practice of plea bargaining is so devised as to give us reason to doubt that those who are convicted of criminal offenses are receiving the punishments they deserve. Except under serendipitous circumstances, plea bargains will never result in a just outcome of a criminal case. Finally, I indicate why we have less reason than we would after a trial to believe that a convict who has "copped a plea" is guilty in the first place.

NORTH CAROLINA v. ALFORD

UNITED STATES SUPREME COURT

Mr. Justice White delivered the opinion of the Court.

On December 2, 1963, Alford was indicted for first-degree murder, a capital offense under North Carolina law.[1] The court appointed an attorney to represent him, and this attorney questioned all but one of the various witnesses who appellee said would substantiate his claim of innocence. The witnesses, however, did not support Alford's story but gave statements that strongly indicated his guilt. Faced with strong evidence of guilt and no substantial evidentiary support for the claim of innocence, Alford's attorney recommended that he plead guilty, but left the ultimate decision to Alford himself. The prosecutor agreed to accept a plea of guilty to a charge of second-degree murder, and on December 10, 1963, Alford pleaded guilty to the reduced charge.

Before the plea was finally accepted by the trial court, the court heard the sworn testimony of a police officer who summarized the State's case. Two other witnesses besides Alford were also heard. Although there was no eyewitness to the crime, the testimony indicated that shortly before the killing Alford took his gun from his house, stated his inten-

400 U.S. 25 (1970)
Locations of deleted citations marked with double asterisk (**). Ed.

[1] Under North Carolina law, first-degree murder is punished with death unless the jury recommends that the punishment shall be life imprisonment:

"A murder which shall be perpetrated by means of poison, lying in wait, imprisonment, starving, torture, or by any other kind of willful, deliberate and premeditated killing, or which shall be committed in the perpetration or attempt to perpetrate any arson, rape, robbery, burglary or other felony, shall be deemed to be murder in the first degree and shall be punished with death: Provided, if at the time of rendering its verdict in open court, the jury shall so recommend, the punishment shall be imprisonment for life in the State's prison, and the court shall so instruct the jury. All other kinds of murder shall be deemed murder in the second degree, and shall be punished with imprisonment of not less than two nor more than thirty years in the State's prison." N.C. Gen. Stat. § 14–17 (1969).

At the time Alford pleaded guilty, North Carolina law provided that if a guilty plea to a charge of first-degree murder was accepted by the prosecution and the court, the penalty would be life imprisonment rather than death. The provision permitting guilty pleas in capital cases was repealed in 1969. See *Parker* v. *North Carolina*, 397 U.S. 790, 792–795 (1970). Though under present North Carolina law it is not possible for a defendant to plead guilty to a capital charge, it seemingly remains possible for a person charged with a capital offense to plead guilty to a lesser charge.

tion to kill the victim, and returned home with the declaration that he had carried out the killing. After the summary presentation of the State's case, Alford took the stand and testified that he had not committed the murder but that he was pleading guilty because he faced the threat of the death penalty if he did not do so.[2] In response to the questions of his counsel, he acknowledged that his counsel had informed him of the difference between second- and first-degree murder and of his rights in case he chose to go to trial.[3] The trial court then asked appellee if, in light of his denial of guilt, he still desired to plead guilty to second-degree murder and appellee answered, "Yes, sir. I plead guilty on—from the circumstances that he [Alford's attorney] told me." After eliciting information about Alford's prior criminal record, which was a long one,[4] the trial court sentenced him to 30 years' imprisonment, the maximum penalty for second-degree murder.[5]

Alford sought post-conviction relief in the state court. Among the claims raised was the claim that his plea of guilty was invalid because it was the product of fear and coercion. After a hearing, the state court in 1965 found that the plea was "willingly, knowingly, and understandingly" made on the advice of competent counsel and in the face of a strong prosecution case. Subsequently, Alford petitioned for a writ of habeas corpus, first in the United States District Court for the Middle District of North Carolina, and then in the Court of Appeals for the

[2] After giving his version of the events of the night of the murder, Alfred stated: "I pleaded guilty on second-degree murder because they said there is too much evidence, but I ain't shot no man, but I take the fault for the other man. We never had an argument in our life and I just pleaded guilty because they said if I didn't they would gas me for it, and that is all." In response to questions from his attorney, Alford affirmed that he had consulted several times with his attorney and with members of his family and had been informed of his rights if he chose to plead not guilty. Alfred then reaffrmed his decision to plead guilty to second-degree murder:

"Q [by Alford's attorney]. And you authorized me to tender a plea of guilty to second-degree murder before the court?

"A. Yes, sir.

"Q. And in doing that, that you have again affirmed your decision on that point?

"A. Well, I'm still pleading that you all got me to plead guilty. I plead the other way, circumstantial evidence; that the jury will prosecute me on—on the second. You told me to plead guilty, right. I don't—I'm not guilty but I plead guilty."

[3] At the state court hearing on post-conviction relief, the testimony confirmed that Alford had been fully informed by his attorney as to his rights on a plea of not guilty and as to the consequences of a plea of guilty. Since the record in this case affirmatively indicates that Alford was aware of the consequences of his plea of guilty and of the rights waived by the plea, no issues of substance under *Boykin* v. *Alabama*, 395 U. S. 238 (1969), would be presented even if that case was held applicable to the events here in question.

[4] Before Alford was sentenced, the trial judge asked Alford about prior convictions. Alford answered that, among other things, he had served six years of a ten-year sentence for murder, had been convicted nine times for armed robbery, and had been convicted for transporting stolen goods, forgery, and carrying a concealed weapon. App. 9–11.

[5] See n. 1, *supra*.

Fourth Circuit. Both courts denied the writ on the basis of the state court's findings that Alford voluntarily and knowingly agreed to plead guilty. In 1967, Alford again petitioned for a writ of habeas corpus in the District Court for the Middle District of North Carolina. That court, without an evidentiary hearing, again denied relief on the grounds that the guilty plea was voluntary and waived all defenses and nonjurisdictional defects in any prior stage of the proceedings, and that the findings of the state court in 1965 clearly required rejection of Alford's claim that he was denied effective assistance of counsel prior to pleading guilty. On appeal, a divided panel of the Court of Appeals for the Fourth Circuit reversed on the ground that Alford's guilty plea was made involuntarily. 405 F. 2d 340 (1968). In reaching its conclusion, the Court of Appeals relied heavily on *United States* v. *Jackson,* 390 U. S. 570 (1968), which the court read to require invalidation of the North Carolina statutory framework for the imposition of the death penalty because North Carolina statutes encouraged defendants to waive constitutional rights by the promise of no more than life imprisonment if a guilty plea was offered and accepted. Conceding that *Jackson* did not require the automatic invalidation of pleas of guilty entered under the North Carolina statutes, the Court of Appeals ruled that Alford's guilty plea was involuntary because its principal motivation was fear of the death penalty. By this standard, even if both the judge and the jury had possessed the power to impose the death penalty for first-degree murder or if guilty pleas to capital charges had not been permitted, Alford's plea of guilty to second-degree murder should still have been rejected because impermissibly induced by his desire to eliminate the possibility of a death sentence.[6] We noted probable jurisdiction. 394 U. S. 956 (1969). We vacate the judgment of the Court of Appeals and remand the case for further proceedings.

We held in *Brady* v. *United States,* 397 U. S. 742 (1970), that a plea of guilty which would not have been entered except for the defendant's desire to avoid a possible death penalty and to limit the maximum penalty to life imprisonment or a term of years was not for that reason compelled within the meaning of the Fifth Amendment. *Jackson* established no new test for determining the validity of guilty pleas. The standard was and remains whether the plea represents a voluntary and intelligent choice among the alternative courses of action open to the defendant. See *Boykin* v. *Alabama,* 395 U. S. 238, 242 (1969); *Machibroda* v. *United States,* 368 U. S. 487, 493 (1962); *Kercheval* v. *United States,* 274 U. S. 220, 223 (1927). That he would not have pleaded except for the opportunity to limit the possible penalty does not necessarily demonstrate that the plea of guilty was not the product of a free and rational

---

[6] Thus if Alford had entered the same plea in the same way in 1969 after the statute authorizing guilty pleas to capital charges had been repealed, see n. 1, *supra,* the result reached by the Court of Appeals should have been the same under that court's reasoning.

choice, especially where the defendant was represented by competent counsel whose advice was that the plea would be to the defendant's advantage. The standard fashioned and applied by the Court of Appeals was therefore erroneous and we would, without more, vacate and remand the case for further proceedings with respect to any other claims of Alford which are properly before that court, if it were not for other circumstances appearing in the record which might seem to warrant an affirmance of the Court of Appeals.

As previously recounted, after Alford's plea of guilty was offered and the State's case was placed before the judge, Alford denied that he had committed the murder but reaffirmed his desire to plead guilty to avoid a possible death sentence and to limit the penalty to the 30-year maximum provided for second-degree murder. Ordinarily, a judgment of conviction resting on a plea of guilty is justified by the defendant's admission that he committed the crime charged against him and his consent that judgment be entered without a trial of any kind. The plea usually subsumes both elements, and justifiably so, even though there is no separate, express admission by the defendant that he committed the particular acts claimed to constitute the crime charged in the indictment.** Here Alford entered his plea but accompanied it with the statement that he had not shot the victim.

If Alford's statements were to be credited as sincere assertions of his innocence, there obviously existed a factual and legal dispute between him and the State. Without more, it might be argued that the conviction entered on his guilty plea was invalid, since his assertion of innocence negatived any admission of guilt, which, as we observed last Term in *Brady,* is normally "[c]entral to the plea and the foundation for entering judgment against the defendant. . . ." 397 U.S., at 748.

In addition to Alford's statement, however, the court had heard an account of the events on the night of the murder, including information from Alford's acquaintances that he had departed from his home with his gun stating his intention to kill and that he had later declared that he had carried out his intention. Nor had Alford wavered in his desire to have the trial court determine his guilt without a jury trial. Although denying the charge against him, he nevertheless preferred the dispute between him and the State to be settled by the judge in the context of a guilty plea proceeding rather than by a formal trial. Thereupon, with the State's telling evidence and Alford's denial before it, the trial court proceeded to convict and sentence Alford for second-degree murder.

State and lower federal courts are divided upon whether a guilty plea can be accepted when it is accompanied by protestations of innocence and hence contains only a waiver of trial but no admission of guilt. Some courts, giving expression to the principle that "[o]ur law only authorizes a conviction where guilt is shown," ** require that trial judges reject such pleas.** But others have concluded that they should not "force any defense on a defendant in a criminal case," particularly when advancement of the defense might "end in disaster. . . ." ** They have argued that, since "guilt, or the degree of guilt, is at times uncertain and elusive," "[a]n accused, though believing in or entertaining doubts respecting his innocence, might reasonably conclude a jury would be convinced of his guilt and that he would fare better in the sentence by pleading guilty. . . ." ** As one state court observed nearly a century ago, "[r]easons other than the fact that he is guilty may induce a defendant to so plead, . . . [and] [h]e must be permitted to judge for himself in this respect." ** 7

This Court has not confronted this precise issue, but prior decisions do yield relevant principles. In *Lynch* v. *Overholser*, 369 U. S. 705 (1962), Lynch, who had been charged in the Municipal Court of the District of Columbia with drawing and negotiating bad checks, a misdemeanor punishable by a maximum of one year in jail, sought to enter a plea of guilty, but the trial judge refused to accept the plea since a psychiatric report in the judge's possession indicated that Lynch had been suffering from "a manic depressive psychosis, at the time of the crime charged," and hence might have been not guilty by reason of insanity. Although at the subsequent trial Lynch did not rely on the insanity defense, he was found not guilty by reason of insanity and committed for an indeterminate period to a mental institution. On habeas corpus, the Court ordered his release, construing the congressional legislation seemingly authorizing the commitment as not reaching a case where the accused preferred a guilty plea to a plea of insanity. The Court expressly refused to rule that Lynch had an absolute right to have his guilty plea accepted, see id., at 719, but implied that there would have been no constitutional error had his plea been accepted even though evidence before the judge indicated that there was a valid defense.

The issue in *Hudson* v. *United States,* 272 U.S. 451 (1926), was whether a federal court has power to impose a prison sentence after accepting a plea of *nolo contendere,* a plea by which a defendant does not expressly admit his guilt, but nonetheless waives his right to a trial and authorizes the court for purposes of the case to treat him as if he were guilty.8 The Court held that a trial court does have such power, and, ex-

---

7 A third approach has been to decline to rule definitely that a trial judge must either accept or reject an otherwise valid plea containing a protestation of innocence, but to leave that decision to his sound discretion. See *Maxwell* v. *United States,* 368 F. 2d 735, 738–739 (CA9 1966).

8 Courts have defined the plea of *nolo contendere* in a variety of different ways, describing it, on the one hand, as "in effect, a plea of guilty," ** and on the other, as a query directed to the court to determine the defendant's guilt.** As a result, it is impossible to state precisely what a defendant does admit when he enters a *nolo* plea in a way that will consistently fit all the cases.

Hudson v. *United States, supra,* was also ambiguous. In one place, the Court called the plea "an admission of guilt for the purposes of the case," id., at 455, but in another, the Court quoted an English authority who had defined the plea as one "where a defendant, in a case not capital, doth not directly own himself guilty . . . ." Id., at 453, quoting 2 W. Hawkins, Pleas of the Crown 466 (8th ed. 1824).

The plea may have originated in the early medieval practice by which defen-

cept for the cases which were rejected in *Hudson,*** the federal courts have uniformly followed this rule, even in cases involving moral turpitude.** Implicit in the *nolo contendere* cases is a recognition that the Constitution does not bar imposition of a prison sentence upon an accused who is unwilling expressly to admit his guilt but who, faced with grim alternatives, is willing to waive his trial and accept the sentence.

These cases would be directly in point if Alford had simply insisted on his plea but refused to admit the crime. The fact that his plea was was denominated a plea of guilty rather than a plea of *nolo contendere* is of no constitutional significance with respect to the issue now before us, for the Constitution is concerned with the practical consequences, not the formal categorizations of state law. See *Smith* v. *Bennett*, 365 U. S. 708, 712 (1961); *Jones* v. *United States*, 362 U. S. 257, 266 (1960). Cf. *Kermarec* v. *Compagnie Generale Transatlantique*, 358 U. S. 625, 630–632 (1959). Thus, while most pleas of guilty consist of both a waiver of trial and an express admission of guilt, the latter element is not a constitutional requisite to the imposition of criminal penalty. An individual accused of crime may voluntarily, knowingly, and understandingly consent to the imposition of a prison sentence even if he is unwilling or unable to admit his participation in the acts constituting the crime.

Nor can we perceive any material difference between a plea that refuses to admit commission of the criminal act and a plea containing a protestation of innocence when, as in the instant case, a defendant intelligently concludes that his interests require entry of a guilty plea and the record before the judge contains strong evidence of actual guilt. Here the State had a strong case of first-degree murder against Alford. Whether he realized or disbelieved his guilt, he insisted on his plea because in his view he had absolutely nothing to gain by a trial and

---

dants wishing to avoid imprisonment would seek to make an end of the matter (*finem facere*) by offering to pay a sum of money to the king. See 2 F. Pollock and F. Maitland, History of English Law 517 (2d ed. 1909). An early 15th-century case indicated that a defendant did not admit his guilt when he sought such a compromise, but merely "that he put himself on the grace of our Lord, the King, and asked that he might be allowed to pay a fine (*petit se admittit per finem*)." *Anon.,* Y. B. Hil. 9 Hen. 6, f. 59, pl. 8 (1431). A 16th-century authority noted that a defendant who so pleaded "putteth hym selfe in *Gratiam Reginae* without anye more, or by Protestation that hee is not guiltie . . . ," W. Lambard, Eirenarcha 427 (1581), while an 18th-century case distinguished between a *nolo* plea and a jury verdict of guilty, noting that in the former the defendant could introduce evidence of innocence in mitigation of punishment, whereas in the latter such evidence was precluded by the finding of actual guilt. *Queen* v. *Templeman*, 1 Salk. 55, 91 Eng. Rep. 54 (K. B. 1702).

Throughout its history, that is, the plea of *nolo contendere* has been viewed not as an express admission of guilt but as a consent by the defendant that he may be punished as if he were guilty and a prayer for leniency. Fed. Rule Crim. Proc. 11 preserves this distinction in its requirement that a court cannot accept a guilty plea "unless it is satisfied that there is a factual basis for the plea"; there is no similar requirement for pleas of *nolo contendere,* since it was thought desirable to permit defendants to plead *nolo* without making any inquiry into their actual guilt. See Notes of Advisory Committee to Rule 11.

much to gain by pleading. Because of the overwhelming evidence against him, a trial was precisely what neither Alford nor his attorney desired. Confronted with the choice between a trial for first-degree murder, on the one hand, and a plea of guilty to second-degree murder, on the other, Alford quite reasonably chose the latter and thereby limited the maximum penalty to a 30-year term. When his plea is viewed in light of the evidence against him, which substantially negated his claim of innocence and which further provided a means by which the judge could test whether the plea was being intelligently entered, see *Mc-Carthy* v. *United States, supra,* at 466–467 (1969),[9] its validity cannot be seriously questioned. In view of the strong factual basis for the plea demonstrated by the State and Alford's clearly expressed desire to enter it despite his professed belief in his innocence, we hold that the trial judge did not commit constitutional error in accepting it.[10]

Relying on *United States* v. *Jackson, supra,* Alford now argues in effect that the State should not have allowed him this choice but should have insisted on proving him guilty of murder in the first degree. The States in their wisdom may take this course by statute or otherwise and may prohibit the practice of accepting pleas to lesser included offenses under any circumstances.[11] But this is not the mandate of the Fourteenth Amendment and the Bill of Rights. The prohibitions against involuntary or unintelligent pleas should not be relaxed, but neither should an exercise in arid logic render those constitutional guarantees counterproductive and put in jeopardy the very human values they were meant to preserve.

The Court of Appeals for the Fourth Circuit was in error to find Alford's plea of guilty invalid because it was made to avoid the possibility of the death penalty. That court's judgment directing the issuance of the

---

[9] Because of the importance of protecting the innocent and of insuring that guilty pleas are a product of free and intelligent choice, various state and federal court decisions properly caution that pleas coupled with claims of innocence should not be accepted unless there is a factual basis for the plea **; and until the judge taking the plea has inquired into and sought to resolve the conflict between the waiver of trial and the claim of innocence.**

In the federal courts, Fed. Rule Crim. Proc. 11 expressly provides that a court "shall not enter a judgment upon a plea of guilty unless it is satisfied that there is a factual basis for the plea."

[10] Our holding does not mean that a trial judge must accept every constitutionally valid guilty plea merely because a defendant wishes so to plead. A criminal defendant does not have an absolute right under the Constitution to have his guilty plea accepted by the court, see *Lynch* v. *Overholser,* 369 U. S., at 719 (by implication), although the States may by statute or otherwise confer such a right. Likewise, the States may bar their courts from accepting guilty pleas from any defendants who assert their innocence. Cf. Fed. Rule Crim. Proc. 11, which gives a trial judge discretion to "refuse to accept a plea of guilty . . . ." We need not now delineate the scope of that discretion.

[11] North Carolina no longer permits pleas of guilty to capital charges but it appears that pleas of guilty may still be offered to lesser included offenses. See n. 1, *supra.*

writ of habeas corpus is vacated and the case is remanded to the Court of Appeals for further proceedings consistent with this opinion.

It is so ordered.

Mr. Justice Black, while adhering to his belief that *United States* v. *Jackson,* 390 U. S. 570, was wrongly decided, concurs in the judgment and in substantially all of the opinion in this case.

Mr. Justice Brennan, with whom Mr. Justice Douglas and Mr. Justice Marshall join, dissenting.

Last Term, this Court held, over my dissent, that a plea of guilty may validly be induced by an unconstitutional threat to subject the defendant to the risk of death, so long as the plea is entered in open court and the defendant is represented by competent counsel who is aware of the threat, albeit not of its unconstitutionality. *Brady* v. *United States,* 397 U. S. 742, 745–758 (1970); *Parker* v. *North Carolina,* 397 U. S. 790, 795 (1970). Today the Court makes clear that its previous holding was intended to apply even when the record demonstrates that the actual effect of the unconstitutional threat was to induce a guily plea from a defendant who was unwilling to admit his guilt.

I adhere to the view that, in any given case, the influence of such an unconstitutional threat "must necessarily be given weight in determining the voluntariness of a plea." *Parker* v. *North Carolina,* 397 U. S., at 805 (dissent). And, without reaching the question whether due process permits the entry of judgment upon a plea of guilty accompanied by a contemporaneous denial of acts constituting the crime,[12] I believe that at the very least such a denial of guilt is also a relevant factor in determining whether the plea was voluntarily and intelligently made. With these factors in mind, it is sufficient in my view to state that the facts set out in the majority opinion demonstrate that Alford was "so gripped by fear of the death penalty"[13] that his decision to plead guilty was not voluntary but was "the product of duress as much so as choice reflecting physical constraint." *Haley* v. *Ohio,* 332 U. S. 596, 606 (1948) (opinion of Frankfurter, J.). Accordingly, I would affirm the judgment of the Court of Appeals.

[12] The courts of appeals have expressed varying opinions on this question. Compare *McCoy* v. *United States,* 124 U. S. App. D. C. 177, 179–180, 363 F. 2d 306, 308–309 (1966); *Bruce* v. *United States,* 126 U. S. App. D. C. 336, 342 n. 17, 379 F. 2d 113, 119 n. 17 (1967); *Griffin* v. *United States,* 132 U. S. App. D. C. 108, 109–110, 405 F. 2d 1378, 1379–1380 (1968); *Maxwell* v. *United States,* 368 F. 2d 735, 739 n. 3 (CA9 1966) (court may accept guilty plea from defendant unable or unwilling to admit guilt), with *United States ex rel. Crosby* v. *Brierley,* 404 F. 2d 790, 801–802 (CA3 1968); *Bailey* v. *MacDougall,* 392 F. 2d 155, 158 n. 7 (CA4 1968); *Hulsey* v. *United States,* 369 F. 2d 284, 287 (CA5 1966) (guilty plea is infirm if accompanied by denial of one or more elements of offense).

[13] *Brady* v. *United States,* 397 U. S., at 750.

PERSPECTIVES ON PLEA BARGAINING

Arnold Enker

Despite the fact that the large majority of criminal cases are disposed of by guilty plea, the major focus of attention to the criminal process traditionally has been upon disputed cases. We have made substantial modifications in the investigatory stages of the process and are devoting ever-increasing attention to pretrial and trial procedures in order to assure a fairer resolution of disputed issues at the trial. Far less attention has been devoted to the dynamics of the guilty plea and its impact on later stages of the proceedings. Even here, to the extent that modifications have been adopted in guilty plea procedures, the focus of attention understandably has been upon the most visible parts of the process, namely, representation by counsel and judicial inquiry at arraignment into "the factual basis for the plea." (Rule 11, Federal Rules of Criminal Procedure.)

Indeed, one gets the impression that our law does not feel quite ready to face up to the theoretical and practical problems involved. Thus, in *Shelton* v. *United States,* 356 U.S. 26 (1958), in which the propriety of the practice of plea bargaining seemed to be squarely presented, after thorough exploration of the issues by a panel of the Fifth Circuit Court of Appeals and then again by that court en banc, the Supreme Court accepted a somewhat dubious confession of error by the Solicitor General and vacated the conviction on the ambiguously stated ground "that the plea of guilty may have been improperly obtained." It is not clear whether the case was reversed because the arraigning judge failed to comply with Rule 11 in his examination to inquire of the defendant— this was the narrow basis for the Solicitor General's confession of error—, or because the Supreme Court determined that the plea in this case was not voluntary, or because the Supreme Court was of the view that any plea induced by a promise concerning the sentence to be imposed is invalid.

More recently, in *Marder* v. *Massachusetts,* 377 U.S. 407 (1964), only three Justices would have noted probable jurisdiction in a case in which the statutory scheme itself—relating admittedly to insignificant parking violations—contained differential penalties for those who admitted the charge and those who chose to defend the case.

From *Task Force Report: The Courts,* issued by the President's Commission on Law Enforcement and Administration of Justice (Washington, D.C., 1967), pp. 108–19. Reprinted by permission of the author.

Likely, this judicial shyness expresses a recognition that we really do not know very much about the practice of plea bargaining. Absent carefully collected factual information about the practice, we are unable to assess its potential dangers, both practical and theoretical, and recommend its improvement or abolition. To some extent, this gap in our information has recently been tightened up by the publication of the findings of the American Bar Foundation's study of the problem in NEW-MAN, CONVICTION—THE DETERMINATION OF GUILT OR INNOCENCE WITHOUT TRIAL (1966). In this paper, based on Newman's findings and other sources, I shall try to evaluate the practice and put it in perspective, assess its dangers and implications, and suggest some—admittedly imperfect—approaches toward improving the process.

I. DESCRIPTION OF PLEA BARGAINING

A. Pleading Guilty to a Reduced Charge

1. "Plea bargaining," or its popular euphemism "the negotiated plea," actually takes on a variety of forms and occurs in varied legal and factual contexts. In what is probably its best known form, the "plea bargain" consists of an arrangement between the prosecutor and the defendant or his lawyer, whereby in return for a plea of guilty by the defendant, the prosecutor agrees to press a charge less serious than that warranted by the facts which he could prove at trial. "Less serious" in this context usually means an offense which carries a lower potential maximum sentence. In such instances the defendant's motivation for pleading guilty is to limit the judge's sentencing discretion to the lesser maximum. Similar results are obtained when the defendant agrees to plead guilty to a given charge in return for a prosecutor's promise not to charge him with being a multiple offender or to drop added counts in a multicount indictment.

The court has no control over the initial charge brought by the prosecutor, so that in cases where such a bargain is struck before any charges have been filed in court, it is not subject to any formal judicial supervision to prevent undesirable reduction of a charge. Presumably a judge has other unofficial ways of expressing his displeasure with a reduced charge, but I have never heard of such judicial expressions. This is probably due to the judge's ignorance of the facts which would warrant a higher charge and to a reluctance to interfere in the conduct of the prosecutor's office. I suppose a judge who disapproves of a low charge could refuse to accept the guilty plea and leave the prosecutor to choose between no prosecution or prosecution for a more serious charge, but that too has been unheard of.

Where the bargain is struck after a higher charge has been filed, there is greater opportunity for judicial control. Still, little control appears to be exercised. New York has a statute which requires the prosecutor to file a statement giving his reasons for accepting a plea to a lesser charge, but a review of the filed statements indicates that they are very vague and general and do not furnish a vehicle for judicial control.[1] A more recent unpublished study in Minneapolis of prosecutors' statements required by a similar statute in Minnesota reveals equally disappointing results. Another reason such statutes are of limited value is that they deal only with pleas to an offense less than that originally charged. As already suggested, the bargain may be struck before any charges have been filed in court. For example, the Minneapolis study disclosed that in the year 1962, out of 91 cases of burglary, only 1 was originally charged as first degree burglary. In the remaining 90 cases the initial charge was third degree burglary.[2] It is difficult to believe that the facts supported a first degree burglary charge in only 1 out of 91 cases. (Compare the comment of one Michigan prosecutor reported in NEWMAN, p. 182, "You'd think all our burglaries occur at high noon.")

As suggested, one reason the court exercises little or no control over charge reduction is that at this early stage of the proceedings, the judge usually has absolutely no information about the crime or the defendant and is in no position to review the prosecutor's judgment. Probably still another reason is that the determination of an appropriate offense category or charge, as distinguished from sentence, is viewed as a matter of prosecutor's discretion. Yet, the ability to control the offense category brings with it control over the sentence, or at least its outside limits. We have never really given any careful thought to the interplay of these forces and roles.[3] When such a problem arose in *United States* v. *Nagelberg*,[4] the Supreme Court, again aided by the Solicitor General's confession of error, failed to grapple with the problem.

Equality of opportunity for such sentencing leniency is also a matter of concern. As would be expected from the above description of prosecutor and judge roles in this instance, judges are not likely to take the initiative in suggesting to the defendant that he use his guilty plea as a bargaining tool. Under the circumstances, the unrepresented defendant, or the defendant represented by counsel inexperienced in criminal matters, may find himself more severely treated than a wiser defendant with an identical background. And even if the judge imposes a light sentence, the felony conviction which might have been avoided may result in collateral disabilities which the judge cannot control.

2. It is equally common for plea bargaining for reduced charges

---

[1] See Weintraub & Tough, *Lesser Pleas Considered*, 32 J. CRIM. L. & CRIMINOLOGY 506 (1939).

[2] First degree burglary carried a minimum sentence of 10 years and second degree 2 years. There was no minimum sentence for third degree burglary. MINN. STAT. §§ 621.07, 621.09, 621.10 (1961) (subsequently repealed).

[3] Compare the judge's power to review a decision to file a nolle prosequi, FED. R. CRIM. P. 48(a), where a similar conflict arises.

[4] 377 U.S. 266 (1964).

to be motivated by the opposite goal, namely, to maximize the judge's sentencing discretion. In this type of agreement the defendant pleads guilty to a lesser charge than is warranted by the facts, not to reduce the potential maximum sentence, but to avoid a legislatively mandated minimum sentence or a legislative direction precluding the availability of probation. A typical example is narcotics prosecutions, where Federal law and some States impose severe mandatory minima for sale. It is common in such instances for defendants who have sold narcotics to plead guilty to a "tax count" in Federal cases or possession of narcotics in State cases, thereby avoiding the minimum sentence.

Because of common judicial antipathy to statutes so limiting their sentencing discretion, the problem of possible judge-prosecutor conflict is not significantly present. In fact, Newman reports that judges sometimes take the initiative in these cases to obtain a reduction of the charges. Other problems arise, however. First of all, the threat of a mandatory sentence places a high price on a not-guilty plea that might induce a defendant not to risk the hazards of a trial. This point will be elaborated upon below. Secondly, as Professor Newman's findings suggest, although the practice of accepting such lesser pleas begins as a discretionary device to individualize sentences, "the pattern of downgrading is such that it becomes virtually routine, and the bargaining session becomes a ritual" (p. 182). Under these circumstances, the public interest in heavy penalties for serious offenders may not always be served. Control in this instance remains, of course, with the prosecutor who can refuse to acquiesce in a request for charge reduction in the case of a serious offender. It is far from clear, however, that this is where such decisions ought to be made.[5] There is a danger, for example, that given two defendants equally guilty of a particular offense, the crucial factor which distinguishes them—the alleged professional character of the one's criminal behavior—is never placed on the record and is determined by the prosecutor on the basis of untested (in court at least) information available only to him. The conviction label becomes a weapon in the hands of the prosecutor to be applied in his uncontrolled discretion against those whom he judges to be dangerous. The "official" facts of the crime bear little relation to the ultimate disposition, which is reached upon extra-record facts. It is, admittedly, not infrequent that the real dispute between the parties is not over those facts which constitute the necessary elements of the crime but over facts which mitigate or aggravate the offense and are relevant only to sentence.

Our law has thus far paid scant attention to the proper procedures for determining these facts other than to accept the position that something less than a trial hearing is permissible.[6] But in those situations, the sentencing judge retains his factfinding powers, and defense counsel

---

[5] See Wechsler, *Sentencing, Correction, and the Model Penal Code*, 109 U. PA. L. REV. 465. 470 (1961).

[6] *Williams* v. *Oklahoma*, 358 U.S. 576, 584 (1959); *Williams* v. *New York*, 337 U.S. 241 (1949). For the barest minimum standards, see *Townsend* v. *Burke*, 334 U.S. 736 (1948).

has a forum in which to present his facts and arguments. Combined with the tendency to require increasing disclosure of the contents of presentence reports,[7] the defendant has the opportunity to argue his case visibly and with a chance of a favorable result. When it is the prosecutor who determines whether to accept a plea to a lesser count or to insist on pressing a charge carrying a mandatory sentence, the judge may be deprived of all sentencing discretion by an invisible decision in a "non-forum." Surely, the resolution of what will often be the sole issue of dispute and the single relevant fact, such as whether the defendant was armed, merits some greater formality and some forum more visible and equally accessible to all defendants.[8]

3. There is a third type of charge reduction which is motivated not by a desire to alter the sentencing powers of the judge but rather to avoid undesirable collateral aspects of a repugnant conviction label. This apparently occurs with some frequency in sex crimes. Thus, to avoid a record of conviction as a rapist, a sexual molester, or a homosexual, the defendant may offer to plead guilty to a charge carrying a vaguer label, such as disorderly conduct. Here, again, there is danger that, apart from sentencing consequences, the risk of having such a repugnant label attached to him may impel an innocent defendant to plead guilty to the nondescript charge. The danger is even greater here, for even the defendant who has a good chance of acquittal at trial may prefer to avoid the adverse publicity of such a trial.

4. Changes in the conviction label to accomplish these varied purposes raise additional problems for the administration of criminal justice. The lack of a comprehensive record of the proceedings and the misleading conviction label undermine attempts to achieve some degree of equality between defendants and may complicate the job of correctional authorities, who receive meager information about the defendant, the factual background of the case, and the judge's objectives, if any, in sentencing. And the unreliability of the conviction label can be misleading to others who have occasion to make reference to it at later stages in the same proceeding or in later proceedings. Thus, a prison classification committee or a parole board, relying on the conviction label in the case of an armed robbery charge reduced to unarmed robbery may mistakenly conclude that the prisoner was unarmed when he committed the robbery and may release a potentially dangerous offender too early. Perhaps the reverse danger is even more present. Because of the prevalence of plea bargaining and reduction of charges, the parole board may assume that all prisoners who pleaded guilty to charges of unarmed robbery were in fact armed. Or, upon a later conviction, a sentencing judge may assume that the earlier crime was in reality armed robbery. A defendant who pleads guilty to an accurate charge

---

[7] See the proposed Rule 32(c), FED. R. CRIM. P.

[8] Compare the remarks of Mr. Justice Fortas, writing for the Court in *Kent* v. *United States*, 383 U.S. 541, 561-63 (1966).

of unarmed robbery, therefore, may in the long run be treated more harshly than he deserves because of an erroneous assumption by others that he bargained to avoid a charge of armed robbery. In other words, where such plea bargaining is widely practiced, conviction records become unreliable and may be misused to the disadvantage of the community or of the defendant.

B. "On the Nose" Guilty Pleas

1. Plea bargaining need not necessarily take the form of a reduction of the charges. A defendant may plead guilty to a charge that accurately describes his conduct in return for a general promise of leniency at sentencing or a more specific promise of probation or of a sentence that does not exceed a specified term of years. To the extent that plea bargaining occurs in Federal courts, except for narcotics cases which carry a mandatory minimum sentence, it usually takes this form. This is probably so because the Federal law contains few lesser included offenses to which charges can be reduced.

In these instances, appearances can be extremely misleading. Superficially, at least, the judge retains complete discretion as to sentence and is able to control the proceedings so as to insure both an accurate guilty plea (protection of the defendant) and a sentence appropriate to the defendant's conduct (protection of the public interest). Closer examination of the process suggests, however, that this may not really be so.

Negotiations usually are handled between the prosecutor and the defendant or his attorney. The judge's isolation from this stage of the negotiations creates a risk that the bargaining will be limited to protection of the interests of the defendant and the prosecutor without anyone being present to protect the "public interest." The defendant's interest in receiving as low a sentence as possible and the prosecutor's interest in maintaining a steady flow of guilty pleas—to preserve a good public image and to induce guilty pleas from other defendants—can easily merge into agreement upon a guilty plea in return for a sentence that is meaningless in terms of the defendant's offense and his need for treatment or control. Related to this is the possibility of inadequate knowledge of the facts, either as to the crime itself or the defendant's background, on the part of the prosecutor who negotiates the guilty plea. Under the pressure of a heavy, time-consuming caseload, the prosecutor may easily be seduced at an early stage of the proceedings, before such facts are more fully developed, by the offer of a quick guilty plea in exchange for a light sentence, only to discover too late that the offense, or the offender, was far more serious than originally thought. It is possible, indeed likely, that the full facts may never be discovered since the quick disposition usually eliminates the need or the impetus for further investigation. Thus, there is a good chance that the judge will never become aware of facts which indicate that the agreement is not in the public interest.

Nor can defense counsel be counted on to provide this protection.

Rarely does a defense attorney conduct a thorough investigation of the case and his client's background; thus he usually provides little additional insight into the causes of the defendant's problems. Also, defense counsel regards his professional responsibility to be exclusively to his client. The public interest in these instances need not necessarily mean a longer sentence; it may include identification of the sources of defendant's problems and the development and suggestion of a program of correctional treatment that is relevant to these problems. But defense counsel, perhaps in part because of legitimate skepticism over the availability of meaningful correctional treatment and of doubts as to the fairness of such programs, seem to regard their duty to the client solely in terms of obtaining for him as lenient a sentence as possible. Perhaps a broader view of the lawyer's role should include within the counseling function the duty to attempt to make the client aware of the fact that he has a problem and of his need for some correctional program. Thus far, however, lawyers have preferred to avoid the welfare implications of their role as counselors and the conflicts this role would create and to limit their role to getting the client "as good a deal" as they can.

Thus, neither prosecutor nor defense counsel is likely to bring before the judge such facts as would undermine the basis for the negotiated agreement. But even if the judge should become aware of such facts through another source, say a presentence report, the dynamics of the present system would prevent close judicial supervision over the negotiated agreement. First of all, the judge's theoretical role as protector of the public interest is limited by judicial reluctance to intervene and repudiate an arrangement accepted by the prosecutor as agent of the state. In other areas of the law it is rare for judges to reject consensual arrangements even when one of the parties represents the public. Thus, it is easy for the judge to sit back and approve anything to which the lawyers agree.

Moreover, it is essential to the successful working of the system that the judge accept the arrangements worked out between defense counsel and the prosecutor. Because of doubts over the legality of the negotiated plea, prosecutors and defense counsel typically avoid all reference in court to the sentence to be imposed until after the plea has been tendered and accepted, and engage in the pious fraud of making a record that the plea was not induced by any promises. Since the judge's sentence remains to be pronounced, the defendant does not achieve the control he sought in negotiating unless he has confidence that the judge will accept the arrangement. The defendant is interested in controlling the exercise of sentencing discretion, not in a lawsuit over a motion to withdraw his guilty plea because of disappointment over the sentence later imposed. The typical unreviewability of the exercise of sentencing discretion only sharpens the point. The credibility of the system requires, then, that the judge hold his power to reject the agreement in careful reserve. If there is to be any effective judicial participation in the process, rather than mere judicial acquiescence in an agreement worked out between the parties, such participation must come at an earlier stage of the proceedings.

Finally, this type of negotiated plea is even less visible than the negotiated plea which results in the reduction of charges. So far as the record reveals, the defendant was charged with a crime appropriate to the acts he committed; he has pleaded guilty to that charge voluntarily; he has asserted in open court that his plea was not induced by any threats or promises, and this assertion has gone unchallenged by his lawyer or the prosecutor; appropriate arguments, pleas, and recommendations have been addressed to the judge at the time of sentencing to influence his decision; and the judge has exercised his discretion and imposed what appeared to him to be the most appropriate sentence based on all of the relevant facts. Not a hint appears on the record to suggest that some relevant facts were not adduced or that the key determinant of the plea decision was not some appropriate peno-correctional end but the prosecutor's desire to induce a guilty plea. Of course, little of this appears in the record when the defendant pleads to a lesser offense, but in that case a comparison of the plea and the original charge suggests at least the possibility of some noncorrectional factor in the process.

The invisibility or low visibility of the process precludes outside control to protect the public interest. It also, to say the least, complicates the process when the defendant, experiencing a change of heart, alleges some abuse in the negotiations. Most such allegations are, probably correctly, suspect. But a system that requires the defendant to deny the negotiations at the very moment he tenders his guilty plea contains potential for overreaching and unfairness. Under such circumstances, it becomes extremely difficult to sift the valid from the false allegations.

2. One further type of plea bargain merits attention. This may be called the "tacit bargain." In this instance, there are no formal or explicit negotiations between the defense and the prosecution. Defendant, aware of an established practice in the court to show leniency to defendants who plead guilty, pleads guilty to the charges in the expectation that he will be so treated. This expectation is almost invariably satisfied without the need to enter into any negotiations or make any explicit promises. To an extent, the areas of concern discussed with respect to other types of plea bargaining are here eliminated or at least mitigated. But, even apart from the fundamental question of the propriety of placing any premium on a guilty plea,[9] some problems remain. Such pleas do not represent a true acknowledgment and acceptance of guilt by the defendant—universally regarded as a first step toward rehabilitation—but are more likely viewed by him as an expedient manipulation of the system. And, again, the overriding desire to keep the calendar moving can easily cause the practice to degenerate into routine and can direct the

[9] For discussion of the propriety of showing leniency to defendants who plead guilty and expression of judicial attitudes toward this practice, see Comment, *The Influence of the Defendant's Plea on Judicial Determination of Sentence*, 66 YALE L.J. 204 (1956); *Pilot Institute on Sentencing*, 26 F.R.D. 231, 285–89 (1960).

judge's attention away from consideration of sentencing goals in his determination.

Cutting across the entire system of plea negotiation is the fear that the low visibility of the proceeding lends itself to possible corrupt manipulation. In actual practice such corruption seems rare. But a real vice in the procedure may be that it often gives the defendant an image of corruption in the system, or at least an image of a system lacking meaningful purpose and subject to manipulation by those who are wise to the right tricks. Cynicism, rather than respect, is the likely result.

II. ADMINISTRATIVE CONSIDERATIONS

The most commonly asserted justification of plea bargaining is its utility in disposing of large numbers of cases in a quick and simple way. The need to induce such summary disposition of cases has been most forcefully stated by Judge Lummus:

> Let us suppose that five hundred cases are on the list for trial at a sitting of court. Of these, one hundred cases are tried, and four hundred defendants plead guilty. Seldom is there time in a sitting to try more than a fifth of the cases on the list. . . . [T]he prosecutor must subordinate almost everything to the paramount need of disposing of his list during the sitting. Rather than dismiss the excess by nolle prosequi, with no penalty, he must induce defendants in fact guilty to plead guilty, in order that some penalty may be imposed. Half a loaf is better than no bread. . . .
>
> If all the defendants should combine to refuse to plead guilty, and should dare to hold out, they could break down the administration of criminal justice in any state in the Union. But they dare not hold out, for such as were tried and convicted could hope for no leniency. The prosecutor is like a man armed with a revolver who is cornered by a mob. A concerted rush would overwhelm him. . . . The truth is that a criminal court can operate only by inducing the great mass of actually guilty defendants to plead guilty.[10]

Administrative need no longer seems to command the consideration it once received when challenged in the name of due process of law. It is easy to minimize administrative convenience and need. Simply increase the staff of prosecutors, judges, defense counsel, and probation officers if the present complement is insufficient to handle the task, it is said. Even if the money were readily available, it would still not be clear that we could call upon sufficient numbers of competent personnel. A lowering of standards in order to man the store adequately may well result in poorer justice. It may also divert both funds and personnel from other

---

[10] LUMMUS, THE TRIAL JUDGE 43–46 (1937).

segments of the criminal process, such as corrections work, where they are arguably more needed.

But there are other reasons to maintain a high proportion of guilty pleas and a low proportion of trials. To suggest the least important of these first, a substantial increase in criminal trials would entail an equally substantial increase in the burden of jury duty on citizens. Many citizens prefer to avoid jury service because it interferes with their private and business lives. Would a disproportionate increase in this burden produce resentment against or a sense of alienation from the criminal process that might be directed against defendants and make other "pro-defendant" reforms less politically acceptable? Probably the best that we can say is that we do not know the answer to this question, but it should cause us to pause before throwing administrative considerations to the winds.

Maximization of adjudication by trial may actually result in more inaccurate verdicts. So long as trials are the exception rather than the rule and are limited, by and large, to cases in which the defense offers a substantial basis for contesting the prosecutor's allegations, the defendant's presumption of innocence and the requirement of proof beyond a reasonable doubt are likely to remain meaningful to a jury. The very fact that the defendent contests the charges impresses upon the jurors the seriousness of their deliberations and the need to keep an open mind about the evidence and to approach the testimony of accusing witnesses with critical care and perhaps even a degree of skepticism. If contest becomes routine, jurors may likely direct their skepticism at the defense. Prosecutors too readily apply the overall, and overwhelming, statistical probability of guilt to individual cases; we do not want jurors to do the same. It makes some sense, then, to screen out those cases where there is no real dispute and encourage their disposition by plea, leaving for trial to the extent possible only those cases where there exists a real basis for dispute.

I shall suggest later that there also are some cases in which the price we pay for contested disposition is the posing to the jury of extreme alternatives, due to the law's need to maintain its generality, under circumstances in which compromise may actually yield a more "rational" result.

III. THE RISK THAT INNOCENT DEFENDANTS MAY PLEAD GUILTY

Thus far we have examined plea bargaining from the impersonal perspective of the "system." Some additional perspective can be gained by viewing the practice from the defendant's point of view. A prominent defense lawyer has put it thusly:

These plea bargains perform a useful function. We have to remember that our sentencing laws are for the most part savage, archaic, and make very little sense. The penalties they set are frequently far too tough. . . .

The negotiated plea is a way by which prosecutors can make value judgments. They can take some of the inhumanity out of the law in certain situations. . . .[11]

And, further:

> If a man is guilty, and the prosecution has a good case, there is little satisfaction to the lawyer or his client in trying conclusions, and getting the maximum punishment. A great deal of good can be done in the plodding everyday routine of the defense lawyer, by mitigating punishment in this manner. Anyone who has ever spent a day in a prison and experienced, even vicariously, the indignity and suffering that incarceration entails realizes full well that the difference between a three-year sentence and a five-year sentence is tremendous, not only for the wrongdoer who is being punished, but for the innocent members of his family who love him, and who suffer humiliation and worse while he is away. This is something that the criminal lawyer can rightfully and usefully do for the "guilty" man. In this regard, the criminal lawyer is daily fulfilling a useful function in our society.[12]

Viewed from this perspective, the negotiated plea is not solely a corrupting inducement offered defendants to waive their constitutional rights but is also a device by which defendants and their counsel can manipulate an imperfect system to mitigate its harshness and excesses. It is all too easy to assert that "there is no such thing as a beneficial sentence for an innocent defendant." [13] There is also no such thing as a beneficial conviction for an innocent man. But innocent men may be convicted at trial as well.

The possibility that innocent defendants might be induced to plead guilty in order to avoid the possibility of a harsh sentence should they be convicted after trial is obviously cause for concern. Because of the emotional potential of this problem, it is easy to overstate. The truth is that we just do not know how common such a situation is. Indeed, this may be the very vice of the current system of plea negotiation. Because of the invisible, negotiated, consensual nature of the handling of the case in terms which avoid exploration of those factors deemed relevant by the law, we do not really know whether there is in fact cause for concern or not. It is this very uncertainty about such serious consequences that creates uneasiness.

[11] Steinberg & Paulsen, *A Conversation With Defense Counsel on Problems of a Criminal Defense,* 7 PRAC. LAW. 25, 31–32 (1961).

[12] Steinberg, *The Responsibility of the Defense Lawyer in Criminal Cases,* 12 SYRACUSE L. REV. 442, 447 (1961).

[13] Comment, *Official Inducements To Plead Guilty: Suggested Morals for a Marketplace,* 32 U. CHI. L. REV. 167, 181 (1964).

Still, perhaps the problem can be put in a better perspective. In the first place, trials, too, may not always result in truthful or accurate verdicts. It is interesting to note that disposition by trial and by negotiated plea are similar in that in neither instance do we have any relatively accurate idea of the incidence of mistaken judgments. On one level, then, the significant question is not how many innocent people are induced to plead guilty but is there a significant likelihood that innocent people who would be (or have a fair chance of being) acquitted at trial might be induced to plead guilty?

Further, concern over the possibility that a negotiated plea can result in an erroneous judgment of conviction assumes a frame of reference by which the accuracy of the judgment is to be evaluated. It assumes an objective truth existing in a realm of objective historical fact which it is the sole function of our process to discover. Some, but by no means all, criminal cases fit this image. For example, this is a relatively accurate description of the issues at stake in a case in which the defendant asserts a defense of mistaken identity. If all other issues were eliminated from the case, there would still exist a world of objective historical fact in which the accused did or did not perpetrate the act at issue. And if he did not, a negotiated guilty plea would represent an erroneous judgment. In this instance, then, the issue suggested is the comparative likelihood of such erroneous decisions as between trial and negotiation.

But not all criminal cases fit the above picture. The conventional dichotomy between adjudication and disposition in which the adjudication process is thought of as one of fact determination tends to obscure the nonfactual aspect of much of the adjudication process. Much criminal adjudication concerns the passing of value judgments on the accused's conduct as is obvious where negligence, recklessness, reasonable apprehension of attack, use of unnecessary force, and the like are at issue. Although intent is thought of as a question of fact, it too can represent a judgment of degrees of fault, for example, in cases where the issue is whether the defendants entertained intent to defraud or intent to kill. In many of these cases, objective truth is more ambiguous, if it exists at all. Such truth exists only as it emerges from the fact-determining process, and accuracy in this context really means relative equality of results as between defendants similarly situated and relative congruence between the formal verdict and our understanding of society's less formally expressed evaluation of such conduct.

The negotiated plea can, then, be an accurate process in this sense. So long as the judgment of experienced counsel as to the likely jury result is the key element entering into the bargain, substantial congruence is likely to result. Once we recognize that what lends rationality to the factfinding process in these instances lies not in an attempt to discover objective truth but in the devising of a process to express intelligent judgment, there is no inherent reason why plea negotiation need be regarded any the less rational or intelligent in its results.

Indeed, it may be that in some instances plea negotiation leads to more "intelligent" results. A jury can be left with the extreme alternatives of guilty of a crime of the highest degree or not guilty of any crime, with no room for any intermediate judgment. And this is likely to occur in just those cases where an intermediate judgment is the fairest and most "accurate" (or most congruent).

Clearly, the line between responsibility and irresponsibility due to insanity is not as sharp as the alternatives posed to a jury would suggest. It may be that such a dividing line exists in some world of objective reality and that the ambiguity arises from the difficulties of accurate factfinding. It is more realistic, however, to view responsibility as a matter of degree at best only roughly expressed in the law's categories of first and second degree murder, manslaughter, etc. The very visibility of the trial process may be one factor that prevents us from offering the jury this compromise in order to preserve the symbolism of uniform rules evenly applied. The low visibility of the negotiated plea allows this compromise which may be more rational and congruent than the result we are likely to arrive at after a trial.[14] While the desire to protect the symbolism of legality and the concern over lay compromises may warrant limiting the jury to extreme alternatives, it does not follow that to allow the defendant to choose such a compromise is an irrational or even a less rational procedure.

There is, moreover, a significant difference between conviction upon trial and by consent that merits further consideration; that relates to the role of defense counsel. Despite defense counsel's best efforts, his innocent client may be convicted at trial. But he cannot be convicted on a plea of guilty without defense counsel's participation and consent. Defendant's consent is also necessary for a guilty plea, but that provides less of an independent check on inaccurate pleas since defendant's prime interest is in minimizing unpleasant consequences. Counsel, on the other hand, as an officer of the court, has a duty to preserve the integrity of the process as well. When the system operates as it is supposed to, defense counsel's control over the plea affords added assurance that the plea is accurate.

We are safe in assuming that the system still works less than ideally. Waiver of counsel is still common in guilty plea cases, and even when the defendant is formally represented, his representation is often perfunctory.[15] But Professor Newman also reports increased inquiry into the factual basis for guilty pleas in all three States studied.[16] This suggests that judges accepting such pleas, if alert to the problem, can ex-

---

[14] The defense of diminished responsibility seeks to accomplish similar ends.

[15] See NEWMAN, CONVICTION—THE DETERMINATION OF GUILT OR INNOCENCE WITHOUT TRIAL 200–05 (1966). These pages contain an excellent discussion of the dynamics of the process and the problems faced by a conscientious attorney.

[16] Id. at 7-21, 233-35.

ercise greater control by refusing to accept waivers and by careful selection of assigned counsel, particularly in those cases in which some lingering doubt as to the defendant's guilt remains.

There is, however, another side to the participation of counsel in the guilty plea. Even counsel may see the occasional practical wisdom of pleading an innocent man guilty. Sworn to uphold the law and at the same time to serve his client's best interests, counsel may be faced with an insoluble human and professional conflict. While such a compromise may serve the defendant's interest in making the best of a bad situation, it can never serve the lawyer's interest in protecting his professional integrity and self-image. At present we have no idea of the extent of this role conflict and its consequences to the profession.[17]

Thus far I have suggested that for those cases in which the key determinant of the plea bargain is experienced counsel's assessment of the chances of conviction, plea bargaining is not likely to impair the accuracy of the guilt determining process. This assumption, of course, does not always prevail. Additional factors may enter into the bargain. Probably the most significant factor is the possibility that the defendant may be convicted of a crime which carries a mandatory nonsuspendible sentence. Where the sentencing judge retains complete discretion in the imposition of sentence, defense counsel is under less pressure to negotiate a plea and is under little pressure to give up a triable defense. If the defense has sufficient merit so that some doubt may linger even after conviction, there may be a fair chance that such doubt will be reflected in the judge's sentence. Because of the rules relating to cross-examination of a defendant, defense counsel are usually of the view that a defendant ordinarily stands little chance of acquittal unless he has a relatively unblemished background. Where sentencing discretion prevails, such a background is likely to result in a light sentence upon conviction. Under such circumstances, a plea bargain has the effect of changing a substantial probability of leniency to a certainty, hardly a sufficient inducement for a man to plead guilty to a crime he has not committed. This becomes even more certain in the case of the defendant with an unblemished background, where the conviction is probably more damaging than any sentence he is likely to receive.

The removal of sentencing discretion by the enactment of mandatory sentences alters the picture completely. Once the defendant has been convicted, lingering doubts as to guilt and the defendant's exemplary prior life can no longer be considered. Under such circumstances, the defendant may be forced to give up a fair chance of acquittal by pleading guilty to a different, usually a lesser, charge upon which the judge can impose a more lenient sentence. The impact of

[17] Lawyers handling divorce cases are often faced with similar conflicts. For a selection of materials related to this problem, see FOOTE, LEVY & SANDER, CASES AND MATERIALS ON FAMILY LAW 682–83, 696–711, 752–69 (1966).

legislatively mandated sentences on plea negotiations was suggested some time ago by prominent writers.[18] Professor Newman's book reports that there was a far greater incidence of bargaining and charge reduction in Michigan, which has legislatively mandated sentences for certain crimes, and in Kansas, whose statutes do not permit the sentencing judge to impose probation as an alternative to a prison term for some crimes, than in Wisconsin, where the legislative sentencing structure leaves judges considerably greater discretion.[19]

An additional extraneous factor influencing counsel's judgment was suggested above, namely, the fear of conviction of a crime carrying a label suggesting abnormality or perversion, and even the fear of going to trial in such a case with its ensuing publicity. Mandatory minimum sentences can be eliminated; adverse publicity of this sort probably cannot. It is difficult to say with confidence that an innocent defendant's plea of guilty to disorderly conduct in such a case is never in the defendant's best interest if he is innocent. It is presumably not in the best interests of the criminal process, but I would hesitate to insist to a client that he owes the system a duty to defend himself and besmirch his family and reputation. In any event, we can encourage greater judicial sensitivity to this problem and closer judicial supervision of the plea in such cases. New Rule 11 of the Federal Rules of Criminal Procedure and the practice in some courts of holding postplea hearings or investigations to develop the facts relating to the offense provide methods for such control.

The discussion in this section has not been designed to suggest that there is no reason for concern over the possibility that innocent persons might be induced to plead guilty by a system of plea negotiations. Rather, my purpose has been to place the problem in what appears to me to be its proper perspective, to demonstrate that there is nothing inherent in such a system that would increase the risks of inaccuracy beyond those present in adjudication by trial, to suggest that plea negotiation has possibilities for more intelligent and more humane disposition of many cases than are available in trial disposition, and to indicate that the problem is not beyond effective judicial control.

IV. VISIBILITY AND INVISIBILITY: SOME SKEPTICAL OBSERVATIONS ON THE NONNEGOTIATED PLEA

At several previous points I have commented on the invisibility or low visibility of key elements of the decision-making process in the case of negotiated pleas. The assumption has been that where there have not

[18] Ohlin & Remington, *Sentencing Structure: Its Effect Upon Systems for the Administration of Criminal Justice*, 23 LAW & CONTEMP. PROB. 495 (1958).

[19] NEWMAN, op. cit. *supra* note 16, at 53–56, 177–84.

been any out-of-court negotiations, where the sentence is truly determined by the judge after argument by counsel and perhaps a presentence investigation, the process is fully visible. I would suggest that the present process for nonnegotiated pleas is not really very visible either. In fact it is less visible to the persons most directly involved, the defendant and his counsel, than the negotiated plea.

Visibility depends on one's vantage point. While the negotiated plea may be of low visibility to the public at large (and to law professors), it is highly visible to the defendant. Whether the factors entering into the bargain are or are not meaningful as sentencing goals, they are at least visible to the defendant and his attorney. The defendant is able to influence the sentence, he may set forth bargaining factors and determine their relevance to the decision, and he may use his bargaining power to eliminate the grossest aspects of sentencing harshness and arbitrariness, be they legislative or judicial. The defendant, if he does not like the bargain, may reject it and stand trial. If he accepts the bargain, he cannot help but feel that his sentence is something that he consented to and participated in bringing about, even if he at the same time resents the process that induced his consent. And while he may find his "correctional treatment" brutal and meaningless on one level, his sentence is meaningful on another level in that at least he participated in it and influenced the final result.

Current sentencing practice for a nonnegotiated plea is to defense counsel, and I suspect to the defendant as well, an even more meaningless, less comprehensible procedure. The defendant and his counsel rarely see the sentencing decision take shape and even more rarely feel that they have participated in its formulation. At the point at which the process is most visible to the public, the imposition of sentence, it is least visible to the defendant. The prosecutor and defense counsel make their arguments and the judge decides. One frequently does not know what influenced the judge and how he went about making up his mind. (When the defendant reaches prison, the prison authorities are often at a similar loss to understand the judge's sentencing goals, although this is in part a product of the division between the probation service, which is an arm of the court, and correctional authorities, who are an arm of the prison.) One often gets the impression that the judge had his mind made up before argument and that counsel played no meaningful role in influencing the final result.

This is particularly true where the judge has had the benefit of a presentence investigation. Armed with all sorts of information and recommendations, and probably having discussed the case in chambers with the probation officer, the judge is rarely influenced by the highly visible argument of counsel. Rather, he has been influenced by the usually invisible report and conference with the probation officer. Even competent defense counsel who has devoted the time since pleading to furnishing the probation officer with helpful information about his client and perhaps has attempted to arrange employment for his client often has little idea how this information was used and whether he has really helped his client. This is particularly true when the defendant is disappointed by the sentence, a not infrequent occurrence. In short, both defendant and defense counsel emerge from the process with a sense of frustration and purposelessness. Often, neither feels he has played any meaningful and influential role in the sentencing process.[20]

The bargain may be looked at then as an attempt by the defendant, and even by his counsel, to preserve their dignity in the process by finding a role for themselves even if it means a sentence based upon criteria logically irrelevant to the goals of the process.

I cannot document these comments. They are merely impressions and observations accumulated during several years of criminal practice. Admittedly this practice was almost entirely on the prosecution side, and my impressions may have been distorted by the fact that office policy forbade us to make any specific recommendations as to sentence. But we were free to present and argue to the court those facts we considered relevant. Still, I always regarded my role in the sentencing process as professionally unsatisfying. With but one or two exceptions, I have rarely had the sense that defense counsel participated very meaningfully either. And on the few occasions that I have served on the defense side, the only occasions on which I had any feeling that I was rendering some professional service to my clients in the sentencing process were when I bargained on their behalf for some sentencing consideration.

In other words, in that moment of dread before a nonnegotiated sentence is imposed, counsel at least, and probably the defendant, have the feeling that they await the pronouncement of an arbitrary fiat which they are helpless to shape. The pronouncement of sentence, particularly if it is an unpleasant one, rarely mitigates this sense, for rarely does a judge articulate any reasons for imposing the sentence he has chosen other than to engage in an occasionally harsh speech excoriating the defendant and his like.

V. THE LEGAL DIALECTIC: VOLUNTARINESS

Current doctrine has it that a guilty plea, to be constitutionally valid, must be voluntary.[21] This notion apparently stems from several

---

[20] Compare the observations of Professor Kadish, *The Advocate and the Expert—Counsel in the Peno-Correctional Process*, 45 MINN. L. REV. 803 (1961):

"Hearings on sentence and release determinations are commonly attenuated interviews when they are given at all." Id. at 804.

"[T]he use of ex parte presentence investigation reports, whose contents are only sometimes made available to the offender, has largely muted the adversary character of sentencing processes." Id. at 806.

"[There exists a] traditional value, associated closely with the root idea of a democratic community, that a person should be given an opportunity to participate effectively in determinations which affect his liberty." Id. at 830.

[21] E.g., *Machibroda v. United States*, 368 U.S. 487 (1962).

sources. Since the Constitution guarantees all defendants a right to trial, the entry of a guilty plea constitutes a waiver of that right which, as with all waivers, must be intelligently and voluntarily made. So viewed, the requirement of voluntariness is a function of the specific rights guaranteed by the sixth amendment.

The requirement of voluntariness may also be viewed as emerging directly from notions of due process. At a minimum, due process requires a fair factfinding procedure designed to find the relevant facts accurately. Conviction by judicial admission satisfies this requirement unless the admission has been induced by unfair means or means which might induce an innocent person to plead guilty.

In addition, the defendant's fifth amendment right not to be compelled to incriminate himself covers not only testimonial self-incrimination but compelled judicial admissions as well. In this context, the requirement of voluntariness bespeaks the ethical and political right of an accused to demand that the state not force him to become the instrument of his own undoing, but be prepared to prove his guilt by so-called objective or extrinsic evidence.

It should be recognized immediately that the term "voluntary" is an exceedingly ambiguous term. This stems not only from the difficulties involved in trying to discover a past state of mind but also from the fact that we do not even have a clear idea of what, if any, psychological facts or experience we are looking for. The choice to plead guilty rather than face the rack is voluntary in the sense that the subject did have a choice, albeit between unpleasant alternatives. The defendant who decides to plead guilty and seek judicial mercy also makes a choice between what are to him two unpleasant alternatives. If we call the first choice involuntary and the second voluntary, what we are really saying is that we are convinced that in the first case almost all persons so confronted will choose to admit their guilt but that the defendant's decision is based on more personal and subjective factors in the second instance.[22]

We also are saying that we approve of judicial mercy but disapprove of the rack. In other words, "voluntariness" expresses not merely judgment of fact but an ethical evaluation. When only certain extreme forms of pressure are disapproved, the difference between those pressures and the milder pressures we are here concerned with is sufficiently great that, while only a matter of degree, the voluntary-involuntary distinction is descriptive and useful. But as milder and less clearly improper inducements fall under the ban, it becomes more difficult to distinguish them from pleas which we regard as valid, at least so long as we are led by our dialectic to look for a nonexistent psychological difference. Thus, it is difficult to distinguish the psychological experience of a defendant who is induced to plead guilty by a prose-

[22] See Bator & Vorenberg, *Arrest, Detention, Interrogation, and the Right to Counsel—Basic Problems and Possible Legislative Solutions*, 66 COLUM. L. REV. 62, 72–73 (1966).

cutor's or judge's promise of sentencing leniency from that of a defendant who is induced to plead guilty by his desire to begin service of his sentence immediately so that he will be released sooner. There is a danger that so long as we adhere to the terminology of voluntariness, our very inability to distinguish these cases will lead us to hold involuntary all pleas induced by any considerations beyond the defendant's sense of guilt and readiness to admit it publicly.

Both at common law and pursuant to recent Supreme Court decisions, a confession is deemed coerced and hence inadmissible if it was induced by any promises or threats. A typical inducement invalidating a confession is the proffer of leniency. Because the terminology and underlying constitutional sources are the same for guilty pleas as for coerced confessions, the inducement test for confessions may be thought to extend to guilty pleas as well.[23] Indeed, because a guilty plea is itself a conviction and leaves the court nothing to do but impose sentence, while a confession is merely evidence which must be corroborated and may be explained, rebutted, or contradicted, some judges might apply an even stricter standard to a guilty plea than to a confession.[24]

To apply the confession cases in this way would be to ignore some vital differences between the two situations. In the first place, even at common law the inducement test was riddled with arbitrary exceptions such as upholding confessions induced by a promise not to arrest or prosecute a relative of the defendant. Secondly, to the extent that it rests on concern for the reliability of the resulting confessions, the extreme sanction of exclusion bespeaks mistrust of the jury's ability to evaluate the confession properly in light of the inducement.[25] As we have suggested above, the accuracy of the guilty plea is not beyond effective judicial inquiry and evaluation.

Also, the particular inducements held improper in the coerced confession cases usually appear against a background of lengthy interrogation and other pressures to confess, factors not usually present when the same inducement is offered for a guilty plea. And in the confession cases, the defendant succumbed to the inducement without the advice of counsel. Any valid system of plea negotiations would presumably require that the defendant have counsel for this and other reasons.[26] Finally, the coerced confession cases must be viewed against the background of secrecy in the interrogation room and the recurring conflict of testimony between police and defendants over where more serious "inducements" had

[23] See, for example, the dissenting opinion in *Shelton* v. *United States,* 246 F. 2d 571 (5th Cir. 1957), *rev'd per curiam,* 356 U.S. 12 (1958).

[24] See ibid. But compare *Haynes* v. *Washington,* 373 U.S. 503 (1963), with *Cortez* v. *United States,* 337 F.2d 699 (8th Cir. 1964).

[25] See the discussion in *Developments in the Law—Confessions,* 79 HARV. L. REV. 938, 954–59 (1966).

[26] See *Davis* v. *Holman,* 354 F.2d 773 (5th Cir. 1965), *cert. denied,* 384 U.S. 907 (1964); *Shupe* v. *Sigler,* 230 F. Supp. 601 (D. Neb. 1964); *Anderson* v. *North Carolina,* 221 F. Supp. 930 (W.D.N.C. 1963).

been offered. Under such circumstances, the very ambiguity and flexibility of the term "voluntariness" made it easy for skeptical courts to grab onto a conceded inducement, albeit a minor one, and hold that this inducement standing by itself rendered the confession involuntary. The coerced confession cases, then, are hardly controlling with respect to plea bargaining which occurs in a wholly different context, despite the similarity of the legal formula.

The fifth amendment approach is more difficult, largely because the ethical principle it expresses often diverges from the accuracy goal of the criminal process, whereas the two tend to converge in the sixth amendment right to trial. Thus, the problem here is in part to determine at what point the preservation of the dignity of all men before the state is undercut by inducements to plead, or what kinds of inducements undermine this dignity. The mere statement of the issue in this form suggests again some room for play, but the problem is complicated by the coerced confession precedents discussed above. But our notions of dignity seem to require that some room be left to the defendant to judge and act intelligently, knowingly, and with competent professional advice in his own self-interest.

Although the sixth amendment guarantees the right to trial, it is not to be assumed that the constitutional scheme requires or even envisions that defendants will always avail themselves of this right. Indeed, as suggested above, the full exercise of this right by all defendants might even thwart some of the goals of the right to trial. Adjudication by trial may be viewed not as a preferred or desired procedure but rather as an available procedure. Its availability to all defendants stands as a check against governmental arbitrariness and as a device for rational factfinding in case of disagreement between the government and the defendant. Defendants then must be informed of and given the tools necessary for the meaningful exercise of this right. It is not necessary, however, that they be encouraged to exercise this right. Again, each single defendant's own self-interest will determine whether or not he should exercise it.

In light of these considerations, including the benefits to both the system and to defendants that can be derived from a controlled system of plea negotiations, it would not be desirable to lay down a broad constitutional dictum forbidding the practice. It would be a mistake to push valid legal, even constitutional, insights to the ultimate of their logic. Accommodation of conflicting interests is a more sensible pursuit.

VI. WHERE DO WE GO FROM HERE?

To recapitulate for a moment, I have suggested that plea bargaining serves several useful ends: It eases the administrative burden of crowded court dockets; it preserves the meaningfulness of the trial process for those cases in which there is real basis for dispute; it furnishes defendants a vehicle to mitigate the system's harshness, whether that harshness stems from callous infliction of excessive punishment or from the occasional inequities inherent in a system of law based upon general rules; and it affords the defense some participation in and control over an unreviewable process that often gives the appearance of fiat and arbitrariness. These are not insignificant accomplishments.

But we have also seen that the system pays a price for these accomplishments. It bears a risk, the extent of which is unknown, that innocent defendants may plead guilty; negotiation becomes directed to the issue of "how many years a plea is worth" rather than to any meaningful sentencing goals; factual information relating to the individual characteristics and needs of the particular defendant are often never developed; and a sense of purposelessness and lack of control pervades the entire process. This is a high price.

Statement of these areas of concern suggests possible remedies designed to encourage the early development and availability of facts concerning the offense and the offender, the candid exchange of attitudes between the parties, and perhaps even the closer and earlier involvement of the judge in the process, i.e., a sort of preplea conference.

Negotiation is not solely a matter of bazaar bargaining. It also involves the narrowing down of areas of disagreement, the recommendation and exploration of alternative courses of action, and the exchange of information, ideas, and insights. Such a process should result in greater disclosure of relevant information than is presently the case. The scheduling of a conference prior to the entry of a guilty plea would eliminate some of the factors discussed above which at present disable the judge from exercising a degree of control. And, it may be hoped, the participation of the judge might direct discussion along more meaningful lines.

Judicial participation is, of course, no panacea. Judges, too, may misdirect their attention to bargaining over the number of counts and years. The earlier use of presentence investigations should also be encouraged. The judge might order such an investigation after the hearing in order to confirm the facts developed and represented at the hearing. Or, the prosecutor and defense counsel might be authorized to request such an investigation before the conference to serve as a basis for discussions.[27]

The suggestion of greater judicial involvement in the process undoubtedly raises some fears.[28] The principal objections relate to the risk that the defendant may be pressured into pleading guilty because of the impression that he will not receive a fair trial if he rejects the judge's recommended disposition.[29] But this cause for concern can be eliminated

[27] Probation investigations are frequently conducted prior to adjudication in juvenile delinquency cases. Under this proposal, a preadjudication investigation would be held only upon the defendant's consent.

[28] See, e.g., *United States* ex rel. *Elksnis* v. *Gilligan*, 256 F. Supp. 244 (S.D.N.Y. 1966).

[29] See Comment, 32 U. CHI. L. REV. 167, 180-83 (1964); Note, *Guilty Plea Bargaining—Compromises by Prosecutors to Secure Guilty Pleas*, 112 U. PA. L. REV. 865, 891-92 (1964).

by requiring that if the defendant rejects the judge's proposal, the trial and sentence shall be before a different judge, a particularly feasible solution in metropolitan courts where the bulk of plea bargaining takes place. Scheduling the trial before a different judge would also eliminate any prejudice that could otherwise result from the judge's reading the probation report and participating in the preplea conference.

It would be a mistake to deny the judge any role in the process of negotiations, particularly since his power of subsequent review seems at present ineffective. It is not contemplated that such a conference would be required for all cases or even ordinarily called at the judge's initiative. Rather, the parties would call such a conference usually after they have reached agreement. In cases in which defense counsel and the prosecutor are agreed upon a disposition, no harm can come from allowing the judge to review their decision before the guilty plea is entered. Such a review may serve to bring up for consideration matters that would otherwise have been ignored by the parties. At worst, the judge will rubber-stamp their agreement.

Even when there is disagreement, a conference might be held if the parties think it could be useful and indicate a desire for it. In such instances, the judge's role in eliciting the relevant facts is likely to be somewhat lessened. Since counsel disagree, each, or at least defense counsel, is likely to adduce all the facts he can in favor of the disposition he is seeking. Such a hearing can be a very real adversary proceeding. Here, too, as in any adversary proceeding, the judge should be alert to elicit any new facts counsel may have ignored, to make use of probation office facilities for investigation if they have not as yet been called upon to open up possible new avenues for exploration, and to offer additional insights into the case. He may be sufficiently persuaded to bring his prestige to the support of one of the parties' views. Such a development could further encourage the use of probation as a sentencing alternative.

The core problem seems to be whether judges can participate in such a process without becoming quasi-prosecutors.[30] What will happen if, notwithstanding his desire to "settle" the case, the judge agrees with the prosecutor's view as to what is an appropriate disposition of the case? Can defense counsel maintain their independence, or might some lawyers feel themselves under pressure to go along with the judge, lest they develop a reputation for being obstructive and damage their position for future clients? When somewhat similar objections were raised against the establishment of public defender offices, they were rejected. And, it should be noted, pressures to cooperate with the judge usually weigh far more heavily upon the prosecutor than upon the defense. If thought necessary, one might require that such a conference be held only at the defense's initiative.

Moreover, the availability of a record of the proceeding should provide added protection. While it would probably be difficult to control

---

[30] See, e.g., *United States* v. *Tateo*, 214 F. Supp. 560 (S.D.N.Y. 1963).

the less formal conference that would follow upon agreement between the parties, the more formal adversary hearing that would follow upon disagreement could and should be entirely "on the record."

Even in the best of worlds, however, negotiation involves some give and take, some compromise. Would it tarnish the image of the law and of the judge to concern him in a procedure that involves compromise? It is no easier to answer this question than those that preceded it. But it may properly be suggested that if there is one area of the law that does not lend itself to the rigidity of either/or, it is sentencing. If we were correct in our suggestion above that adjudication is not always a search for objective truth, the point is all the more valid with respect to disposition, and our search for meaningfulness must be directed not so much to the result as to the process of decision making.

The answers to the above questions are far from clear. They are problematic. Still, the suggestions for new directions seem to be worth careful experimentation. When the parties agree on a disposition, the emphasis should be on improved early factfinding, largely through the probation service, with some greater measure of judicial control. Where there is disagreement, there should be available, perhaps only at defendant's option, opportunity for argument and conference with the judge before a plea is entered.

VII. THE ROLE OF DEFENSE COUNSEL

It is likely that the key participant in any scheme of negotiated pleas would be defense counsel. I suggested earlier that defense counsel typically take a narrow view of their role in representing their clients: to do their best within honorable means to secure an acquittal and to do their equal best after conviction to obtain for the client as "light" a term as possible. The implications of a lawyer's role as counselor are ignored.

This is not the place to explore the possibilities of altering that professional self-image. But it is appropriate to suggest, at least, that it is particularly timely now as a role is being found for the lawyer at more and more stages of the total criminal process that new thought be given to the nature of that role. Is it also the lawyer's function to suggest to his client his need of and the availability of correctional devices which may aid him? Is it his duty to the client to get the client to understand himself better, to advise him that there are procedures and techniques available today for such indepth study in many cases? Should he advise his client that the development of such information and the formulation of a correctional program are more in his long-term interest than the year less in jail he can probably get from hard bargaining?

This is not to suggest, of course, that the ultimate decision as to which course to pursue is to be the lawyer's. Decisions in issues of such moment and consequence must under our system remain in the hands of the defendant.[31] The question is whether it is counsel's duty to explore these issues with his client and perhaps even advise his client which course the lawyer thinks he ought to follow.

Implicit in the foregoing is the requirement that counsel have a thorough understanding of correctional theories and practices—their successes and failures, be trained in the understanding of human behavior so that he may identify the sources of his client's difficulties, and be familiar with the public and private agencies to which the client may be referred for more professional assistance. Such professional skills are vital to the lawyer even today, when he plays a more limited role. Yet it is the rare criminal lawyer who has any real grasp of the correctional aspects of the criminal process. This should be an area of concern to the bar and the law schools in the training of future lawyers.[32]

SOME CONCLUDING OBSERVATIONS

In a very significant sense, the problems involved in the plea bargaining process reflect the context in which it arises, the broader sentencing process. The absence of "legal standards to govern the exercise of individualized correction,"[33] both procedural and substantive, the subjectivism and unreviewability of most sentencing decisions, and the failure to articulate goals beyond the most general and unhelpful are not only attributes of plea bargaining but are endemic to the entire peno-correctional process. It is precisely because of this ambiguity in the total process that it lends itself to the kind of manipulation described above.

The ultimate answers to the problems outlined in this paper cannot come from a mere tinkering with the process of negotiations but must be sought in improvement of the total process. One line of inquiry could be directed toward the development of standards which could serve as frames of reference for individual cases. More precise factfinding might be another approach. Adjudication is, of course, a form of factfinding directed to correctional decision making, but the definitional elements of a given crime represent the minimally relevant facts. They are in a sense jurisdictional facts designed at best merely to indicate generally that the case is appropriate to the correctional process. But they do not carry us very far along that process. A listing of facts deemed relevant to the determination of an appropriate sentence for various crimes[34] would provide an agenda or reference points for argument and decision, and

---

[31] Cf. *Brookhart* v. *Janis*, 384 U.S. 1, 7–8 (1966).

[32] Cf. the observations of Professor Newman, *Functions of the Police, Prosecutor, Court Worker, Defense Counsel, Judge in Aiding Juvenile Justice*, 13 JUV. CT. JUDGES J. 6, 11–12 (1962).

[33] Kadish, *supra* note 21, at 828.

[34] See, e.g., MODEL PENAL CODE §§ 7.01-.04, 210.6(3), (4) (Proposed Official Draft 1962).

would provide a basis for review. Such a listing might serve as a sort of checklist in negotiated pleas to direct the negotiations along more desired lines.

At the same time attention must be given to the development of new types of correctional programs so that defendant and his counsel might themselves become interested in seeking correction of the defendant's problems rather than merely getting as light a sentence as possible. Exploration of these suggestions is, of course, beyond the scope of this paper. But it is important to stress the point at which the two groups meet and to suggest the broader context in which solutions must be sought.

CRIMINAL JUSTICE AND THE NEGOTIATED PLEA

KENNETH KIPNIS

In recent years it has become apparent to many that, in practice, the criminal justice system in the United States does not operate as we thought it did. The conviction secured through jury trial, so familiar in countless novels, films, and television programs, is beginning to be seen as the aberration it has become. What has replaced the jury's verdict is the negotiated plea. In these "plea bargains" the defendant agrees to plead guilty in exchange for discretionary consideration on the part of the state. Generally, this consideration amounts to some kind of assurance of a minimal sentence. The well-publicized convictions of Spiro Agnew and Clifford Irving were secured through such plea bargains. In 1974 in New York City, 80 percent of all felony cases were settled as misdemeanors through plea bargains.[1] Only 2 percent of all felony arrests resulted in a trial.[2] It is at present a commonplace that plea bargaining could not be eliminated without substantial alterations in our criminal justice system.

Plea bargaining involves negotiations between the defendant (through an attorney in the standard case) and the prosecutor as to the

From *Ethics* 86 (1976): 93–106. © 1976 by the University of Chicago. Reprinted by permission of the publisher, the University of Chicago Press.

[1] Marcia Chambers, "80% of City Felony Cases Settled by Plea Bargaining," *New York Times* (February 11, 1975), p. 1.

[2] Tom Goldstein, "Backlog of Felonies Rose Sharply Here Despite Court Drive," *New York Times* (February 12, 1975), p. 1.

conditions under which the defendant will enter a guilty plea.[3] Both sides have bargaining power in these negotiations. The prosecutor is ordinarily burdened with cases and does not have the wherewithal to bring more than a fraction of them to trial. Often there is not sufficient evidence to ensure a jury's conviction. Most important, the prosecutor is typically under administrative and political pressure to dispose of cases and to secure convictions as efficiently as possible. If the defendant exercises the constitutional right to a jury trial, the prosecutor must decide whether to drop the charges entirely or to expend scarce resources to bring the case to trial. Since neither prospect is attractive, prosecutors typically exercise their broad discretion to induce defendants to waive trial and to plead guilty.

From the defendant's point of view, such prosecutorial discretion has two aspects: it darkens the prospect of going to trial as it brightens the prospect of pleading guilty. Before negotiating, a prosecutor may improve his bargaining position by "overcharging" defendants[4] or by developing a reputation for severity in the sentences he recommends to judges. Such steps greatly increase the punishment that the defendant must expect if convicted at trial. On the other hand, the state may offer to reduce or to drop some charges, or to recommend leniency to the judge if the defendant agrees to plead guilty. These steps minimize the punishment that will result from a guilty plea. Though the exercise of prosecutorial discretion to secure pleas of guilty may differ somewhat in certain jurisdictions and in particular cases, the broad outlines are as described.

Of course a defendant can always reject any offer of concessions and challenge the state to prove its case. A skilled defense attorney can do much to force the prosecutor to expend resources in bringing a case to trial.[5] But the trial route is rarely taken by defendants. Apart from prosecutorial pressure, other factors may contribute to a defendant's willingness to plead guilty: feelings of guilt which may or may not be connected with the charged crime; the discomforts of the pretrial lockup as against the comparatively better facilities of a penitentiary; the costs of going to trial as against the often cheaper option of consenting to a plea; a willingness or unwillingness to lie; and the delays which are almost always present in awaiting trial, delays which the defendant may

[3] Often the judge will play an important role in these discussions, being called upon, for example, to indicate a willingness to go along with a bargain involving a reduction in sentence. A crowded calendar will make the bench an interested party.

[4] In California, for example, armed robbers are technically guilty of kidnapping if they point a gun at their victim and tell him to back up. Thus, beyond the charge of armed robbery, they may face a charge of kidnapping which will be dropped upon entry of a guilty plea (see Albert W. Alschuler, "The Prosecutor's Role in Plea Bargaining," *University of Chicago Law Review* 36 [Fall 1968]: 88).

[5] Arthur Rosett, "The Negotiated Guilty Plea," *Annals of the American Academy of Political and Social Science* 374 (November 1967): 72.

sit out in jail in a kind of preconviction imprisonment which may not be credited to a postconviction sentence. It is not surprising that the right to a trial by jury is rarely exercised.

If one examines the statistics published annually by the Administrative Office of the U.S. Courts,[6] one can appreciate both the size of the concessions gained by agreeing to plead guilty and (what is the same thing) the size of the additional burdens imposed upon those convicted without so agreeing. According to the 1970 report, among all convicted defendants, those pleading guilty at arraignment received average sentences of probation and/or under one year of imprisonment. Those going to a jury trial received average sentences of three to four years in prison.[7] If one looks just at those convicted of Marijuana Tax Act violations with no prior record, one finds that those pleading guilty at arraignment received average sentences of probation and/or six months or less of imprisonment while those going to trial received average sentences more than eight times as severe: four to five years in prison.[8] Among all Marijuana Tax Act convictions, defendants pleading guilty at the outset had a 76 percent chance of being let off without imprisonment, while those who had gone to trial had only an 11 percent chance.[9] These last two sets of figures do not reflect advantages gained by charge reduction, nor do they reflect advantages gained by electing a bench trial as opposed to a jury trial. What these figures do suggest is that the sentences given to convicted defendants who have exercised their constitutional right to trial are many times as severe as the sentences given to those who do not. In *United States* v. *Wiley* [10] Chief Judge Campbell laid to rest any tendency to conjecture that these discrepancies in sentences might have explanations not involving plea bargains.

> . . . I believe, and it is generally accepted by trial judges throughout the United States, that it is entirely proper and logical to grant some defendants some degree of leniency in exchange for a plea of guilty. If then, a trial judge grants leniency in exchange for a plea of guilty, it follows, as the reverse side of the same coin, that he must necessarily forego leniency, generally speaking, where the defendant stands trial and is found guilty.
>
> . . . I might make general reference to a "standing policy" not to consider probation where a defendant stands trial even though I do not in fact strictly adhere to such a policy.

No deliberative body ever decided that we would have a system in which the disposition of criminal cases is typically the result of nego-

---

[6] Administrative Office of the United States Courts, *Federal Offenders in the United States District Courts* (Washington, D.C., 1970).

[7] Ibid., pp. 57, 59.

[8] Ibid., pp. 57, 65.

[9] Ibid., p. 60.

[10] 184 F. Supp. 679 (N.D. Ill. 1960).

tiations between the prosecutor and the defendant's attorney on the conditions under which the defendant would waive trial and plead guilty to a mutually acceptable charge. No legislature ever voted to adopt a procedure in which defendants who are convicted after trial typically receive sentences far greater than those received by defendants charged with similar offenses but pleading guilty. The practice of plea bargaining has evolved in the unregulated interstices of our criminal justice system. Its development has not gone unnoticed. There is now a substantial literature on the legality and propriety of plea bargaining.[11] But though philosophers do not often treat issues arising in the area of criminal procedure, there are problems here that cry for our attention. In the preceding pages I have been concerned to sketch the institution of plea bargaining. In what follows I will raise some serious questions about it that should concern us. I will first discuss generally the intrinsic fairness of plea bargains and then, in the final section, I will examine critically the place of such bargains in the criminal justice system.

I

As one goes through the literature on plea bargaining one gets the impression that market forces are at work in this unlikely context. The terms "bargain" and "negotiation" suggest this. One can see the law of supply and demand operating in that, other things being equal, if there are too many defendants who want to go to trial, prosecutors will have to concede more in order to get the guilty pleas that they need to clear their case load. And if the number of prosecutors and courts goes up, prosecutors will be able to concede less. Against this background it is not surprising to find one commentator noting: [12] "In some places a 'going rate' is established under which a given charge will automatically be broken down to a given lesser offense with the recommendation of a given lesser sentence." Prosecutors, like retailers before them, have begun to appreciate the efficiency of the fixed-price approach.

The plea bargain in the economy of criminal justice has many of the important features of the contract in commercial transactions. In

---

[11] Some of the most significant treatments of plea bargaining are Alschuler; Arnold Enker, "Perspectives on Plea Bargaining," in *Task Force Report: The Courts*, by the President's Commission on Law Enforcement and Administration of Justice (Washington, D.C., 1967), p. 108; "The Unconstitutionality of Plea Bargaining," *Harvard Law Review* 83 (April 1970): 1387; Donald J. Newman, *Conviction: The Determination of Guilt or Innocence without Trial* (Boston, 1966); Abraham S. Blumberg, *Criminal Justice* (Chicago, 1967); National Advisory Commission on Criminal Justice Standards and Goals, *Courts* (Washington, D.C., 1973); American Bar Association Project on Minimum Standards for Criminal Justice, *Standards Relating to Pleas of Guilty, Approved Draft* (New York, 1968).

[12] Rosett, p. 71.

both institutions offers are made and accepted, entitlements are given up and obtained, and the notion of an exchange, ideally a fair one, is present to both parties. Indeed one detects something of the color of consumer protection law in a few of the decisions on plea bargaining. In *Bailey* v. *MacDougal* [13] the court held that "a guilty plea cannot be accepted unless the defendant understands its consequences." And in *Santo Bello* v. *New York* [14] the court secured a defendant's entitlement to a prosecutorial concession when a second prosecutor replaced the one who had made the promise. Rule 11 of the Federal Rules of Criminal Procedure (effective August 1, 1975) requires that "if a plea agreement has been reached by the parties which contemplates entry of a plea of guilty or nolo contendere in the expectation that a specific sentence will be imposed or that other charges before the court will be dismissed, the court shall require the disclosure of the agreement in open court at the time the plea is offered." These procedures all have analogues in contract law. Though plea bargains may not be seen as contracts by the parties, agreements like them are the stuff of contract case law. While I will not argue that plea bargains are contracts (or even that they should be treated as such), I do think it proper to look to contract law for help in evaluating the justice of such agreements.

The law of contracts serves to give legal effect to certain bargain-promises. In particular, it specifies conditions that must be satisfied by bargain-promises before the law will recognize and enforce them as contracts. As an example, we could look at that part of the law of contracts which treats duress. Where one party wrongfully compels another to consent to the terms of an agreement the resulting bargain has no legal effect. Dan B. Dobbs, a commentator on the law in this area, describes the elements of duress as follows: "The defendant's act must be wrongful in some attenuated sense; it must operate coercively upon the will of the plaintiff, judged subjectively, and the plaintiff must have no adequate remedy to avoid the coercion except to give in. . . . The earlier requirement that the coercion must have been the kind that would coerce a reasonable man, or even a brave one, is now generally dispensed with, and it is enough if it in fact coerced a spineless plaintiff." [15] Coercion is not the same as fraud, nor is it confined to cases in which a defendant is physically compelled to assent. In Dobbs' words: "The victim of duress knows the facts but is forced by hard choices to act against his will." The paradigm case of duress is the agreement made at gunpoint. Facing a mortal threat, one readily agrees to hand over the cash. But despite such consent, the rules of duress work to void the effects of such agreements. There is no legal obligation to hand over the cash and, having given it over, entitlement to the money is not lost.

13 392 F.2d 155 (1968).

14 404 U.S. 257 (1971).

15 Dan B. Dobbs, *Handbook on the Law of Remedies* (Saint Paul, 1973), p. 658.

The gunman has no legal right to retain possession even if he adheres to his end of the bargain and scraps his murderous plans.

Judges have long been required to see to it that guilty pleas are entered voluntarily. And one would expect that, if duress is present in the plea-bargaining situation, then, just as the handing over of cash to the gunman is void of legal effect (as far as entitlement to the money is concerned), so no legal consequences should flow from the plea of guilty which is the product of duress. However, Rule 11 of the Federal Rules of Criminal Procedure requires the court to insure that a plea of guilty (or nolo contendere) is voluntary by "addressing the defendant personally in open court, determining that the plea is voluntary and not the result of force or promises *apart from a plea agreement*" (emphasis added). In two important cases (*North Carolina* v. *Alford* and *Brady* v. *United States*) [16] defendants agreed to plead guilty in order to avoid probable death sentences. Both accepted very long prison sentences. In both cases the Supreme Court decided that guilty pleas so entered were voluntary (though Brennan, Douglas, and Marshall dissented). In his dissent in *Alford,* Brennan writes: ". . . the facts set out in the majority opinion demonstrate that Alford was 'so gripped by fear of the death penalty' that his decision to plead guilty was not voluntary but was the 'product of duress as much so as choice reflecting physical constraint.' " In footnote 2 of the *Alford* opinion, the Court sets out the defendant's testimony given at the time of the entry of his plea of guilty before the trial court. That testimony deserves examination: "I pleaded guilty on second degree murder because they said there is too much evidence, but I ain't shot no man, but I take the fault for the other man. We never had an argument in our life and I just pleaded guilty because they said if I didn't they would gas me for it, and that is all." The rule to be followed in such cases is set out in *Brady:* "A plea of guilty entered by one fully aware of the direct consequences, including the actual value of any commitments made to him by the court, prosecutor or his own counsel, must stand unless induced by threats (or promises to discontinue improper harassment), misrepresentation (including unfilled or unfillable promises), or perhaps by promises that are by their very nature improper as having no proper relationship to the prosecutor's business (e.g. bribes)." Case law and the Federal Rules both hold that the standard exercise of prosecutorial discretion in order to secure a plea of guilty cannot be used to prove that such a plea is involuntary. Even where the defendant enters a guilty plea in order to avert his death at the hands of the state, as in *Alford,* the Court has not seen involuntariness. Nevertheless, it may be true that some guilty pleas are involuntary in virtue of prosecutorial inducement considered proper by the Supreme Court.

Regarding the elements of duress, let us compare the gunman situation with an example of plea bargaining in order to examine the volun-

[16] 400 U.S. 25 (1970) and 397 U.S. 742 (1970), respectively.

tariness of the latter. Albert W. Alschuler, author of one of the most thorough studies of plea bargaining, describes an actual case:

> San Francisco defense attorney Benjamin M. Davis recently represented a man charged with kidnapping and forcible rape. The defendant was innocent, Davis says, and after investigating the case Davis was confident of an acquittal. The prosecutor, who seems to have shared the defense attorney's opinion on this point, offered to permit a guilty plea to simple battery. Conviction on this charge would not have led to a greater sentence than thirty days' imprisonment, and there was every likelihood that the defendant would be granted probation. When Davis informed his client of this offer, he emphasized that conviction at trial seemed highly improbable. The defendant's reply was simple: "I can't take the chance." [17]

Both the gunman and the prosecutor require persons to make hard choices between a very certain smaller imposition and an uncertain greater imposition. In the gunman situation I must choose between the very certain loss of my money and the difficult-to-assess probability that my assailant is willing and able to kill me if I resist. As a defendant I am forced to choose between a very certain smaller punishment and a substantially greater punishment with a difficult-to-assess probability. As the size of the certain smaller imposition comes down and as the magnitude and probability of the larger imposition increases, it becomes more and more reasonable to choose the former. This is what seems to be occurring in Alschuler's example: "Davis reports that he is uncomfortable when he permits innocent defendants to plead guilty; but in this case it would have been playing God to stand in the defendant's way. The attorney's assessment of the outcome at trial can always be wrong, and it is hard to tell a defendant that 'professional ethics' require a course that may ruin his life." Davis's client must decide whether to accept a very certain, very minor punishment or to chance a ruined life. Of course the gunman's victim can try to overpower his assailant and the defendant can attempt to clear himself at trial. But the same considerations that will drive reasonable people to give in to the gunman compel one to accept the prosecutor's offer. Applying the second and third elements of duress, one can see that, like the gunman's acts, the acts of the prosecutor can "operate coercively upon the will of the plaintiff, judged subjectively," and both the gunman's victim and the defendant may "have no adequate remedy to avoid the coercion except to give in." In both cases reasonable persons might well conclude (after considering the gunman's lethal weapon or the gas chamber) "I can't take the chance." A spineless person would not need to deliberate.

That prosecutors could exercise such duress apparently seemed plain to the authors of the *Restatement of Contracts*.[18] Their summariza-

---

[17] Alschuler, p. 61.
[18] American Law Institute, *Restatement of Contracts* (Saint Paul, 1933), p. 652.

tion of the law of contracts, adopted in 1932 by the American Law Institute, contained the following: "A threat of criminal prosecution . . . ordinarily is a threat of imprisonment and also . . . a threat of bringing disgrace upon the accused. Threats of this sort may be of such compelling force that acts done under their influence are coerced, and the better foundation there is for the prosecution, the greater is the coercion." While it is always true that even in the most desperate circumstances persons are free to reject the terms offered and risk the consequences, as Morris Raphael Cohen put it: "such choice is surely the very opposite of what men value as freedom." [19]

Indeed if one had to choose between being in the position of Davis's client and facing a fair-minded gunman, I think that it would be reasonable to prefer the latter. While the law permits one to recover money upon adverting to the forced choice of the gunman, it does not permit one to retract a guilty plea upon adverting to the forced choice of the prosecutor. This is the impact of *Brady* and Rule 11.

Note that the duress is not eliminated by providing defendants with counsel. While a good attorney may get better concessions and may help in the evaluation of options, in the end the defendant will still have to decide whether to settle for the smaller penalty or to risk a much heavier sentence. One does not eliminate the injustice in the gunman situation by providing victims with better advice.

Nor does it help matters to insure that promises of prosecutorial concessions are kept. The gunman who violates his part of the bargain—murdering his victims after they give over their money—has compounded his wrongdoing. Reputations for righteousness are not established by honoring such bargains.

Nor is it legitimate to distinguish the prosecutor from the gunman by saying that, while the gunman is threatening harm unless you hand over the cash, the prosecutor is merely promising benefits if you enter a guilty plea. For, in the proper context, threats and promises may be intertranslatable. Brandishing his pistol, the holdup man may promise to leave me unharmed if I hand over the cash. Similarly, the prosecutor may threaten to "throw the book" at me if I do not plead guilty to a lesser charge. In the proper context, one may be compelled to act by either form of words.

One might argue that not all "hard choices" are examples of duress. A doctor could offer to sell vital treatment for a large sum. After the patient has been cured it will hardly do for her to claim that she has been the victim of duress. The doctor may have forced the patient to choose between a certain financial loss and the risk of death. But surely doctors are not like gunmen.

Two important points need to be made in response to this objection. First, the doctor is not, one assumes, responsible for the diseased

[19] Morris Raphael Cohen, "The Basis of Contract," in *Law and the Social Order* (New York, 1933), p. 86.

condition of the patient. The patient would be facing death even if she had never met the doctor. But this is not true in the case of the gunman, where both impositions are his work. And in this respect the prosecutor offering a plea bargain in a criminal case is like the gunman rather than like the doctor. For the state forces a choice between adverse consequences that it imposes. And, of course, one cannot say that in the defendant's wrongdoing he has brought his dreadful dilemma upon himself. To do so would be to ignore the good reasons there are for the presumption of innocence in dispositive criminal proceedings.

Second, our laws do not prohibit doctors from applying their healing skills to maximize their own wealth. They are free to contract to perform services in return for a fee. But our laws do severely restrict the state in its prosecution of criminal defendants. Those who framed our constitution were well aware of the great potential for abuse that the criminal law affords. Much of the Constitution (especially the Bill of Rights) checks the activity of the state in this area. In particular, the Fifth Amendment provides that no person "shall be compelled in any criminal case to be a witness against himself." If I am right in judging that defendants like Alford and Davis's client do not act freely in pleading guilty to the facts of their cases, that the forced choice of the prosecutor may be as coercive as the forced choice of the gunman, that a defendant may be compelled to speak against himself (or herself) by a prosecutor's discretion inducing him to plead guilty, then, given the apparent constitutional prohibition of such compulsion, the prosecutor acts wrongfully in compelling such pleas. And in this manner it may be that the last element of duress, wrongfulness, can be established. But it is not my purpose here to establish the unconstitutionality of plea bargaining, for it is not necessary to reach to unconstitutionality to grasp the wrongfulness of that institution. One need only reflect upon what justice amounts to in our system of criminal law. This is the task I will take up in the final section of this paper.

II

Not too long ago plea bargaining was an officially prohibited practice. Court procedures were followed to ensure that no concessions had been given to defendants in exchange for guilty pleas. But gradually it became widely known that these procedures had become charades of perjury, shysterism, and bad faith involving judges, prosecutors, defense attorneys and defendants. This was scandalous. But rather than cleaning up the practice in order to square it with the rules, the rules were changed in order to bring them in line with the practice. There was a time when it apparently seemed plain that the old rules were the right rules. One finds in the *Restatement of Contracts:* [20] ". . . even if the

[20] American Law Institute, p. 652.

accused is guilty and the process valid, so that as against the State the imprisonment is lawful, it is a wrongful means of inducing the accused to enter into a transaction. To overcome the will of another for the prosecutor's advantage is *an abuse of the criminal law which was made for another purpose"* (emphasis added). The authors of the *Restatement* do not tell us what they were thinking when they spoke of the purpose of the criminal law. Nonetheless it is instructive to conjecture and to inquire along the lines suggested by the *Restatement*.

Without going deeply into detail, I believe that it can be asserted without controversy that the liberal-democratic approach to criminal justice—and in particular the American criminal justice system—is an institutionalization of two principles. The first principle refers to the intrinsic point of systems of criminal justice.

> A. Those (and only those) individuals who are clearly guilty of certain serious specified wrongdoings deserve an officially administered punishment which is proportional to their wrongdoing.

In the United States it is possible to see this principle underlying the activities of legislators specifying and grading wrongdoings which are serious enough to warrant criminalization and, further, determining the range of punishment appropriate to each offense; the activities of policemen and prosecutors bringing to trial those who are suspected of having committed such wrongdoings; the activities of jurors determining if defendants are guilty beyond a reasonable doubt; the activities of defense attorneys insuring that relevant facts in defendants' favor are brought out at trial; the activities of judges seeing to it that proceedings are fair and that those who are convicted receive the punishment they deserve; and the activities of probation officers, parole officers, and prison personnel executing the sentences of the courts. All of these people play a part in bringing the guilty to justice.

But in liberal-democratic societies not everything is done to accomplish this end. A second principle makes reference to the limits placed upon the power of the state to identify and punish the guilty.

> B. Certain basic liberties shall not be violated in bringing the guilty to justice.

This second principle can be seen to underlie the constellation of constitutional checks on the activities of virtually every person playing a role in the administration of the criminal justice system.

Each of these principles is related to a distinctive type of injustice that can occur in the context of criminal law. An injustice can occur in the outcome of the criminal justice procedure. That is, an innocent defendant may be convicted and punished, or a guilty defendant may be acquitted or, if convicted, he or she may receive more or less punishment than is deserved. Because these injustices occur in the meting out of punishment to defendants who are being processed by the system, we can refer to them as internal injustices. They are violations of the first principle. On the other hand, there is a type of injustice which occurs when basic liberties are violated in the operation of the criminal justice system. It may be true that Star Chamber proceedings, torture, hostages, bills of attainder, dragnet arrests, unchecked searches, *ex post facto* laws, unlimited invasions of privacy, and an arsenal of other measures could be employed to bring more of the guilty to justice. But these steps lead to a dystopia where our most terrifying nightmares can come true. However we limit the activity of the criminal justice system in the interest of basic liberty, that limit can be overstepped. We can call such infringements upon basic liberties external injustices. They are violations of the second principle. If, for example, what I have suggested in the previous section is correct, then plea bargaining can bring about an external injustice with respect to a basic liberty secured by the Fifth Amendment. The remainder of this section will be concerned with internal injustice or violations of the first principle.

It is necessary to draw a further distinction between aberrational and systemic injustice. It may very well be that in the best criminal justice system that we are capable of devising human limitations will result in some aberrational injustice. Judges, jurors, lawyers, and legislators with the best of intentions may make errors in judgment that result in mistakes in the administration of punishment. But despite the knowledge that an unknown percentage of all dispositions of criminal cases are, to some extent, miscarriages of justice, it may still be reasonable to believe that a certain system of criminal justice is well calculated to avoid such results within the limits referred to by the second principle.[21] We can refer to these incorrect outcomes of a sound system of criminal justice as instances of aberrational injustice. In contrast, instances of systemic injustice are those that result from structural flaws in the criminal justice system itself. Here incorrect outcomes in the operations of the system are not the result of human error. Rather, the system itself is not well calculated to avoid injustice. What would be instances of abberrational injustice in a sound system are not aberrations in an unsound system: they are a standard result.

This distinction has an analogy in the area of quality control. Two vials of antibiotic may be equally contaminated. But depending upon the process used to produce each, the contamination may be aberrational or systemic. The first sample may come from a factory where every conceivable step is taken to insure that such contamination will not take place. The second vial may come from a company which uses a cheap manufacturing process offering no protection against contamination. There is an element of tragedy if death results when all possible pre-

---

[21] My discussion here owes much to John Rawls' treatment of "imperfect procedural justice" in his *A Theory of Justice* (Cambridge, 1971), pp. 85–86.

cautions have been taken: there just are limits to human capability at our present level of understanding. But where vital precautions are dropped in the name of expediency, the contamination that results is much more serious if only because we knew it would take place and we knew what could be done to prevent it. While we have every reason to believe that the first sample is pure, we have no reason to believe that the second sample is uncontaminated. Indeed, one cannot call the latter contamination accidental as one can in the first case. It would be more correct to call it an accident if contamination did not take place in the total absence of precaution.

Likewise, systemic injustice in the context of criminal law is a much more serious matter than aberrational injustice. It should not be forgotten that the criminal sanction is the most severe imposition that the state can visit upon one of its citizens. While it is possible to tolerate occasional error in a sound system, systematic carelessness in the administration of punishment is negligence of the highest order.

With this framework in mind, let us look at a particular instance of plea bargaining recently described by a legal aid defense attorney.[22] Ted Alston has been charged with armed robbery. Let us assume that persons who have committed armed robbery (in the way Alston is accused of having committed it) deserve five to seven years of prison. Alston's attorney sets out the options for him: "I told Alston it was possible, perhaps even probable, that if he went to trial he would be convicted and get a prison term of perhaps five to seven years. On the other hand, if he agreed to plead guilty to a low-grade felony, he would get a probationary sentence and not go to prison. The choice was his." Let us assume that Alston accepts the terms of the bargain and pleads guilty to a lesser offense. If Alston did commit the armed robbery, there is a violation of the first principle in that he receives far less punishment than he deserves. On the other hand, if Alston did not commit the armed robbery, there is still a violation of the first principle in that he is both convicted of and punished for a crime that he did not commit, a crime that no one seriously believes to be his distinctive wrongdoing. It is of course possible that while Alston did not commit the armed robbery, he did commit the lesser offense. But though justice would be done here, it would be an accident. Such a serendipitous result is a certain sign that what we have here is systemic injustice.

If we assume that legislatures approximate the correct range of punishment for each offense, that judges fairly sentence those who are convicted by juries, and that prosecutors reasonably charge defendants, then, barring accidents, justice will *never* be the outcome of the plea-bargaining procedure: the defendant who "cops a plea" will never receive the punishment which is deserved. Of course legislatures can set punishments too high, judges can oversentence those who are convicted by

22 Robert Hermann, "The Case of the Jamaican Accent," *New York Times Magazine* (December 1, 1974), p. 93 (© The *New York Times* Company).

juries, and prosecutors can overcharge defendants. In these cases the guilty can receive the punishment they deserve through plea bargaining. But in these cases we compensate for one injustice by introducing others that unfairly jeopardize the innocent and those that demand trials.

In contrast to plea bargaining, the disposition of criminal cases by jury trial seems well calculated to avoid internal injustices even if these may sometimes occur. Where participants take their responsibilities seriously we have good reason to believe that the outcome is just, even when this may not be so. In contrast, with plea bargaining we have no reason to believe that the outcome is just even when it is.

I think that the appeal that plea bargaining has is rooted in our attitude toward bargains in general. Where both parties are satisfied with the terms of an agreement, it is improper to interfere. Generally speaking, prosecutors and defendants are pleased with the advantages they gain by negotiating a plea. And courts, which gain as well, are reluctant to vacate negotiated pleas where only "proper" inducements have been applied and where promises have been understood and kept. Such judicial neutrality may be commendable where entitlements are being exchanged. But the criminal justice system is not such a context. Rather it is one in which persons are justly given, not what they have bargained for, but what they deserve, irrespective of their bargaining position.

To appreciate this, let us consider another context in which desert plays a familiar role; the assignment of grades in an academic setting. Imagine a "grade bargain" negotiated between a grade-conscious student and a harried instructor. A term paper has been submitted and, after glancing at the first page, the instructor says that if he were to read the paper carefully, applying his usually rigid standards, he would probably decide to give the paper a grade of D. But if the student were to waive his right to a careful reading and conscientious critique, the instructor would agree to a grade of B. The grade-point average being more important to him than either education or justice in grading, the student happily accepts the B, and the instructor enjoys a reduced workload.

One strains to imagine legislators and administrators commending the practice of grade bargaining because it permits more students to be processed by fewer instructors. Teachers can be freed from the burden of having to read and to criticize every paper. One struggles to envision academicians arguing for grade bargaining, suggesting that a quick assignment of a grade is a more effective influence on the behavior of students, urging that grade bargaining is necessary to the efficient functioning of the schools. There can be no doubt that students who have negotiated a grade are more likely to accept and to understand the verdict of the instructor. Moreover, in recognition of a student's help to the school (by waiving both the reading and the critique), it is proper for the instructor to be lenient. Finally, a quickly assigned grade enables the guidance personnel and the registrar to respond rapidly and appropriately to the student's situation.

What makes all of this laughable is what makes plea bargaining outrageous. For grades, like punishments, should be deserved. Justice in retribution, like justice in grading, does not require that the end result be acceptable to the parties. To reason that because the parties are satisfied the bargain should stand is to be seriously confused. For bargains are out of place in contexts where persons are to receive what they deserve. And the American courtroom, like the American classroom, should be such a context.

In this section, until now I have been attempting to show that plea bargaining is not well calculated to insure that those guilty of wrongdoing will receive the punishment they deserve. But a further point needs to be made. While the conviction of the innocent would be a problem in any system we might devise, it appears to be a greater problem under plea bargaining. With the jury system the guilt of the defendant must be established in an adversary proceeding and it must be established beyond a reasonable doubt to each of twelve jurors. This is very staunch protection against an aberrational conviction. But under plea bargaining the foundation for conviction need only include a factual basis for the plea (in the opinion of the judge) and the guilty plea itself. Considering the coercive nature of the circumstances surrounding the plea, it would be a mistake to attach much reliability to it. Indeed, as we have seen in *Alford*, guilty pleas are acceptable even when accompanied by a denial of guilt. And in a study of 724 defendants who had pleaded guilty, only 13.1 percent admitted guilt to an interviewer, while 51.6 percent asserted their innocence.[23] This leaves only the factual basis for the plea to serve as the foundation for conviction. Now it is one thing to show to a judge that there are facts which support a plea of guilty and quite another to prove to twelve jurors in an adversary proceeding guilt beyond a reasonable doubt. Plea bargaining substantially erodes the standards for guilt and it is reasonable to assume that the sloppier we are in establishing guilt, the more likely it is that innocent persons will be convicted. So apart from having no reason whatever to believe that the guilty are receiving the punishment they deserve, we have far less reason to believe that the convicted are guilty in the first place than we would after a trial.

In its coercion of criminal defendants, in its abandonment of desert as the measure of punishment, and in its relaxation of the standards for conviction, plea bargaining falls short of the justice we expect of our legal system. I have no doubt that substantial changes will have to be made if the institution of plea bargaining is to be obliterated or even removed from its central position in the criminal justice system. No doubt we need more courts and more prosecutors. Perhaps ways can be found to streamline the jury trial procedure without sacrificing its virtues.[24] Certainly it would help to decriminalize the host of victimless

[23] Blumberg, p. 91.

[24] John Langbein has suggested that we look to the German legal system to see how this might be done. See his "Controlling Prosecutorial Discretion in Germany," *University of Chicago Law Review* 41 (Spring 1974): 439.

crimes—drunkenness and other drug offenses, illicit sex, gambling, and so on—in order to free resources for dealing with more serious wrong-doings. And perhaps crime itself can be reduced if we begin to attack seriously those social and economic injustices that have for too long sent their victims to our prisons in disproportionate numbers. In any case, if we are to expect our citizenry to respect the law, we must take care to insure that our legal institutions are worthy of that respect. I have tried to show that plea bargaining is not worthy, that we must seek a better way. Bargain justice does not become us.

Notes on Legal Materials

What follows is a brief guide to some of the most important materials that a student may encounter in looking through legal literature. My intention is to give a general sense of what is there and how to find it.

MATERIALS ON LEGAL RESEARCH

Legal research is a subject in itself and a number of books are available which give it the treatment it is due. Among these are *Fundamentals of Legal Research* by Jacobstein and Mersky (Foundation Press, Inc.), *Effective Legal Research* by Price and Bitner (Little, Brown and Company), *Legal Research in a Nutshell* by Morris L. Cohen (West Publishing Co.), *How to Find the Law* by William R. Roalfe (West Publishing Co.), and *A Guide to Legal Research* by Surrency, Feld and Crea (Oceana Publications, Inc.). The standards for legal citation and abbreviation are set out in a booklet entitled *A Uniform System of Citation* which is published and distributed by the Harvard Law Review Association, Gannett House, Cambridge, Massachusetts, 02138.

JUDICIAL OPINIONS

Judicial opinions are the main subject matter in many if not most law school courses and, along with the Constitution and the statutes, they are the primary sources of the law. Seven of these opinions are reprinted in this text. A typical judicial opinion sets out a decision arrived at by articulating rules of law covering the facts of the particular case that has come before the court. Once a court has laid down a rule of law in a particular fact situation, that court and others below it will be bound to adhere to the rule in cases where the facts are substantially similar.

Law students are invariably asked to "brief cases," that is, to summarize legal opinions. The general forms of such briefs differ somewhat from instructor to instructor and, moreover, different interpretations of the same case are not at all uncommon. Indeed, coloring an interpretation of a case is an important part of advocacy. Nevertheless, practice in briefing cases does develop skill in comprehending legal materials and does direct attention to some of the salient considerations that judges take into account. A typical brief would contain answers to the following questions:

1) What *facts* are relevant to the court's decision in the case?
2) What legal *issues* or questions are presented by the facts?
3) What is the *holding* of the court? What rules of law does the case stand for?
4) What is the court's *reasoning*? What justification does the court provide for its action in the case?

CASEBOOKS

These are the basic textbooks used in most law school classes. They consist largely of excerpts of judicial opinions from appellate level cases. (Thousands of these excerpted opinions are analyzed and discussed in the course of a law school education.) Casebooks are occasionally useful in directing one to the most significant opinions in a particular area. Because the law changes constantly some casebooks are updated periodically by means of paperbound supplements.

CASE REPORTS

The complete opinions are to be found in the case reports of which there are many series. The legal profession has its own system of citation which, once understood, permits the easy location of a particular opinion in the thousands of volumes of a law library. Often the same opinion will appear in two or more series. For example, the citation for the Washington Supreme Court opinion in *DeFunis* v. *Odegaard* is 82 Wn. 2d 11, 507 P. 2d 1169 (1973). What this means is that the case was decided in 1973 and the opinion is to be found in the second series of the official Washington Reports in volume 82 on page 11 and also in the Pacific Reporter, second series, in volume 507, on page 1169. Sometimes given with the date is information about the court where the decision was made. The abbreviations for some of the most important series are as follows:

A. 2d	Atlantic Reporter, Second Series
A.L.R.	American Law Reports
Am. Dec.	American Decisions
Atl.	Atlantic Reporter
Cal. Rptr.	California Reporter
F. 2d	Federal Reporter, Second Series
Fed.	Federal Reporter
F. Supp.	Federal Supplement
L. Ed.	Lawyers Edition, U.S. Supreme Court Reports
N.E.	North Eastern Reporter
N.W.	North Western Reporter
N.Y.S. 2d	N.Y. Supplement Reporter, Second Series
Pac.	Pacific Reporter
P. 2d	Pacific Reporter, Second Series
S.E.	South Eastern Reporter
So.	Southern Reporter
Sup. Ct.	Supreme Court Reporter (U.S.)
S.W.	South Western Reporter
U.S.	United States Supreme Court Reports

It is difficult to overstate the amount of primary source material which is generated by judicial opinions. A law library may have tens of thousands of volumes of case reports alone. Not surprisingly, there are several important series of law books—*Shepard's Citations* and the various digests, for example—that mainly serve to direct researchers to the opinions in the various reports that are relevant to certain cases or points of law. The use of these books is explained in the texts cited in the first main section of these notes.

TREATISES AND LEGAL ENCYCLOPEDIAS

Treatises and legal encyclopedias may also be used to direct a researcher to cases. What distinguishes them is that they set out in an expository way the substance of the law. Although all treatises are summaries of the statutory and case law in a particular area, some are interpretative and critical as well. Some are extremely detailed multi-volume treatments: *Williston's Law of Contracts* for example. Many are kept up-to-date by means of supplementary material which is inserted in a pocket at the back of the text and several use a loose-leaf format for the same purpose. Some of the single-volume treatises—those in the Hornbook Series (West Publishing Co.), for example—are especially useful to law students as supplements to casebooks.

Worth mentioning in this context are the course outlines which are prepared for law students. Although these are not at all authoritative and are not used to locate cases, they are sometimes useful in getting the sense of an area of law quickly and conveniently. Gilbert law summaries are a well-known series.

Somewhat similar to treatises are the various Restatements that have been prepared by committees working under the auspices of the American Law Institute. Covering torts, contracts, agency, property and several other topics, they are part of a movement to codify and standardize American law.

Corpus Juris Secundum (C.J.S.), *American Jurisprudence* (Am. Jur.) and *American Jurisprudence* 2d are attempts to state comprehensively the body of American case law. These legal encyclopedias are useful research tools and several have been prepared which cover the laws of particular states. Needless to say, encyclopedias are constantly being updated.

PERIODICALS

There are hundreds of periodicals which specialize in legal matters and hundreds more which often carry articles about law. Of particular importance are the law reviews which are sponsored by law schools and edited by law students working under faculty supervision. The *Index to Legal Periodicals* and the *Index to Periodical Articles Related to Law* are invaluable in gaining access to all of this literature. Articles in periodicals are cited in much the same way as cases. Thus an article at 81 Yale L.J. 980 is to be found in volume 81 of the *Yale Law Journal* on Page 980.

LAW DICTIONARIES

A dictionary of legal terminology is practically indispensable to the novice. *Law Dictionary* by Steven H. Gifis (Barron's Educational Series, 1975) is inexpensive, up-to-date, and adequate for most purposes. *Ballentine's Law Dictionary* edited by William S. Anderson (Lawyers Co-operative Publishing Co., 1969) is probably the most useful one where more complete coverage is required. The most comprehensive guide to the specialized meanings which have been given to terms in judicial opinions is the 46-volume *Words and Phrases*. This is a particularly valuable research tool for work in law and legal philosophy. As with encyclopedias and treatises, it can be used to locate cases.

Glossary of
Legal Terminology

The words defined below are unfamiliar expressions which appear in the course of this textbook and which are not explained in context. Included are definitions which are relevant to the usage in this volume: other meanings are not listed.

AGENT: A person who, by mutual consent, acts for another person who is known as the PRINCIPAL.

APPELLANT: A person commencing a proceeding in a reviewing court in order to have set aside a decision of a lower court. Sometimes called the "plaintiff in error." See APPELLEE.

APPELLEE: A person prevailing in a lower court and seeking, in an appellate proceeding, to have the reviewing court uphold the lower court decision. Sometimes called the "defendant in error." See APPELLANT.

CERTIORARI: An undertaking by a higher court to review a case which has been decided by a lower court.

COMMON LAW: A body of law deriving from the decisions of the courts rather than from legislation.

DEFENDANT: In civil proceedings, the party who is sued; the party responding to the complaint of the PLAINTIFF. In criminal proceedings, the person who is charged with a crime; the "accused."

DICTUM: A statement in the course of a legal opinion which does not bear on the determination of the case.

EX ABUNDANTE CAUTELA: Out of abundant caution.

FELONY: A major criminal offense. See MISDEMEANOR.

FELONY MURDER: A homicide which is first degree murder in virtue of its occurrence in the commission of an independent felony or attempt to commit such a felony. The usual mental elements of first degree murder need not be proved.

INDICTMENT: A formal accusation by a grand jury by which criminal proceedings are commenced. See INFORMATION.

INFORMATION: A formal accusation by a prosecutor by which criminal proceedings are commenced. See INDICTMENT.

LESSEE: One who holds property in virtue of a lease; a tenant. See LESSOR.

LESSOR: One who leases property to another; a landlord. See LESSEE.

MISDEMEANOR: A minor criminal offense. See FELONY.

MOTION IN ARREST OF JUDGMENT: An application to the court to withhold judgment after the verdict because of a defect on the record.

NOLLE PROSEQUI: A formal declaration by the prosecutor that he or she will not further prosecute a particular case.

PARI PASSU: Without preference.

PLAINTIFF: One who initiates a law suit. See DEFENDANT.

PRINCIPAL: One who authorizes another to act on his or her behalf. See AGENT.

REMAND: To send back a case to the original court for further action.

TESTATOR: A person who makes a will.

WRIT OF HABEAS CORPUS: A written order by a higher court challenging the legal authority by which a person is being detained in jail or prison.

Selected Supplementary Readings

I. STRICT LIABILITY IN THE CRIMINAL LAW

AUSTIN, J. L., "A Plea for Excuses," in *Philosophical Papers*. London: Oxford University Press, 1961.

BEARDSLEY, ELIZABETH LANE, " 'Excusing Conditions' and Moral Responsibility," in *Determinism and Freedom in the Age of Modern Science,* ed., Sidney Hook. New York: New York University Press, 1958. A reply to the Hart article reprinted in this book.

BECKER, LAWRENCE C., "Criminal Attempt and the Theory of the Law of Crimes," *Philosophy and Public Affairs,* 3 (1974): 262.

BENTHAM, JEREMY, *An Introduction to the Principles of Morals and Legislation.* Oxford: Basil Blackwell, 1948.

BERGER, F. R., "Excuses and the Law," *Theoria,* 31 (1965): 9.

BRANDT, RICHARD, "A Utilitarian Theory of Excuses," *Philosophical Review,* 78 (1969): 337.

COOPER, DAVID, "Responsibility and the System," in *Individual and Collective Responsibility,* ed., Peter A. French. Cambridge: Schenkman Publishing Company, 1972.

EZORSKY, GERTRUDE, ed., *Philosophical Perspectives on Punishment.* Albany: State University of New York Press, 1972.

EZORSKY, GERTRUDE, "Punishment and Excuses," in *Punishment and Human Rights,* ed., Milton Goldinger. Cambridge: Schenkman Publishing Company, 1974.

FEINBERG, JOEL, *Doing and Deserving.* Princeton: Princeton University Press, 1970.

HALL, JEROME, *General Principles of Criminal Law,* Second Edition. Indianapolis: Bobbs-Merrill Company, Inc., 1960.

HART, *Aims of the Criminal Law,* 23 LAW & CONTEMP. PROB. 401 (1958).

HART, H. L. A., *Punishment and Responsibility: Essays in the Philosophy of Law.* New York: Oxford University Press, 1968.

HOLMES, O. W., *The Common Law,* ed., Mark D. Howe. Boston: Little, Brown and Company, 1964.

HOULGATE, LAURENCE D., "Excuses and the Criminal Law," *Southern Journal of Philosophy,* 13 (1975): 187.

HOWARD, COLIN, *Strict Responsibility.* London: Sweet & Maxwell, 1963.

JACOBS, FRANCIS G., *Criminal Responsibility.* London: Weidenfeld and Nicolson, 1971.

LaFAVE, WAYNE, R. and AUSTIN W. SCOTT, JR., *Criminal Law.* St. Paul: West Publishing Co., 1972.

LYONS, DANIEL, "Is Hart's Rationale for Excuses Workable?" *Dialogue,* 8, (1969): 496.

LYONS, DANIEL, "On Sanctioning Excuses," *Journal of Philosophy,* 66 (1970): 646.

MURPHY, JEFFRIE G., "Involuntary Acts and Criminal Liability," *Ethics,* 81 (1971): 332.

MURPHY, JEFFRIE, G., "Marxism and Retribution," *Philosophy and Public Affairs,* 2 (1973): 217.

MUELLER, *On Common Law Mens Rea,* 42 MINN L. REV. 1043 (1958).

NOWELL-SMITH, P. H., "On Sanctioning Excuses," *Journal of Philosophy,* 67 (1970): 609.

PACKER, HERBERT, *The Limits of the Criminal Sanction.* Stanford: Stanford University Press, 1968. Contains a critical discussion of *Dotterweich.*

PACKER, *Mens Rea and the Supreme Court,* 1962 SUP. CT. REV. 107. Contains a critical discussion of *Dotterweich.*

SAYRE, *Public Welfare Offenses,* 33 COLUM. L. REV. 55 (1933).

SIEGLER, FREDERICK ADRIAN, "Lyons on Sanctioning Excuses," *Journal of Philosophy,* 67 (1970): 620.

STONE, CHRISTOPHER D., *Where the Law Ends: The Social Control of Corporate Behavior*. New York: Harper & Row, Publishers, 1975.

THALBERG, IRVING, "Hart on Strict Liability and Excusing Conditions," *Ethics*, 81 (1971): 150.

WALKER, OWEN S., "Why Should Irresponsible Offenders be Excused?" *Journal of Philosophy*, 66 (1969): 279.

WASSERSTROM, H. L. A. *Hart and the Doctrine of Mens Rea and Criminal Responsibility*, 35 U. CHI. L. REV. 92 (1967).

WILLIAMS, GLANVILLE, *Criminal Law: The General Part*, Second Edition. London: Stevens & Sons Limited, 1961.

WILLIAMS, GLANVILLE, *The Mental Element in Crime*. Jerusalem: Magnes Press, 1965.

II. THE ENFORCEMENT OF COMMUNITY STANDARDS

BAYLES, MICHAEL, "Comments on Feinberg: Offensive Conduct and the Law," in *Issues in Law and Morality*, eds., Norman S. Care and Thomas K. Trelogan. Cleveland: Case Western Reserve Press, 1973.

COHEN, M. R., "Moral Aspects of the Criminal Law," in *Reason and Law*. Glencoe: The Free Press, 1950. Also at 49 YALE L. J. 987 (1940).

DEVLIN, PATRICK, *The Enforcement of Morals*. London: Oxford University Press, 1965.

DWORKIN, *Lord Devlin and the Enforcement of Morals*, 75 YALE L.J. 986 (1966).

GUSSFIELD, *On Legislating Morals: The Symbolic Process of Designating Deviance*, 56 CALIF. L. REV. 55 (1968).

HART, H. L. A., "Immorality and Treason," *Listener*, 62 (1959): 162.

HART, H. L. A., *Law, Liberty, and Morality*. Stanford: Stanford University Press, 1963.

HART, *Social Solidarity and the Enforcement of Morality*, 35 U. CHI. L. REV. 1 (1967).

HENKIN, *Morals and the Constitution: The Sin of Obscenity*, 63 COLUM. L. REV. 391 (1963).

HUGHES, *Morals and the Criminal Law*, 71 YALE L. J. 662 (1962).

KRISTOL, IRVING, "Pornography, Obscenity, and the Case for Censorship," *New York Times Magazine*, March 28, 1971, p. 24.

LOUCH, A. R., "Sins and Crimes," *Philosophy,* 43 (1968): 38.

MILL, JOHN STUART, *On Liberty.* Indianapolis: Bobbs-Merrill Company, Inc., 1956.

NAGEL, ERNEST, "The Enforcement of Morals," *Humanist,* 28 (May/June 1968): 20. Reprinted in *Ethics and Public Policy,* ed., Tom L. Beauchamp. Englewood Cliffs: Prentice-Hall, Inc., 1975.

PENNOCK, J. ROLAND and JOHN W. CHAPMAN, eds., *The Limits of Law.* New York: Lieber-Atherton, 1974.

ROSTOW, EUGENE V., "The Enforcement of Morals," in *The Sovereign Prerogative.* New Haven: Yale University Press, 1962.

SARTORIUS, *The Enforcement of Morality,* 81 YALE L.J. 891 (1972).

SCHWARTZ, *Morals Offenses and the Model Penal Code,* 63 COLUM. L. REV. 669 (1963).

SKOLNICK, *Coercion to Virtue: The Enforcement of Morals,* 41 S. CAL. L. REV. 590 (1968).

STEPHEN, J., *Liberty, Equality, Fraternity.* London: Smith Elgard and Co., 1873.

WASSERSTROM, RICHARD, ed., *Morality and the Law.* Belmont: Wadsworth Publishing Company, Inc., 1971.

III. THE DUTY TO RENDER AID

AMES, *Law and Morals,* 22 HARV. L. REV. 97 (1908).

CALABRESI & MALAMED, *Property Rules, Liability Rules, and Inalienability Rules: One View of the Cathedral,* 85 HARV. L. REV. 1089 (1972).

D'AMATO, *The "Bad Samaritan" Paradigm,* 70 NW. U. L. REV. 298 (1975).

DYKE, *The Duty to Aid One in Peril: Good Samaritan Laws,* 15 HOW. L. J. 672 (1969).

FITZGERALD, P. J., "Acting and Refraining," *Analysis,* 27 (1967): 133.

FLETCHER, *Fairness and Utility in Tort Theory,* 85 HARV. L. REV. 537 (1972).

FLETCHER, *Theory of Criminal Negligence: A Comparative Analysis,* 119 U. PA. L. REV. 401 (1971).

FRANKLIN, *Vermont Requires Rescue: A Comment,* 25 STAN. L. REV. 51 (1972).

HALL, JEROME, *General Principles of Criminal Law,* Second Edition Indianapolis: Bobbs-Merrill Company, Inc., 1960.

HART, H. L. A. and A. M. HONORÉ, *Causation in the Law.* London: Oxford University Press, 1959.

HUGHES, *Criminal Omissions,* 67 YALE L.J. 590 (1958).

LaFAVE, WAYNE R. and AUSTIN W. SCOTT, JR., *Criminal Law.* St. Paul: West Publishing Co., 1972.

LYONS, DANIEL, "The Odd Debt of Gratitude," *Analysis,* 29 (1969): 92.

MACK, ERIC, "Causing and Failing to Prevent," *Southwestern Journal of Philosophy,* 7 (1976): 83. Contains a discussion of the Harris article reprinted in this book.

McCLOSKEY, J. J., "Human Needs, Rights and Political Values," *American Philosophical Quarterly,* 13 (1976): 187.

NAGEL, *Libertarianism Without Foundations,* 85 YALE L. J. 136 (1975). Thomas Nagel's review of *Anarchy, State, and Utopia* by Nozick.

NOTE, *Good Samaritans and Liability for Medical Malpractice,* 64 COLUM. L. REV. 1301 (1964).

NOZICK, ROBERT, *Anarchy, State, and Utopia.* New York: Basic Books, Inc., Publishers, 1974.

POSNER, *Strict Liability: A Comment,* 2 J. LEG. STUD. 205 (1973).

PROSSER, WILLIAM L., *Handbook of the Law of Torts,* Fourth Edition. St. Paul: West Publishing Co., 1971.

RATCLIFFE, JAMES M., ed., *The Good Samaritan and the Law.* New York: Doubleday & Co., 1966.

RUDOLPH, *The Duty to Act: A Proposed Rule,* 44 NEB. L. REV. 499 (1965).

SCHEID, *Affirmative Duty to Act in Emergency Situations—The Return of the Good Samaritan,* 3 JOHN MARSHALL J. PRACT. & PROC. 1 (1969).

TERRY, *Negligence,* 29 HARV. L. REV. 40 (1916).

THOMSON, JUDITH JARVIS, "A Defense of Abortion," *Philosophy and Public Affairs,* 1 (1971): 47.

TRAMMELL, R. L., "Saving Life and Taking Life," *Journal of Philosophy,* 72 (1975): 131.

WILLIAMS, GLANVILLE, *Criminal Law: The General Part,* Second Edition. London: Stevens & Sons Limited, 1963.

IV. THE PROSECUTION OF THE CONSCIENTIOUS VIOLATOR

BEDAU, HUGO ADAM, ed., *Civil Disobedience: Theory and Practice.* New York: Pegasus, 1969.

BEDAU, HUGO ADAM, "Military Service and Moral Obligation," *Philosophy and Political Action,* eds., Virginia Held, Kai Neilsen and Charles Parsons. New York: Oxford University Press, 1972.

BICKEL, ALEXANDER M., *The Morality of Consent.* New Haven: Yale University Press, 1975.

BLACK, *Problems of the Compatibility of Civil Disobedience with American Institutions of Government,* 43 TEXAS L. REV. 492 (1965).

BROCK, DAN W., "Amnesty and Morality," *Social Theory and Practice,* 3 (1974): 131.

COHEN, CARL, *Civil Disobedience: Conscience, Tactics, and the Law.* New York: Columbia University Press, 1971.

COHEN, CARL, "Conscientious Objection," *Ethics,* 4 (1968): 269. A postscript to this piece, treating *Sisson* and several other draft cases, appears along with the original article in *Philosophy for a New Generation,* Second Edition, ed., A. K. Bierman and James A. Gould. New York: Macmillan Company, 1973.

COHEN, MARSHALL, "Liberalism and Disobedience," *Philosophy and Public Affairs,* 1 (1972): 283.

COX, ARCHIBALD, "Direct Action, Civil Disobedience, and the Constitution," in *Civil Rights, the Constitution, and the Courts.* Cambridge: Harvard University Press, 1967.

DOUGLAS, WILLIAM O., *Points of Rebellion.* New York: Vintage Press, 1970.

DWORKIN, GERALD, "Non-neutral Principles," *Journal of Philosophy,* 71 (1974): 491.

DWORKIN, RONALD, "A Theory of Civil Disobedience," in *Ethics and Social Justice,* eds., Howard E. Kiefer and Milton Munitz. New York: New York University Press, 1968.

FORTAS, ABE, *Concerning Dissent and Civil Disobedience.* New York: New American Library, 1968.

GENDIN, SIDNEY, "Governmental Toleration of Civil Disobedience," in *Philosophy and Political Action,* eds., Virginia Held, Kai Neilsen and Charles Parsons. New York: Oxford University Press, 1972.

GREENAWALT, *A Contextual Approach to Disobedience,* 70 COLUM. L. REV. 48 (1970).

HALL, ROBERT T., "Legal Toleration of Civil Disobedience," *Ethics,* 81 (1971): 128.

HALL, ROBERT T., *The Morality of Civil Disobedience.* New York: Harper and Row, 1970.

HOOK, SIDNEY, ed., *Law and Morality.* New York: New York University Press, 1964. Part I treats the general area of civil disobedience.

HOOK, SIDNEY, "Social Protest and Civil Disobedience," *Humanist,* 27 (1967): 157.

HATFIELD, MARK O., *Not Quite So Simple.* New York: Harper & Row, 1968. Chapter Seven contains a discussion of civil disobedience.

HUGHES, *Civil Disobedience and the Political Question Doctrine,* 43, N.Y.U.L. REV. 1 (1968).

JOHNSON, CONRAD D., "Moral and Legal Obligation," *Journal of Philosophy,* 72 (1975): 315.

KADISH, MORTIMER R. and SANFORD H. KADISH, *Discretion to Disobey: A Study of Lawful Departures from Legal Rules.* Stanford: Stanford University Press, 1973.

KINOY, ARTHUR, "The Role of the Radical Lawyer and Teacher of Law," in *Law Against the People,* ed., Robert Lefcourt. New York: Vintage Books, 1971.

MONIST, 54 (October, 1970). The topic for this issue is "Legal Obligation and Civil Disobedience."

MURPHY, JEFFRIE G., ed., *Civil Disobedience and Violence.* Belmont: Wadsworth Publishing Company, Inc., 1971.

Note, *Sentencing in Cases of Civil Disobedience,* 68 COLUM. L. REV. 1508 (1968).

PEPPERS, DONALD A., "War Crimes and Induction: A Case for Selective Nonconscientious Objection," *Philosophy and Public Affairs,* 3 (1974): 129.

RAWLS, JOHN, "The Justification of Civil Disobedience," in *Civil Disobedience: Theory and Practice,* ed., Hugo Adam Bedau. New York: Pegasus, 1969.

SCHAEFER, STEPHEN, *The Political Criminal: The Problems of Morality and Crime.* New York: The Free Press, 1974.

SINGER, PETER, *Democracy and Disobedience.* London: Oxford University Press, 1973.

VAN DEN HAAG, ERNEST, *Political Violence and Civil Disobedience.* New York: Harper & Row, Publishers, 1972. Appendix B is a critique of Dworkin.

WALZER, MICHAEL, "The Obligation to Disobey," *Ethics,* 77 (1967): 163.

WASSERSTROM, *The Obligation to Obey the Law,* 10 U.C.L.A.L. REV. 780 (1963).

WOLFF, ROBERT PAUL, "Four Questions on the Draft," in *Philosophy: A Modern Encounter.* Englewood Cliffs: Prentice-Hall, Inc., 1971.

WYZANSKI, CHARLES E. JR., "It is quite right that the young should talk about us as hypocrites. We are." *Saturday Review,* 51 (July 20, 1968):14.

WYZANSKI, CHARLES E. JR., "On Civil Disobedience," *Atlantic Monthly,* 221 (February 1968): 58. Reprinted in *Civil Disobedience: Theory and Practice,* ed., Hugo Adam Bedau. New York: Pegasus, 1969.

ZINN, HOWARD, *Disobedience and Democracy.* New York: Random House, 1968. A critique of Fortas' views.

V. PREFERENTIAL TREATMENT

ALEXANDER & ALEXANDER, *The New Racism,* 9 SAN DIEGO L. REV. 190 (1972).

AUERBACH, JEROLD S., *Unequal Justice: Lawyers and Social Change in Modern America.* New York: Oxford University Press, 1976. An historian discusses discrimination within the legal profession.

BAYLES, MICHAEL, "Compensatory Reverse Discrimination in Hiring," *Social Theory and Practice,* 2 (1973): 301.

BAYLES, MICHAEL, "Reparations to Wronged Groups," *Analysis,* 33 (1973): 182.

BEDAU, HUGO ADAM, "Compensatory Justice and the Black Manifesto," *Monist,* 56 (1972): 20.

BEDAU, HUGO ADAM, ed., *Justice and Equality.* Englewood Cliffs: Prentice-Hall, Inc., 1971.

BITTKER, BORIS, *The Case for Black Reparations*. New York: Random House, 1973.

BLACKSTONE, WILLIAM T., "Reverse Discrimination and Compensatory Justice," *Social Theory and Practice*, 3 (1975): 253. Discusses *De-Funis*.

BLUMROSEN, *Stranger in Paradise: Griggs v. Duke Power Co. and the Concept of Employment Discrimination*, 71 MICH L. REV. 59 (1972).

BOXILL, BERNARD R., "The Morality of Reparation," *Social Theory and Practice*, 2 (1972): 113.

COHEN, MORRIS R., "Property and Sovereignty," in *Law and the Social Order*. New York: Harcourt Brace & World, Inc., 1933.

COLEMAN, JULES, "Justice and Preferential Hiring," *Journal of Critical Analysis*, 5 (1973): 27. A criticism of the Thomson article reprinted in this book.

COWAN, J. L., "Inverse Discrimination," *Analysis*, 33 (1972): 10.

DANIELS, ROGER, *Concentration Camps, USA: Japanese Americans and World War II*. New York: Holt, Rinehart and Winston, 1971.

"DeFunis Symposium," 75 COLUM. L. REV. 483 (1975).

"DeFunis: The Road Not Taken" (Symposium), 60 VA. L. REV. 917 (1974).

DWORKIN, RONALD, "The DeFunis Case: The Right to Go to Law School," *New York Review of Books*, 23 (February, 1976): 29. An exchange of letters on this article appears in *The New York Review of Books* of July 15, 1976 at page 45.

ELY, *The Constitutionality of Reverse Racial Discrimination*, 41 U. CHI. L. REV. 723 (1974).

EZORSKY, GERTRUDE, "Fight Over University Women," *New York Review of Books*, 21 (May, 1974): 32.

FISS, *A Theory of Fair Employment Laws*, 38 U. CHI. L. REV. 235 (1970).

FISS, OWEN M., "Groups and the Equal Protection Clause," *Philosophy and Public Affairs*, 5 (1976): 107.

FRIED, MARLENE GERBER, "In Defense of Preferential Hiring," *Philosophical Forum*, 5 (1973-1974): 309.

FULLINWIDER, ROBERT K., "Preferential Hiring and Compensation," *Social Theory and Practice*, 3 (1975): 307.

GIBBARD, ALLEN, "Natural Property Rights," *Nous*, 10 (1976): 77.

GLAZER, NATHAN, *Affirmative Discrimination*. New York: Basic Books, 1976.

GINGER, ANN FAGAN, ed., *DeFunis versus Odegaard and the University of Washington: The University Admissions Case, The Record*, three volumes. Dobbs Ferry: Oceana Publications, Inc., 1974. This set contains virtually the complete record of the litigation in *DeFunis*.

GOLDMAN, ALAN H., "Affirmative Action," *Philosophy and Public Affairs*, 5 (1976): 178.

GOLDMAN, ALAN H., "Limits to the Justification of Reverse Discrimination," *Social Theory and Practice*, 3 (1975): 289.

GROSS, BARRY R., ed., *Reverse Discrimination*. Buffalo: Prometheus Books, 1977.

HELD, VIRGINIA, "Reasonable Progress and Self Respect," *Monist*, 57 (1973): 12.

HONORÉ, A. M., "Ownership," in *Oxford Essays in Jurisprudence*, ed., A. G. Guest. Oxford: Oxford University Press, 1961.

HUGHES, *Reparations for Blacks*, 43 N.Y.U.L. REV. 1073 (1968).

KAPLAN, *Equal Justice in an Unequal World: Equality for the Negro— The Problem of Special Treatment*, 61 NW. U. L. REV. 363 (1966).

MARTIN, MICHAEL, "Pedagogical Arguments for Preferential Hiring and Tenuring of Women Teachers in the University," *Philosophical Forum*, 5 (1974-1975): 325.

MAVRODES, GEORGE L., "Property," *Personalist*, 53 (1974): 245.

NAGEL, THOMAS, "Equal Treatment and Compensatory Discrimination," *Philosophy and Public Affairs*, 2 (1973): 348.

NICKEL, J. W., "Discrimination and Morally Relevant Characteristics," *Analysis*, 32 (1972): 113.

NICKEL, *Preferential Policies in Hiring and Admissions: A Jurisprudential Approach*, 75 COLUM. L. REV. 534 (1975).

O'NEIL, ROBERT M., *Discriminating Against Discrimination: Preferential Admissions and the DeFunis Case*. Bloomington: Indiana University Press, 1975.

O'NEIL, *Preferential Admissions: Equalizing the Access of Minority Groups to Higher Education*, 80 YALE L. J. 699 (1971).

RAWLS, JOHN, *A Theory of Justice*, Cambridge: Harvard University Press, 1971.

SHER, GEORGE, "Justifying Reverse Discrimination in Employment," *Philosophy and Public Affairs,* 4 (1975): 159.

SHINER, ROGER, "Individuals, Groups, and Inverse Discrimination," *Analysis,* 33 (1973): 185.

SILVESTRI, PHILIP, "The Justification of Inverse Discrimination," *Analysis,* 33 (1973): 31.

SIMON, ROBERT, "Preferential Hiring: A Reply to Judith Jarvis Thomson," *Philosophy and Public Affairs,* 3 (1974): 316.

SOWELL, THOMAS, " 'Affirmative Action' Reconsidered," *Public Interest,* 42 (1976): 47.

STONE, CHRISTOPHER D. *Should Trees Have Standing? Toward Legal Rights for Natural Objects.* New York: Avon Books, 1975.

TAYLOR, PAUL W., "Reverse Discrimination and Compensatory Justice," *Analysis,* 33 (1973): 177.

THALBERG, IRVING, "Justifications of Institutional Racism," *Philosophical Forum,* 3 (1972): 243.

THALBERG, IRVING, "Reverse Discrimination and the Future," *Philosophical Forum,* 5 (1973–1974): 294.

TREBILCOT, JOYCE, "Sex Roles: The Argument from Nature," *Ethics,* 85 (1975): 249.

TUSSMAN & TENBROEK, *The Equal Protection of the Laws,* 37 CALIF. L. REV. 341 (1949).

VETTERLING, MARY K., "Some Common Sense Notes on Preferential Hiring," *Philosophical Forum,* 5 (1973–1974): 320.

VIEIRA, *Racial Imbalance, Black Separatism, and Permissible Classification by Race,* 67 MICH. L. REV. 1553 (1969).

WASSERSTROM, RICHARD, "The University and the Case For Preferential Treatment," *American Philosophical Quarterly,* 13 (1976): 165.

VI. PLEA BARGAINING

ALSCHULER, *The Defense Attorney's Role in Plea Bargaining,* 84 YALE L.J. 1179 (1975).

ALSCHULER, *The Prosecutor's Role in Plea Bargaining,* 36 U. CHI. L. REV. 50 (1968).

ALSCHULER, *The Supreme Court, The Defense Attorney, and the Guilty*

Plea, 47 U. COLO. L. REV. 1 (1975). See Section III on voluntary waiver of the right to trial.

American Bar Association's Project on Minimum Standards for Criminal Justice, *Standards Relating to Pleas of Guilty, Approved Draft.* New York: Institute of Judicial Administration, 1968.

BEDFORD, SYBILLE, *The Faces of Justice.* New York: Simon and Schuster, 1961. Describes judicial proceedings in several European countries.

BLUMBERG, ABRAHAM, *Criminal Justice.* Chicago: Quadrangle Books, 1967. A sociological study of the criminal justice system in a metropolitan area.

COHEN, MORRIS RAPHAEL, "The Basis of Contract," in *Law and the Social Order.* New York: Harcourt, Brace and Company, 1933.

DALZELL, *Duress by Economic Pressure,* 20 N.C.L. REV. 237 (1942).

DAWSON, *Economic Duress—An Essay in Perspective,* 45 MICH. L. REV. 253 (1947).

DAWSON, ROBERT O., *Sentencing: The Decision as to Type, Length and Conditions of Sentence.* Boston: Little, Brown and Company, 1969.

FRANKFURT, HARRY, "Coercion and Moral Responsibility," in *Essays on Freedom of Action,* ed., Ted Honderich. London: Routledge & Kegan Paul, Ltd., 1973.

LANGBEIN, *Controlling Prosecutorial Discretion in Germany,* 41 U. CHI. L. REV. 439 (1974).

LYONS, DANIEL, "Welcome Threats and Coercive Offers," *Philosophy,* 50 (1975): 425.

KADISH, SANFORD, "The Crisis of Overcriminalization," *Annals of the American Academy of Political and Social Science,* 374 (1967): 157.

KLEINIG, ROBERT, *Punishment and Desert.* The Hague: Martinus Nijhoff, 1973. Contains bibliography on punishment.

KOEN & NEWMAN, *Two Perspectives on the Agnew Plea Bargain,* 10 CRIM. L. BULL. 80 (1974).

MORRIS, NORVAL, *The Future of Imprisonment.* Chicago: University of Chicago Press, 1974.

National Advisory Commission on Criminal Justice Standards and Goals, *Courts.* Washington, D.C.: U. S. Government Printing Office, 1973.

NEWMAN & NEMOYER, *Issues of Propriety in Negotiated Justice,* 47 DENVER L. J. 367 (1970).

NEWMAN, DONALD J., *Conviction: The Determination of Guilt or Innocence Without Trial.* Boston: Little, Brown and Company, 1966.

NOZICK, ROBERT, "Coercion," in *Philosophy, Politics and Society,* Fourth Series, eds., Peter Laslett, W. G. Runciman and Quentin Skinner. New York: Harper & Row Publishers, Inc., 1972.

Note, *The Unconstitutionality of Plea Bargaining,* 83 HARV. L. REV. 1387 (1970).

PARKER, *Plea Bargaining,* 1 AM. J. CRIM. L. 187 (1972).

REMINGTON, FRANK J. et al., *Criminal Justice Administration: Cases and Materials.* Indianapolis: Bobbs-Merrill Company, Inc., 1969.

ROSETT, ARTHUR, "The Negotiated Guilty Plea," *Annals of the American Academy of Political and Social Science,* 374 (November, 1967): 72.

ROSETT, ARTHUR and DONALD R. CRESSEY, *Justice by Consent.* Philadelphia: J. P. Lippincott Company, 1976. Contains bibliographical notes on plea bargaining.

VON HIRSCH, ANDREW, "Giving Criminals Their Just Deserts," *Civil Liberties Review,* 3 (April/May 1976): 23.

VON HIRSCH, ANDREW, *Doing Justice: The Choice of Punishments.* New York: Hill & Wang, 1976. The report of the Committee for the Study of Incarceration.

WILLIAMS, GLANVILLE, *The Proof of Guilt: A Study of the English Criminal Trial.* London: Stevens & Sons Limited, 1955.

WISHINGOOD, *The Plea Bargain in Historical Perspective,* 23 BUFFALO L. REV. 499 (1974).